ICELAND

JENNA GOTTLIEB

NORWEGIAN SEA

Grímsey

Raufarhöfn

Þistilfjörður

Kópasker

85

Bakkaflói

ðlufjörður

Skjálfandi

Ólafsfjörður

85

Bakkafjörður

Grenivík

Húsavík

Vopnafjörður

Ivík

82

87

864

Vopnafjörður

Laugar

Akureyri

85

917

Bakkagerði

1

Reykjahlíð

1

94

Mývatn

Seyðisfjörður

Egilsstaðir

93

Neskaupstaður

F26

Hallormsstaður

1

96

Eskifjörður

Reyðarfjörður

Fáskrúðsfjörður

96

ofsjökull

Hálslón

Kvíslavatn

F26

Djúpivogur

Vatnajökull

1

Þórisvatn

Langisjór

Öræfajökull

Höfn

1

Kirkjubæjarklaustur

0   25 mi

204

0   25 km

1

© AVALON TRAVEL

Contents

DISCOVER
Iceland

S cale the heights of soaring mountaintops. Dive into some of the clearest water in the world. Hike the rim of a remote volcano that rises from an Arctic desert. Witness a rainbow materialize over a thundering waterfall. Iceland is a place not just to see, but to experience.

Iceland is revered for its breathtaking landscapes, unrivaled trekking, and Arctic wildlife. Four major national parks and a dozen smaller reserves protect these resources. Vatnajökull National Park makes up 13 percent of the country and protects the largest glacier in the world outside the poles. Geothermal pools, like the famous milky waters of the Blue Lagoon, bubble up from beneath the earth and provide a place to soak away your worries.

If city life is more your speed, Reykjavík is waiting for you. Stroll the capital's streets and explore the galleries, coffeehouses, intimate concert

Clockwise from top left: horses roaming the landscape; the Icelandic national costume; colorful downtown Reykjavík; lava from the eruption of Holuhraun; old wooden fishing boat in the Westfjords; aerial view of Reykjavík.

venues, and music shops—you can't help but feel the city's creative energy. Handcrafted local beers replace specialty coffees as the drink of choice come evening time, when low-key daytime hangouts morph into pulsing parties that fuel Reykjavík's thriving nightlife scene.

In summer, the days seem endless—the sun shines for nearly 24 hours around the summer solstice. Winter tourism is increasing, with visitors lured by the chance to hunt the northern lights, yet another of Iceland's spectacular natural wonders. Watching the lights flicker in the sky, changing colors, disappearing and popping up again stronger and brighter, makes braving the wind and rain worth it.

There are endless possibilities. For scenery and adventure, Iceland is unmatched.

Clockwise from top left: northern lights appearing in the west; campsite at Álftavatn on the Laugavegurinn Trail; Húsavík; Siglufjörður.

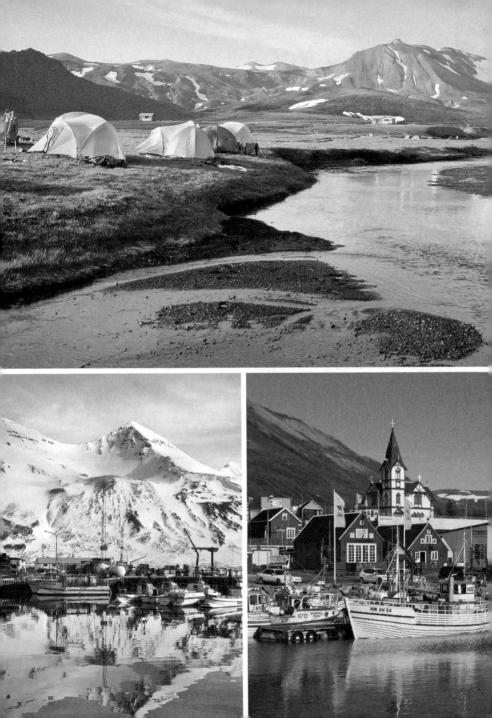

Planning Your Trip

Where to Go

Reykjavík

Home to two-thirds of Iceland's population, the capital city is the **cultural and social hub** of the country, with an energy that is separate from the rest of the country. Here you'll find chic hotels, eclectic restaurants, and top-notch shopping on the main street **Laugavegur**—not to mention a thriving **art scene** and vibrant **nightlife.** Pay a visit to the great church **Hallgrímskirkja**, the placid pond **Tjörnin** near city hall, and, for a taste of history, the **National Museum of Iceland.** A trip to the **old harbor** is also a must—take in a concert at the striking glass hall **Harpa,** or head out on a **whale-watching** tour.

Reykjanes Peninsula and the South

Outside of Reykjavík, the Reykjanes Peninsula and nature sights in South Iceland get the most traffic on the island. The **Reykjanes Peninsula** is home to charming fishing villages, **Keflavík** airport, and the **Blue Lagoon**, where you can

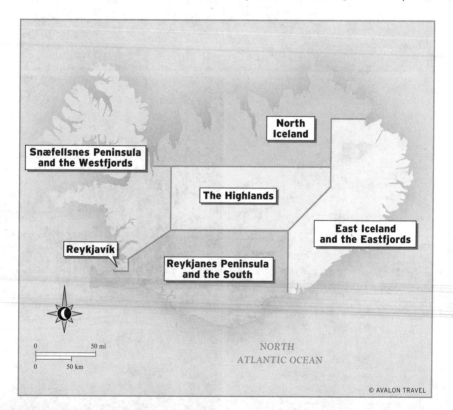

© AVALON TRAVEL

take a healing dip in the milky heated water. The 300-kilometer Golden Circle route encompasses three key sights: the powerful waterfall Gullfoss, the bubbling geothermal phenomenon Geysir, and the history-steeped national park Þingvellir. Some of the best hiking trails in the country are in the south. A favorite is the Laugavegurinn trail, where you can see towering mountains, vast glaciers, hot springs, roaring rivers, and stunning waterfalls.

Snæfellsnes Peninsula and the Westfjords

Called "Iceland in miniature" by locals, the Snæfellsnes Peninsula has a bit of everything: quaint fishing towns, spectacular mountains, hiking, whale-watching, and even a glacier you can walk on—Snæfellsjökull, world famous as the starting point of Jules Verne's *A Journey to the Center of the Earth*. Endless coastlines, offbeat museums, and beautiful rocky landscapes await in the Westfjords. For outstanding bird-watching, visit the Látrabjarg cliffs in summer to check out thousands of nesting puffins.

North Iceland

Iceland's "second city," low-key Akureyri offers beautiful botanical gardens, first-rate hotels and restaurants, and a booming art scene. It's the perfect place to base yourself for a visit to the north. The Mývatn region lures visitors with its birdlife-rich lake, gorgeous hiking trails, vast lava fields, enormous craters, soaring mountains, and the soothing Mývatn Nature Baths. Jökulsárgljúfur National Park offers a number of treasures, including the gigantic canyon Ásbyrgi and Dettifoss, the largest waterfall in Iceland. Húsavík has some of the best whale-watching opportunities on the island, with a chance to see as many as 12 species of whale.

East Iceland and the Eastfjords

Looking for the "ice" in Iceland? Head to East Iceland, where the giant white Vatnajökull glacier will take your breath away. Drive or hike right up into the glacier's edge in Skaftafell National Park, where you'll see snowcapped mountains, green fields, and black-sand beaches. Hikers can scale Mount Snæfell, the highest mountain (excluding glaciers) in Iceland,

whale-watching in Húsavík

with spectacular views spanning from the highlands to the sea. Weave through the unspoiled Eastfjords, where each fjord has its own charm. The east is the most remote part of the island, and summer is the only practical time to tour this region.

The Highlands

The uninhabited interior draws adventure seekers and avid hikers with its unique and unforgiving landscape. Iceland's largest glaciers (Vatnajökull, Langjökull, and Hofskjökull) are the backdrop to the highlands, with dramatic scenery cut by wind and ice. Hike the rim of Mount Askja, a volcano with a pale blue lake-filled crater and sensational views. Askja emerges from the eerie, isolate Ódáðahraun lava field, the largest desert in Europe. You have to stay abreast of the weather forecast in the highlands—it can snow any day of the year here.

When to Go

Iceland is a year-round destination, but when to visit depends on what you want to do and what you'd like to see. For instance, winter is not the time to go hiking, but the lower airfare and hotel prices during the off season, as well as the lure of northern lights, draw many people over the winter.

Summer (June-August)

The summer is the high season and offers the best weather to explore all of Iceland's outdoor jewels. The summer is perfect for outdoor activities such as hiking, diving, whale-watching, glacier-walking, bird-watching, and swimming. The landscape is green and lush and the days long. The midnight sun has to be seen to be believed. June-August is also the best time to embark on a Ring Road trip, as the roads are the best this time of year, and the weather is not likely to cause too many problems. That said, it's important to

two of Iceland's natural wonders—the midnight sun and waterfalls

Chasing the Northern Lights

The biggest winter attraction in Iceland is the northern lights. People travel from around the world to catch a glimpse of the green, white, blue, and red lights dancing in the night sky. The phenomenon is caused by solar winds, which push electronic particles to collide with molecules of atmospheric gases, causing an emission of bright light.

There's something very special about bundling up in your warmest winter gear, trekking outside the main towns to avoid bright lights, and hunting for the aurora borealis. The best time to see northern lights is from October to March. Forecasts predict visibility at www.vedur.is, the national weather website. When the forecast is strong, it's best to drive (or take a tour bus) to a dark area and look up. It doesn't have to be far—just outside city center where the lights are low. Northern lights tours are offered by Reykjavik Excursions (www.re.is).

northern lights over a moss-covered lava field

northern lights over Mount Kirkjufell on the Snæfellsnes Peninsula closely monitor the weather forecast for wind or heavy rain.

While the summer offers the best weather and the freedom to explore the island, it comes at a price. Airfare and hotel rates are highest during the summer, and there is a summer rush of tourists.

Autumn (September-October)

The autumn attracts travelers who want to **avoid the tourist crush** of the summer but still want to explore some of the countryside and enjoy outdoor activities. There is still plenty of daylight, and **hiking** is still viable in the autumn, but you must monitor the weather because storms can pop up. It's also possible to see **northern lights** this time of year; check the forecast for the dancing green lights at www.vedur.is.

The autumn is perfect for a long weekend in **Reykjavík.** This time of year is also known for local festivals in the capital city, such as the Reykjavík International Film Festival in September and the music festival Iceland Airwaves at the end of October.

Winter (November-March)

Iceland's **low season,** winter isn't a bad time to visit if you are willing to go with the flow, as the weather can be unpredictable at best and punishing at worst. The pluses are that airfare and hotel prices are the lowest of the year, you won't battle crowds anywhere, and this is the best time to catch a glimpse of the **northern lights.** Other popular outdoor activities during the winter are **riding snowmobiles and horses** and **skiing** up north.

The downside to winter travel is, unsurprisingly, the **changeable, challenging weather.** You will likely encounter wind, rain, snow, sleet, and everything in between. Travel to the countryside is limited in the winter as **many roads are closed,** and even open roads can have tough conditions.

Spring (April-May)

April and May fall in between the low winter season and high summer season and are a good option for **budget-conscious** travelers. You have a crack at **decent weather** without paying the extraordinary summertime prices. That said, the weather is unpredictable, so a visit in April can feel like winter—it's **hit or miss.** But if the weather is pleasant enough, you can enjoy hikes, horse riding, whale-watching, and all that Reykjavík has to offer.

autumn in Reykjavík

horses in winter

Before You Go

Visas and Officialdom

Visitors to Iceland must arrive with a valid **passport** that expires no sooner than three months after your intended departure date. Travelers from the United States, Canada, Australia, New Zealand, United Kingdom, and Ireland do not require a visa for trips shorter than 90 days. However, if you would like to stay longer, you need to procure a permit from the Directorate of Immigration (www.utl.is), which is very difficult to get. There are different, more lenient rules for residents of European Union and European Economic Area countries.

Getting There

Flying into Iceland is a pretty seamless experience. The country's main carrier, **Icelandair** (www.icelandair.com), serves more than 30 destinations in the United States, Canada, and Europe. Iceland's accessibility has been a main selling point as a travel destination, as the country is just five hours from New York City and about three hours from London.

For those traveling from mainland Europe, a **ferry** can be a great option, especially if you want to bring a car, camper, or bicycle for the trip. **Smyril Line** (www.smyril-line.fo) runs a ferry to Iceland from Denmark, Norway, and the Faroe Islands. The ferry drops you off in Seyðisfjörður in East Iceland, which is convenient if you're traveling with a car and want to spend time in the countryside. But if you want to stay in the south, where Reykjavík and the Golden Circle attractions are, a ferry may not be the best option.

Getting Around

Having access to a **car** gives you the ultimate freedom in seeing the island on your own schedule (but expect to pay dearly, especially in summer). If you plan to stay in Reykjavík for most of your trip, or want to do short day trips in the southern or western parts of the country, it's not necessary to rent a car. You can book **tours** and travel by **bus.**

relaxing in the Blue Lagoon

The Best of Iceland

For this recommended itinerary, you will drive clockwise around Iceland. The **Ring Road (Route 1)** encircles the island, connecting many of the most popular attractions. Paved for most of its 1,332-kilometer length, it's the most accessible route around the country.

Keep in mind that it's always necessary to check road conditions before you head out in your car. Because the weather can be so challenging, it's ideal to plan a trip around the Ring Road in the **summer.** Despite snow removal during the winter, snowfall can close parts of the route in the east and north.

Day 1: Soak in the Blue Lagoon

After landing at **Keflavík International Airport**, take the Fly Bus or pick up your rental car and drive east on Route 41 to **Reykjavík.** If you are arriving in the morning or afternoon, head south on Route 43 and make a stop at the **Blue Lagoon** near Grindavík to soak in the soothing, geothermally heated water. Revived from jet lag, you're ready to experience the capital city's epic nightlife.

Days 2-3: Head North to Akureyri

From Reykjavík, drive north on the Ring Road to **Borgarnes** and visit the **Settlement Center** to get a taste of Iceland's rich history. Head north again on the Ring Road and then east on Route 518 to **Húsafell** to check out the gorgeous waterfalls of **Hraunfossar**, where the water flows out of lava formations tumbling to the river below. Circle back to the Ring Road and continue driving north to **Akureyri,** where you will spend the next three nights. Spend Day 3 exploring the city's botanical gardens, shops, and restaurants.

Day 4: Hike and Bird-Watch in Mývatn

From Akureyri, head east on the Ring Road to the **Mývatn region** with its mighty lake, vast

Winter Wonders

Sure, Iceland's winter weather can be challenging. But you'll be rewarded with truly unique experiences that make it all worthwhile.

- **Hunt for northern lights:** The main season to see northern lights is October to March. You can book a guided tour or venture out on your own.

- **Soak in the Blue Lagoon:** The most popular tourist attraction in Iceland is popular for a reason—it's a soothing, special experience. The winter is no exception. It's eerie and beautiful to soak during light snowfalls or while watching northern lights dance above on clear nights.

- **Ride majestic Icelandic horses:** Icelandic horses are hardy creatures that are beautiful to ride along the snowy white landscape. Akureyri-based tour company **Saga Travel** (www.sagatravel.is) offers horse-riding day tours from Akureyri and Mývatn.

- **Go cross-country skiing up north:** Iceland isn't known for its skiing, but it does have a well-maintained ski area up north, not too far from Akureyri. The **Hlíðarfjall** ski area (www.hlidarfjall.is) has more than a dozen well-kept trails.

- **Take a glacier walk:** Tour operators offer the unique opportunity to hike on a glacier. They supply all the necessary equipment and provide pick-ups at your hotel or guesthouse. **Icelandic Mountain Guides** (www.mountainguides.is) offers a year-round guided tour walking on a glacier in Skaftafell National Park.

- **Ride snowmobiles:** It's spectacular to glide atop the pristine white snow on crisp and clear winter days. **Vatnajökull Travel** (www.vatnajokull.is) features a year-round tour that includes snowmobile rides on Vatnajökull glacier, the biggest glacier in Europe.

- **Embark on an art museum crawl in Reykjavík:** If the weather outside is frightful, head indoors to explore Iceland's modern artists, like Erró, and old masters such as Jóhannes Kjarval at the **Reykjavík Art Museum.**

- **Tour the Golden Circle:** Iceland's number one tour is available year-round. Book a bus tour or drive the 300-kilometer route yourself. The frozen **Gullfoss** falls and the vast landscape in winter white are gorgeous.

going for a glacier walk

Dettifoss falls

lava fields, gigantic craters, and unique rock formations. Go hiking, watch the rich birdlife, and soak in the decadent **Mývatn Nature Baths.** On the way back from Mývatn to Akureyri, be sure to stop at the glorious waterfall **Goðafoss.** Spend the night in Akureyri.

Day 5: Whale-Watch in Húsavík

Head northeast via Route 85 to **Húsavík,** a placid seaside town known for its spectacular **whale-watching** and comprehensive **Húsavík Whale Museum.** From Húsavík, head south on Route 85 to **Ásbyrgi,** the horseshoe-shaped gorge with towering rock walls and raw nature. Then head to the tremendous waterfall **Dettifoss,** where you will feel the crushing force of the glacial water tumbling below. Continue south on Route 85 to link back up with the Ring Road and drive on to the eastern town **Egilsstaðir,** where you will spend the night.

Days 6-7: Explore the Glacial East

From Egilsstaðir, drive south on the Ring Road to **Vatnajökull glacier,** Europe's largest ice cap, and **Jökulsárlón,** a glacier lagoon. Spend the night in **Höfn.** On Day 7, head to **Skaftafell National Park** to take in the black sands and glacial landscape. If you're feeling adventurous and the weather is pleasant, consider a glacier walk tour. Continue west on the Ring Road to **Vík,** where you will spend the night.

Day 8: Tour the Golden Circle

From Vík, continue west on the Ring Road, starting with a visit to the fishing village **Skógar,** where you can see the waterfall **Skógafoss,** one of the tallest in Iceland. Then tour the **Golden Circle,** a trio of must-see sights. Head west on the Ring Road and north on Route 35 to visit the geothermal area of **Geysir,** where the hot spring Strokkur erupts every 5-7 minutes. Next visit nearby **Gullfoss,** Iceland's most famous and most photographed waterfall. Head west on Routes 35, 37, 365, and 36 to **Þingvellir National Park**—it's a geological wonder and also home to the birthplace of democracy in Iceland. Drive southwest on Route 36 to Reykjavík to spend the night.

Day 9: Hang Out in Reykjavík

Spend as much time in Reykjavík as possible before heading back to Keflavík for your flight. For suggestions for a longer stay in the city, see page 20. If you only have time for a quick coffee, check out Reykjavík's oldest coffeehouse, Mokka, or pick up one of Reykjavík's famous hot dogs at Bæjarins Beztu Pylsur. Drive back to Keflavík.

Get Yourself in Hot Water

Water serves as a constant tourist attraction in Iceland, from waterfalls to boat trips and hot springs.

A trip to Iceland would not be complete without visiting the Blue Lagoon just outside of Grindavík. Against a backdrop of lava fields, the manmade hot spring soothes and exhilarates at the same time. And that goes for any weather conditions—rain, snow, or sunshine. Soaking within the deep mist is a unique experience, a little eerie, and one you will remember—and talk about—for ages.

Up north, the Mývatn Nature Baths feel secluded in comparison to the Blue Lagoon, with fewer people and more room to wade. The water comes from the National Power Company's borehole in Bjarnaflag, scorching when it arrives to the basin next to the manmade bathing lagoon but cooling significantly before filtering into the lagoon. The bottom of the lagoon contains minerals that are beneficial to the skin. The bathing experience is divine, relaxing every inch of your body.

Tourists who visit swimming pools will quickly see how they are an integral part of Icelandic culture. It's common to see families, friends, and coworkers relaxing in a hot tub and talking about politics, music, or the latest movies. The pools are also a great alternative to outdoor activities when the weather is particularly bad—which can happen in Iceland at any time, in any season.

An important note: It is required to shower before you enter the pool or hot tub. Icelanders shower, sans bathing suit, in gender-divided locker rooms, and you're expected to do the same. Just go with the flow.

Mývatn Nature Baths

The Best of Reykjavík

With quaint museums, cool music venues, and top-notch restaurants, small Reykjavík makes a big impression.

Day 1

Explore downtown Reykjavík and all the shops, galleries, restaurants, and coffeehouses the city has to offer. Walk down the street Skólavörðustígur to the landmark church Hallgrímskirkja to check out the amazing interior, beautiful organ, and view from the top. Grab coffee or lunch on Skólavörðustígur at Café Babalu, which makes tasty lattes and light meals like crepes and panini. The street is also where you can pick up a traditional Icelandic sweater at the Handknitting Association of Iceland.

Walk down the main street, Laugavegur, and pop into shops like Hrím for Icelandic design and Mál og Menning for books, T-shirts, and other tourist wares. Walk toward city hall and stroll around the manmade pond Tjörnin, where you can check out swans, ducks, and other birds that call the pond home.

For dinner, consider one of the city's trendy restaurants, like Fiskfelagid for the freshest catch of the day or Buddha Café for Asian fusion. Reykjavík nightlife is epic, and venues like Húrra and Kex Hostel are perfect to check out local DJs or live bands and to dance the night away.

Day 2

Reykjavík's harbor has a lot to see. Have breakfast at Café Haiti and watch boats enter the harbor. Sign up for a whale-watching or bird-watching excursion to have a chance to see minke whales, dolphins, fin whales, blue whales, and seabirds (depending on the season). Once back on land, take a walk over to the Saga Museum

Reykjavík

the amazing pipe organ of Hallgrímskirkja

to learn about Iceland's history and enjoy a coffee and snack or light meal at the in-house café, **Kol & Salt.** Walk over to **Harpa** concert hall to take in a concert or just check out the amazing interior and architecturally significant exterior.

Walk back downtown and check out the **Reykjavík Art Museum,** then have dinner at the wildly popular restaurant **Osushi**, which features delicious sushi. Stop by **Bar 11** to hear some local live music.

Day 3

Go to **Mokka** café on **Skólavörðustígur** for breakfast—the waffles with homemade jam and fresh cream are delightful. Visit Reykjavík's best record shops: Head to **12 Tónar,** a few stores up from Mokka, and then walk to **Lucky Records** near Hlemmur bus station.

Instead of going directly to the airport, sign up for a bus transfer to the **Blue Lagoon** to enjoy the glorious milky water. Then head to Keflavík for your flight.

Harpa concert hall

whale-watching near Húsavík

Iceland offers some of the best whale-watching and bird-watching opportunities in the world's northern reaches. But there's more to the island's wildlife than just the star attractions—seals and reindeer are also worth seeking out.

WHALES

Several whale-watching tour companies operate around the island. Some head out year-round, while others are restricted to the summer. The main whale-watching destinations are in the south (Reykjavík), west (Grundarfjörður), and north (Dalvík and Húsavík).

- **Reykjavík:** Operating from Reykjavík's harbor, whale-watching tours give you the chance to see minke, blue, and fin whales as well as dolphins and porpoises (year-round).

- **Grundarfjörður:** This western town is the best shot you have to catch a glimpse of orcas (it's possible to see orcas year-round, but your best bet is during the winter months).

- **Dalvík:** It's possible to see humpback whales, minke whales, blue whales, harbor porpoises, and dolphins on tours leaving from the harbor of this small northern fishing town (year-round).

a puffin on Heimaey

- **Húsavík:** The unofficial whale-watching capital on the island has seen several species from its shores, including minke, humpback, pilot, northern bottlenose, sperm, sei, fin, orca, and blue whales (mid-May to late October).

PUFFINS

From April to August, it's possible to see puffins in several parts of the country.

- **Heimaey:** Thousands of visitors flock to this island off the south coast to walk along the sea cliffs and spend time with its puffin population (June to August).

- **Látrabjarg:** In West Iceland, trails allow you to access the colossal Látrabjarg cliffs, where puffins gather to nest in intricate crevices (May to August).

- **Borgarfjörður Eystri:** Get a close view of puffins at this fjord in East Iceland, with a great observation platform connected to a small islet that the birds love (mid-April to mid-August).

- **Flatey:** This western island is a good place to spot migrating puffins in the summer (June to August).

SEALS

Six species of seal have been spotted off the coasts of Iceland. The most common sightings are of gray seals and harbor seals. The remaining four species (hooded, harp, bearded, and ringed seals) are hit or miss. In the summer, you have a good chance of spotting gray seals and harbor seals around the Vatnsnes Peninsula in the north. The peninsula is also home to the Icelandic Seal Center, which offers wonderful exhibits about these creatures. The center's staff has information on the best sites for seal-watching opportunities.

REINDEER

Iceland's reindeer herds live only in East Iceland. The best places to view them during the summer are the areas around Mount Snæfell.

reindeer in Egilsstaðir, East Iceland

Iceland Getaway

If you don't have a lot of time, it's possible to see some of the country's highlights in four short days.

Day 1

After landing at **Keflavík International Airport,** either pick up your rental car or take the Fly Bus into **Reykjavík.** If you are arriving in the morning or afternoon, make a stop at the **Blue Lagoon** near Grindavík for a soothing soak. Head to Reykjavík and check into your hotel, guesthouse, or hostel. Explore some of Iceland's **nightlife** by taking in a concert at **Harpa** concert hall or having a couple of drinks at **Kex Hostel,** a favorite among locals and tourists.

Day 2

Spend the day exploring Reykjavík, including the landmark church **Hallgrímskirkja,** the **Saga Museum,** the **Reykjavík Art Museum,** the **National Gallery of Iceland,** and the numerous cafés, galleries, and shops in downtown Reykjavík.

Day 3

Spend a day in the **Snæfellsnes Peninsula** exploring charming fishing villages and the mighty **Snæfellsjökull glacier,** which appeared in Jules Verne's classic tale *A Journey to the Center of the Earth.* Visitors will get to see interesting rock formations, black-sand beaches, and thriving birdlife.

Day 4

Before your flight, spend some time in Reykjavík, exploring unique **galleries** like **Spark Design Space** and top-notch **shopping** like **66 North** and **Geysir** for gifts and quality clothes to bring back home.

the doors of Hallgrímskirkja in Reykjavík

Stykkishólmur on the Snæfellsnes Peninsula

Reykjavík

Look for ★ to find recommended
sights, activities, dining, and lodging.

Highlights

© AVALON TRAVEL

★ **Listasafn Reykjavíkur (Reykjavík Art Museum):** It's actually three museums in one, with one dedicated to sculpture, one to contemporary art, and one that houses the works of beloved Icelandic artist Jóhannes Kjarval. If you buy a ticket to one museum, you can visit the other two on the same day (page 30).

★ **Hallgrímskirkja:** The "Church of Hallgrímur" is a striking national monument dedicated to Hallgrímur Pétursson, one of Iceland's most cherished and celebrated poets. Its tower offers spectacular views (page 31).

★ **Listasafn Íslands (National Gallery of Iceland):** The largest collection of Icelandic art on the island has everything from classic portraits to gorgeous landscapes (page 35).

★ **Tjörnin:** Close to Reykjavík City Hall, this pond is a lovely place to take a stroll and enjoy the birdlife (page 36).

★ **Harpa:** This striking concert hall features individual glass panels that light up during the darkness of winter (page 36).

★ **Sólfar (Sun Voyager):** The large Viking boat sculpture by the sea has been delighting photographers and tourists for decades (page 37).

★ **Perlan:** This unique dome-shaped building has one of the best views of the city, with an outdoor deck and huge mounted binoculars to check out the city below (page 39).

★ **Hiking Mount Esja:** The 914-meter-high Esja is perfect for hikers who don't have the time to venture far from the city. An easy climb on basalt rock climaxes with gorgeous views out to sea (page 66).

Reykjavík is having a moment. Relatively affordable airfares are drawing weekenders from both sides of the Atlantic, giving Iceland's capital city a chance to show off its urban appeal and highly individualistic style.

Reykjavík's history dates back to AD 874, when Ingólfur Arnarson from Norway established the first settlement in Iceland. The city slowly grew over the centuries, and in 1786, Reykjavík was established as an official trading town; 1786 is considered the city's official founding date.

Today, Reykjavík has a lot of people, cars, and trees, in stark contrast to the rest of the country. Roughly 200,000 of Iceland's 330,000 residents live in the capital city. Though it's small, its energy mimics that of New York City or Berlin. Reykjavík residents are known to have two lives: They work by day and become musicians, artists, or poets by night. While strolling on Reykjavík's main street, Laugavegur, you'll see street art among the high-end shops, musicians playing impromptu concerts outside coffeehouses, and small art galleries boasting original "Icelandic Design." It's undeniably a creative place.

While Reykjavík can seem quite urban with its galleries and restaurants, nature is never too far away. The air is unbelievably clean (unlike in many urban areas), and whales can be seen passing by the harbor during the summer.

PLANNING YOUR TIME

Given its small size, Reykjavík can be "done" in 1-2 days depending on your level of interest. Some travelers treat Reykjavík as their starting point before heading out on the Ring Road or booking day trips into the countryside, while others travel to Reykjavík specifically for the nightlife and art scene.

ORIENTATION

Reykjavík is the most compact capital city in all of Europe. City center and the old harbor are situated in the northern half of the city, and the main bus station (BSÍ) is in the south. Most of the hotels, museums, shops, and restaurants are in the northern half, and tourists

---

Previous: downtown Reykjavík; a park near the Alþingishúsið. **Above:** Hallgrímskirkja.

Central Reykjavík

© AVALON TRAVEL

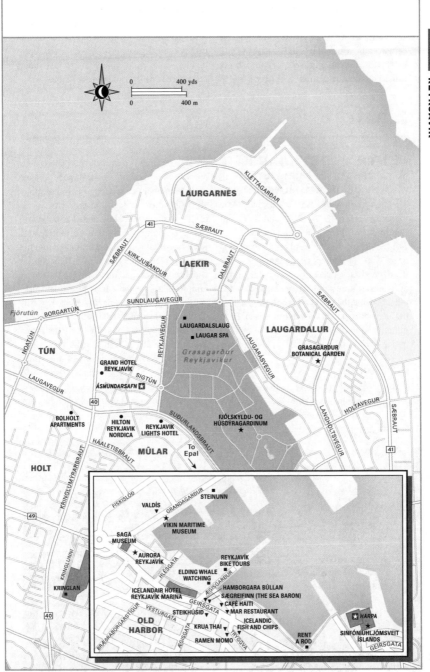

don't have to venture far outside city center on short trips to Reykjavík.

The main street in central Reykjavík is Laugavegur, which starts in the east. As you move west, it eventually becomes Bankastræti, which ends up Austurstræti. The streets tend to have long names, and there isn't a grid system in place, but the city is small enough that you won't get too lost. Hlemmur bus station on the east end of Laugavegur is Strætó's main depot downtown. It can connect you to just about anywhere in central and greater Reykjavík.

Sights

CENTRAL REYKJAVÍK
★ Listasafn Reykjavíkur (Reykjavík Art Museum)

The **Reykjavík Art Museum** is actually three museums (Hafnarhús, Kjarvalsstaðir, and Ásmundarsafn) in three different locations. Admission is 1,200ISK, and each museum is open 10am-5pm daily. It's important to note that if you purchase a ticket to any one of the three museums, you are granted free admission to the other two. But the free entry is only available on the same day your ticket was purchased. Each museum is pretty small and you can hit all three in one day, as an hour at each is enough time.

HAFNARHÚS

Hafnarhús (Tryggvagata 17, tel. 354/590-1200, www.listasafnreykjavikur.is), which focuses on contemporary art, is the crown jewel of the three museums, in part because of its permanent collection of Erró paintings and prints. Erró, an Icelandic pop artist, is one of the most celebrated modern Icelandic artists. The museum's collection is extensive, and works are regularly rotated to make room for new works. His work ranges from light pop art with bright colors and interesting characters to samples of line sketches from his earlier work. While the art can be playful, the artist also tackles political and social issues in his work. The museum also houses works from other Icelandic artists, as well as rotating exhibitions of foreign painters, designers, and visual artists. You get a sense that this is Reykjavík's version of New York's Museum of Modern Art. The museum is based in a nondescript

Reykjavík's stunning setting

white-block building, and the interior has three floors of exhibitions. The ground floor holds the souvenir shop and coat check along with a large open space for exhibits. The upper floors are dedicated to exhibitions.

KJARVALSSTAÐIR

Kjarvalsstaðir (Flókagata 24, tel. 354/517-1290, www.listasafnreykjavikur.is) is the place to go if you're looking to explore the works of Icelandic painter Jóhannes Kjarval (1885-1972), who is best known for his dark and moody paintings of Iceland's landscape. Kjarval was a master of capturing Iceland's raw nature in the winter light. The majority of Kjarval's collection was left to the city of Reykjavík after his death. The other wing of the museum features various Icelandic artists, ranging from well-known modern artists to some of Iceland's best and brightest art students. The museum is one level with a coffeehouse in the middle of the two wings. The high ceilings and wall of windows by the coffeehouse make for an interesting space. A large outdoor field behind the museum sometimes serves as a spot for sculpture exhibitions. The museum is on the small size, so budget an hour to check out the art.

ÁSMUNDARSAFN

Ásmundarsafn (Sigtún, tel. 354/553-2155, www.listasafnreykjavikur.is) is an impressive sculpture museum featuring only the works of Ásmundur Sveinsson (1893-1982), who worked with materials including wood, copper, and iron. Ásmundur's work is housed in a gorgeous stark white domed building. It's small, so you only need an hour or less to explore the work, but it's an hour well spent. An exhibit features what his workshop looked like, as well as renderings of projects, and his masterpiece, a chair carved out of wood. The detail of the chair is spectacular. An outdoor sculpture garden features interesting works among trees, shrubs, and flowers.

Þjóðmenningarhúsið (Culture House)

Culture House (Hverfisgata 15, tel. 354/545-1400, www.thjodmenning.is, 11am-5pm daily, 1,000ISK) is a stately white neo-classic building that first opened to the public in 1909 as a museum. It is home to significant medieval manuscripts, including unique sagas, narratives, and poems from early settlers. Guided tours of exhibitions on Mondays and Fridays at 3pm last about an hour, or you can tour on your own. Rotating exhibitions throughout the year can include paintings, photography, or literary works. The exhibits do an excellent job of placing the manuscripts, literature, and artwork in context, giving visitors a great overview. Be sure to check the website to see what's on view. Culture House also plays host to conferences, gatherings, and readings throughout the year, including Reykjavík's annual design festival, DesignMarch, in the spring. The cafeteria serves light meals, and the traditional meat soup is delicious.

★ Hallgrímskirkja

Hallgrímskirkja (Hallgrímstorg, tel. 354/510-1000, www.hallgrimskirkja.is, 9am-9pm daily June-Aug., 9am-5pm daily rest of year, free) is one of the most photographed, and most visited, sites in Reykjavík. The "Church of Hallgrímur" is a national monument dedicated to Hallgrímur Pétursson, one of the most cherished and celebrated poets of Iceland, who lived 1614-1674. It's a modern structure, made out of concrete, that has basalt-style columns at the bottom coming to a point at the top.

Standing at 73 meters, the Lutheran church was designed by state architect Guðjón Samúelsson, and work started on the church in 1945. Completed in 1986, the church is a must-see for tourists. The interior is home to a gorgeous organ constructed by Johannes Klais Organworks in Germany, as well as beautiful stained-glass windows. Concerts ranging from choirs to organ performances are frequently held at the church. Be sure to check the website for upcoming concerts. An annual Christmas concert features traditional songs sung in English. It's an active church that holds services.

Downtown Reykjavík

© AVALON TRAVEL

Hallgrímskirkja

The highlight of a trip to Hallgrímskirkja for many is a visit to the **tower** (9am-9pm daily June-Aug., 9am-5pm daily rest of year, 800ISK) at the top, which has spectacular views of the city. An elevator takes you to the tower.

Einar Jónsson Museum

The **Einar Jónsson Museum** (Eiríksgata 1, tel. 354/561-3797, www.lej.is, 1pm-5pm daily June-mid-Sept., 1pm-5pm Sat.-Sun. mid-Sept.-Nov. and Feb.-May, closed Dec.-Jan., 1,000ISK) houses the works of one of Iceland's most celebrated sculptors, Einar Jónsson (1874-1954). Situated across the street from Hallgrímskirkja, the museum features work ranging from Christian-themed sculptures to those depicting Iceland's rich folklore. Einar worked almost entirely with plaster, which was rare for the period. The outdoor sculpture garden is beautiful, whether the sun is shining or it is under a layer of snow. The garden makes the museum a very special visit. Plan to spend about an hour checking out the art inside, and if the weather is nice, spend additional time outside in the garden.

Hið Íslenzka Reðasafn (Icelandic Phallological Museum)

The **Icelandic Phallological Museum** (Laugavegur 116, tel. 354/561-6663, www.phallus.is, 10am-6pm daily, 1,000ISK) is just as weird as it sounds. Guests can view the penises of 200 Icelandic animals, including the arctic fox, walrus, seal, and polar bear. After the museum was moved to its current location in Reykjavík (from Húsavík in North Iceland), the curator unveiled his latest acquisition—a human member. The museum has members on display in glass cases, and preserved bones of certain mammals are hanging on the wall. The highlight is also a unique photo op: the huge whale specimen on display. Some people find the museum humorous, while others are a bit freaked out. Looking for unique postcards, T-shirts, and souvenirs? Look no further.

Spark Design Space

Spark Design Space (Klapparstígur 33, tel. 354/552-2656, www.sparkdesignspace.com, 10am-6pm Mon.-Fri., noon-4pm Sat., free) was a welcome addition to the Reykjavík gallery scene. Before Spark opened in 2010, Reykjavík did not have a gallery dedicated to product design, which is surprising for such a design-conscious city. The gallery has rotating exhibitions ranging from poster design to home goods to 3D printer demonstrations. Spark plays a role in local events and festivals; it's a venue during Reykjavík's annual spring design festival, DesignMarch. Just off Laugavegur, the main street in downtown Reykjavík, Spark is in a great location among cool shops and popular bars.

Þjóðminjasafn Íslands (National Museum of Iceland)

The **National Museum of Iceland** (Suðurgata 41, tel. 354/530-2200, www.nationalmuseum.is, 10am-5pm daily May-mid-Sept., 11am-5pm Mon., 10am-5pm Tues.-Sun. mid-Sept.-Apr., 1,500ISK) is Reykjavík's main heritage and history museum, housing everything from tools and clothing of the settlement era to models of Viking-era ships. This is the best museum in the city to get insight on the history of the Icelandic nation and its people. The artifacts and exhibitions are well presented with clear information in English. Budget about two hours to take in all exhibits.

Saga Museum

The **Saga Museum** (Grandagardi 2, tel. 354/511-1517, www.sagamuseum.is, 10am-6pm daily, 2,000ISK) moved to its new location in 2014 after being housed in Perlan for years. With the move came a bigger and reinvigorated museum, with 17 exhibits ranging from Iceland's first inhabitants to the nation's conversion to Christianity to the reformation. Special emphasis is placed on important characters in Iceland's history, such as Ingólfur Arnarson, who is believed to be the first settler in Iceland. There are interactive displays as well as artifacts on view and even a Viking dress-up area that is great for kids. They can play with replicas of traditional clothing and plastic swords. An audio guide in English, German, French, or Swedish is available to accompany your walk around the museum. The in-house café, **Kol & Salt,** serves light meals, coffee, and a selection of wine and beer. The cakes are very tempting. It's best to budget two hours for this museum.

Norræna Húsið (Nordic House)

Nordic House (Sturlugata 5, tel. 354/551-7030, www.nordichouse.is, 11am-5pm Sun.-Wed., 11am-9pm Thurs.-Sat., free) is home to a library, café, and numerous cultural events

the National Gallery of Iceland

during the year. For instance, literary and film festivals are held at the building, as well as fashion and music events. Most tourists visit Nordic House for the structure itself. The building, which was opened in 1968, was designed by noted Finnish architect Alvar Aalto, and several of his signature traits are reflected in the design, including the use of tile, white, and wood throughout the building. The exterior features a one-story design with a blue ceramic rooftop.

Ljósmyndasafn Reykjavíkur (Reykjavík Museum of Photography)

The Reykjavík Museum of Photography (Tryggvagata 15, tel. 354/563-1790, www.photomuseum.is, noon-7pm Mon.-Thurs., 1pm-5pm Fri.-Sun., free) has an extensive collection of photographs, as well as items and documents related to the practice of photography, from professional and amateur photographers in Iceland. The collection is divided into three categories: landscape, press, and portrait photography. The museum is small, but there are a lot of treasures to be found, including the oldest photo in the museum's collection, a landscape photo, which dates from 1870. Iceland's most famous landscape photographer, Ragnar Axelsson, regularly has photos on exhibit.

★ Listasafn Íslands (National Gallery of Iceland)

If you have time for only one art museum, the National Gallery of Iceland (Fríkirkjuvergur 7, tel. 354/515-9600, www.listasafn.is, 10am-5pm Tues.-Sun. mid-May-mid-Sept. 15, 11am-5pm Tues.-Sun. mid-Sept.-mid-May, 1,000ISK) should be it due to its large and varied collection. The National Gallery houses the country's main collection of Icelandic art, with particular emphasis on 19th- and 20th-century Icelandic and international art. Here you will see everything from traditional landscape paintings to art depicting the sagas to works by modern Icelandic artists. Works from international artists on display include some from Pablo Picasso and Richard Serra. The stately white building is a stone's throw from Tjörnin (The Pond), so if the weather is fair, taking a leisurely stroll after visiting the museum is quite nice.

Raðhús (Reykjavík City Hall)

Reykjavík's City Hall (Tjarnagata 11, tel. 354/411-1111, www.visitreykjavik.is) is more than just a building that houses the mayor and other officials. Built in 1992, the large white structure has a wall of windows overlooking the pond. On the ground floor, visitors

City Hall

will find an information desk with maps and tourist brochures, as well as a cozy café with a great view of the pond and city. A large hall is often used for art exhibitions and markets, and a huge model of Iceland is a favorite among tourists and is worth a visit.

★ Tjörnin

Tjörnin (The Pond) is a small body of water, rich with birdlife, situated next to the Reykjavík City Hall building. Its scenic strip of colorful houses begs to be photographed. When the weather is nice, a walk around the pond, which is about 1.5 kilometers around, is delightful. Sculptures and benches dot the perimeter. Birdlife is plentiful, with arctic terns, ducks, seagulls, and swans. Feeding the birds is not allowed, so don't be that tourist who empties a bag of stale bread at the edge. In the winter, the pond freezes and becomes popular for ice skating.

Alþingishúsið (Parliament House)

The Alþingishúsið is the meeting place of the national parliament members of Iceland. While Iceland's democracy dates back to the year 930, and parliament members met at Þingvellir, the parliament was moved to Reykjavík in 1844. Situated near Austurvöllur park, the stone building was designed by Danish architect Ferdinand Meldahland and built in 1881. Currently, only the debating chamber and a few small meeting rooms are actually located in the building. It's not possible to attend sessions of parliament. Offices of most of Alþingi's members are in other buildings in the area around Austurvöllur, which is actually the address of the building.

OLD HARBOR

Reykjavík's old harbor has been undergoing a transformation over the past few years, and it's become a dynamic place to visit, with shops, museums, new hotels, and the Ólafur Elíasson-designed Harpa concert hall.

★ Harpa

Reykjavík's newest landmark, Harpa (Austurbakki 2, tel. 354/528-5000, www.harpa.is) is a striking glass structure that hosts rock concerts, operas, the Icelandic Symphony, and international conferences. Designed by Icelandic/Danish artist Ólafur Elíasson, the concert hall's exterior features individual glass panels that light up during the darkness of winter. Individual glass panels sometimes blink in a pattern, or simply

Reykjavík harbor

change colors. The building is particularly striking since it's so close to the water in the harbor area. Since opening its doors in 2011, Harpa has been lauded by design organizations and magazines around the world, even earning the title of "Best Performance Venue of 2011" by *Travel & Leisure* magazine. There are daily guided tours of the building available for 1,750ISK, but it's also a fun place to explore and take pictures, even if you're not going to attend a concert or conference. A café on the bottom floor serves coffee, soft drinks, light meals, and cakes, and a formal restaurant on the fourth floor has stunning views of the harbor. Two shops also occupy the first floor: the record shop 12 Tónar and the design shop Epal.

Höfði House

Höfði House (Borgartún) is one of Reykjavík's most historically significant buildings and worth a photo or two. Built in 1909, the stately white building was initially used as a consulate for France, and later served as a sort of guesthouse for famous folks passing through including Winston Churchill, the Queen of England and even actress Marlene Dietrich. Perhaps its most famous use was as the backdrop for the 1986 meeting between U.S. president Ronald Reagan and the head of the Soviet Union, Mikhail Gorbachev, that effectively ended the Cold War. Today, Höfði is owned by the City of Reykjavík and is currently used for official receptions and meetings. Although the house is unfortunately not open to the public, visitors are welcome to explore the exterior of the building.

★ Sólfar (Sun Voyager)

Situated near a coastal path popular with cyclists and runners is *Sólfar* (by the street called Sæbraut), a huge aluminum sculpture that resembles a Viking ship. Before Harpa was built, *Sólfar* was the top spot to take photos near the harbor. But, it's still a big draw for tourists and definitely worth a visit. Icelandic sculptor Jón Gunnar Árnason was inspired by undiscovered territory and chasing the sun, hence the name the *Sun Voyager*. The sculpture was unveiled in 1990, just months after Jón Gunnar's death. The view of Mount Esja, the sea, and passing boats is the perfect backdrop for photos. On clear days, you can see the town of Akranes across the bay.

Aurora Reykjavík

Aurora Reykjavík (Grandagarður 2, tel. 354/780-4500, www.aurorareykjavik.is,

Harpa

9am-9pm daily, 1,600ISK) gives you a chance to check out northern lights in any season. If you can't make it to Iceland in the wintertime, this is the next best thing. The multimedia exhibition gives a history of the aurora borealis, stories of northern lights from around the world, and an introduction to northern lights photography. The highlight of the center is a 13-minute film that shows some of the most majestic northern lights displays over the island.

Vikin Maritime Museum

Vikin Maritime Museum (Grandargarður 8, tel. 354/517-9400, www.maritimemuseum. is, 10am-5pm daily, 1,300ISK) is Reykjavík's main museum devoted to the city's fishing history. The main exhibitions show the progression from rowboats to modern trawlers and describe the trading vessels used, trading routes, and the construction of Reykjavík's harbor. There are daily tours of the coastal vessel *Odinn* available at 11am, 1pm, 2pm, and 3pm that last about an hour. The exhibitions cover the city's fishing history going back to the settlement to present day. The museum café has great views of the harbor and offers an outdoor eating area when the weather cooperates.

OUTSIDE THE CITY CENTER
Fjölskyldu- og Húsdýragarðinum (Reykjavík Zoo)

The Reykjavík Zoo (Laugardalur, tel. 354/575-7800, www.mu.is, 10am-6pm daily June-late Aug., 10am-5pm daily late Aug.-May, adults 750ISK, children 5-12 550ISK, children 4 and under free) is more park than zoo. You won't see monkeys or polar bears, but exhibits house horses, pigs, goats, sheep, and other farm animals. The main attraction is a pair of seals. It's a pleasant place to walk around and bring children, but it isn't much of a tourist destination. In other words, if you're not on a long trip with small children, you can skip the zoo and not feel bad about it. Inside is a tiny aquarium that houses mainly fish. In the summer months, you'll see Icelandic families taking a stroll, looking at the animals, and visiting a small play area for children. There isn't an official petting zoo, but it's common to see parents holding their children up to pet horses in a penned area.

Grasagardur Reykjavíkur (Reykjavík Botanical Garden)

The Reykjavík Botanical Garden

Reykjavík Zoo

(Laugardalur, tel. 354/411-8650, www.grasa-gardur.is, 10am-10pm daily May-Sept., 10am-3pm daily Oct.-Apr., free) is a beautiful spot tucked away in a quiet part of the city. East of downtown Reykjavík, the neighborhood is more residential. During the summer months, the garden is chock-full of bright flowers, hardy plants, peaceful ponds, and thriving birdlife. The café within the garden, Café Flora, is a little known spot among tourists. There, you will find locals sipping on coffee drinks and enjoying light meals while taking in the view from grand windows. If you're not visiting in the summer, you can skip the garden.

★ Perlan

Perlan (Öskjuhlíð, tel. 354/562-0200, www.perlan.is, free) was a unique addition to Reykjavík's skyline in 1991. The dome-shaped structure named "The Pearl" offers one of the best views of the city skyline. It houses a café that serves coffee and light meals, a souvenir shop next to the café, and an outdoor viewing platform (10am-10pm) that overlooks the city. The main attraction, however, is a rotating fine-dining restaurant on the top floor that completes a full rotation every two hours.

Sports and Recreation

BIKING

Reykjavík is a wonderful city to see by bicycle. That is, when the weather holds up. Over the past few years, there has been an initiative to designate more bike lanes and establish more places to lock up your bicycle along the streets. This isn't Amsterdam (perhaps the most bike-friendly city in Europe), but Reykjavík has come a long way. If you're in town and would like to rent a bike for an independent ride, or join a tour, Reykjavík Bike Tours (Ægisgarður 7, tel. 354/694-8956, www.icelandbike.com) will get you going. Their "Classic Reykjavík Bike Tour" covers about seven kilometers and takes a good 2.5 hours for 5,500ISK. Along the tour, you will see the University of Iceland campus, Reykjavík's Catholic cathedral, the parliament house, the old harbor, and more. Bicycle rentals start at 3,500ISK for four hours.

FISHING

If you'd like to try your hand at reeling in one of Iceland's freshest fish during the summer, you can rent equipment at Reykjavík harbor from Rent a Rod (tel. 354/869-2840, www.rentarod.is, 10am-6pm Mon.-Fri., 11am-5pm Sat.-Sun. June-Aug.). For 5,000ISK, you can rent a rod with wheel and line for two hours, including bait, single-use gloves, map of the harbor, and a life vest. You can catch trout, salmon, cod, pollock, and haddock. The staff could also arrange for fishing day tours out of the harbor. For sea angling tours, check out Elding Whale Watching (Ægisgarður 5, tel. 354/519-5000, www.whalewatching.is), which offers a tour with a "gourmet" twist, where you can cook and eat your catches on board the boat. The tour is available May-August. The tour is about three hours, departs daily from Reykjavík harbor at 11am, and costs 13,500ISK.

WHALE-WATCHING

Whale-watching is in some ways the best part of natural Reykjavík, in that you get to see a slice of nature just minutes from shore. Elding Whale Watching (Ægisgarður 5, tel. 354/519-5000, www.whalewatching.is) offers tours all year-round and boasts a 95 percent chance of seeing whales in the summer, and 80 percent chance in the winter. The guides are enthusiastic and the business is one of the oldest at the harbor. Tourists relish the sightings of minke and humpback whales, dolphins, porpoises, and various seabirds, including puffins and arctic terns. Make sure you dress warmly, even in the summer, as it can get quite cold on the open waters. Tours are about three hours long and cost 8,500ISK for adults and 4,250ISK for children. **Special Tours** (Ægisgarður 13, tel. 354/560-8800, www.specialtours.is) also runs year-round tours from Reykjavík harbor, with five daily departures May-August and one or two daily departures the remainder of the year. Tours are about three hours long and cost 8,500ISK per person.

BIRD-WATCHING

For bird-watchers, the "Puffin Express" tour, which leaves from Reykjavík harbor May through mid-August, is operated by **Special Tours** (tel. 354/560-8800, www.specialtours.is). The owners have been running bird-watching tours since 1996, provide binoculars on board, and have a 100 percent sighting success rate. The guides have a soft spot for the funny black and white birds with the brilliant beaks and take great pride in telling you all about them. A one-hour boat tour is 5,000ISK for adults and 2,500ISK for children.

SWIMMING

Swimming is a central part of Icelandic culture, and if you don't visit a pool or two during your stay in Iceland, you're missing out. Icelanders treat the pools as places for social gatherings. Visitors will see groups of friends and/or family in the pools and relaxing in hot tubs, chatting, laughing, and catching up. Each pool has its own character and local flavor, and some pools are more child-friendly than others, with slides and bigger areas designated for children. And, for roughly $5, it's a great way to spend a few leisurely hours. The pools listed here are recommended.

Laugardalslaug (Sundlaugavegur 30, tel. 354/411-5100, 7am-10pm Mon.-Fri., 8am-8pm Sat.-Sun., 600ISK) is the biggest pool facility in Reykjavík, and the one that gets the most tourists. The heated 50-meter outdoor pool is a big draw, along with the hot tubs, steam bath, and sauna. It's very crowded in the summer months (June-August) and can be loud

because the giant water slide in the children's pool is a favorite among local kids.

Sundhöllin (Barónstígur, tel. 354/551-4059, 7am-10pm Mon.-Fri., 8am-7pm Sat.-Sun., 600ISK) is the only indoor pool in Reykjavík and popular among locals and tourists alike. The 25-meter pool was recently renovated, and the outdoor sundeck overlooking Hallgrímskirkja is a great spot to spend a couple of hours when the sun is shining. Sudhöllin also has a steam room and two hot tubs. Given its proximity to the city center, the pool gets a good amount of traffic.

Vesturbæjarlaug (Hofsvallagata 104, tel. 354/566-6879, 7am-10pm Mon.-Fri., 8am-10pm Sat.-Sun., 600ISK) is situated in a quiet neighborhood west of the city center. If you're looking to beat the crowds and experience the pool culture among locals, this is the spot. Facilities include a 25-meter pool, a few hot tubs, and a sauna.

SPAS

If you're after something more luxurious than a local swimming pool, there are a couple of spas in Reykjavík where you can relax and get treatments. Many tourists opt to spend an afternoon at the Blue Lagoon near Grindavík, and several buses depart from the bus station BSÍ (www.bsi.is). But if you want to beat the crowds, a local spa is a great option.

Laugar Spa (Sundlaugavegur 30A, tel. 354/553-0000, www.laugarspa.is, 6am-11pm Mon.-Fri., 8am-9:30pm Sat., 8am-7:30pm Sun.) is Reykjavík's largest private spa, offering an extensive menu of treatments including facials, body massage and scrub, tanning treatments, waxing and nail services, and clay wrap treatments. The spa is marketed as an "aquatic heaven," and it's as good as it sounds. The entrance to the spa is reminiscent of a cave, with the soothing sound of water drops falling from a six-meter-wide waterfall. Inside, six sauna rooms are kept at different temperatures, each with its own unique theme. The treatment rooms feature muted hues and calming music. There is a gym on-site, as well as a café serving fresh, healthy meals.

The **Soley Natura Spa** at Icelandair Hótel Reykjavík Natura (Nautholsvegur 2, tel. 354/444-4085, www.icelandairhotels.com, 10am-8pm Mon.-Fri., 10am-7pm Sat., noon-5pm Sun.) arrived on the scene in 2011. The spa has an earthy atmosphere with natural hues and lots of wood furnishings. It's Scandinavian to a T. Guests have access to a heated pool, hot tub, and sauna before and after treatments. Massage options include lymphatic massage, hot stone massage, reflexology, and pregnancy massage. Beauty treatments include waxing services, manicures and pedicures, and facials.

Entertainment and Events

NIGHTLIFE

Reykjavík may be small, but its nightlife is epic. Whether you're up for some live music, want to dance, or are interested a classic pub crawl, Reykjavík will not disappoint. The main drag, Laugavegur, is ground zero for the hottest clubs and bars in town. If you are up for dancing, Kiki Queer Bar is your spot. If you fancy a whiskey bar, Dillon is the place. If you want to catch a hot Reykjavík band performing live, Húrra is your best bet. Be prepared for it to be a late night and for your wallet to take a hit. Locals don't venture out until around midnight, and drinks are expensive. Expect to pay upwards of New York City and London prices for alcohol. For that reason, cocktail bars are scarce and beer is the favored beverage. But, for such a small city, you can't help but be impressed by the number of hot spots catering to different genres. Your biggest challenge will be narrowing down your options!

Dance Clubs

Austur (Austurstræti 7, tel. 354/568-1907, 8pm-1am Thurs., 8pm-4:30am Fri.-Sat.) was once the hottest club in Reykjavík, but a dress code and competition from other clubs have knocked Austur down a couple of pegs. It's still a place to go, mingle with locals, and dance the night away with current and trendy dance music.

Boston (Laugavegur 28B, tel. 354/577-3200, 4pm-1am Mon.-Thurs., 4pm-3am Fri.-Sat.) is best known as a hangout for local artists, writers, hipsters, and hangers-on. The bar has an unassuming exterior, but inside await good drinks and hot music, mainly rock. If there's a concert on the night you go, expect to stand shoulder to shoulder. It's a tight spot and doesn't take too long to draw a big crowd.

Hressingarskálinn (Austurstræti 22, tel. 354/561-2240, www.hresso.is, 9am-1am Sun.-Thurs., 10am-4am Fri.-Sat.), simply known as Hresso, is a casual restaurant by day, serving up hamburgers and sandwiches. Free Wi-Fi attracts writers, tourists, and locals, who are known to spend hours sipping endless cups of coffee. By night, Hresso transforms into a dance club, with hot DJs and live bands. Expect current and trendy dance music.

Lebowski Bar (Laugavegur 20, tel. 354/552-2300, www.lebowski.is, 11:30am-1am Sun.-Thurs., 11:30am-4am Fri.-Sat.) not so subtly pays homage to the Coen brothers' movie *The Big Lebowski*. Inside there is bowling paraphernalia, posters from the film, and even a rug hanging on the side of the bar. It's a casual eatery during the day, like many of Reykjavík's bars, but at night it transforms into a pretty wild scene, playing the latest dance music. There's a dance floor in the back end of the bar.

Bars

Celtic Cross (Hverfisgata 26, tel. 354/511-3240, 11am-1am Sun.-Thurs., 11am-5am Fri.-Sat.) has Guinness on tap, which is the only thing that makes this place remotely Irish despite wood paneling and Irish ale ads on the walls. But, locals come for the Guinness and it attracts tourists as well. Crowds are known to be rowdy on the weekends.

The English Pub (Austurstræti 12b, tel. 354/578-0400, www.enskibarinn.is, noon-1am Mon.-Fri., noon-4:30am Sat.-Sun.) is part English pub, part sports bar. There's a nice selection of Icelandic and foreign beer, and Guinness is on tap. If there's a soccer game being played anywhere in the world, it will likely be shown on one of the many screens in the bar. If there's an English league game on, expect a crowd of expats, tourists, and locals.

Kaffibarinn (Bergstaðastræti 1, tel. 354/551-1588, 5pm-1am Sun.-Thurs., 3pm-3am Fri.-Sat.) has been a Reykjavík institution since scenes from the indie film *101 Reykjavík* were filmed in the bar. Damon Albarn, the Blur frontman, used to own a stake in the bar. It's a tiny bar, with a rich red exterior, that gets jam-packed during the weekends, but it's one of those places that it's cool to say you were there. Expect trendy dance music to be blaring as you enter.

Micro Bar (Austurstræti 6, tel. 354/847-9084, 4pm-midnight daily) is a beer lover's paradise. The bar carries about 80 different beers from countries including Belgium, Germany, Denmark, and the United States. The big draws are the wide selection of Icelandic beers on tap and the number of Icelandic craft beers available. Stop by and try a local stout, pale ale, or lager. The atmosphere is relaxed and relatively quiet, with dim lighting and a large wood bar. You'll find locals at one of the tables enjoying a beer and conversation with a friend.

Gay and Lesbian

Kiki Queer Bar (Laugavegur 22, tel. 354/571-0194, www.kiki.is, 8pm-1am Thurs., 8pm-4:30am Fri.-Sat.) is Reykjavík's only gay bar and was a welcome addition to the scene when it opened its doors in early 2013. Many locals will tell you this is *the* place to go to dance because it attracts some of the best local and visiting DJs. You can expect music ranging from Madonna to Lady Gaga and everything in between.

Lebowski Bar

Live Music

Bar 11 (Hverfisgata 18, tel. 354/690-6021, noon-1am Sun.-Thurs., noon-3am Fri.-Sat.) has earned its reputation as Reykjavík's leading rock bar by featuring a steady stream of up-and-coming rock bands as well as local favorites. The decor is dark, with skulls and black furnishings, but the attitude is light and fun.

Café Rósenberg (Lækjargata 2, tel. 354/551-8008, 11am-1am Sun.-Thurs., 11am-3am Fri.-Sat.) is known to host jazz, pop, rock, and folk acts from all around Iceland. You have a good chance to catch local favorites like KK, Ellen, and Svavar Knutur here, as well as international acts. The staffers are warm and friendly music lovers who take pride in booking varied acts and running a laid-back café that serves classic Icelandic comfort food.

Dillon (Laugavegur 30, tel. 354/511-2400, 2pm-1am Sun.-Thurs., 2pm-3am Fri.-Sat.) looks and feels like a dive bar. Rockers, metalheads, and hipsters unite, listening to live

Kiki Queer Bar

bands and sipping the fine collection of whiskeys available. When there isn't live music, locals DJs keep the music flowing. The interior is a little rough, with lots of wood and not many places to sit, and the music is always loud.

Húrra (Tryggvagata 22, tel. 354/691-9662, 5pm-1am Sun.-Thurs., 5pm-4:30am Fri.-Sat.) is a colorful spot featuring a steady stream of Iceland's hottest bands taking the stage, playing everything from rock and dance to pop and hip hop, depending on the night.

Kex Hostel (Skulagata 28, tel. 354/561-6060, www.kexhostel.is) has become a Reykjavík institution over the past few years. The hostel, which used to be home to a biscuit factory, is a great space, complete with mid-century furniture, vintage wall maps, and a lot of curiosities. A small stage in the entryway hosts up and coming bands while guests drink and hang out at the bar. A back room serves as a concert space for more formal concerts. If you're in your 20s and aren't bothered by hipsters, this is your place. Since this is a hostel,

it's open 24 hours, so check listings at www.grapevine.is for concert times.

Loft Hostel (Bankastræti 7, tel. 354/553-8140, www.lofthostel.is) opened in 2013 and has quickly earned a reputation as a place to see and be seen. The fourth-floor bar/café hosts up and coming bands, established live acts, and DJs. An outdoor deck overlooks Bankastræti and is packed with locals and tourists alike when the sun is shining during the day, and filled with mingling concertgoers at night. Since this is a hostel, it's open 24 hours, so check listings at www.grapevine.is for concert and event times.

PERFORMING ARTS
Íslenska Óperan (Icelandic Opera)
The **Icelandic Opera** (Ingólfsstræti 2A, tel. 354/511-6400, www.opera.is) has been thriving since productions moved in 2011 to the exquisite Harpa concert hall by the harbor. Productions have become more elaborate, and entire runs have been selling out. If you are an opera fan, check the website to see the current and upcoming shows. Past performances include *Carmen, Il Trovatore, La Boheme,* and *The Magic Flute.*

Sinfóníuhljómsveit Íslands (Icelandic Symphony Orchestra)
The **Icelandic Symphony Orchestra** (Austurbakki 2, tel. 354/545-2500, www.sinfonia.is) consists of 90 full-time members and performs about 60 concerts each season, including subscription concerts in Reykjavík, family concerts, school concerts, and recordings, as well as local and international tours. Based in the Harpa concert hall, the symphony has performed works by Igor Stravinsky, Sergei Rachmaninoff, and Pyotr Tchaikovsky.

Þjóðleikhúsið (National Theater of Iceland)
The **National Theater of Iceland** (Hverfisgata 19, tel. 354/551-1200, www.

leikhusid.is) has been a Reykjavík mainstay since its opening in 1950. The emphasis is on Nordic/Scandinavian plays and musicals, but some foreign works are translated into Icelandic. For instance, in 2014, the theater put on a production of the Monty Python musical *Spamalot* in the 500-seat main stage. The exterior is a cold, concrete-gray building, but inside is a different story. The interior is modern, the theaters comfortable, and there's a lovely lounge area with plush seats and small tables where you can have a drink and wait for the show to begin.

FESTIVALS AND EVENTS
Spring

Launched in 2009, the **Reykjavík Fashion Festival** (www.rff.is) showcases fashion lines from established designers as well as up-and-comers every March for four days. Along with runway shows and special exhibitions, the festival welcomes international designers as guest speakers. In 2014, Calvin Klein was a guest.

Coinciding with the Reykjavík Fashion Festival is **DesignMarch** (www.design-march.is), a broader event that covers everything from product design to graphic design. With pop-up stores around the city and exhibitions held in museums and open-air spaces, the festival attracts people from around the world to check out the latest and greatest in Icelandic design.

You may not expect Reykjavík to be a blues town, but don't tell that to locals. The **Reykjavík Blues Festival** (www.blues.is) is a week-long festival held in early April. It mixes local talent with acclaimed international acts like Michael Burks, Lucky Peterson, Pinetop Perkins, and Magic Slim and the Teardrops.

Gamers rejoice! The **EVE Fanfest** takes over the city every May, celebrating the beloved video game *EVE*, which is the creation of local company CCP. Thousands of gamers, nerds, and curious locals gather, attend round-table discussions, play live tournaments, and indulge in a pub crawl.

Summer

Delighting locals and tourists since 1970, the **Reykjavík Arts Festival** (www.artfest.is) manages to keep the program fresh, showcasing visual and performance artists from around the globe. The festival spans two weeks over late May/early June and holds events in different cultural venues as well as outdoor exhibitions.

Reykjavík Pride (www.reykjavikpride.com) is a citywide celebration of human rights, diversity, and culture. It garners a huge turnout every year. Each August, the city hosts rainbow-themed events ranging from concerts to guest speakers. It's known as the highest-profile event for Iceland's gay, lesbian, bisexual, and transgender community. Hundreds of volunteers organize the event, and people from around the country congregate to celebrate their fellow citizens.

Since 1990, the **Reykjavík Jazz Festival** (www.reykjavikjazz.is) has been delighting horn section enthusiasts. International artists like Aaron Parks and Chris Speed are invited to put on concerts and jam with locals over five days in mid-August. There are off-venue free events throughout the city, and this is a popular festival among the locals. Main concerts take place at the concert hall Harpa.

Independent choreographers launched the **Reykjavík Dance Festival** (www.reykjavikdancefestival.com) in 2002, and the annual event is still going strong today. The focus is on bringing contemporary dance closer to the people. The week-long event held every August showcases local talent as well as international dancers.

Reykjavík Culture Night (www.menningarnott.is) has the darling slogan "come on in," which is a reference to the old-fashioned customs of hospitality. Culture Night actually starts during the day, with select residents opening up their properties to offer waffles and coffee to their neighbors and visitors. Hundreds of events around the city range from cultural performances to free museum events. The festival culminates with a huge outdoor concert that features some of the biggest names in Icelandic rock and pop music. It's held at the end of August.

Fall

Beginning at the end of September, the **Reykjavík International Film Festival** (www.riff.is) takes place over 11 days, during which films from more than 40 countries are screened. They range from short films to full-length features and documentaries, and the festival is a great venue to discover new talent. Invited special guests have included American director Jim Jarmusch and English director Mike Leigh. **Iceland Airwaves** (www.icelandairwaves.is) has been delighting music lovers since 1999. The five-day festival, held in late October/early November, has hosted an impressive list of performers, including Sigur Rós, Björk, and Of Monsters and Men, as well as international artists including Robyn, Kraftwerk, and Flaming Lips. There are also off-venue performances held for free in bars, bookstores, record shops, and coffeehouses— so if you don't score tickets to the festival, you can still check out some amazing music. A detailed off-venue schedule is published along with on-venue appearances.

Winter

Sónar Reykjavík (www.sonarreykjavik.com) is the new kid on the block in Reykjavík music festivals. Launched in 2013, Sónar features rock, pop, punk, electronic, and dance music performances in Harpa concert hall. Artists have included GusGus, Squarepusher, and Hermigervill. The festival takes place in middle of February.

The annual **Reykjavík Food & Fun Festival** (www.foodandfun.is) showcases the culinary exploits of world-renowned chefs collaborating with local Icelandic chefs. There are competitions, exhibitions, and lots of eating. It takes place at the end of February.

Shopping

Reykjavík may not strike you as a shopping destination, but there are quite a few local brands, like clothing labels 66 North and Cintamanti, that are quite popular. The high street in the city, Laugavegur, is chock-full of design shops, jewelers, boutiques, and bookstores. If you're up for some shopping, be sure to take a stroll on Laugavegur.

ART/DESIGN

Aurum (Bankstræti 4, tel. 354/551-2770, www.aurum.is, 10am-6pm Mon.-Fri., 11am-5pm Sat.-Sun.) is the place to go for unique Icelandic jewelry. Shoppers are treated to an impressive display of rings, necklaces, and earrings made from silver, gold, or lava stones. Aurum's jewelry is distinctively Icelandic, with pieces inspired by the raw nature of the island. An adjoining part of the store is dedicated to modern toys for kids, knitwear, accessories, and home goods.

Epal (Skeifan 6, tel. 354/568-7733, www.epal.is, 10am-6pm Mon.-Fri., 11am-4pm Sat., closed Sun.) is the original design store in Iceland, stocking everything from furniture to light fixtures to bedding and small goods. At Epal, which was founded in 1975, you'll find Icelandic designers as well as international brands, including Fritz Hansen, Georg Jensen, Marimekko, OK Design, and Tin Tin. Other than the main location at Skeifan, Epal has two other stores at Keflavík International Airport and Harpa concert hall.

Foa (Laugavegur 2, tel. 354/571-1433, 11am-6pm daily) is a new addition to the Laugavegur design store scene. Since opening its doors in late 2013, Foa has carried "indie" design brands that can't be found in many other stores. For instance, there are hand-carved wooden swans by local artist Bjarni Þór on sale as well as small woolen goods for kids and individual letterpress cards. It's a fun store to wander around and pick up something unique.

Hrím (Laugavegur 25, tel. 354/553-3003, www.hrim.is, 10am-6pm Mon.-Sat., 1pm-5pm Sun.) is where you go for one-stop shopping for design lovers, whether you're looking for accessories, playful paper goods, or housewares. There is an emphasis on Icelandic design, especially when it comes to jewelry and home goods, but there are also foreign-made items as well. For instance, Hrím has an impressive Lomography camera display for those looking for lo-fi film or a new Diana plastic camera. The staff is friendly and eager to help you find that perfect purchase.

Hrím Eldhus (Laugavegur 32, tel. 354/553-2002, 10am-6pm Mon.-Sat., 1pm-5pm Sun.) was opened in 2014 after the success of parent shop Hrím, down the block. Eldhus, which means kitchen in Iceland, focuses on modern design accessories for the kitchen and dining room. The adorable store stocks goods from local Icelandic designers as well as designers from its Scandinavian and Nordic neighbors. This store is stocked with nothing you really need, but everything you want.

Kraum (Aðalstræti 10, tel. 354/517-7797, www.kraum.is, 9am-6pm Mon.-Fri., 10am-5pm Sat., noon-5pm Sun.) has been voted "the best place to stock up on local design" by local newspaper *The Reykjavík Grapevine* for five years in a row. Kraum stocks everything from the adorable independent children's clothing line As We Grow to handbags made from fish leather. They also carry pillows, jewelry, candleholders, and woolen goods. If you're going to visit one design shop in Reykjavík, it should be Kraum, as it has the largest and most diverse selection of goods.

BOOKSTORES

Reykjavík was named a UNESCO City of Literature in 2012, and the title was well deserved. Locals like to boast that 1 in 10 Icelanders will publish a book in their lifetime and that Iceland has the highest number of Nobel Prize winners for literature per capita. That would be one winner—Halldór Laxness for *Independent People.* Due to the importance of literature to the city and the exceptionally high literacy rate of citizens, Reykjavík boasts an unusually high number of bookstores.

Eymundsson (Austurstræti 18, tel. 354/540-2000, www.eymundsson.is,

Hrím design store

10am-10pm daily) is the oldest and largest bookstore chain in Reykjavík, dating back to 1872. The main shop on Austurstræti has four levels, with an impressive magazine section, tourist books on Iceland, and a large English-language book section.

IÐA (Lækjargata 2A, tel. 354/511-5001, www.ida.is, 9am-10pm daily) has a huge souvenir section that you see upon walking through the door. There are Iceland-related books, T-shirts, postcards, stuffed toys, and keychains. Walk a little farther and you will see an impressive array of art, travel, and design books, along with classic literature in English and a fine magazine collection. The top floor is home to a café that serves excellent coffee and a nice choice of light meals.

Mál og Menning (Laugavegur 18, tel. 354/515-2500, www.malogmenning.is, 9am-10pm daily), which means "Language and Culture," is a favorite among Reykjavík locals. The three-level store sells fun tourist wares on the ground floor next to the magazine section. Upstairs is a collection of art and photography books, along with hundreds of English-language novels and nonfiction reads. The top floor also houses a café, where people sip lattes as they flip through magazines and newspapers. The bottom floor sells office and craft supplies.

MUSIC

Icelandic music is more than Björk and Sigur Rós, and a few choice music shops will help you discover local favorites as well as up-and-coming Icelandic artists.

A lot more than a record shop, 12 Tónar (Skólavörðustígur 15, tel. 354/511-5656, www.12tonar.is, 11am-6pm daily) is a place to mingle with other music lovers and sample new Icelandic music with private CD players and headphones, all while sipping on a complimentary cup of coffee. The shop was founded in 1998 and is an integral part of Reykjavík's music culture; the owner also runs an independent music label, and the shop is often used as a music venue during Reykjavík's annual autumn music festival, Iceland Airwaves.

If you like vinyl, Lucky Records (Rauðarárstígur 10, tel. 354/551-1195, www.luckyrecords.is, 9am-10pm Mon.-Fri., 11am-10pm Sat.-Sun.) is the place for you. The shop has the largest collection of new and used vinyl in the city, with an extensive Icelandic selection as well as foreign rock, pop, hip-hop,

coffee at Mál og Menning bookshop

jazz, soul, and everything else you could imagine. Bands and DJs frequently play free concerts at the shop, and it's a fun place to spend a couple of hours. There's a turntable and headphones, with which you're welcome to sample used records.

Smekkleysa (Bad Taste) Records (Laugavegur 28, tel. 354/534-3730, www. smekkleysa.net, 11am-6pm daily) was born from the legendary Smekkleysa record label that has released albums from the Sugarcubes, Sigur Rós, and scores of other Icelandic artists. Its record shop, while small, has a great collection of Icelandic music on CD and vinyl, as well as a DVD section, box sets, and classical music on CD.

CLOTHING/KNITWEAR

Perhaps Iceland's best known and oldest brand, **66 North** (Bankastræti 5, tel. 354/535-6600, www.66north.com, 9am-9pm Mon.-Sat., 10am-9pm Sun.) has been keeping Icelanders warm since 1926. You will find hats, rainwear, gloves, fleece, vests, and parkas in colors ranging from basic black (a favorite among Icelanders) to lava orange. Heavy parkas cost an arm and a leg (around $500), but you pay for the Thermolite insulation and design details. If you're not looking to make a fashion investment, you can grab a hat for about $20.

Cintamani (Bankastræti 7, tel. 354/533-3390, www.cintamani.is, 9am-10pm daily) has been dressing Icelanders in colorful, fashionable designs since 1989. Ranging from base layers to outerwear, Cintamani is a bit more playful than 66 North with more prints and brighter colors. The emphasis is not just on style, but warmth as well with top-notch insulation.

Farmers & Friends (Holmasloð 2, tel. 354/552-1960, www.farmersmarket.is, 10am-6pm Mon.-Fri., 11am-4pm Sat.) is the flagship store of the wildly popular Farmer's Market clothing label. If you are looking for sweaters other than the traditional garb available at Handprjónasamband Íslands (Handknitting Association of Iceland), Farmer's Market offers everything from cardigans to capes in stylish colors and patterns. The label, which was launched in 2005, is focused on combining classic Nordic design elements with a modern aesthetic.

Geysir (Skólavörðustígur 16, tel. 354/519-6000, www.geysir.com, 10am-7pm Mon.-Sat., 11am-5pm Sun.) features clothes that combine beauty with the utility of Icelandic wool. Warm sweaters, cardigans, capes and

12 Tónar music shop

blankets are on offer at the flagship Reykjavík shop, not too far from Hallgrímskirkja. The clothes have a traditional look with some modern twists.

Handprjónasamband Íslands (Handknitting Association of Iceland) (Skólavörðustígur 19, tel. 354/552-1890, www.handknit.is, 9am-6pm Mon.-Fri., 9am-4pm Sat., 11am-4pm Sun.) is a collective of Icelanders that knit and sell sweaters, scarves, shawls, hats, mittens, and other woolen goods. If you are looking for an authentic, traditional Icelandic sweater, and are willing to pay top dollar, this is your place. There are a lot of colors and patterns to choose from in an array of sizes.

Kolaportið (Tryggvagata 19, tel. 354/562-5030, www.kolaportid.is, 11am-5pm Sat.-Sun.) is Reykjavík's only flea market, and, boy, do they go all out in this space. You can find everything from secondhand traditional Icelandic sweaters, to used CDs and vinyl records, to books and even fresh and frozen fish. It's a very popular place to stop by and it's usually packed, regardless of the weather or season.

KronKron (Laugavegur 63b, tel. 354/562-8388, www.kronbykronkron.com, 10am-6pm Mon.-Thurs., 10am-6:30pm Fri., 10am-5pm Sat.) is a hip shop that focuses on up and coming designers. Fashions range from fun and flirty to chic and modern. You can find elegant dresses, fashion forward sweaters and unique accessories. The clientele ranges from teens to young professionals, which shows the range of duds available.

Steinunn (Grandagarður 17, tel. 354/588-6649, www.steinunn.com, 11am-6pm Mon.-Fri., 1pm-4pm Sat., closed Sun.) is a modern, signature collection by Steinunn Sigurðardóttir that features a love of knits, detail and craft. Popular among Icelandic women, the clothes are sleek, chic and feminine, and are frequently shown during the Reykjavík Fashion Festival in the spring. The label was launched in 2000 after Steinnun cut her teeth in New York working for the likes of Calvin Klein and Ralph Lauren.

GIFTS AND SOUVENIRS

Álafoss (Laugavegur 8, tel. 354/562-6303, www.alafoss.is, 9am-10pm daily) is best known for its huge factory wool store in the Reykjavík suburb Mosfellsbær, but this small downtown outpost is great for picking up yarn for knitting projects and small wool souvenirs to bring home. You can find socks, hats, magnets, shot glasses, soft toys, candy, and

Handknitting Association of Iceland

handmade Icelandic soap, among many other goodies.

Blue Lagoon (Laugavegur 15, tel. 354/420-8849, www.bluelagoon.com, 10am-6pm Mon.-Fri., 10am-4pm Sat., 1pm-5pm Sun.) is a tiny shop on the main street that carries all of the Blue Lagoon's skin-care line. If you can't make it to the actual Blue Lagoon near Grindavík, don't fret, because you can take home some of the essence that makes the site so special. The shop is decked out in cool blue hues and lots of lava stones, and the shelves are filled with everything from a nourishing algae mask to mineral bath salts.

The Little Christmas Shop (Laugavegur 8, tel. 354/552-2412, 10am-6pm Mon.-Fri., 10am-5pm Sat., 10:30am-2pm Sun.) is a small shop where it's Christmas all year-round. A pair of stone Santa shoes outside the store draws you into a world of Christmas tree ornaments, ceramic Yule Lads figurines, soft toys, dishes, and just about everything with a Christmas theme. No matter what the season, it's a joyous shop to visit and will get you buying Christmas ornaments in July.

Polar Bear Gift Store (Laugavegur 38, tel. 354/578-6020, www.isbjorninn.is, 10am-8pm daily) is bound to catch your attention due to the huge toy polar bear models outside the store. While polar bears are not indigenous to Iceland, don't let that fact stop you from checking out the cute wares inside. You can pick up T-shirts, hats, magnets, keychains, and other souvenirs. The selection of souvenirs does not focus on polar bears, but the huge stuffed polar bears outside the store tend to draw in tourists.

Ravens (Laugavegur 15, tel. 354/551-1080, www.ravens.is, 10am-7pm Mon.-Sat., 11am-5pm Sun.) is a unique shop that houses all sorts of good stuff that you can't find anywhere else. You can find arctic fur, authentic Inuit art, lambskin rugs, custom-made knives, sculptures, and leather accessories. You won't find mass-produced souvenirs here.

The Viking (Hafnarstræti 3, tel. 354/551-1250, www.theviking.is, 9am-7pm Mon.-Fri., 9am-6pm Sat.-Sun.) is exactly what you would expect from a souvenir shop in Reykjavík. T-shirts, mugs, stuffed puffins and polar bears, wool products, Viking helmets, and

The Little Christmas Shop

just about everything in between can be found here. If you're looking for unique and sophisticated trinkets, this isn't your spot. But, if you're up for fun and affordable items, you will likely find them here.

Vínberið (Laugavegur 43, tel. 354/551-2475, 9am-6pm Mon.-Fri., 10am-6pm Sat., noon-5pm Sun.) is a sweets shop stocked with everything from chocolates to rhubarb toffee. There's a good mix of local and foreign brands, and it would be almost impossible to not find something you like. Gift options include treats wrapped in pretty packaging. In the back there are spices and baking products, and in the summer there is frequently a mini outdoor fruit market just outside the shop. One sweet that is wildly popular among Icelanders is black licorice. You can find a selection of licorice candies with or without a chocolate coating.

SHOPPING MALLS

Kringlan (Kringlunni 4-12, tel. 354/568-9200, www.kringlan.is, 10am-6:30pm Mon.-Wed., 10am-9pm Thurs., 10am-7pm Fri.,

10am-5pm Sat.-Sun.), which is a short bus ride from downtown Reykjavík, resembles just about any mall in America. There are clothing stores, a bank, a movie theater, and a food court packed with teenagers and shoppers. If the weather is particularly bad and you want to get some shopping done, it's a good destination. There's a 66 North shop in Kringlan, as well as some other Icelandic brands. Kringlan is a five-minute drive east from downtown Reykjavík, and it can be reached by Strætó bus numbers 1, 2, 3, 4, 6, 13, and 14. One-way bus fare is 350ISK, and it takes about 10 minutes from downtown Reykjavík.

Smáralind (Hagasmári 1, tel. 354/528-8000, www.smaralind.is, 11am-7pm Mon.-Thurs., 11am-9pm Fri., 11am-6pm Sat., 1pm-6pm Sun.) is located in the Reykjavík suburb Kópavogur and is one of the main shopping centers in the region for locals. You will find everything from Adidas sneakers to Levi's, but for double the price than back home. However, it offers a movie theater and an entertainment area with rides for kids if that strikes your fancy.

Accommodations

Accommodations in Reykjavík fall into three categories: hotels, guesthouses, and self-catering apartments. The city isn't known for luxurious hotels, but there are a few "upmarket" choices; however, they remain "no-frills" when compared to other cities in Europe. By and large, expect to pay a lot during the high season (June-August). While most of the options are downtown, there are a few outside the 101 postal code. However, given how small Reykjavík is, most options are within walking distance or are within a short bus ride to downtown.

HOTELS
Under 25,000ISK

Fosshótel Baron (Baronsstígur 2-4, tel. 354/562-3204, www.fosshotel.is, rooms from

21,000ISK) may not be pretty from the exterior, but it's clean, convenient, and in a good location in downtown Reykjavík. The 120 rooms range from standard singles and doubles to apartment-style accommodations that have kitchenettes and mini refrigerators. The lobby looks a little depressing, but the accommodating staff and the location make up for it. Guests have access to free Wi-Fi, free and plentiful parking, and an adequate included breakfast.

★ Hótel Frón (Laugavegur 22A, tel. 354/511-4666, www.hotelfron.is, rooms from 20,000ISK) couldn't have picked a better location if they tried. Located on the high street Laugavegur, the hotel has single, double, and apartment-style studios that are clean, bright, and comfortable. The apartments come with a small kitchen, and a couple of them feature Jacuzzi bathtubs. The downside, however, is the proximity to bars on Laugavegur, which means it can be quite noisy on Friday and Saturday nights.

Hótel Klöpp (Klapparstígur 26, tel. 354/595-8520, www.centerhotels.is, rooms from 17,000ISK) offers fresh rooms on a quiet corner in city center. Some rooms feature warm, bright hues including red walls, while others are stark white, clean, and cool. All rooms have hardwood floors and small private bathrooms. Guests have access to free Wi-Fi, assistance with booking tours is provided, and the friendly staff even offers a northern lights wake-up service in the winter when the aurora borealis is visible.

Reykjavík Lights Hotel (Suðurlandsbraut 16, tel. 354/513-9000, www.keahotels.is, rooms from 18,000ISK) is a concept design hotel with 105 rooms, including singles, doubles, triples, and group rooms. Just past the reception area is an airy lobby that houses a bar and the common eating area. Rooms are large, featuring Nordic-style decor and luxurious beds. The bathrooms are modern and stark white with showers. Located outside of city center, it's about a 10-minute walk to downtown.

Radisson Blu Saga Hotel (Hagatorg, tel. 354/525-9900, www.radissonblu.com, rooms from 22,000ISK) has a dynamite location in city center, close to the Reykjavík Art Museum and Iceland's infamous Bæjarins Beztu Plysur hot dog stand. Rooms are larger than average, many with a maritime theme that's charming. Beds are lush, and the 209 rooms are stocked with bath products from Anne Semonin. Amenities include free Wi-Fi, access to the spa and health center, and two in-house restaurants: Grillið for fine dining and Restaurant Skrudur for more casual meals.

Icelandair Hótel Reykjavík Natura (Hlídarfótur, tel. 354/444-4500, www.icelandairhotels.com, rooms from 19,500ISK) underwent a renovation in 2012, transforming itself from what was just the hotel near the domestic city airport to a hotel with a fantastic spa and eclectic restaurant. It pays homage to Reykjavík's rich art culture with murals and sculptures throughout the building. Built in 1964, the hotel has been a favorite among business travelers due to its proximity to the airport, conference facilities, and indoor swimming pool. The in-house restaurant Satt offers a delicious breakfast buffet and meals throughout the day. The main attractions, for many, are the indoor pool and Soley Natura Spa, where guests can get massages, manicures, pedicures, and facial treatments. The hotel is a 20-minute walk to downtown Reykjavík, but guests are given free passes for the city bus, which stops just outside the hotel.

Over 25,000ISK

Centrum Plaza Hotel (Aðalstræti 4, tel. 354/595-8500, www.centerhotels.is, rooms from 28,000ISK) is in the heart of Reykjavík. Many of the 180 rooms have spectacular views of the city, but with that comes quite a bit of noise during the weekends. The rooms are cozy and sparsely decorated but clean and bright. The bathrooms are small, with a shower, and each room has a flat-screen TV and free Wi-Fi. The clientele is a mix of business and leisure travelers. A lounge downstairs tends to be sleepy because of the proximity of popular bars downtown.

Award-winning boutique hotel **101 Hotel** (Hverfisgata 10, tel. 354/580-0101, www.101hotel.is, rooms from 58,000ISK) is quite posh for Reykjavík. Indeed, the World Travel Awards named 101 Hotel the top boutique hotel in Iceland. Rooms are modern and chic with a black-and-white color palette, wood floors, and in-room fireplaces. It's cozy and stylish at the same time. And while the rooms are pricey, the amenities are pretty great. Each room has a large walk-in shower, flat-screen TV with satellite channels, free high-speed Wi-Fi, a CD/DVD player with a Bose iPod sound dock, and bathrobes and slippers. The restaurant offers an eclectic menu with creations ranging from mussels and pomme frites to Icelandic cod with saffron risotto.

Grand Hotel Reykjavík (Sigtún 38, tel. 354/514-8000, www.grand.is, rooms from 30,000ISK) is a huge 311-room high-rise hotel just a few minutes from downtown Reykjavík. This is a favorite among business travelers and conference attendees because the hotel has meeting rooms and conference facilities. The rooms are large, with hardwood floors and comfortable yet uninspiring furnishings. The restaurant is pricey; dishes range from lamb filets with mushrooms to duck breast with parsnip.

Hilton Reykjavík Nordica (Suðurlandsbraut 2, tel. 354/444-5000, www. hiltonreykjavik.com, rooms from 36,000ISK) is a 252-room four-star hotel situated in the financial district, about a 10-minute walk to downtown Reykjavík. It attracts business travelers as well as families and individuals thanks to its comfortable rooms, top-notch service, luxurious spa, and memorable in-house restaurant, Vox. If it's not important to be in the thick of downtown Reykjavík, Hilton Reykjavík is a good option.

Hlemmur Square (Laugavegur 25, tel. 354/415-1600, www.hlemmursquare.com, rooms from 38,000ISK) bills itself as an upmarket hostel. As the name suggests, the hotel is right next to Hlemmur bus station, which is downtown's most extensive bus station, providing bus transfers to just about every part of the city. Other than being in a killer location, Hlemmur Square has a popular lounge that attracts not just hotel guests, but locals. This is a great spot for 20-somethings to meet fellow travelers and socialize.

★ **Hótel Borg** (Posthússtræti 9-11, tel. 354/551-1440, www.hotelborg.is, rooms from 40,500ISK) is a popular choice for celebrities and politicians passing through Reykjavík. Why? Built in 1930, the 56-room four-star downtown Reykjavík hotel is elegant, modern, and steeped with old-time charm. Hotel Borg's rooms have custom-made furniture, flat-screen satellite TV, and very comfortable beds. The in-house restaurant Silfur is a favorite, and a café/bar serves light meals.

Hotel Holt (Bergstaðastæti 37, tel. 354/552-5700, www.holt.is, rooms from 40,500ISK) offers spacious, tastefully decorated rooms, some with a balcony. Holt is one of the few hotels in downtown Reykjavík that offer room service, and its service and

Hótel Borg

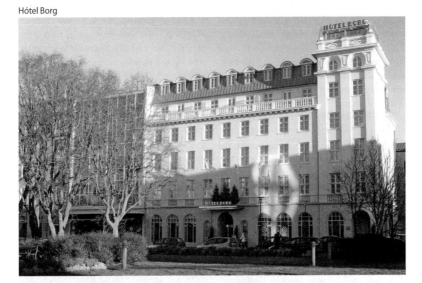

amenities are comparable to upscale hotels in large European cities. Guests also have free access to Iceland's largest health club (World Class Fitness), free parking, free Wi-Fi, and a staff eager to assist with tour bookings and recommendations for sights and restaurants.

★ **Icelandair Hótel Reykjavík Marina** (Myrargata 2, tel. 354/560-8000, www.icelandairhotels.com, rooms from 38,000ISK) opened its doors in 2012, and the hotel is in a great location by the harbor district, close to the whale-watching tours, restaurants, and museums. One of the most design conscious of the Icelandair Hótels chain, Reykjavík Marina features art throughout the lobby, restaurant, and rooms. You can see everything from murals by local Icelandic artists to impressive wood sculptures. The rooms are minimalist and modern, the staff warm, and the hotel is home to one of the hippest hotel bars in the city, Slipp Bar.

Kvosin Hotel (Kirkutorg 4, tel. 354/571-4460, www.kvosinhotel.is, rooms from 43,000ISK) is a gorgeous modern boutique hotel situated close to the pond and parliament in downtown Reykjavík. Rooms come in four adorably described sizes: normal, bigger, biggest, and larger than life. All rooms feature mini refrigerators, a Nespresso machine, Samsung Smart TV, and skin-care amenities from Aveda. The rooms are sleek and Scandinavian cool with accents from local Icelandic designers. Breakfast is included and served downstairs at the Bergsson restaurant, which is known for its delicious breakfast and brunch options.

Radisson Blu 1919 Hotel (Posthússtræti 2, tel. 354/599-1000, www.radissonblu.com, rooms from 38,000ISK) is an 88-room hotel that occupies a central location in the capital. Built in 1919, the hotel has undergone a couple of renovations, but it has maintained a lot of its charm. The rooms are large, with hardwood floors, sizable bathrooms, comfortable beds, and free high-speed Wi-Fi. Guests who reserve a suite are treated to a king-size bed, Jacuzzi bathtub, and bathrobe with slippers. Guests also have access to a fitness center with some basic machines. The in-house restaurant is dynamite, with a menu ranging from fresh fish caught off of Iceland's shores to lamb filets and duck breast entrées.

GUESTHOUSES
Under 25,000ISK

Reykjavik Hostel Village (Flókagata 1, tel. 354/552-1155, www.hostelvillage.is, rooms from 15,000ISK) offers rooms in five different residential houses. Rooms include dorm accommodations, singles, doubles, triples, and apartment-style studios. The decor is simple, with neutral colors and wood furnishings. It's a five-minute walk to Laugavegur, the main drag, and the prices are reasonable, making this a great option for budget travelers.

★ **Loft Hostel** (Bankastræti 7, tel. 354/553-8140, www.lofthostel.is, beds from 20,000ISK) opened in 2013 and has quickly earned a reputation as a place to be and be seen. The rooms range from dorm accommodation to privates, but the big draw is the fourth floor bar/café that hosts up-and-coming bands, established live acts, and DJs. An outdoor deck overlooks Bankastræti in downtown Reykjavík, and it is packed with locals and tourists alike when the sun is shining.

Sunna Guesthouse (Thórsgata 26, tel. 354/511-5570, www.sunna.is, rooms from 19,000ISK) offers several types of accommodations: one- and two-bedroom apartments, studios, rooms with private bathrooms, and rooms with shared bathroom facilities. All rooms are decorated in a light, minimalist style with muted colors and wood furniture. The location is key, as it's right across the street from Hallgrímskirkja in downtown Reykjavík. Guests have access to a shared kitchen to prepare meals, and a breakfast buffet is included in the price. The breakfast accommodates vegetarians as well as those with gluten allergies.

Salvation Army (Kirkjustræti 2, tel. 354/561-3203, www.guesthouse.is, rooms from 14,000ISK) is only open to tourists during the summer months because it serves as a dorm for university students between

September and May. But when it's open, it's a great budget option for travelers. There are private rooms as well as dorms available in the heart of Reykjavík. Rooms and common areas are clean and convenient. Please keep in mind that because the facilities are so well-managed and in a killer location, the hostel tends to sell out for the summer, so if you're interested, book early.

Over 25,000ISK

The **Adam Hotel** (Skólavörðustígur 42, tel. 354/896-024, www.adam.is, rooms from 25,000ISK) underwent a significant face-lift, and each room now has a private bathroom. Rooms are small and no-frills, but the location is terrific, with several rooms overlooking Hallgrímskirkja in downtown Reykjavík. Guests tend to be young, and the hotel is a great spot to meet fellow travelers. All rooms have free Wi-Fi.

★ **Kex Hostel** (Skulagata 28, tel. 354/561-6060, www.kexhostel.is, rooms from 28,000ISK) is a lot more than a hostel; it's ground zero for music lovers, hipsters, and the beautiful people of downtown Reykjavík to congregate, meet for drinks, and listen to live music. The hostel offers rooms ranging from private rooms to dorm accommodations, all with shared bathroom facilities. But, most people don't stay for the style or comfort of the rooms, but for the experience Kex has to offer. The front lounge houses vintage wall maps, vintage midcentury furniture, and a small stage for live bands to plug in and play. The back room is a converted gym that hosts concerts, fashion and vinyl markets, and even food festivals. Staying at Kex means you're staying for the atmosphere, the experience.

APARTMENTS
Under 25,000ISK

Bolholt Apartments (Bolholt 6, tel. 354/517-4050, www.stay.is, rooms from 15,000ISK) offers comfortable, simple rooms just a 10-minute walk from downtown Reykjavík, which makes this well-managed apartment complex very popular. Guests have private bathrooms, small kitchenettes, and access to free Wi-Fi and free parking. A common lounge has a pool table and a couple of sofas great for unwinding and meeting fellow travelers. Bolholt is a great option for independent, budget travelers.

Einholt Apartments (Einholt 2, tel. 354/517-4050, www.stay.is, rooms from 15,000ISK) has stylish, minimalist apartments with private bathrooms and kitchenettes. Its clientele ranges from more mature travelers to 20-something backpackers. Einholt is a great downtown spot for the independent traveler to spend a couple of nights or a longer stay to get to know Reykjavík.

The options at **Reykjavík4You Apartments** (Laugavegur 85, www.reykjavik4you.com, rooms from 25,000ISK) are great spaces in a central location. Studios and one- and two-bedroom apartments are available, and all are stocked with well-equipped kitchens, spacious bathrooms, and bright decor. Apartments are clean and comfortable, with lots of light in the summer months.

Room with a View (Laugavegur 18, tel. 354/552-7262, www.roomwithaview.is, rooms from 20,000ISK) is right next to the popular bookstore Mál og Menning and near all the great bars downtown. Rooms range from small singles to three-bedroom apartments for groups. Rooms are clean and modern, some with private bathroom facilities. Guests have access to two hot tubs as well as a common kitchen area. Be advised that because of the proximity of bars and restaurants, it can be quite noisy on Friday and Saturday nights. If you're looking for a quiet room on a sleepy street, this isn't it.

Food

Reykjavík's culinary charm may be surprising to some. While there are traditional Icelandic restaurants serving up fresh fish and tender lamb filets, there are also fantastic eateries specializing in food you may not expect to see in Iceland. For instance, there's an impressive collection of Asian and Mediterranean restaurants, which have authentic menus that incorporate the great ingredients found in Iceland. If you're in the mood for tapas, there's a place to have an exquisite meal. Craving sushi? You will not be disappointed. As for Icelandic cuisine, there are upmarket restaurants catering to foodies as well as fast food joints offering quick, affordable bites.

ASIAN

Asía (Laugavegur 10, tel. 354/562-6210, www.asia.is, 11am-11pm daily, 1,500ISK) doesn't strive to be authentic and is comparable to American-style Chinese food. The outside is a bit tacky, with sketched palm trees and a yellow painted exterior, and the inside isn't much better with knickknacks and a kitschy style. The food, however, is fine and the prices are reasonable. The menu consists of shrimp, chicken, beef, and lamb options, and a few specials are offered.

Bambus (Borgartún 16, tel. 354/517-0123, www.bambusrestaurant.is, 11:30am-11pm Mon.-Fri., 5pm-10pm Sat.-Sun., 1,750ISK) is a delightful Asian fusion restaurant mixing Thai, Japanese, and Indian influences. You will find dishes incorporating everything from curry to teriyaki and coconut milk. A salad with chicken, sweet chili, and mango is spectacular. The restaurant is decorated in a minimalist Asian-influenced style.

Buddha Café (Laugavegur 3, tel. 354/571-5522, www.buddha.is, 4:30pm-10pm Mon., 11:45am-10pm Tues.-Thurs., 11:45am-11pm Fri.-Sat., closed Sun., 2,300ISK) combines Japanese and Chinese flavors to create unique and memorable dishes. The sushi menu has mainstays like California and avocado rolls, but some of the more adventurous rolls are divine, including shrimp tempura with coriander sweet chili sauce. Main courses range from fresh fish to wok-fried beef in oyster sauce. During the week, a three-course lunch special is a steal for under 2,000ISK.

Gandhi Restaurant (Posthusstræti 17, tel. 354/511-1691, www.gandhi.is, 5:30pm-10pm daily, 3,000ISK) features the creations of two chefs from southwest India. Combining local Icelandic ingredients with traditional Indian spices, the menu offers authentic dishes like chicken vindaloo and fish masala as well as vegetarian options. The food is fresh and perfectly spiced. The butter chicken is gorgeous, rivaling that of top Indian restaurants you'd find in London.

Krua Thai (Tryggvagata 14, tel. 354/561-0039, www.kruathai.is, 11:30am-9:30pm Mon.-Fri., noon-9:30pm Sat., 5pm-9:30pm Sun., 1,500ISK) has all your favorite Thai classics, ranging from chicken pad thai to spring rolls and noodle soups. During weekdays, the restaurant has a three-course lunch special for just 1,400ISK.

Noodle Station (Skólavörðustígur 21, tel. 354/551-3199, charin_79@hotmail.com, 11am-11pm daily, 1,100ISK) is a popular spot for Reykjavík natives, students, and tourists. People flock to the tiny shop for one of the tastiest and cheapest meals you can find in downtown Reykjavík. Noodle soup is available with chicken or beef or as a vegetarian option. The smell of spices wafting down Skólavörðustígur will draw you in.

Osushi (Pósthússtræti 13, tel. 354/561-0562, www.osushi.is, 11:30am-10pm Mon.-Thurs., 11:30am-11pm Fri.-Sat., 3pm-10pm Sun., bites from 300-500ISK) is a sushi train with bites snaking their way around. Diners are treated to everything from deep-fried shrimp tempura rolls to tuna sashimi and grilled eel bites. For kids, there are chicken teriyaki kebabs, spring rolls, and even a chocolate mousse for dessert.

Ramen Momo (Tryggvagata 16, tel. 354/571-0646, www.ramenmomo.is, 11:30am-9pm Mon.-Sat., noon-5pm Sun., 1,200ISK) is an adorable hidden restaurant not too far from the harbor. Owned and operated by a Tibetan immigrant, Ramen Momo serves up glorious chicken, beef, or vegetarian ramen soup and dumplings. The nondescript eatery has an authentic feel to it, and your taste buds will thank you.

Sushibarinn (Laugavegur 2, tel. 354/552-4444, www.sushibarinn.is, 11:30am-10pm Mon.-Sat., 5pm-10pm Sun., rolls from 1,400ISK) has not only sushi roll staples like California, volcano, and shrimp tempura rolls, but also some creative combinations, including the Rice Against the Machine roll, which has salmon, cream cheese, red onions, and chili. For those who are inclined, whale sushi is on the menu as well.

Sushi Samba (Þingholtsstræti 5, tel. 354/568-6600, www.sushisamba.is, 5pm-11pm Sun.-Thurs., 5pm-midnight Fri.-Sat., rolls from 2,500ISK) combines Japanese and South American elements to create inventive and delicious sushi rolls and entrées. You'll find traditional fresh seafood like tuna, salmon, crab, lobster, and shrimp, along with South American influences like spicy salsa, jalapeño mayo, and chimichurri. Main entrées include baked vanilla-infused cod and grilled beef tenderloin with mushroom sauce, jalapeño, and coriander.

ICELANDIC

Bergsson Mathús (Templarasund 3, tel. 354/571-1822, www.bergsson.is, 7am-9pm Mon.-Fri., 7am-5pm Sat.-Sun., 1,400ISK) is known for its fantastic brunch menu and light, flavorful dishes. Try the roast beef on a bed of salad or the spinach lasagna. The eatery is also a popular coffee spot for locals.

★ **Borg Restaurant** (Póshússtræti 9, tel. 354/578-2020, www.borgrestaurant.is, 7am-1am daily, 4,000ISK) has been a fixture on the Reykjavík foodie scene for years. Located on the ground floor of Hótel Borg, the restaurant is owned and operated by world-renowned chef Völundur Völundarson, who has been featured on cooking shows around the world. The cuisine is fresh and the food local, with fish dishes ranging from blue ling to salmon and plaice. A tasting menu features the chef's choice of nine courses.

Einar Ben (Veltusundi 1, tel. 354/511-5090, www.einarben.is, 5:30pm-10pm Mon.-Fri., 5pm-10pm Sat.-Sun., 4,000ISK) is named after the Icelandic literary hero Einar Benediktsson, but tourists don't flock to the restaurant for that reason. The cozy atmosphere, friendly staff, and stellar location in city center, along with fresh fish and local lamb, make this a winner among tourists. It accommodates large groups.

Fjalakötturinn (Aðalstræti 16, tel. 354/514-6060, www.fjalakotturinn.is, lunch 11:30 am-2pm daily, dinner 6pm-10:30pm Sun.-Thurs., 6pm-11pm Fri.-Sat., 3,800ISK) is housed inside Hotel Centrum in downtown Reykjavík, but it's not only a popular place for hotel guests to visit. The inventive food, modern decor, intimate tables, and gorgeous pictures of Iceland's landscape make this spot a winner. Fresh fish including salmon, trout, catfish, and lobster is on the menu, as well as rack of lamb.

Iðnó (Vonarstræti 3, tel. 354/562-9700, www.idno.is, noon-10pm daily, entrées from 7,000ISK) is a historic building that currently houses local theater productions as well as a fine restaurant. Situated close to Tjörnin and City Hall, the restaurant is pricey, but the food is memorable. The smoked salmon on blinis with caviar is exquisite, as is the ginger-glazed breast of duck. The restaurant is often used to host private parties and family gatherings in a huge banquet room.

★ **Lækjarbrekka** (Bankastræti 2, tel. 354/551-4430, www.laekjarbrekka.is, 11:30am-10pm daily, entrées from 3,000ISK) occupies a historic building that has undergone quite a few transformations since it was built in 1834, including a bakery. Today, Lækjarbrekka is one of the best-known downtown restaurants catering to tourists. Fresh fish dishes are on the menu as well as some of Iceland's most adventurous cuisine. You'll find fermented shark, whale meat, puffin, and Icelandic horse filets on offer. For tamer choices, the pan-fried filet of lamb and arctic char are splendid.

Perlan (Öskjuhlíð, tel. 354/562-0200, www.perlan.is, 10am-11pm daily, mains from 4,200ISK) occupies the top floor of the architecturally significant building, providing breathtaking views of the city. If you are in town on New Year's Eve, this is a great place to have a late dinner. The food is classic, with fresh ingredients and nothing too outrageous. There is whale meat on the menu, but most people opt for the fresh rainbow trout or the glorious cod with rye bread and potatoes, a traditional, hearty Icelandic meal.

Restaurant Reykjavík (Vesturgata 2, tel. 354/552-3030, www.restaurantreykjavik. is, 6pm-10pm daily, mains from 4,000ISK) is known for its fantastic fish buffet, which starts every day at 6pm. This is a favorite among tourists looking to sample traditional Icelandic fish dishes as well as international classics. The restaurant is housed in a huge yellow building with lots of tables, so you're not likely to have to wait for a table. The fish buffet features everything from salmon, cod, lobster, fish balls, trout, and caviar to shrimp and crab specialties. An à la carte menu offers beef, lamb, fish, and vegetarian options.

MEDITERRANEAN

Gamla Smiðjan Pizzeria (Lækjargata 8, tel. 354/578-8555, www.gamlasmidjan.is, 11:30am-10pm daily, 1,500ISK) is a wildly popular pizza place among the locals, which is telling. While Reykjavík isn't known for its pizza, this place is pretty darn good. You have a choice of an obscene number of toppings, ranging from classic pepperoni to more exotic options like tuna fish and banana. It has a laid-back atmosphere and decent service.

Hornið (Hafnartsræti 15, tel. 354/551-3340, www.hornid.is, 11am-11:30pm daily, large pizzas from 1,790ISK) looks like a bistro from the outside with yellow and blue walls, and the interior reveals a relaxed atmosphere with friendly service and yummy pizzas. Classic pizzas include pepperoni, four cheese, and vegetable, but there are also adventurous creations like the Pizza Pecatore, which has shrimp, mussels, and scallops on top. If you're not up for pizza, entrées include salted cod with risotto and filet of lamb with vegetables.

Ítalía (Laugavegur 11, tel. 354/552-4630, www.italia.is, 11:30am-11:30pm daily, pasta dishes from 2,400ISK) is a cute Italian restaurant right on the main street, Laugavegur. The owners boast a menu that offers classics like spaghetti Bolognese, lasagna, and mushroom ravioli as well as options that incorporate local ingredients, like smoked salmon with toasted bread and pan-fried salted cod with onions. Pizza and calzone are also on the menu.

Tapas Barinn (Vesturgata 3b, tel. 354/551-2344, www.tapas.is, 5pm-11:30pm Sun.-Thurs., 5pm-1am Fri.-Sat., 3,500ISK) was a welcome addition to the Reykjavík restaurant scene. There are so many delightful choices, but if you'd like a taste of the chef's best Icelandic dishes, go for the "gourmet feast" where the chef prepares dishes with smoked puffin, Icelandic sea trout, lobster tails, grilled Icelandic lamb, minke whale with cranberry sauce, and pan-fried blue ling with lobster sauce. The seven plates, along with a shot of the famous Icelandic spirit Brennivin and a chocolate *skyr* mousse dessert will only set you back 6,690ISK. If you would like more traditional tapas, there are lots of options, including salmon and bacon-wrapped scallop bites.

Uno (Hafnarstræti 1, tel. 354/561-3131, www.uno.is, 11:30am-11pm Sun.-Thurs., 11:30am-midnight Fri.-Sat., mains from 2,800ISK) is an elegant Italian restaurant that has a lovely terrace out front where locals and tourists are seen sipping coffees and cocktails when the sun is shining. The interior is very cozy, with leather armchairs in the lounge and warm hues and artwork decorating the walls. The menu makes it hard to decide with so many tasty options. You could go traditional

the Sea Baron restaurant

are comfortable couches in the lounge, where you're welcome to sip a cocktail while waiting for a table. The food is flawless, ranging from pan-fried prime lamb and oxtail with artichoke puree to blackened monkfish and fried langoustine with lobster spring rolls.

Humarhúsið (Amtmannsstígur 1, tel. 354/561-3303, www.humarhusid.is, 11am-10pm Mon.-Sat., 5pm-10pm Sun., mains from 4,400ISK) or "The Lobster House" is the place for—you guessed it—lobster. You can't make a bad choice: grilled lobster tails with garlic butter, lobster soup, slow cooked monkfish and smoked lobster with potato salad, lobster tempura, and lots of other options. If you're not a fan of lobster, don't fret. There are lamb, pork, and other fish options on the menu.

Icelandic Fish & Chips (Tryggvagata 11, tel. 354/551-1118, www.fishandchips.is, noon-9pm daily, mains from 1,290ISK) serves up a wonderful range of fresh seafood: cod, plaice, blue ling, haddock, red fish, wolf fish, and shellfish. For an authentic Icelandic fish-and-chips meal, go for the cod. The biggest draws, however, are the "skyronnaise dips," in which Iceland's famous soft cheese, *skyr*, is blended with an array of spices, including basil, coriander, ginger, and tarragon. The truffle and tarragon dip is heavenly.

MAR Restaurant (Geirsgata 9, tel. 354/519-5050, www.marrestaurant.com, 11:30am-11pm daily, mains from 3,900ISK) offers South American-inspired dishes ranging from prosciutto-wrapped monkfish with fennel seeds to lamb filet with leeks, carrots, and beets. The banana crème brûlée with chocolate sorbet is recommended for dessert. The atmosphere is casual, with wood tables and minimalist design, and its harbor location is great.

★ **Sægreifinn (Sea Baron)** (Geirsgata 8, tel. 354/553-1500, www.saegreifinn.is, 11:30am-10pm daily, mains from 1,200ISK) has been a Reykjavík institution for years. With its prime location by the harbor, the Sea Baron is known for its perfectly spiced, fresh lobster soup, which comes with a side of bread and butter. Fish kebabs on offer include

with chicken rigatoni or try something more exotic, like black linguine with mussels, scallops, and olives.

SEAFOOD

★ **Fish Market** (Aðlstræti 12, tel. 354/578-8877, www.fiskmarkadurinn.is, 6pm-11:30pm daily, mains from 4,300ISK) stands out among a number of fantastic seafood restaurants in Reykjavík. What makes Fish Market special is the combination of ingredients the chef employs. For instance, the grilled monkfish comes with crispy bacon, cottage cheese, tomato yuzu pesto, and crunchy enoki mushrooms. It's a vision, as is the salted cod with lime zest with potato puree, dried cranberries, and celery salad.

Fiskfelagid (Fish Company) (Vesturgata 2a, tel. 354/552-5300, www.fiskfelagid.is, 5:30pm-midnight daily, entrées from 3,800ISK) has a striking, chic interior with modern wooden tables and chairs, candleholders throughout the space, and personal notes and photos adorning the walls. There scallops, monkfish, and cod. There is also whale meat available if you're inclined. Inside, visitors will find a hut-like atmosphere with fishing relics, photos, and equipment. There's a net hanging from the ceiling, and there are charming knickknacks displayed lovingly by the 90-year-old owner.

STEAKHOUSES

Argentina (Barónsstígur 11A, tel. 354/551-9555, www.argentina.is, 6pm-midnight Sun.-Thurs., 5:30pm-1am Fri.-Sat., mains from 3,900ISK) is warm and inviting the second you step through the door, with leather couches, a roaring fireplace, and the smell of choice cuts of meat wafting through the air. You can choose from rib eye, T-bone, slow-cooked ox flank, beef rump, porterhouse, and peppered beef tenderloin, among other cuts. Chicken, lamb, and seafood round out the menu, as well as an excellent wine list.

Steikhúsið (Tryggvagata 4, tel. 354/561-1111, www.steik.is, 5pm-10pm Sun.-Wed., 5pm-11pm Thurs.-Sat., steaks from 3,650ISK) opened in 2012, but it has already made a big impact on Reykjavík's restaurant scene. Guests can choose from beef rib eye, porterhouse, and T-bone cuts or lamb filets, with tasty sauces including béarnaise, creamy pepper, and blue cheese. There are also fish entrées on offer as well as a dynamite hamburger with brie, pickled vegetables, mango chutney, chipotle, and bacon. For the adventurous, the surf-and-turf features minke whale and horse meat grilled in a coal oven.

FAST FOOD

★ **Bæjarins Beztu Pylsur (The Town's Best Hot Dog)** (Tryggvatagata 1, tel. 354/511-1566, www.bbp.is, 11:30am-12:30am Sun.-Thurs., 11:30am-4am Fri.-Sat., 380ISK) is a place that you have to visit. Even if you don't eat hot dogs, you should get a look at the tiny shack that has been delighting tourists, locals, food critics, and even U.S. president Bill Clinton for years. Located close to the harbor, the hot dog stand serves up lamb meat hot dogs, with fresh buns and an array of toppings. If you're out for a late-night bar crawl and get hungry, keep in mind that the stand is open until 4am on the weekend.

Grillhusið (Tryggvagata 20, tel. 354/562-3456, www.grillhusid.is, 11:30am-10pm Sun.-Thurs., 11:30am-11pm Fri.-Sat., 1,500ISK) is part diner, part TGI Friday's, with Americana displayed on the walls and an extensive menu ranging from hamburgers to fish-and-chips to salads and sandwiches. They have an interesting array of burgers on offer, and the lamb/béarnaise burger is a personal favorite.

Hamborgara Búllan (Geirsgata 1, tel. 354/511-888, www.bullan.is, 11:30am-9pm daily, burgers from 730ISK) is a corner burger joint situated in the old harbor district, close to where the whale-watching tours depart. The food is tasty, the service quick, and the decor a little kitschy, making this a great spot to grab a quick bite to eat. A special includes a hamburger, fries, and soda for 1,590ISK, which is pretty cheap for a meal in downtown Reykjavík.

Hlölla Bátar (Ingólfstorg, tel. 354/511-3500, www.hlollabatar.is, 11:30am-10pm daily, sandwiches from 890ISK) has hot and cold hero/hoagie sandwiches on offer, including barbecue, curry, ham and cheese, and veggie boats. It's a great place to get something quick to eat, fuel up, and continue exploring the city.

Islenska Hamborgarafabrikkan (Icelandic Hamburger Factory) (Höfðatún 2, tel. 354/575-7575, www.fabrikkan.is, 11am-10pm Sun.-Thurs., 11am-midnight Fri.-Sat., burgers from 1,695ISK) is a wildly popular hamburger joint. It has the look and feel of a casual eatery, but the hamburgers are pretty special. They range from classic hamburgers with lettuce, cheese, and tomatoes to more creative concoctions like the surf-and-turf, which combines a beef patty with tiger prawns, garlic, Japanese seaweed, cheese, lettuce, tomatoes, red onions, and garlic-cheese sauce. Other options include chicken and lamb, as well as a whale meat burger.

Roadhouse (Snorrabraut 56, tel. 354/571-4200, www.roadhouse.is, 11:30am-9:30pm

Mon.-Thurs., 11:30am-11pm Fri.-Sat., noon-9:30pm Sun., burgers from 1,895ISK) does its best to depict an American-style hamburger joint. It's kitschy, cute, and familiar, with Americana hanging on the walls, ranging from old license plates to Elvis Presley posters. The food is exceptional "fast food," with choice burgers featuring everything from crumbled blue cheese to jalapeños and fried onions. A favorite among Icelanders is the Texas mac-and-cheese burger, with a patty, macaroni and cheese, bacon, and barbecue sauce piled on top. The pork baby-back ribs are memorable.

COFFEEHOUSES

Café Babalu (Skólavörðustígur 22, tel. 354/555-8845, www.babalu.is, 11am-11pm daily, 500ISK) is a charming coffeehouse decorated with vintage furniture, lots of wood furnishings, and kitschy knickknack goodness. Other than coffee drinks, the two-floor café serves light meals including soup, panini, and crepes. This is a favorite among tourists, and in the summer months, there's an outdoor eating area on the second floor.

Café Haiti (Geirsgata 7, tel. 354/588-8484, www.cafehaiti.is, 8am-8pm Mon.-Thurs., 8am-11pm Fri., 9am-11pm Sat., 9am-8pm Sun., light meals from 950ISK) is owned and operated by a delightful Haitian woman who has called Iceland home for years. The atmosphere is warm and inviting, with comfortable couches and chairs among the tables and even a little stage area upfront for regular concerts that take place. In addition to coffee and tea, light meals of soup and sandwiches are available, as well as sweet treats like cakes and cookies. A house favorite is specially brewed Arabic coffee that takes some time, but it's well worth the wait.

C Is for Cookie (Tysgata 8, tel. 354/578-5914, 9am-6pm Mon.-Fri., 11am-5pm Sat., noon-5pm Sun., 500ISK) is a nondescript café on a quiet side street in the city. For that reason, along with a stellar cup of coffee, it's a favorite among locals. When the weather is good, people congregate in a park adjacent to the coffeehouse and at tables and chairs outside. Freshly baked treats include Icelandic pancakes, brownies, and, of course, cookies.

Kaffitár (Bankastræti 8, tel. 354/511-4540, www.kaffitar.is, 7:30am-6pm Mon.-Sat., 9am-5pm Sun., 500ISK) is the closest thing Iceland has to a coffee chain like Dunkin Donuts or Starbucks. There are locations in

Café Babalu

city center, Keflavík airport, and a smattering of other sites. They also sell coffee beans and ground coffee in supermarkets and takeout coffee at gas stations. The city center location is bright, colorful, and usually crowded. The coffee is fresh and the cakes and other sweets are delicious. You can't go wrong at Kaffitár.

Mokka (Skólavörðustígur 3A, tel. 354/552-1174, www.mokka.is, 9am-6:30pm daily, 500ISK) is the oldest coffeehouse in Reykjavík and still has a faithful following today. It's busy all day, with tourists as well as artists, writers, and other famous folks stopping by for a cup of coffee and Mokka's famous waffles with fresh cream and homemade jam. Art and photography exhibitions are frequently held at the coffeehouse, so stop by and have a look at the walls.

Reykjavík Roasters (Karastigur 1, tel. 354/517-5535, www.reykjavikroasters.is, 8am-6pm Mon.-Fri., 9am-6pm Sat.-Sun., 500ISK) is a charming corner coffeehouse situated in a great part of town. Just a stone's throw from Hallgrímskirkja, Reykjavík Roasters is a great spot to sit down for a coffee to break up a busy day of sightseeing. Decorated with vintage couches and chairs and wood tables with delicate tablecloths, the coffeehouse is packed with tourists and locals chilling out, drinking lattes and getting some good free Wi-Fi. During the summer months, when the weather is cooperating, there's an outside sitting area to all guests to enjoy their drinks while soaking in the sun.

Stofan Café (Vesturgata 3, tel. 354/863-8583, 101stofan@gmail.com, 9am-midnight Mon.-Thurs., 9am-1am Fri.-Sat., 10am-11pm Sun., 500ISK) moved to a larger space in 2014, closer to the harbor, and with more space came more couches, chairs, and tables to accommodate the growing number of fans of this hot spot. The café serves coffee drinks, local beers, and cakes and light meals. It's common to catch locals enjoying their drinks while curling up with a good book on a vintage armchair.

Mokka

VEGETARIAN

Gló (Engjateigi 19, tel. 354/553-1111, www.glo.is, 11am-9pm daily, 2,500ISK) has a spectacular menu featuring not just vegetarian and vegan options, but also a killer raw food selection. Expect to see staples like tofu and hummus served in creative ways, and there's also a great salad bar. The meat dish option can be great if you're traveling with a carnivore. The decor is modern and chic and the staff friendly.

ICE CREAM

Eldur og Is (Skólavörðustígur 2, tel. 354/571-2480, 1,000ISK) offers soft-serve and Italian-style ice cream with flavors including the basics: vanilla, chocolate, and strawberry, as well as coffee, pistachio, and several others. A crepe bar inside has delicious combinations, including the Nutella and nut special crepe. This place has a central location and a good reputation, so it can be a bit crowded. The sofas and armchairs inside make it very comfortable.

Valdis (Grandagarður 21, tel. 354/586-8088, www.valdis.is, noon-11pm daily, from 330ISK) draws a crowd during sun-soaked summer days and the dim, windy dog days of winter. It's always busy here and for good reason. The harbor location and its creative and delicious ice cream flavors make this a favorite among locals and tourists. Flavors include coconut, white chocolate, vanilla coffee, Oreo, and local favorites black licorice and rhubarb. During the summer, there are tables and chairs outside the shop, where scores of people enjoy their cones.

Information and Services

VISITORS CENTERS

Around Iceland (Laugavegur 18b, tel. 354/561-9161, www.aroundiceland.is, 8am-7pm daily) is a lively tourist office with the regions of Iceland separated in different exhibitions. The sections are Reykjavík, West, South, East, and North Iceland, and brochures are available to help you explore each region. The friendly staff is eager to help you book afternoon, day, or multiday tours ranging from a Golden Circle tour (including visits to Gullfoss, Geysir, and Þingvellir) to hiking tours in North Iceland. There's something for everyone. In the front is an eclectic array of souvenirs, including jewelry and woolen goods, and in the back is a cozy coffeehouse with armchairs, sofas, coffee drinks, and light meals.

The Reykjavík **tourist information center** (Aðalstræti 2, tel. 354/590-1550, www.visitreykjavik.is, 8:30am-7pm daily June-mid-Sept., 9am-6pm Mon.-Fri., 9am-4pm Sat.-Sun. mid-Sept.-May) is a one-stop shop for all your tourist needs. The building is thought of as a hub, with brochures available for every region of the island and information on every tour on offer. You can pick up maps and purchase tickets to events.

MEDIA

The *Reykjavík Grapevine* is Iceland's only English-language newspaper, and it's geared toward tourists, hipsters, and music-loving locals. There are listings for bands and DJ club dates, information about what's on at museums and art galleries, and articles ranging from humorous to informative to sarcastic on what's going on in Reykjavík. To get the pulse of the city, pick up a copy in bookstores, museums, and shops, or check it out online at www.grapevine.is. In summertime, the newspaper comes out every other week, and in the winter it's monthly.

EMERGENCY SERVICES

The telephone number for emergencies is 112. If you are having a medical emergency, are stranded by car trouble, or are experiencing a safety issue or any other pressing, dire emergency, dial this number.

MEDICAL SERVICES

Landspitali (Norðurmýri, tel. 354/543-1000, www.landspitali.is) is the national hospital of Iceland. It houses day-patient units, an emergency room, and clinical services. If you are experiencing a medical emergency, dial 112 for an ambulance.

For a pharmacy, visit **Lyf og Heilsa** (Haaleitisbraut 68, tel. 354/581-2101, 8am-midnight Mon.-Fri., 10am-midnight Sat.-Sun.). Keep in mind that "over the counter" medication and aspirin are only available at a pharmacy, not in supermarkets or convenience stores like in other countries.

Transportation

GETTING THERE

Air

Iceland isn't as difficult to reach as you may think. Smack dab in the mid-Atlantic, Reykjavík is just a short flight for many North Americans and Europeans, about five hours from New York City and three hours from London. The majority of international travel is handled through **Keflavík International Airport** (KEF), which is about 50 minutes west of Reykjavík.

Reykjavík City Airport (Þorragata 10, tel. 354/569-4100, www.isavia.is) is the city's domestic airport, with regional connections to towns throughout the country, including Akureyri and the Westfjords. The only international flights are to the Faroe Islands and Greenland.

Several airlines have offices in Reykjavík: **Air Iceland** (Reykjavíkurflugvöllur, tel. 354/570-3000, www.airiceland.is), **Eagle Air** (Reykjavíkurflugvöllur, tel. 354/562-4200, www.eagleair.is), **Icelandair** (Reykjavíkurflugvöllur, tel. 354/505-0100, www.icelandair.is), and **Wow Air** (Katrinartun 12, tel. 354/590-3000, www.wowair.is).

GETTING TO AND FROM THE AIRPORT

The **Fly Bus** (tel. 354/580-5400, www.flybus.is) runs regularly from **Keflavík International Airport** to **BSÍ** (Vatnsmýrarvegur 10, tel. 354/562-1011, www.bsi.is), Reykjavík's main bus station, where you can get a shuttle to your hotel in Reykjavík. It takes about 50 minutes to get from Keflavík to BSÍ bus station, and buses depart about 40 minutes after flights land. One-way tickets cost 1,950ISK. (BSÍ is also the main departure site for day-tour bus trips with various companies, including Reykjavik Excursions.) **Taxis** are also available at Keflavík; the fare from the airport to Reykjavík is upward of 12,000ISK.

Strætó (www.straeto) bus numbers 15 and 19 stop at the **Reykjavík City Airport** near the Air Iceland and Eagle Air terminals, respectively. Taxis are also available on-site.

GETTING AROUND

Bus

Reykjavík's bus system is convenient, reliable, and an affordable way to get around the city. The bus system, called **Strætó** (www.straeto.is), which means "street" in Icelandic, runs about 30 bus lines within the city center as well as to outlying Reykjavík areas like Kópavogur and Hafnarfjörður. The bright yellow buses cost 400ISK per ride within the city limits, and you can ask for a free bus transfer if you need to switch buses to get to your destination. You must pay with exact change; bus drivers don't make change. Buses run daily 7am-11pm. Be sure to check the website at www.straeto.is for information on holiday schedules and delays due to weather.

If you plan to use the bus a fair amount, you can buy nine tickets for 3,500ISK at **Hlemmur bus station** (Laugavegur, tel. 354/540-2701). Hlemmur is Strætó's central downtown station, where you can catch or connect to any bus you're looking for. Think of it as Reykjavík's equivalent of New York's Times Square subway station. Another great option is the **Reykjavík Welcome Card,** which grants you free access to the city's swimming pools, almost all the city's museums, and unlimited city bus rides. You can purchase a card for one or three days for 1,000ISK and 2,500ISK, respectively. If you will be spending a lot of time in Reykjavík, this is a great option to save a lot of money. Cards can be purchased at tourist offices and bus stations.

Strætó's blue long-distance buses depart from **Mjodd station** (tel. 354/557-7854), eight kilometers southeast of city center, traveling to several regions around the country.

Taxi

The two things you need to know about taxis in Reykjavík is that they are expensive and you have to call ahead for one. Hreyfill (tel. 354/588-5522, www.hreyfill.is) and BSR (tel. 354/561-0000, www.taxireykjavik.is) are two popular taxi companies in the city. Taxis arrive 5-10 minutes after you call, and the price on the meter is inclusive—you don't tip in Iceland. It's rare to spend less than 2,000ISK on a taxi ride, even for short distances. Cab prices rival those in New York City. There are a couple of cab stations downtown where you don't have to call ahead—just outside Hlemmur bus station and near Lækjartorg. They are hard to miss as the line of taxis can be 10 deep.

Car

There is no shortage of rental car companies in Iceland eager to rent you a car, and many of them make it quite easy, with offices at Keflavík International Airport, BSÍ bus station, and around the city. They include the following: Avis (Knarrarvogur 2, tel. 354/591-4000, www.avis.is), Budget (Vatsmýrarvegur 10, tel. 354/562-6060, www.budget.is), Europcar (Hjallahrauni 9, tel. 354/565-3800, www.europcar.is), and Hertz (Reykjavík City Airport, tel. 354/505-0600, www.hertz.is).

Be advised that parking isn't easy in Reykjavík. Most locals have cars, and street parking can take some time. However, there are several parking garages and lots available around the city, and parking at a garage will cost less than 100ISK per hour.

Bicycle

Reykjavík has taken great strides in becoming more bicycle-friendly over the past few years. There are new bicycle lanes throughout the city as well as new bike racks to lock up your ride outside shops. Be aware that bike theft is rampant, so be proactive and lock up your bicycle. Don't leave it unattended and unlocked. It'll disappear. Other than bike theft, the only other concern for cyclists is weather, which changes often. You can start your ride during calm and sunny skies, but within minutes that could change with rain and wind.

One of the most central and most popular bike rental companies in Reykjavík is Borgarhjol Bike Rental (Hverfisgata 50, tel. 354/551-5653, www.borgarhjol.is), close to the main street Laugavegur. Bike rentals begin at 2,600ISK for four hours.

Walking

Reykjavík is an inherently walkable city, depending on the weather, of course. Because of its small size, it's a perfect city to roam, to pop into quaint shops, visit museums, and photograph the many statues around the city. You can start at the harbor and make your way to Tjörnin, up to Hallgrímskirkja, and beyond.

A new walking tour was launched in 2013 by I Heart Reykjavík (Mjóahlíð 14, tel. 354/854-4476, www.iheartreykjavik.net) that is designed to tell you about the history of Reykjavík and some of the quirky characters who inhabit the city. It's a three-hour tour for 5,000ISK, and you can book at www.tours.iheartreykjavik.net. Tours are offered daily.

Greater Reykjavík

MOSFELLSBÆR

Just 15 minutes from downtown Reykjavík, Mosfellsbær is a quaint, placid town with a picturesque bay, beautiful mountains, and clean streams and rivers. About 9,000 people live in Mosfellsbær, and it feels remote enough to feel like you're closer to the countryside, but it's also close enough to get downtown.

Sights
ÁLAFOSS WOOL FACTORY SHOP
The **Álafoss Wool Factory Shop** (Álafossvegur 23, tel. 354/566-6303, www. alafoss.is, 9am-6pm Mon.-Fri., 9am-4pm Sat.) is home to the Álafoss wool brand, which was established in 1896. The shop sells wool skeins, scarves, hats, sweaters, and blankets, along with some other small goods. You can also purchase a sheep skin as well as other Icelandic design products. The shop is located in the old factory house by the Álafoss waterfall, which was used to drive the mills of the old factory. For decades it was the leading manufacturer and exporter of Icelandic wool products. You can visit to experience this important side of Iceland's industrial history and get a look at an exhibition of old knitting machinery and photographs from the early days. The prices are comparable to downtown Reykjavík prices, but the selection is better and bigger.

GLJÚFRASTEINN
Gljúfrasteinn (Pósthólf 250, tel. 354/568-8066, www.gljufrasteinn.is, 9am-5pm daily June-Aug., 10am-5pm Tues.-Sun. Sept.-May, 800ISK) was the home of Icelandic novelist and national treasure Halldór Laxness. Laxness, who was awarded the Nobel Prize for Literature in 1955 for his novel *Independent People,* lived at this home from 1945 until his death in 1998. It has been preserved as a museum, giving visitors a glimpse into his life, including his library and study, where he wrote several of his works. There is a short multimedia presentation about his life and work, available in English, Icelandic, and Swedish. Guided tours of the house and grounds take about an hour. You can purchase many of his books at the museum, translated into English and German. The house, which is a white two-story concrete building, is well preserved, but it feels lived in with lots of personal artifacts decorating the home, including books, clothing, and furniture.

Sports and Recreation
★ HIKING MOUNT ESJA
Standing 914 meters high, Mount Esja looms over Reykjavík, and it's a favorite among locals and the subject of thousands of picturesque photographs snapped by tourists. Hiking Esja is a popular pastime and a few paths ascend the mountain. The most popular path begins at the car park, which is at about 780 meters. From there, you can cross the Mógilsa stream, which leads to a steeper stretch named "steinnin." The hike is eight kilometers round-trip and it's considered easy, but be aware that the last stretch to the top is pretty steep. There are handrails to lessen the challenge. When you reach the top of this path, there is a guestbook to sign. It's fun to read through all the names and see where people have traveled from to climb the mountain.

Please be careful before you head out. Make sure you check the weather forecast and let your guesthouse or hotel know of your plans. Remember that the weather can be fickle. It can be beautiful out with sunny skies, but it could turn very windy and rainy. Make sure you bring water, proper footwear, and waterproof clothing with you.

Getting to Esja is pretty easy, even if you don't have access to a car. It's just 20 minutes (10.7 kilometers) north of Mosfellsbær and is accessible from Route 1. Drive through Mosfellsbær and you will see the signs

Greater Reykjavík

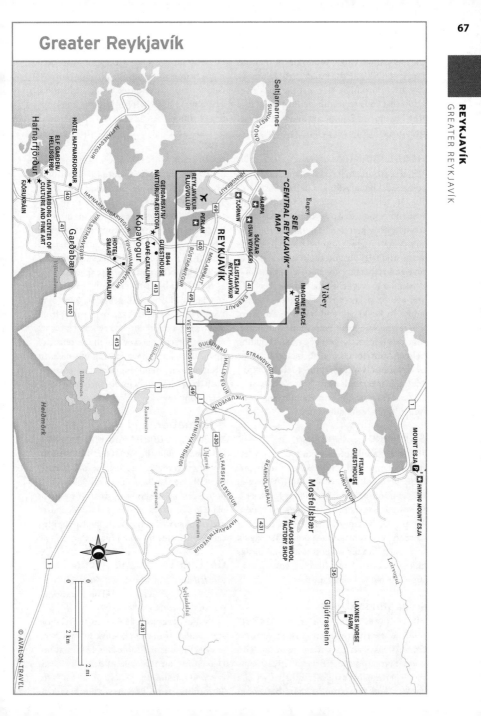

© AVALON TRAVEL

pointing to the car park. By bus, you can take the Strætó 57 bus (www.straeto.is) from the bus station Mjodd in Reykjavík. The bus fare is 800ISK and the bus departs 12 times a day. It's a 30-minute ride. Let the bus driver know that you are heading to the base of Esja (the bus stop is Esjumelar) and you will get dropped off at the car park.

HORSE RIDING

If you're staying in Reykjavík and want to do some local horse riding, Laxnes Farm (off Rte. 36, tel. 354/566-6179, www.laxnes.is) is just a 15-minute drive northeast from downtown Reykjavík. Icelandic horses are available to ride for different tour lengths. The staff is warm and friendly and shows a great deal of love and respect for the horses they care for. A popular tour is called the "Laxnes Special"; you will be picked up at your hotel or guesthouse in Reykjavík and taken to the farm, where you will meet your guide and horse. You are given all the gear you need, including helmets, rain clothes, and boots, and are taken on a glorious two-hour riding tour (9,900ISK) that has spectacular landscape views. The Laxnes Farm is close to Halldór Laxness's home, but they are not related.

SWIMMING

If you're planning to stay in town for a few hours or more, check out the local swimming pool, called Varmárlaug (Þverholt 2, tel. 354/566-6754, 6:30am-8pm Mon.-Fri., 9am-6pm Sat.-Sun. in summer, 4pm-9pm Mon.-Fri. in winter, 600ISK). The pool isn't as impressive as some of the pools in Reykjavík city center, but the water is warm and the facilities are clean. You're likely to see locals taking a dip, but not many tourists.

Accommodations

Fitjar Guesthouse (Fitjar, tel. 354/691-5005, www.fitjarguesthouse.com, rooms from 9,000ISK) is a six-room guesthouse on a quiet street in Mosfellsbær. Three rooms have private bathroom facilities with a shower, and three rooms share bathroom accommodations. Rooms are clean and comfortable, but the decor is nothing to write home about. This is a great spot to spend a night before you continue on your journey. Guests have access to free Wi-Fi, a television, a common, fully equipped kitchen, and laundry facilities.

Food

Kaffihúsið Álafossi (Álafossvegur 27, tel. 354/566-8030, www.alaborg.is, 11am-10pm Mon.-Fri., 11am-7pm Sat., noon-7pm Sun., 1,500ISK) is a cozy coffeehouse right next to the Álafoss Wool Factory Shop. It serves light meals ranging from soups to sandwiches. The staff is warm and there's interesting artwork from local Icelandic artists adorning the walls. The coffee and cakes are splendid.

Mosfellsbakarí (Háholt 13-15, tel. 354/566-6145, www.mosbak.is, 7am-6pm Mon.-Fri., 8am-4pm Sat.-Sun., pastries from 600ISK) is a decadent bakery known for its chocolate creations. Located in the center of town, the bakery does roaring business. In addition to its indulgent cakes and pastries, the bakery offers light meals, including sandwiches and soup.

Information and Services

Mosfellsbær's tourist information office is based inside the Mosfellsbær public library (Þverholt 2, tel. 354/566-6822, www.mosfellsbaer.is, 9am-5pm daily), which is housed inside a shopping area. It's a great place to stop to gather some tourist brochures and maps as well as buy some food at the grocery store inside the shopping center.

Getting There and Around

Mosfellsbær is just a 15-minute drive from downtown Reykjavík. It's 14 kilometers northeast of Reykjavík via Route 49.

By bus, take the 15 bus to the Haholt stop, which is in the center of town. Check www.straeto.is for more bus information. Depending on the time of day, buses run every 30 minutes to every hour, and it takes 30 minutes from downtown Reykjavík to

Mosfellsbær. A single ride on the bus is 400ISK.

KÓPAVOGUR

Kópavogur is a quiet suburb home to families, young professionals, and immigrants, and it attracts people traveling on business or shoppers headed to the Smáralind mall or the island's only IKEA. There are a couple of museums worth checking out for local art and history.

Sights
GERÐARSAFN (KÓPAVOGUR ART MUSEUM)

The Kópavogur Art Museum (Hamraborg 4, tel. 354/570-0440, www.gerdarsafn.is, 11am-5pm Tues.-Sun., 500ISK) is named Gerðarsafn in Icelandic, after sculptor Gerður Helgadóttir, who passed away in 1975. In 1977, her heirs donated roughly 1,400 of her works to the municipality of Kópavogur on the condition that a museum bearing her name would be opened. Gerður's black-iron works in the 1950s made her a pioneer of three-dimensional abstract art in Iceland. Around 1970 Gerður returned to working with plaster, terra cotta, and concrete, using simple circles with movement in many variations. The museum opened in 1994. Other works on display range from contemporary to landscape art. It's a pretty museum with varied works of art, and it's worth a visit if you're in the neighborhood.

NÁTTÚRÚFRÆÐISTOFA (NATURAL HISTORY MUSEUM)

The Natural History Museum (Hamraborg 6A, tel. 354/570-0430, www.natkop.is, 10am-7pm Mon.-Thurs., 11am-5pm Fri., 1pm-5pm Sat., free) opened its doors in 2002 and is a great place to bring kids to learn about the animals and geology of Iceland. The museum exhibitions fall into two categories: zoological and geological. The geology section, where you learn about the major rock types and minerals of Iceland, is of more interest to adults. The zoological part focuses on the mammals, fish, birds, and invertebrates of Iceland. It's

educational and entertaining, and kids love it due to the various exhibitions on seals, foxes, and cute birds like puffins.

Sports and Recreation
SWIMMING

The Kópavogur Swimming Pool (Borgarholtsbraut 17, tel. 354/540-0470, 6:30am-10pm Mon.-Fri., 8am-7pm Sat.-Sun., 500ISK) is frequented by locals and their children and has a very family-friendly atmosphere. Amenities include a 50-meter outdoor pool, two smaller indoor pools, three water slides, seven hot pots, and a steam bath. You aren't likely to see crowds or tourists, so if you're looking to just swim, this is a good spot.

Accommodations

Hótel Smári (Hlíðarsmára, tel. 354/558-1900, www.hotelsmari.is, rooms from 25,000ISK) is a 48-room block hotel situated right next to the huge mall Smáralind. The rooms are in need of an update, as they have an 1980s style with carpeting, orange hues, ad shiny lamps. But the rooms are clean and spacious, and comfortable for a short stay.

BB44 Guesthouse (Borgarholtsbraut 44/Nýbýlavegur 16, tel. 354/554 4228, www.bb44.is, doubles 11,300ISK) offers eight guest rooms in two locations. The single, double, and family rooms have free Wi-Fi, shared kitchen facilities, and free parking. Rooms are very basic, with standard beds, desks, and simple chairs. The location is prime, just a 10-minute walk from downtown Kópavogur, where there are museums, restaurants, and the town's swimming pool. Guests have access to a hot tub at the guesthouse.

Food

Café Catalina (Hamraborg 11, tel. 354/554-2166, www.catalina.is, 11am-9pm Mon.-Fri., noon-3am Sat.-Sun., 1,500ISK) offers Icelandic comfort food at decent prices. The menu includes mashed fish with rye bread, fishballs with potatoes and onion sauce, and Icelandic meat soup. Other options include hamburgers, sandwiches, and soups. There's live music on the weekends, which draws plenty of locals.

Smáralind (Hagasmara 1, tel. 354/528-8000, www.smaralind.is, 11am-7pm Mon., Wed., and Fri., 11am-9pm Thurs., 11am-6pm Sat., 1pm-6pm Sun.) is Iceland's largest shopping mall, and in addition to a food court, there are casual eateries TGI Friday's and Café Adesso, coffee shop Kaffitár, and Serrano, which serves Mexican-style food.

Information and Services

The town's **service and administration center** (Fannborg 2, tel. 354/570-1500) is open 8am-4pm Monday-Thursday and 8am-3pm Friday.

Getting There and Around

Kópavogur is just a 10-minute ride south from downtown Reykjavík by car. You take Route 40 to Route 49 and it's 5 kilometers.

City buses go to Kópavogur, including buses 1, 2, and 28. Buses leave every 30 minutes or so, the fare is 400ISK for one way, and it takes about 20 minutes by bus. Check www.straeto.is for more bus information.

HAFNARFJÖRÐUR

Hafnarfjörður is a picturesque fishing town that about 30,000 people call home. Attractions include a scenic harbor, pretty parks, and the famous Viking Village, a restaurant and hotel that plays host to numerous Viking-related events.

Sights
ELF GARDEN

The **Elf Garden,** which is operated by local artist Ragnhildur Jónsdóttir in **Hellisgerði Park** (Höfuðborgarsvæði, tel. 354/585-5500, free), is cheesy to some but charming to many others. For 2,000ISK, Ragnhildur will take you on an hour-long "elf walk," where she will tell you about the folklore of the *huldufólk* and their role in literature and Iceland's culture. To book an elf walk, call 354/694-3153 or send an email to elves@elfgarden.is. After the walk you can visit the little **Elf Garden house** (tel. 354/694-3153, www.elfgarden.is) to continue the talk, enjoy the artwork inspired by elves, and get some *huldufólk* coffee and elf tea. The house's visitors area is quaint and cozy, with a small table, a few chairs, and a large window

Hafnarfjörður

overlooking the park. Even if you don't go on the elf walk, the park is a lovely place to spend a couple of hours, walking along the path through trees, tiny caves, lava rocks, and around a pretty pond.

HAFNARFJÖRÐUR MUSEUM
Hafnarfjörður Museum (Vesturgata 8, www.hafnarfjordur.is, 11am-5pm daily June-Aug., 11am-5pm Sat.-Sun. rest of year, 600ISK) houses a collection of cultural artifacts and photographs that are significant to the town. The museum consists of six houses and nine exhibitions that showcase how life was in the town in the old days. The six houses date from 1803 to 1906 and include the oldest house in the town, Sivertsen's House.

HAFNARBORG CENTER OF CULTURE AND FINE ART
Hafnarborg Center of Culture and Fine Art (Strandgata 34, tel. 354/555-0800, www.hafnarborg.is, noon-5pm Wed.-Mon., 500ISK) consists of two exhibition galleries with rotating exhibitions ranging from contemporary art from modern Icelandic artists to works by some of the island's most celebrated artists of years past.

FJÖRUKRÁIN (VIKING VILLAGE)
Fjörukráin (Viking Village) (Strandgata 55, tel. 354/565-1213, www.vikingvillage.is) is great fun for kids and adults alike. The closest thing Iceland has to a theme park, the Viking Village celebrates the island's history, with a sense of humor. It's kitschy, with lots of Viking horns, reproduced wood huts, and wooden furnishings. Guests can stay at the hotel, visit the gift shop, stay for a meal at the restaurant, or just check out the decor.

The Viking Village takes center stage every mid-June when the space hosts the **Viking Festival,** which takes place over five days. There are performances of jousts with participants in Viking costumes, food stands, metalwork demonstrations, and woolen goods and jewelry for sale.

Sports and Recreation
SWIMMING
Take a dip with the locals at the Suðurbæjarlaug pool (Hringbraut 77, tel. 354/565-3080, 6:30am-9:30pm Mon.-Fri., 8am-5:30pm Sat.-Sun., 500ISK), which has an outdoor pool with a water slide, a steam bath, and a few hot tubs.

HORSE RIDING
This town is a lovely place to ride a horse. With its rolling landscape and picturesque views, it doesn't get much better than this in the greater Reykjavík area. Íshestar (Sörlaskeið 26, tel. 354/555-7000, www.ishestar.is) is a local company that offers an array of tours. They provide transportation to the riding center from your accommodation and all gear needed to ride. A half-day tour goes for about 17,000ISK.

Accommodations
Hótel Hafnarfjörður (Reykjavíkurvegur 72, tel. 354/540-9700, www.hhotel.is, rooms from 16,000ISK) is a 70-room hotel with comfortable rooms ranging from single rooms to family suites. The hotel has a business traveler/corporate feel to it, but you can't beat the amenities and location. Rooms feature neutral hues, simple furnishings, and private bathrooms. Some rooms have a kitchenette for self-catering needs. Continental breakfast, Wi-Fi, parking, and access to a nearby fitness center are included in the price.

Hótel Viking (Strandgata 55, tel. 354/565-1213, www.vikingvillage.is, rooms from 18,300ISK) at the Viking Village has 42 hotel rooms and 14 "Viking cottages" next to the hotel. All rooms and cottages include private bathrooms, comfortable beds, televisions, and stylish Viking accessories. The hotel features artworks from Iceland, Greenland, and the Faroe Islands, which is a lot of fun. Guests have access to free Wi-Fi, free parking, and a hot tub on-site. Breakfast is included in the price.

Food

Fjörugarðurinn (Viking Restaurant) (Strandagata 55, tel. 354/565-1213, www.fjorukrain.is, 2,400ISK) at the Viking Village is a restaurant that serves traditional Icelandic fare like lamb and fish dishes in a fun, Viking-themed atmosphere. There are lots of wood furnishings and medieval accents displayed throughout the space. You can book a Viking performance in advance for large groups for a fee, which includes the guests being "kidnapped" from their bus, brought into a "cave" in the restaurant, served mead, escorted to dinner, and entertained with singing and music. The restaurant is open for dinner 6pm-10pm daily.

Osushi (Reykjarvíkurvegur 60, tel. 354/561-0562, www.osushi.is, 11:30am-9:30pm Mon.-Thurs., 11:30am-10pm Fri.-Sat., 3pm-9:30pm Sun., bites from 300ISK) is the Hafnarfjörður outpost of the popular downtown Reykjavík sushi train. Individual bites on offer range from fresh salmon farmed from Iceland's shores to eel and shrimp-based pieces.

Súfistinn (Strandgata 9, tel. 354/565-3740, 8am-11:30pm Mon.-Thurs., 8am-midnight Fri., 10am-midnight Sat., 1pm-midnight Sun., 800ISK) is a cozy café that sells stellar coffee drinks, fresh pastries, and light meals. Situated by the central downtown shopping area and performance hall, it's a perfect place to grab a blueberry muffin and latte or a soup or sandwich.

Information and Services

The tourist information center is situated in **Hafnarfjörður Town Hall** (Strandgata 6, tel. 354/585-5555, www.hafnarfjordur.is, 8am-5pm Mon.-Fri. year-round, 10am-3pm Sat.-Sun. June-Aug.). You can arrange for transportation, buy tickets to local tours, and peruse brochures about the town's sights.

Getting There and Around

Hafnarfjörður is just a 15-minute drive south from downtown Reykjavík. It's an 11-kilometer drive, and you take Route 40 to get there.

City bus 1 stops in town. Check www.straeto.is for bus schedules and information.

VIÐEY ISLAND

Viðey is a little gem of an island accessible by ferry. Historically, the island was inhabited by an Augustine monastery from 1225 to 1539 and was the center for a pilgrimage in the Middle Ages. The island is home to one of the oldest buildings in Iceland— **Viðeyjarstofa** (Höfuðborgarsvæði), which dates back to 1755 and served as a home to many of Iceland's most powerful men over generations. The building is a white stone building with a black roof, and it's open to the public. The island, which is just 1.6 square kilometers in size, hosts unspoiled nature with vast stretches of grassy plains and rich birdlife, as well as the John Lennon Peace Tower, an installation created by Yoko Ono.

Imagine Peace Tower

The **Imagine Peace Tower** (www.imaginepeacetower.com) is an outdoor installation created by artist Yoko Ono in memory of her late husband, John Lennon. A light beams from a structure into the sky, visible from miles away. It was unveiled on Viðey on October 9, 2007, which was Lennon's 67th birthday. It's lit every year from October 9, Lennon's birthday, until December 8, the anniversary of Lennon's death. The words "imagine peace" are inscribed on the structure in 24 languages. The base of the tower is 10 meters wide, and the beam of light reaches 4,000 meters into the sky.

Viðey Island

Getting There and Around

In the summer, **Elding** (tel. 354/533-5055, www.videy.com) operates a ferry with eight daily departures mid-May through September from Skarfabakki pier, Harpa, and Ægisgarður pier. Ferries run in the afternoon. During the rest of the year the ferry runs three departures on Saturdays and Sundays from Skarfabakki to Viðey. The ferry ride costs 1,100ISK and is just about 10 minutes.

Reykjanes Peninsula and the South

While South Iceland attracts the most tourists out of any region, it still feels untouched and exotic in many places—a hiker's paradise.

Glaciers, mountains, and two active volcanoes (Katla and Hekla) beckon tourists to visit. A wide and diverse region, the south is home to well-known sights like Þingvellir National Park and the Geysir hot springs, both on the popular Golden Circle tour, and lesser-known gems like the Laugavegurinn hiking trail, an area with colorful mountains, waterfalls, and lava-shaped landscapes.

The terrain is rugged and even desert-like in some areas, with most of the ground consisting of heather, moss, and lichen covering lava stones for miles. Visitors have an uninterrupted view of the landscape due to the lack of trees. But the hiking trails are well developed and the land mostly level, making for a relatively easy hiking locale. The trails are situated in picturesque regions with plenty of bird-watching opportunities in the summer.

Steeped in history, Þingvellir National Park is commonly referred to as the site of the world's first democracy. It's said that a group of settlers first gathered and met as a democratic legislature here close to a millennium

ago. Geology buffs will be thrilled to visit the Mid-Atlantic Ridge, a fault line that lies in Þingvellir. Visitors can literally plant one foot on Europe's side and the other in North America. Outside of Reykjavík, Þingvellir is the most visited site in Iceland.

Home to Iceland's only international airport, the Reykjanes Peninsula is one part of the country that visitors are sure to see. Reykjanes is also home to the famous heated waters of the Blue Lagoon, where you can soak away your jet lag.

PLANNING YOUR TIME

The dynamic Reykjanes Peninsula and southern coast region is defined by its vast lava fields, numerous hot springs, geothermal energy, and rugged landscape. Most tourists plan to visit at least two sites other than Keflavík airport—the Mid-Atlantic Ridge at Þingvellir National Park and the glorious Blue Lagoon, where you can soak in geothermally heated water.

If you are planning to spend one night in

Look for ★ to find recommended
sights, activities, dining, and lodging.

Highlights

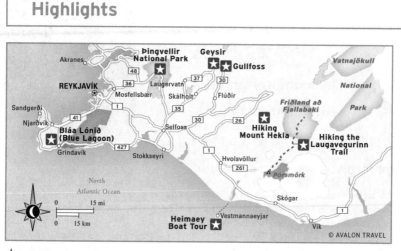

© AVALON TRAVEL

★ **Bláa Lónið (Blue Lagoon):** This gorgeous, geothermally heated spring heals the skin and soothes the body (page 82).

★ **Þingvellir National Park:** This park appeals to both geology buffs and history enthusiasts, as it's home to the rift valley that marks the crest of the Mid-Atlantic Ridge as well as the site where Iceland's first parliament gathered (page 86).

★ **Geysir:** Make a trip to the Geysir site to see the Strokkur geyser shoot steam and boiling water up to 30 meters. The natural phenomenon occurs every 10 minutes or so (page 90).

★ **Gullfoss:** This towering waterfall is 32 meters high, with white water tumbling over basalt rocks amid a lush green backdrop in the summer or stark white snow in the winter. If you have time to see only one waterfall in Iceland, this should be it (page 91).

★ **Hiking Mount Hekla:** One of Iceland's most active volcanoes offers stunning views. On clear days you can see as far as the ice-capped Vatnajökull glacier (page 98).

★ **Hiking the Laugavegurinn Trail:** This 55-kilometer, four-day hike is one of the most popular trails on the island. Hikers will see vast glaciers, bubbling hot springs, and towering mountains (page 101).

★ **Heimaey Boat Tour:** Take a tour from the harbor of lovely Heimaey, the only inhabited island in the Westman Islands, to see rocky lava coastline, bird cliffs, and ocean caves (page 108).

Reykjanes Peninsula and the South

the region, it's recommended to base yourself in Keflavík, where there are several guesthouses and hotels, as well as the largest selection of restaurants and shops on the peninsula. From Keflavík, you are close to attractions such as the Blue Lagoon, Garður lighthouses, and the Viking World museum.

The southern coast is home to the Golden Circle, arguably the most popular tour on the island. It takes you to three sites: the towering Gullfoss waterfall, Þingvellir National Park, and Geysir. The Golden Circle can be accomplished in one day, either by a bus tour or independently using a rental car.

Plan to spend at least an afternoon on the Reykjanes Peninsula (likely, at the Blue Lagoon) and at least one day exploring the coast.

Reykjanes Peninsula

The Reykjanes Peninsula is home to a striking, dramatic landscape that has lava fields for miles, volcanic craters, geothermal waters and hot springs, and lava caves. The region is also a hotbed for outdoor activities, including horse riding, hiking, and bathing in hot springs.

REYKJANESBÆR (KEFLAVÍK AND NJARÐVÍK)

Reykjanesbær is where every tourist's journey begins in Iceland, as it is home to the country's only international airport, Keflavík.

During World War II, British and American troops arrived in Iceland and built the country's first airport base. Situated in between the United States and continental Europe, Iceland's location served the Allies well. Some may be surprised to learn that the last American troops left the island only in 2006.

While it may be tempting to get off the plane and get on a bus straight to Reykjavík, Reykjanesbær, which is a municipality that includes the towns **Keflavík** and **Njarðvík,** is a great place to explore. Lava fields for miles, coupled with majestic sea cliffs and accessible hiking trails, make the region a perfect place to roam. Throw on some hiking boots and have your camera ready. It's also a great spot for bird-watching during the summer months, when you can see arctic terns and gannets.

Sights
REYKJANES FOLK MUSEUM
Reykjanes Folk Museum (Duusgata 2-8, Keflavík, tel. 354/421-6700, www.reykjanes. is, 11am-6pm daily, 500ISK) hosts a variety of exhibits highlighting the town's rich history as one of Iceland's main commercial ports, and it remains so today. A museum housed in a stone turf-roofed farm cottage shows how life was lived in the region at the turn of the 20th century. On display are reconstructed rooms

the rugged coastline of Reykjanes

Reykjanes Peninsula

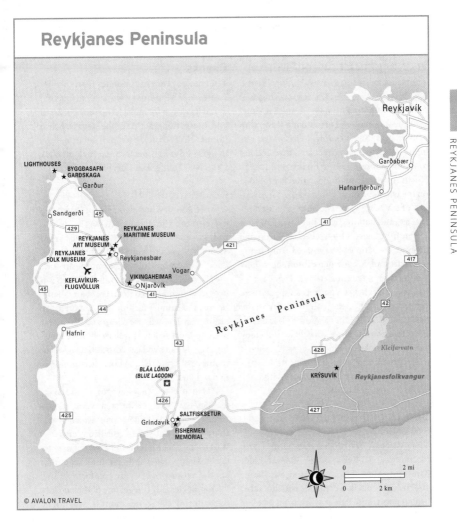

© AVALON TRAVEL

with vintage furnishings and artifacts, including furniture, cooking equipment, and work gear for fishermen.

REYKJANES ART MUSEUM

The **Reykjanes Art Museum** (Duusgata 2-8, Keflavík, tel. 354/421-6700, www.listasafn.reykjanesbaer.is, noon-5pm Mon.-Fri., 1pm-5pm Sat.-Sun., free) is a charming museum that hosts exhibitions of local artists and crafters. The museum gives a taste of the local and eclectic art scene. Check out contemporary art as well as traditional paintings of the rolling landscape.

REYKJANES MARITIME CENTER

The **Reykjanes Maritime Center** (Duusgata 2, Keflavík, tel. 354/421-6700, noon-5pm Mon.-Fri., 1pm-5pm Sat.-Sun., free), which opened in 2002, houses 100 model boats built by a retired local sailor, Grímur Karlsson. Models on display include masted schooners of the mid-19th century and steam-powered trawlers of the 20th century. Information is available on the types of boats and when they were used.

VIKINGAHEIMAR (VIKING WORLD)

The museum Viking World (Vikingabraut 1, Njarðvík, tel. 354/894-2874, www.vikingaheimar.com, 1pm-4pm Mon.-Wed. and Sat.-Sun., 1,200ISK) is centered around a Viking ship exhibit. The ship *Íslendingur (Icelander)* was built in 2000 to sail to Greenland from Iceland to commemorate Leifur Eiríksson's trip to North America, and information is provided on the trip. It's a great photo op of a large replica of a Viking ship. The ship is housed inside a grand building with huge windows not too far from shore. Lifted several feet from the ground, the ship can be viewed from many interesting angles. A video exhibit shows how Viking ships were constructed. There are tables and chairs below, and you can spend some time gazing at the boat with the ocean in the background. When the weather is pleasant, it's great to sit on the large grass field and enjoy a coffee from the café inside. For kids, there's a "settlement zoo" exhibit, which allows children to get up close and personal with baby lambs, calves, and birds.

Sports and Recreation
SWIMMING

The Vatnaveröld Swimming Pool (Sunnubraut 31, Keflavík, tel. 354/421-1500, 7am-8pm Mon.-Fri., 8am-6pm Sat.-Sun., 400ISK) in Keflavík is complete with hot tubs, heated pools, and a great swimming area for children. It's a wildly popular spot for locals and gives you a peek into an integral part of Icelandic society.

WHALE-WATCHING

During the summer months (June-September), Airport Whale Watching (tel. 354/421-7777, www.dolphin.is, 8,000ISK for 3-hour trip) runs a tour from Keflavík Harbor. You have a chance to see dolphins and minke, fin, orca, sei, and humpback whales. The tours are three hours long on a large, 90-person vessel. If you do not see any whales or dolphins,

you will be given a free voucher for another tour.

Events

The major touring music festival All Tomorrow's Parties (www.atpfestival.com) found its way to Iceland a few years ago. Local and international acts take the stage at Ásbrú (former NATO base) in Keflavík for three days in early July. Past performers include Nick Cave, Neil Young, and Interpol.

Accommodations

One of the busiest hostels outside of Reykjavík, FIT Hostel (Fitjabraut 6A, Keflavík, tel. 354/421-8889, www.fithostel.is, beds from 4,000ISK) is where many begin their journey. Located just a few minutes from the airport, the 100-bed hostel offers rooms that sleep 2-6 people, common kitchen areas, shared bathrooms, and laundry facilities. It's not pretty by any means, but beds are cheap and it's a great place to meet fellow travelers who are looking to share rides and gas costs. Private double rooms cost 7,900ISK, and dorm accommodation is 4,000ISK.

At Hótel Berg (Bakkavegur 17, Keflavík, tel. 354/422-7922, www.hotelberg.is, rooms from 11,000ISK), the 17 rooms are comfortable and have flat-screen televisions and free Wi-Fi. The decor is a bit old-fashioned, with tasseled lampshades and grandmother quilts, but the queen-size beds are comfortable and the rooms clean. If you get one of the two loft suites during the winter months, you might catch a glimpse of the northern lights from the skylight.

The 68 rooms at Hótel Keflavík (Vatnsvegur 12, Keflavík, tel. 354/420-7000, www.hotelkeflavik.is, rooms from 34,000ISK) are a bit small, but each has a private bathroom, comfortable beds, and great views of the landscape. Guests are treated to a warm and helpful staff. An in-house restaurant serves traditional Icelandic fare and some international favorites.

Keflavík's 20-room, centrally located modern hotel, Hótel Keilir (Hafnargata 37,

Keflavík, tel. 354/420-9800, www.eng.hotelkelir.is, rooms from 14,900ISK), boasts minimalist decor, average-sized rooms, and small bathrooms. A family suite is available that comfortably sleeps five people.

Icelandair Hótel-Keflavík (Hafnargata 57, Keflavík, tel. 354/421-5222, www.icelandairhotels.com, rooms from 32,000ISK) is just 10 minutes from the airport and a 15-minute drive to the Blue Lagoon. The 60-room hotel offers modern and comfortable rooms, an in-house spa, and a restaurant.

Food

Situated in the heart of the town, Langbest (Hafnargata 62, Keflavík, tel. 354/421-4777, www.langbest.is, 11:30am-9:30pm daily, 1,000ISK) serves up pizza, sandwiches, and fish-and-chips. It's a great place to stop for something quick and affordable.

Housed in Icelandair Hótel's Keflavík location, Vocal Restaurant (Hafnargata 57, Keflavík, tel. 354/421-5222, www.icehotels.is, 5am-10pm daily, 1,900ISK) is known for serving classic fish and meat dishes. Expect to see classic Icelandic cod, salmon, and lamb recipes on the menu. It opens for breakfast at 5am for early birds.

Information and Services

Reykjanesbær's tourist office (Hafnargata 57, tel. 354/421-6777, www.reykjanes.is, 10am-10pm daily June-Aug., 10am-4pm daily Sept.-May) is based in an office in the Reykjanesbær library.

Getting There and Around

Reykjanesbær is 49 kilometers southwest from Reykjavík. By car, take Route 41 to reach the region. It's about a 45-minute drive.

The Fly Bus (tel. 354/580-5400, www.flybus.is) runs regularly from Keflavík International Airport to the BSÍ bus station in Reykjavík, where you can get a shuttle to your hotel in Reykjavík. It takes about 50 minutes to get from Keflavík to BSÍ bus station, and buses depart about 40 minutes after flights land. One-way tickets cost 1,950ISK.

If you are staying in Reykjanesbær, be sure to contact your hotel or guesthouse to see if there is a shuttle to pick you up at the airport. If not, taxis are available at the airport.

There are tours for sights in Reykjanesbær, but if you want the freedom to roam, renting a car is essential.

GARÐUR

Garður is a placid seaside town on the northwest tip of Reykjanes and a great place to spend a couple of hours. Garður is best known for a pair of lighthouses. On sunny summer days, you can see locals and tourists picnicking by the lighthouses, basking in the sun and enjoying the serenity and scenery. The lighthouses are a great spot to catch a glimpse of the northern lights in the winter, as the location is away from the bright lights of downtown.

Sights
LIGHTHOUSES

The main highlight of Garður is the two lighthouses, each with unique charm. The older, more traditional red-striped lighthouse was built in 1847, and the newer square-designed one was built in 1944 in a more modern Nordic design. This is a popular destination to stop and take a photo. Fishing boats can often be seen from shore, and there is rich birdlife in the region, ranging from hordes of seagulls circling in the summer months to ravens dominating the skies in the winter. It's also common to see arctic terns and gannets in the summer months. In the winter, the lighthouses appear against a backdrop of mist and mystery, and if you're lucky, you will see northern lights dancing in the night sky.

BYGGÐASAFN GARÐSKAGA (FOLK MUSEUM)

The Byggðasafn Garðskaga (Folk Museum) (Skagabraut 100, tel. 354/422-7220, www.svgardur.is, 1pm-5pm daily Apr.-Oct., open by appointment the rest of the year, free) is based in the rugged landscape with thriving birdlife. The quaint museum houses items that were essential for the livelihood of residents on both land and sea, including tools, fishing items, and maps. It offers a window into what life was like in past generations, reminding visitors that life in Iceland was not easy for early settlers. The museum also has an extensive collection of 60 functional engines provided by local resident Guðni Ingimundarson.

Sports and Recreation
CAMPING
There is a **free campground** (Skagabraut, tel. 354/422-7220) situated close to the two lighthouses. Campers have access to running water and toilets.

Accommodations and Food
Guesthouse Garður (Skagabraut 46, tel. 354/660-7894, www.guesthousegardur.is, apartments from 26,000ISK) is a charming guesthouse with seven apartments ranging from studios to two-bedrooms available year-round. Close to the harbor, the apartments have private kitchens, bathrooms with showers, free Wi-Fi, and satellite TV. The friendly staff can help arrange for local tours, including golfing, bird-watching, and fishing. The cozy guesthouse is just a 10-minute drive to Keflavík airport.

Getting There and Around
Garður is 55 kilometers west of Reykjavík. By car, take Route 41 to Route 45.

ELDEY ISLAND
Situated about 15 kilometers southwest from the southernmost tip of the Reykjanes Peninsula, Eldey Island is made up of sheer cliffs that jut out of the ocean and reach 77 meters high. Birdlife thrives on the island; Eldey has one of the biggest gannet bird colonies in the world. In recent years, an estimated 70,000 gannets have bred on the island from June to August. The best view of the island is from the Reykjanes Lighthouse; the GPS coordinates are N 63.8151, W 22.7033.

GRINDAVÍK
Grindavík is a placid fishing town steeped in fish trade history. Many of the same families have been trolling these waters for generations, and visitors can see fishers hauling their daily bounty of cod out of the harbor by day and dine on the local catch at night. The Grindavík area's greatest claim to fame, however, is the giant manmade geothermal expanse of the Blue Lagoon.

Sights
★ BLÁA LÓNIÐ (BLUE LAGOON)
Located 23 kilometers south of Keflavík International Airport, the **Blue Lagoon** (Svartsengi, tel. 354/420-8800, www.bluelagoon.com, 7:30am-9pm daily June-Aug., 10am-8pm daily Sept.-May) draws visitors from around the world, to soak in the glorious, healing waters amid a dreamlike atmosphere.

A trip to the Blue Lagoon in the winter is eerie and wonderful. Watching as snow falls from the jet-black December sky, or as northern lights dance across it, while soaking in the heated water is sublime. But the heated water, which ranges 37-39°C (98-102°F), is heavenly during any time of year. The milky waters and the misty air during the summer are lovely, especially on sunny days.

The water is not deep, less than five feet, and the bottom is covered with white silica mud, the result of a natural process of re-condensation. It's common to see visitors cover their faces with the mud, as it's very good for your skin. The gift shop sells Blue Lagoon skin products that have ingredients ranging from silica mud to algae found in other parts of Iceland.

For those not interested in taking a soak, there are two steam baths on the property, as well as a dry sauna and massage area. Spa treatments are also available.

Many tours feature a visit to the Blue Lagoon, but if you're traveling independently, it makes sense to visit right after you fly in or before you head home, as it's very close to Keflavík airport. A rejuvenating soak is a great way to kick off your trip or end it on a relaxing note.

The entrance fee is 6,000ISK for adults, 3,000ISK for teenagers, 3,000ISK for senior citizens, and children under the age of 13 are admitted free. Because of the increase in tourism over the past few years, the Blue Lagoon now requires that you book a time slot ahead of your arrival. Thousands of people visit the site every day, and it could be quite crowded during summer months. If you don't bring your own towel, you can rent one at the front desk, along with swimsuits and bathing caps.

SALTFISKSETUR (SALTFISH MUSEUM)

The Saltfish Museum (Hafnargata 12A, tel. 354/420-1190, www.saltfisksetur.is, 9am-6pm daily, entrance 500ISK) is a museum that tells you exactly what Iceland's fish trade was like from 1770 to 1965, when saltfish ceased to be Iceland's top export. Photos, fishing equipment, and even a full-size fishing boat from the early 20th century are on display, explaining the importance of saltfish to Iceland, economically and culturally. If you're curious about the region, would like to learn more about processing saltfish in the olden days, or would like to get a look at an old-school fishing boat, be sure to stop by.

FISHERMEN MEMORIAL

A sad part of Iceland's fishing history is the stories of men that went out to sea to never return. There's a moving memorial in downtown Grindavík, in the main garden near the Saltfish Museum, showing a mother with her son and daughter waiting for their fisherman husband/father to return home from sea. It's a reminder that the fish used for consumption and trade has come at a high price for many families over the years. The memorial was created by sculptor Ragnar Kjartansson.

Sports and Recreation
BIKING

Reykjanes has several well-maintained trails perfect for cycling. Arctic Adventures (tel. 354/562-7000, www.adventures.is) operates a popular mountain biking tour that departs from Reykjavík by bus. Biking begins at the Blue Lagoon. The easy bike ride takes tourists on trails that run along volcanic craters, rugged lava fields, and bubbling hot springs throughout the peninsula. The tour runs mid-May-mid-September for 33,000ISK and

the Blue Lagoon

ends with a dip in the soothing, geothermally heated water at the Blue Lagoon.

CAMPING

Tourists can camp from mid-May to mid-September at Grindavík's Campsite (Austurvegur 26, tel. 354/660-7323, 1,200ISK) by the harbor. A popular campsite, Grindavík's location offers laundry facilities, a common eating area, and a playground for children that has swings and a spider net for climbing. The campsite accommodates tents, RVs, and campers, with access to hookups. The grassy field is an open space with beautiful views of mountains. There's also a paved entrance to the campsite and a large parking area. Close by is an area to empty camper port-a-potties.

GOLF

Just four kilometers southwest from the Blue Lagoon, Húsatóftir Golf Course (Húsatóftum, tel. 354/426-8720, paller@grindavik.is, 5,000ISK) is an 18-hole golf course where visitors can golf from late May to early September, depending on the weather. The course sits on a scenic part of the southern part of the country with picturesque views of the landscape. However, the course can be busy with locals during the high season of June-July. Be sure to call ahead for a tee time.

SWIMMING

Grindavík is home to one of the best pools in South Iceland. The Grindavík Swimming Pool (Austurvegur 1, tel. 354/426-7555, www.grindavik.is, 7am-8pm Mon.-Fri., 10am-5pm Sat.-Sun. June-Aug., 400ISK) has a 25-meter pool, hot tubs, tanning beds, a water slide, children's pool, and fitness center.

Accommodations

The ★ Blue Lagoon Clinic (Svartsengi, tel. 354/420-8806, www.bluelagoon.com/Clinic, doubles from 46,000ISK) is a luxurious hotel connected to the Blue Lagoon specializing in treating psoriasis and eczema. Guests travel to the healing waters from around the world

in the hope of treating skin diseases through specialized treatments. The clinic has 15 rooms that offer comfortable beds, modern decor, and beautiful views of the lagoon. To stay at the clinic, guests must have a form completed by a dermatologist citing that you have a form of psoriasis or eczema.

Open all year long, Guesthouse Borg (Boragarhraun 2, tel. 354/895-8686, www.guesthouseborg.com, rooms from 14,000ISK) is a basic, no-frills guesthouse in the center of Grindavík. The seven-room guesthouse has shared kitchen facilities, bathrooms, and washing machines, and is a five-minute drive from the Blue Lagoon. It's a clean and comfortable place to stay, but nothing to write home about.

The 32-room guesthouse Northern Light Inn (Grindavíkurvegur 1, tel. 354/426-8650, www.nli.is, doubles from 34,500ISK) offers cozy, bright, rooms with free Wi-Fi, satellite TV, and stunning views. An in-house restaurant offers classic Icelandic fare with plenty of fish and lamb dishes as well as a couple of vegetarian options. A conference area attracts business travelers, but the proximity to the Blue Lagoon is a big draw for tourists.

Food

Bryggjan (Miðgarður 2, tel. 354/426-7100, www.kaffibryggjan.is, 11am-6pm daily, 600ISK) is Grindavík's main coffee house and a favorite among locals and tourists alike. The cozy eatery is light on decor but known for its light meals, sandwiches, and soups. The lobster soup is delicious and affordable at just 600ISK.

The ★ Lava Blue Lagoon Restaurant (Svartsengi, tel. 354/420-8800, www.bluelagoon.com, noon-8:30 pm daily, entrées from 5,900ISK) is very much a spa restaurant; ingredients are fresh and local, and the recipes are healthy. You will find fresh vegetables and fish as well as lean meats. The menu accommodates a host of dietary requirements. You will dine in a minimalist atmosphere with cool hues and modern accents.

Mamma Mía (Víkurbraut 31, tel. 354/426-7860, 5pm-10pm Mon.-Thurs.,

11:30am-11:30pm Fri.-Sun., entrées from 1,400ISK) is Grindavík's only pizzeria. It serves up classics like margherita and pepperoni but also does some specialty pies with interesting ingredients, including tuna fish and pineapple. Hamburgers, sandwiches, and salads are also available. It's a family-friendly restaurant, one that locals and their kids frequent often. You can eat in or do takeaway.

★ Salthúsið (Stamphólsvegur 9, tel. 354/426-9700, www.salthusid.is, noon-10pm daily mid-May-mid-Sept., entrées from 2,400ISK), or "The Salt House," is a favorite among local fishers, residents, and tourists. There's a lot of saltfish on the menu, but guests can also choose from lamb and chicken dishes, as well as burgers, sandwiches, and fish-and-chips from this quiet eatery. The garlic-roasted lobster with salad and garlic bread is delicious. If you have room, be sure to check out the decadent dessert menu, which includes deep-fried bananas with vanilla ice cream and caramel sauce, and French chocolate cake with fresh cream.

Information and Services

The tourist information center is located in the Saltfish Museum (Hafnargata 12A, tel. 354/420-1190, 10am-5pm daily). The gas station N1 and grocery chain Netto are situated downtown on Víkurbraut.

Getting There and Around

By car, Grindavík is 50 kilometers from Reykjavík. Drivers should take Route 41 west to Route 43 south. It's about a 40-minute drive.

There are three daily departures from BSÍ bus station (www.bsi.is) in Reykjavík to Grindavík all year-round from the company Reykjavík Excursions (tel. 354/580-5400, www.re.is) for 3,900ISK. There are return buses to Reykjavík as well. The buses go to the Blue Lagoon as well as the center of Grindavík (about 1.25 hours).

KRÝSUVÍK

The Krýsuvík geothermal area, which is 35 kilometers south of Reykjavík, is popular among geology buffs and hikers. Gurgling mud pools amid the yellow, red, and orange clay-like earth are intertwined with dancing steam and hot springs. The many hiking paths allow you to feel lost in the outer space-like atmosphere. The region gives you a great sense of Iceland's raw, natural geothermal energy, which powers much of the island. Take some time to roam, but be sure to stay within the designated roped-off areas to avoid getting burned by spray and steam. To get to the region, take Route 42 from Reykjavík. It's about a 40-minute drive.

The Golden Circle

If you ask an Icelander which tour you should take if you want a taste of Iceland outside of Reykjavík, you will most likely hear the "Golden Circle" tour. Encompassing the three most commonly visited sights in South Iceland, the Golden Circle gives you a slice of Icelandic history at Þingvellir, a view of Iceland's bubbling geothermal activity at Geysir, and a peek of a roaring, powerful waterfall at Gullfoss. The sights are classically Icelandic, and postcard perfect, whether in summer or winter. Because of the popularity

of the sights, it's pretty easy to get there. You can pre-book a tour through many tourism companies, or simply go to Reykjavík's main bus terminal, BSÍ (Vatnsmýrarvegur 10, Reykjavík, tel. 354/562-1011, www.bsi.is), and buy a same-day ticket through Reykjavik Excursions (tel. 354/580-5400, www.re.is) for 9,500ISK for an eight-hour tour. If you want to rent a car and view the sights independently, take Route 1 past the town of Selfoss, then Route 30 to Gullfoss, then Route 35 to Geysir, and Routes 37, 365, and 36 to Þingvellir. In

The Golden Circle

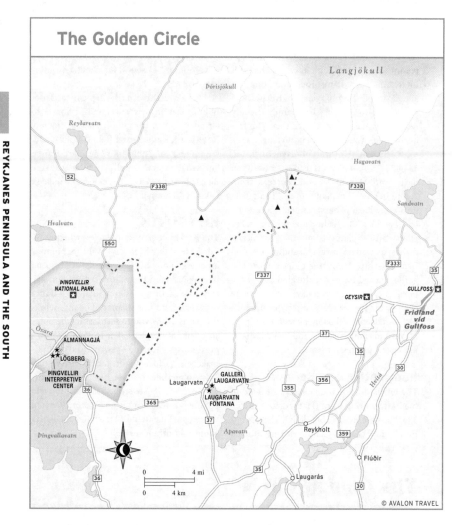

© AVALON TRAVEL

total, the Golden Circle is a 300-kilometer circular route, leaving from and returning to Reykjavík.

★ ÞINGVELLIR NATIONAL PARK

The birth of Iceland as a nation began at Þingvellir. Literally translated to "Parliament Plains," Þingvellir is the site of Iceland's first general assembly, which was said to be established in the year 930, and the meeting place of the Icelandic parliament until 1798.

Many significant sights are at Þingvellir, including Almannagjá (All Man's Gorge) and Lögberg (Law Rock). Icelanders made sure that Þingvellir is a protected national park by establishing it as such in 1930.

Visitors also come to the area for its geological significance, as it is the site of a rift valley that marks the crest of the **Mid-Atlantic Ridge** and is home to Þingvallavatn, the largest natural lake on the island, which has a surface area of 84 square kilometers.

Sights

ÞINGVELLIR INTERPRETIVE CENTER

The **Þingvellir Interpretive Center** (tel. 354/482-2660, www.thingvellir.is, 9am-5pm daily year-round, free) gives a great overview of the national park, its history, and its geological significance. Stop in to see the interactive display and then pick up hiking maps at the information center next door.

ALMANNAGJÁ

The moss-covered, stony landscape is home to Almannagjá (All Man's Gorge), which is the tallest cliff face and the original backdrop to the Alþing. This rock structure is considered the edge of the North American plate, which visitors can get a look at up close. It's an impressive sight, so be sure you have your camera ready.

LÖGBERG (LAW ROCK)

Lögberg (Law Rock) is a popular site within the park. Iceland's Commonwealth period ran from 930 till 1262, and during that time, the Law Rock was the center of the Alþing (parliament). A man known as the "law speaker" proclaimed the laws of the Commonwealth, was required to memorize the laws, and had three years to recite all of them. At the Law Rock, members of the Alþing gave speeches and held significant events, including where the calendar was confirmed for the year as well as legal rulings. It's where Icelandic democracy began.

ÖXARÁ RIVER

The Öxará (Axe) River flows over seemingly endless lava fields, emitting a haunting mist in the winter months. It's serene and eerie until it reaches the waterfall Öxaráfoss, where the water tumbles and roars over the cliffs. At the river's edge, visitors can see a church and farmhouse, which is the official summer residence of Iceland's prime minister. The church, **Þingvallakirkja,** is a charming wood church in traditional Icelandic design that dates from 1859. Tourists can visit the church 9am-5pm daily from mid-May to early September. Visitors can go inside, take photos, and sit on a pew and reflect. The interior features a wooden pulpit and bells from earlier churches. There's a small cemetery behind the church where celebrated poets Einar Benediktsson and Jonasa Hallgrimsson are buried.

Þingvellir National Park

Sports and Recreation

DIVING

Scuba diving in the naturally filtered, pure water of Þingvallavatn lake is sublime. While some may think that diving in Iceland sounds strange, a growing number of tourists are opting to take a dip and check out what lies within the clear lake. Surveying the underwater basalt walls, multicolored algae, and sloping sands is magical. Don't even think about going in without a drysuit, as the water temperature hovers around 3°C (37°F). Diving is possible year-round, and day tours start at 35,000ISK. There are rules to obey, so don't attempt to dive without a guide. Dive Iceland (Ásbúðartröð 17, Hafnarfjörður, tel. 354/699-3000, www.dive.is) offers a two-tank dive package for about 35,000ISK.

FISHING

Boats are not allowed on the lake, but fishing permits are sold at the information center. Tourists have a chance of catching arctic char and brown trout. Be sure to obey the rules and pay for the permit. The fishing season at the lake runs from May 1 to September 15, and permits are about 30,000ISK.

HIKING

Þingvellir is lovely for the casual hiker. Acres of flat lava fields make it an easy hike, but be sure to be careful of open rock fissures along the way, because you could fall in. There are scores of foot trails and plenty of interesting rock formations and rugged landscape to see. You can get information about trails and the surrounding area at the visitors center. If you're looking to scale some small mountains, check out Mount Syðstasúla (1,085 meters), which is in the northern region of the park and is the easiest to climb. The view from the top is spectacular.

HORSE RIDING

Þingvellir is a popular spot for riding horses, with several trails that offer the chance to check out some of the more beautiful and geologically significant areas of the park.

Most tours cost about 12,500ISK and last for 3-4 hours. Seeing the region by horseback is a beautiful way to survey the land. Reykjavik Excursions (tel. 354/580-5400, www.re.is) offers a horse-riding day tour in Þingvellir for 19,900ISK.

Accommodations and Food

Þingvellir National Park's only hotel, Valholl Hotel, unfortunately burned down in 2009. However, there are hotels to stay at in nearby Laugarvatn and Selfoss. If you would like to stay within the park limits, your only option is camping at one of Þingvellir's five campgrounds in two sections of the park: at the Leirar section of the park, which is a five-minute walk from the Þingvellir information center, and in Vatnskot section, which is by Lake Þingvallavatn. The Leirar campground is divided into four campsites: Fagrabrekka, Syðri-Leirar, Hvannabrekka, and Nyrðri-Leirar. The Vatnskot campground is situated at an abandoned farm by the lake. All campsites have access to toilets, electricity, and cooking facilities. The difference in the two sections is not about amenities, but whether you want to camp close to the lake or stay closer to the information center. Both sections have great landscape views and spacious fields. The campgrounds are open June 1-Septembter 1, and it costs 1,300ISK per person.

Information and Services

The tourist information center (tel. 354/482-2660, www.thingvellir.is, 9am-7pm daily May-Oct., 9am-5pm daily Nov.-Apr.) is next to the main campground.

Getting There and Around

Þingvellir is 46 kilometers northeast of Reykjavík. By car, take Route 36, which will take you to the northern part of the park.

While there is no public transportation available to get to the park, a number of tours include a stop at Þingvellir. Check out Reykjavik Excursions (tel. 354/580-5400, www.re.is) for daily departures.

LAUGARVATN

Laugarvatn, or "Bathing Waters," is a lake situated between Þingvellir and the geothermal hot spot of Geysir. Historically, members of Iceland's parliament (Alþing) visited the springs due to the proximity to where parliament met at Þingvellir for hundreds of years. The lake's water temperature hovers around 104°F, making it a unique and warm swimming experience.

Sights
GALLERI LAUGARVATN
When not enjoying the soothing hot springs or vast landscape, steal away for a few minutes at Galleri Laugarvatn (Haholt 1, tel. 354/486-1016, www.gallerilaugarvatn.is, 1pm-5pm daily), a charming little gallery that features local handicrafts, ranging from glass tea light holders to unique paper crafts.

LAUGARVATN FONTANA
The Laugarvatn Fontana (Hverabraut 1, tel. 354/486-1400, www.fontana.is, 11am-9pm daily, 3,200ISK entry fee) is worth a stop before or after you visit geothermal hot spot Geysir. The facility's sauna captures the steam just as it escapes from the earth. Tourists and locals can be seen basking in the natural sauna and hot springs, enjoying the geothermal energy up close and personal. For something really unique to the region, each day at 2:30pm there is a planned walk to the on-site geothermal bakery from the reception area. Visitors can experience the geothermal bakery firsthand and see as the staff digs out rye bread that has been buried in the ground, left to bake naturally from the geothermally heated earth. After the walk, you can try the bread, served hot from the ground with some butter. It's delicious!

Sports and Recreation
SWIMMING
Situated downtown, the Laugarvatn Swimming Pool (Hverabraut 2, tel. 354/486-1251, 10am-10pm Mon.-Fri., 10am-6pm Sat.-Sun. June-mid-Aug., 5pm-8pm Mon., Wed., and Fri., 1pm-5pm Sat. mid-Aug.-May, 500ISK) is popular among locals, but it's a nice break from the summer tourist rush at the Fontana spa nearby. Head here if you would like a quiet spot to take a dip.

Accommodations
Location is key for Hótel Edda ML Laugarvatn (Skólatún, tel. 354/444-4810, www.hoteledda.is, mid-June-mid-Aug., rooms from 11,100ISK), as this 101-room hotel is a popular stop for those touring the Golden Circle. Rooms are basic and no-frills, with double beds, IKEA-style furniture, and crisp white bedding. Thirty-two rooms have private bathrooms, while the rest share facilities, and there is free Wi-Fi in common areas. Guests get a 10 percent discount for the geothermal steam baths at the nearby Fontana spa.

Efstidalur II (Bláskógabyggð, tel. 354/486-1186, www.efstidalur.is, rooms from 14,000ISK) is a charming farmhouse bed-and-breakfast with an in-house restaurant, friendly staff, and horse rentals. Situated close to the Fontana spa, the B&B is also in the proximity of the Golden Circle.

One of the busiest hostels in South Iceland, Laugarvatn Youth Hostel (Dalsel, tel. 354/486-1215, www.laugarvatnhostel.is, open all year, double rooms from 10,900ISK) sleeps 140 people in single, double, and family rooms. Ten rooms have private bathroom facilities, while the rest share. Kitchen and laundry facilities are available, and the staff is very warm and helpful. There's also a big hot tub on the property.

Food
At Restaurant Linden (Lindarbraut 2, tel. 354/486-1262, www.laugarvatn.is, noon-10pm daily in summer, entrées from 1,800ISK), owner and head chef Baldur Öxdal Halldórsson has created an upscale, fine dining experience in a town with fewer than 300 residents. Guests have a lot of choices, from Icelandic mainstays to more exotic fare, with dishes ranging from reindeer meat burgers and pan-fried arctic char to tender lamb

filets and smoked cod. The classic decor and friendly staff make this little restaurant a treasure. You won't find typical tourist fare here.

Getting There and Around

Laugarvatn is just 77 kilometers northeast from Reykjavík and is easily accessible by car and bus. If driving, take Route 37, which heads toward Gullfoss and Geysir. Turn off on Route 354, which will take you to Laugarvatn.

The Stræto bus company (tel. 354/540-2700, www.straeto.is) has one daily departure to Laugarvatn year-round, leaving from the Mjodd bus terminal (tel. 354/587-0230) in Reykjavík. The trip is about 2.5 hours, and it costs 1,400ISK.

★ GEYSIR

Iceland's geysers are the most obvious demonstration of the island's natural geothermal energy. A bubbling pool of hot water in clay-like earth erupts into a mountain of steam, delighting spectators.

Historically, Geysir is the most famous of Iceland's geysers; it's actually the source of the word "geyser." Geologists theorized that in the 13th century earthquakes stirred the underground workings of the natural hot springs, causing them to gush, releasing pressure, steam, and water up to 20 meters into the air.

Visitors to the site today aren't going to see Geysir erupt, as the geyser hasn't blown since 2005; it's been rendered dormant. But don't fret, because Geysir's nearby cousin, Strokkur (Churn), erupts every seven minutes or so, delighting tourists. The churning, gurgling pool of water turning out a rush of pressure is an impressive sight. Be sure to have your camera ready.

Crowds gather at Strokkur to watch the frequent eruptions. Please be careful and stay behind the ropes or you may get hit with hot spray.

After walking around the geothermal area, stop at the visitors center (10am-5pm May-Aug., noon-4pm Jan.-Apr. and Sept.-Dec.). It has a short multimedia exhibition about the geology of the region, a small café serving refreshments, and a souvenir shop.

Sports and Recreation
CAMPING

About 100 meters from the Geysir area is a campground (tel. 354/480-6800, 1,000ISK) that has hot showers, pool access, and a common barbecue area. Hótel Geysir operates the campsite, and you pay at the Geysir Shops just

the Strokkur geyser erupting

across from the campgrounds. For an additional 500ISK you can have access to electricity, and the use of the swimming pool and hot tub at Hótel Geysir will run you an additional 500ISK.

Accommodations and Food

You can't stay any closer to the geysers than at the **Hótel Geysir** (Geysir, tel. 354/480-6800, www.geysircenter.is, rooms from 18,000ISK). The property features posh suites that have huge Jacuzzi tubs and luxurious beds right across the way from the geysers. Guests can also stay in chalets on the property that are essentially double rooms. The decor is a bit rustic, but the rooms are comfortable. Visitors have access to an outdoor swimming pool and hot tub, and the geysers are just two minutes away. The in-house restaurant (8am-10pm daily) serves up delicious dishes ranging from fresh Icelandic cod to lamb and beef entrées. A lunch buffet is popular among tourists. A three-course dinner menu will run you about 7,000ISK.

Guesthouse Geysir (Haukadalur, tel. 354/486-8733, www.geysirgolf.is, double rooms from 16,000ISK) doesn't have the perks of the Hótel Geysir, but the guesthouse has single, double, and triple rooms, as well as sleeping bag accommodations and free breakfast in the summer months. Guests also have access to a kitchen to prepare and store their food. The guesthouse is next to a nine-hole golf course. It's clean and comfortable and adequate for a quick stay.

Getting There and Around

Geysir is about a 1.5-hour drive east from Reykjavík. You start out on Route 1, then take Route 35, which takes you directly to the site.

SBA-Norðurleið bus service (tel. 354/550-0770, www.sba.is) passes by Geysir daily during its highland route toward Akureyri. You can request a stop at the site. The ride from Reykjavík is about 2.5 hours (4,600ISK). The bus runs during the summer only.

★ GULLFOSS

The thundering, roaring waterfall of Gullfoss epitomizes the raw beauty of Iceland. Gullfoss (Golden Falls) tumbles into the Hvíta (White) River, which is a perfect name given the turbulent white water. There are three levels of water at the falls, ranging from 11 meters to 21 meters, meeting at a 70-meter gorge. If you get too close, expect to get soaked.

Because of Iceland's changing weather, you

Gullfoss

have a good chance to see a rainbow over the falls, making for a perfect snapshot of your visit. Plan to walk around the site, enjoying not only the wonder of the falls, but also the beautiful surrounding landscape. In the summer, there are miles of lush green grass and frequent rainbows on sunny/rainy days. Be careful; it could be slippery.

No matter what time of year, there are scores of tour buses and independent drivers visiting the falls, and that's for a very good reason. It's gorgeous.

There is currently a fight between landowners and the Icelandic government over whether to charge visitors a fee to visit the falls. At the time of writing, it was undecided and still in the courts.

An on-site café includes a souvenir shop and offers some brochures about the surrounding area.

Accommodations and Food

A short walking distance from the falls and parking area, **Gullfosskaffi (Gullfoss Café)** (tel. 354/486-6500, www.gullfoss.is, 9am-9:30pm daily, entrées from 1,200ISK) is the place to go when you're in the area.

The Icelandic lamb meat soup on the menu is a winner, and a favorite among visitors, but sandwiches, cakes, and coffee are also available.

Hótel Gullfoss (Brattholt, tel. 354/486-8979, www.hotelgullfoss.is, rooms from 21,000ISK) is situated perfectly, just three kilometers from the falls in a remote area. The resort-like atmosphere is comfortable and a great place to spend the night while touring the Golden Circle. Every room has a private bathroom and is classically furnished with comfortable beds. An in-house restaurant and hot tub out back make for a comfortable stay.

Getting There and Around

By car, Gullfoss is 115 kilometers northeast from Reykjavík. The drive takes about 1.5 hours on Route 35.

If you plan to travel by bus, **SBA-Norðurleið** (tel. 354/550-0770, www.sba.is) makes one daily stop to and from Gullfoss on its Kjölur (Highlands) route. The ride from Reykjavík is about 3.25 hours (4,800ISK). The bus runs during the summer only.

The Southern Coast

If you're after hot springs and quirky museums, and you have some time to spend before you head to the Golden Circle, look no farther than the southern coast. Small towns like Hveragerði and Selfoss have unique charm—Hveragerði's claim to fame is as the hot springs capital of Iceland. Selfoss is frequently used as a home base when exploring the Golden Circle, but there are a couple of museums to check out.

HVERAGERÐI

Some Icelanders affectionately call Hveragerði the "Capital of Hot Springs." It's just 20 minutes outside of Reykjavík, so tourists have no reason not to stop by the region, especially as

the town is on the way to the Golden Circle of Gullfoss, Geysir, and Þingvellir. Given its proximity to Reykjavík and its healing hot springs, the town is an all-year destination. After a visit to the springs, think about taking a peek at some of the local greenhouses populating the geothermal area. Tomatoes, cucumbers, and bell peppers are popular greenhouse-grown veggies in the region.

Sights
HVERAGARÐURINN GEOTHERMAL PARK

People flock to Hveragerði for one main reason—hot springs. Whether they're under blue skies and sunshine or rain, wind, and

The Southern Coast

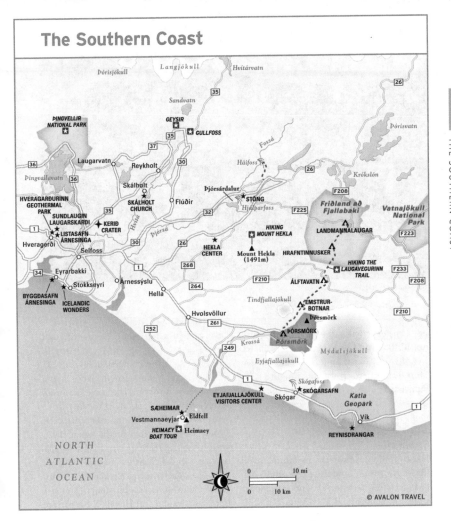

snow, the hot springs beckon visitors from around the world. The central geothermal area is in the center of town (Hveramörk 13, 9am-11am and 5pm-8pm Mon.-Thurs., 2pm-4pm Sat.-Sun., free). The natural phenomenon is hypnotizing to watch, as water bubbles to the top of the water surface. It's a constant reminder that Iceland sits on a hotbed of natural, geothermal energy. Follow the path between geysers and hot pools, and at the end of the walk, you can soak your feet in one of the hot springs.

LISTASAFN ÁRNESINGA (LA ART MUSEUM)

The **Listasafn Árnesinga (LA Art Museum)** (Austurmork 21, tel. 354/483-1727, www.listasafnarnesinga.is, noon-6pm daily, closed mid-Dec. to mid-Jan., free) offers several different exhibitions throughout the year, ranging from modern to traditional art from Icelandic artists local to the region. The museum also has a children's section, focusing on art for young visitors. It's a cute place to visit, especially if you are traveling with children.

the southern coast

SPA

For a spa experience, the NLFÍ Health and Rehabilitation Clinic (Grænumörk 10, tel. 354/483-0300, www.hnlfi.is, 7:30am-4:30pm Mon.-Fri.) offers treatments ranging from mud baths and acupuncture to massage. Come to relax and pamper yourself.

Sports and Recreation

CAMPING

Just two minutes from the swimming pool, the Hveragerði Campsite (Reykjamork, tel. 354/483-4605, www.reykjamork-camping@ simnet.is) is open mid-May-Sept., 1,200ISK. Visitors have access to a washing machine, toilets, and 220-volt electricity. There are about 80 spots on the large field, and the campsite accommodates tents, RVs, and campers.

GOLF

A nine-hole golf course is located in a picturesque part of the town, against a backdrop of hot springs. Open from May to August, the Hveragerði Golf Course (Gufudalur, tel. 354/483-5090, 3,000ISK) rents clubs and golf carts, and runs a café with light meals. Call ahead for a tee time.

HIKING AND BIKING

Several trails between Hveragerði and Þingvallavatn lead up to Mount Hengill, which is 68 kilometers north of Hveragerði. The 803-meter Mount Hengill gives hikers a view of the vast volcanic landscape. There are several active hot spots along the way, so be sure to stick to the trail. Bring your camera and a good pair of boots to roam the region. If you are interested in renting a bicycle, Hveragerði-based Iceland Activities (tel. 354/777-6263, www.icelandactivities.is) rents bikes in the region and organizes daily bike tours. Day tours last 4-5 hours and cost 11,900ISK per person. Before you head out for a hike, be sure to check the weather forecast and let your hotel/guesthouse know of your whereabouts.

SWIMMING

If hot springs aren't your bag, there's a lovely swimming pool downtown. The heated pool Laugaskarð (Reykjamörk, tel. 354/483-4113, 400ISK) is open 7am-8:30pm daily in summer, 10am-5:30pm daily in winter.

Accommodations

The 17-room boutique hotel Frost og Funi

(Hverahvammur, tel. 354/483-4959, www. frostogfuni.is, rooms from 17,000ISK) is nestled in the heart of Hveragerði. Each room, which is adorned with art from local Icelandic artists, has private shower facilities and comfortable beds. Guests have access to a spa next to the river that offers treatments, hot tubs, and a swimming pool. The included breakfast is delicious.

Situated close to the Ring Road, Frumskógar (Frumskógar 3, tel. 354/896-2780, www.frumskogar.is, double rooms from 15,000ISK) is a family-run guesthouse that offers five double rooms, one single room, and six apartments. Rooms are clean and comfortable, but no-frills. The friendly staff is happy to recommend activities, tours, and places to see. All rooms have free Wi-Fi, and breakfast is available for an extra cost.

Food

Dalakaffi (Jokutunga, tel. 354/862-8522, www.dalakaffi.is, 9am-6pm daily, 500ISK) is a quaint coffee shop that offers delicious cakes, fresh bread, and light meals. Located near the geothermal park, this is a great place to stop for a quick bite to eat.

The Hótel Örk (Breiðamörk 1C, tel. 354/483-7000, www.hotel-ork.is, 8am-10pm daily, entrées from 3,100ISK) has the ambience of a midrange banquet hall, but the food does not disappoint. You will find a plethora of lamb and fish dishes, but the lobster soup is something special, as is the pan-fried duck breast dish. The restaurant is a favorite among locals, and they often hold wedding receptions, birthdays, and other special occasions at the restaurant.

Located close to the geothermal park area, Hverabakari (Breidumork 10, tel. 354/894-4879, hverabak@gmail.com, 8:30am-6pm Mon.-Fri., 9am-6pm Sat.-Sun., 600ISK) is known for its "hot spring bread," which is a rye bread baked in the earth, utilizing the natural geothermal heat of the area. There are other delicious treats to sample, including cakes and doughnuts.

Information and Services

The South Iceland regional information center (Sunnumörk 2-4, tel. 354/483-4601, www.south.is, 9am-5pm Mon.-Fri., noon-4pm Sat.-Sun.) is right off Route 1.

Getting There and Around

Hveragerði is 40 kilometers southeast of Reykjavík. The drive takes about 35 minutes on Route 1.

The Strætó 51 bus (tel. 354/540-2700, www.straeto.is) from Mjodd bus station in Reykjavík makes about 10 daily stops to Hveragerði year-round, stopping at the Shell gas station downtown. The bus ride is about 55 minutes.

SELFOSS

Located close to Gullfoss, Geysir, and Þingvellir, Selfoss is considered a hub in South Iceland for many tourists and locals. Many visitors make a stop here to fill up their gas tanks, get a bite to eat, or rest their head in one of the town's nice hotels or guesthouses. While the town's proximity to the Ring Road and sights in the countryside is a plus, Selfoss has a few attractions of its own that are definitely worth checking out. History buffs will want to drop by the Heritage Museum, which features exhibitions of life in the town and the surrounding sights.

Sights
BYGGÐASAFN ÁRNESINGA (HERITAGE MUSEUM)

Byggðasafn Árnesinga (Heritage Museum) (Eyrargötu 50, tel. 354/483-1504, www.husid.com, 11am-5pm daily May-Sept., 700ISK) is one of Iceland's oldest buildings. Built in 1765, the house was home to a local Danish merchant and his large family and business. Merchant families lived in the house for nearly two centuries. Today, the museum gives a peek into what life was like in Iceland in the 1870s, with the decor, furniture, tools, and housewares of years past.

KERIÐ CRATER

The Kerið crater, which is just 15 kilometers north of Selfoss, is a cool place to stop and take a photo due to the sheer size of the crater lake. The collapsed scoria cone is 70 meters deep and is used for farming fish. There's a nice path along the rim to get a good view, but be careful and stay on the path.

SKÁLHOLT CHURCH

The site of the Skálholt church (tel. 354/486-8870, www.skalholt.is) has great significance in Iceland's history. Gissur the White, a wealthy political figure, played a big role in the Christianization of Iceland and the future status of the church. He built the first church in Iceland at Skálholt around the year 1000. His son, Ísleifur (1006-1080), chose Skálholt as the site of the first Episcopal see in Iceland, and the first bishopric was founded here in 1056 for southern Iceland.

In the 12th century, bishop Klængur Þorsteinsson built a great cathedral at Skálholt, and it served as a cultural center up to the Reformation in 1550. The last Catholic bishop of Iceland, Jón Arason, was executed at Skálholt in 1550, along with his two sons, because he opposed the Reformation forced upon Iceland by King Christian III of Denmark. A memorial stands at the site of the execution. Today, Skálholt is visited for the cathedral, the tomb of bishops, the museum, and the collection of ancient books in the tower, which tourists can view. In the summer months, there are cultural events and concerts held for locals and tourists. The church on the site today dates from 1963 and is a large, stark white church with a dark top. The design is sharp, clean, and classically Nordic. It's a sacred historical site for many Icelanders.

Admission is free, and tourists can visit 9am-6pm daily. There's a church service every Sunday at either 11am or 2pm.

Skálholt is 39 kilometers northeast of Selfoss. The drive takes about 35 minutes on Route 35.

Sports and Recreation
GOLF

The Kidjaberg Golf Course (Kidjaberg, tel. 354/486-4495, 8am-10pm daily in summer, 5,000ISK) in Selfoss offers an 18-hole course with glorious views near the Hvitá River. A clubhouse and restaurant are on-site. Be sure to call ahead for a tee time, as this is a popular course among locals.

Skálholt church

HORSE RIDING

Sólhestar (Borgargerdi, tel. 354/892-3066, www.solhestar.is) offers horse tours ranging from 1-hour rides for 7,000ISK to customized all-day tours for 20,000ISK. Tours feature trails along scenic hot springs, looming volcanoes, remote beaches, and gorgeous waterfalls.

SWIMMING

The Sundhöll Selfoss (Bankavegur, tel. 354/480-1960, sundh@arborg.is, 6:30am-9:30pm Mon.-Fri., 9am-7pm Sat.-Sun., 600ISK) is a pool open year-round; towel and swimsuit rentals are available.

Accommodations

★ Hótel Selfoss (Eyrarvegur 2, tel. 354/480-2500, www.selfosshotel.is, rooms from 37,500ISK) offers a stylish interior that you'd expect in Reykjavík but are delighted to see in the countryside. The 99-room hotel provides large rooms, spacious bathrooms, and chic decor. Ten rooms are specifically designed for people with disabilities, and it is one of the most wheelchair-friendly hotels on the island. Business travelers are attracted to the hotel for its conference center, while those looking for luxury are thrilled about the in-house spa, which offers a number of treatments. The staff aims to please and is happy to chat and give recommendations about local sites.

Hótel Fosstún (Eyrarvegur 26, tel. 354/480-1200, www.fosstun.is, open June-mid-Aug., apartments from 22,500ISK) is an apartment hotel with options ranging from double apartments to larger family apartments that provides guests with an independent stay. The no-frills facility features 32 rooms with standard beds, full kitchens, and private bathrooms with a shower. A washing machine is available for use, and there is free parking. A breakfast buffet is included.

Selfoss Hostel (Austurvegur 28, tel. 354/660-6999, www.selfosshostel.is, rooms from 10,000ISK) is one of the nicer hostels on the island. The 60-bed facility has spacious rooms, a common kitchen, small gym, and helpful staff. The hostel has a friendly atmosphere. Guests often meet up with fellow travelers and plan excursions together. Washing machines are available for use, and sheets are provided. A hot tub out back is a nice touch.

Food

Hafið Bláa (Thorlákshöfn, tel. 354/483-1000, www.hafidblaa.is, 11am-10pm daily, entrées from 1,200ISK), which translates to "The Blue Sea," is a seaside café where you can grab a quick coffee and cake or sit and enjoy a light meal and the beautiful view. The cream of mushroom soup is memorable. Lobster soup, arctic char, and salted cod are also on the menu.

Menam (Eyrarvegur 8, tel. 354/482-4099, www.menam.is, 11am-2pm and 5pm-10:30pm daily, entrées from 1,500ISK) is a nice little Thai restaurant that serves classic chicken, lamb, beef, and seafood dishes. The chicken pad thai is delicious.

Riverside Restaurant (Eyrarvegur 2, tel. 354/480-2500, www.hotelselfoss.is, 7am-10pm daily, entrées from 3,600ISK) is Hótel Selfoss's in-house restaurant. Guests are treated to fresh, local ingredients and eclectic recipes in an elegant dining atmosphere. The sesame fried salmon and bacon-covered monkfish are recommended. Vegetarian dishes are available.

Information and Services

The tourist information center (Austurvegur 2, tel. 354/480-1990, www.arborg.is, 10am-7pm daily June-Aug.) is a great place to pick up pamphlets, arrange tours, and ask the staff questions.

Getting There and Around

Selfoss is 57 kilometers southeast from Reykjavík. By car, Selfoss is off of the familiar Route 1. The drive takes about 40 minutes.

If you're traveling by bus, the Strætó 51 bus (tel. 354/540-2700, www.straeto.is) leaves from bus station Mjodd in Reykjavík several times a day. The ride takes about 50 minutes and costs 1,600ISK. Buses stop and pick up near the main circle (Austurvegur) downtown.

STOKKSEYRI

This small town was home to a thriving fish business, but today, it's more of a tourist town with a couple of kitschy museums.

Sights
THE GHOST CENTRE
The small Ghost Centre (Hafnargata 9, tel. 354/483-1202, www.icelandicwonders.com, 1pm-6pm daily June-late Aug., by request rest of year, 2,000ISK) is a fun museum dedicated to Iceland's most famous ghosts and their stories. During the tour, which takes about 40 minutes, you hear all about 24 ghost stories through a device and headphones that can be listened to in English, French, German, Russian, Japanese, or Icelandic. While you listen to the ghost stories, you look at displays about the various ghosts. The ghosts include mountainside ghosts, ancient ghosts, ghosts in animal disguises, infant ghosts, and sea ghosts. There's a Ghost Bar at the end of the tour, where you can order a drink and absorb everything you just took in. It's all in good fun, but it's not recommended for children under the age of 12.

ICELANDIC WONDERS
Icelandic Wonders (Hafnargata 9, tel. 354/483-1202, www.icelandicwonders.com, 1pm-6pm daily June-late Aug., by request rest of year, 1,500ISK) is right next door from the Ghost Centre. Instead of ghosts, this exhibition focuses on Iceland's rich folklore, including elves, trolls, the Yule Lads (Iceland's version of Santa Claus), and northern lights. There's something for everyone at this charming museum, and it is much more child-friendly than the Ghost Centre.

Getting There and Around
Stokkseyri is 65 kilometers southeast of Reykjavík and accessible by Route 1. The drive takes about 45 minutes.

Southwest Iceland

Southwest Iceland is home to grand beauty like Europe's largest glacier, Vatnajökull, and quiet spots like black-sand beaches in Vík. Outdoor activities like hiking, bird-watching, and jeep tours are popular things to do in the region.

MOUNT HEKLA

Hekla's claim to fame is being the most active volcano in the country today. And that's no easy feat, as there are 35 volcanoes currently active in Iceland. Hekla (Hood) should not be confused with nearby Eyjafjallajökull, which wreaked havoc for air travel across Europe in 2010. Climbing 1,491 meters, Hekla has erupted five times in the last hundred years and more than 20 times since Iceland was settled in the 10th century. Its last eruption was in 2000, and local scientists expect it to erupt in the near future, as there have been thousands of tremors in recent months. What makes Hekla somewhat unique is it's a cone volcano, which is less common in Iceland than fissure volcanoes.

Sights and Recreation
★ HIKING MOUNT HEKLA
Scaling Hekla is not as daunting as it looks. In a moderately challenging 3.5 hours or so, you will reach the summit from a seven-kilometer trail. Along the way, you will cross rough lava fields and see ice and snow as the peak gets nearer. At the top, the view is jaw dropping. On clear days, you will see all of the Fjallabak mountains up to Vatnajökull glacier, Europe's largest glacier.

Now for some crucial safety tips. The ideal time to make the climb is August-September, when it's not likely that you will encounter a lot of snow at the top. Always make sure you check weather conditions before you head out and let people (like the concierge of your hotel) know of your travel plans. Also check in with the **tourist information center** in Hella (Thrudvangur 6, tel. 354/487-4800). Make sure you have an adequate amount of drinking water, appropriate clothing, and a charged mobile phone.

HEKLA CENTER

The **Hekla Center** (Leirubakki, tel. 354/487-8700, www.leirubakki.is, 10am-9pm daily May-Sept., 600ISK) was opened in 2007 to give visitors a comprehensive look at one of the island's most active volcanoes over the years. The exhibition emphasizes the influence of the volcano on the inhabited areas close to it, including Landsveit, Holt, and Rangárvellir. The center has special educational materials for children as well as tourist information in English. An on-site café offers light meals and coffee. It's an essential place to stop and read up on the region.

Getting There and Around

By car from Reykjavík, head southeast on Route 1 and then take Route 26. The journey from Reykjavík is 93 kilometers, which takes about 1.5 hours.

For those interested in going by bus during the summer months, **Reykjavik Excursions** (tel. 354/580-5400, www.re.is) runs a daily bus that goes to Landmannalaugar, which passes Hekla. The tour takes 12 hours and costs 17,900ISK.

ÞJÓRSÁRDALUR

Þjórsárdalur is a flat valley, but it's quite lush due to its proximity to the Þjórsá River. The region has a lot of pumice because of the numerous eruptions from Mount Hekla over the years.

Sights
HÁIFOSS

Háifoss, a beautiful waterfall near Mount Hekla, drops from a height of 122 meters, making it the second highest waterfall on the island. Located against the backdrop of the Þjórsá River, Háifoss is a wonderful place to stop and take a picture. It is possible to hike to the waterfall (about a six-hour moderate hike), but there is a parking lot above the waterfall, which makes it a car-friendly stop along the way to your next destination. If you are planning to hike it, make sure you

REYKJANES PENINSULA AND THE SOUTH
SOUTHWEST ICELAND

hiking Mount Hekla

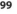

have proper footwear and adequate drinking water. A well-maintained trail starts from the car park. From Selfoss, take the Route 1 for 14 kilometers to Route 30 for 18 kilometers to Route 32 for about 43 kilometers.

HJÁLPARFOSS

Hjálparfoss is another gorgeous waterfall near Mount Hekla. It is about 30 kilometers east of the village Flúðir and can be reached by a gravel road off Route 32 that winds through the Vikrar lava fields.

STÖNG

Stöng, a settlement-era farm, was completely buried by Hekla's eruption in the year 1104. A reconstructed 11th-century longhouse called Þjóðveldisbær was erected in this protected valley (tel. 354/488-7713, www.thjodveldisbaer.is, 10am-6pm daily early June-Aug., remainder of the year open by appointment, 750ISK). For those looking to see a traditional "turf house" with grass on the roof, this is the place to go. The farm, as legend tells it, was the residence of Gaukur á Stöng from *Njál's Saga*. History buffs will want to make a stop at the farm; go inside and take a look.

Sports and Recreation
SWIMMING

After erecting the local dam, the Búrfell hydroelectric station used its extra cement to build the open-air Þjórsárdalur Swimming Pool (tel. 354/488-7002, 10am-9pm daily June-Aug., 550ISK).

Getting There and Around

Þjórsárdalur is 118 kilometers east of Reykjavík. It's accessible by Route 32, but keep in mind that a four-wheel-drive jeep is needed to get around some choppy parts by the river. It is not recommended to venture out in a compact car, as the chance of getting stranded is high. The drive takes about 1.5 hours. Be sure to check weather forecasts before heading out on your journey.

ÞÓRSMÖRK AND LANDMANNALAUGAR

The Þórsmörk (Thor's Woods) region offers a spectacular view of the landscape, ranging from towering mountains to scores of glacial streams and miles of black sand. Be advised that making it to the region is no easy feat. Do not venture out in a compact car. Because of the Krossá River, it is a wet and turbulent ride that requires a jeep.

Þórsmörk

★ Hiking the Laugavegurinn Trail

The wildly popular hiking route from the Landmannalaugar region to the Þórsmörk area is a 55-kilometer four-day hike that attracts backpackers and hikers from around the world. If you're coming to Iceland to hike just one trail, this is the one. Its popularity stems from the variety of landscape along the way: bubbling hot springs, vast glaciers, beautiful mountains, stunning waterfalls, and roaring rivers.

At night, hikers can rest their heads in mountain huts, which span the duration of the trail. The huts mark the starting and ending points of each leg of the trail.

To reserve huts, visit the **Volcano Huts** website at www.volcanohuts.com. Huts can sleep 2-16 people, and beds start at 6,500ISK. Huts have running water, cooking facilities, a sauna, pool, and showers. There are campsites that adjoin the mountain huts and are also operated by Volcano Huts. The facilities include a cooking area, toilets, and running water. It's always a good idea to call ahead for camping, and it's required to call ahead for mountain huts.

For more information about the Laugavegurinn Trail, contact **Ferðafélag Íslands (Iceland Touring Association)** (www.fi.is).

DAY 1: LANDMANNALAUGAR TO HRAFNTINNUSKER

The Landmannalaugar-Hrafntinnusker leg of the hike spans 12 kilometers, and its estimated walking time is 4-5 hours. It's considered moderately challenging. The trail goes through a rugged lava field, which makes this leg a bit more challenging, to the slopes of the volcano Brennisteinsalda. The landscape offers every color of the rainbow, from deep green moss to the bluest skies to yellow and red earth. After about four hours, you will reach a hot spring, Stórihver, which surges with activity, steam bubbling to the surface. The remainder of the day 1 trail to the Hrafntinnusker hut at Höskuldsskáli might be challenging depending on weather conditions, so be sure to monitor the forecast for snow and wind.

DAY 2: HRAFNTINNUSKER TO ÁLFTAVATN

The Hrafntinnusker-Álftavatn part of the trail is 12 moderately challenging kilometers, with an estimated walking time of about five hours. You start out going through a valley

Landmannalaugar

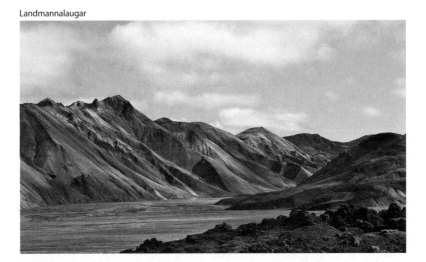

with some small gorges and dips in the land, but be careful where you step, because they may be filled with snow or ice. If the weather is good, a climb up to Mount Háskerðingur (1,032 meters) will treat you to a spectacular view of the landscape and the road ahead. The trail continues through a region rich with mountains and glaciers. As you get closer to the Grashagakvísl River, the colors become more vibrant because there's more bright green moss and lichen alive along the river banks. It's a beautiful place to stop, take some pictures, and soak up the scenery.

DAY 3: ÁLFTAVATN TO EMSTRUR

The third day from Álftavatn to Emstrur is a little longer at 15 kilometers and an estimated walking time of seven hours. The moderately challenging trail starts out over the ridge Bratthals, passes into the Hvanngil gorge, and crosses the Bratthalskvísl River by bridge. The landscape is vast and serene. As you continue on to the Kaldaklofskvísl River, there is a bridge for hikers. Past the bridge, you have two options as the trail splits. One branch leads east to Mælifellssandur, and the other path leads south to Emstrur. Most people opt for the southern trail to Emstrur because it's a bit more scenic with mountain views and an interesting rocky landscape. Less than one kilometer from Kaldaklofskvísl from the southern trail, there's another river, Nyrðri Emstruá, where there is a bridge to cross.

DAY 4: EMSTRUR TO ÞÓRSMÖRK

The last leg of the hike, from Emstrur to Þórsmörk, is 15 kilometers, with an estimated walking time of seven hours. Hikers start out by navigating the canyon of Syðri-Emstruá. It's important to note that there is a steep path down to the bridge, so please be aware and be careful where you step while descending. Next, hikers will come across the Almenningar region and will have to cross the Þröngá River. After wading through the river, it's a 30-minute walk to the Langidalur huts in Þórsmörk.

TIPS

It can be quite cold and snowy, so it's important to closely monitor the weather and hike in good conditions. Even if there isn't snow, the wind can be unforgiving. Be sure to dress warmly and have good boots. The ideal months for this hike are June and July.

Getting There and Around

Landmannalaugar is 193 kilometers southeast of Reykjavík. Take Route 1 to Route 26 to F225. It's about a 3.5-hour drive.

If starting the hike at Þórsmörk, it's important to note that it is not easy to reach when compared to other destinations in the south. However, it's worth the effort if you're looking for untouched and unspoiled land. There are significantly fewer visitors to Þórsmörk. You will need a jeep to navigate these roads; do not attempt the trip in a compact car.

Þórsmörk is 157 kilometers southeast from Reykjavík. It's reachable from Route 1 to Route 249 by jeep. The drive takes about 3.5 hours.

By bus, Trex (tel. 354/587-6000, www.trex.is) has daily departures in the summer from Reykjavík to Þórsmörk and to Landmannalaugar for 6,800ISK per person, and it's about a four-hour ride. Reykjavik Excursions (www.re.is) offers bus service daily in the summer from Reykjavík to and from Landmannalaugar and to and from Þórsmörk for 13,000ISK for a bus passport.

EYJAFJALLAJÖKULL

Eyjafjallajökull became Iceland's most famous volcano after its last eruption in 2010 halted air travel across Europe, stranding tens of thousands of people. For locals, it was a treat to hear foreign newscasters struggle to pronounce the name of the volcano on the nightly news. Clips were regularly shown on Icelandic TV. (For the record, it's pronounced EYE-ya-fyat-lah-YOH-kuht.)

Before Eyjafjallajökull made worldwide headlines, the volcano had been a popular destination to explore, and it remains so today, with a rugged and icy landscape.

Eyjafjallajökull is completely covered by an ice cap, which led to the extreme ash cloud after its latest eruption. Magma hitting the ice created the ash cloud. The ice cap covers an area of about 100 square kilometers, which feeds several outlet glaciers. When people joke that "Iceland is green, and Greenland is icy," those who visit the Eyjafjallajökull region will think again. There is a lot of ice in Iceland. The ice cap is the fourth largest glacier in Iceland.

Eyjafjallajökull is a stratovolcano that ascends 1,651 meters at its highest point. The volcano is fed by a magma chamber under the mountain, and it is part of a chain of volcanoes stretching across Iceland. Its nearest active neighbors are Katla to the north and Heimaey and Eldfell to the south. The volcano is thought to be related to Katla, in that eruptions of Eyjafjallajökull have generally been followed by eruptions of Katla. However, Katla did not erupt following Eyjafjallajökull's 2010 eruption. Scientists closely monitor the volcanoes' activity, measuring size and frequency of tremors.

Eyjafjallajökull (Iceland Erupts) Visitors Center

The visitors center (Rte. 1, tel. 354/487-5757, www.icelanderupts.is, 750ISK) opened on April 14, 2011, which was exactly one year after the start of the Eyjafjallajökull eruption. Situated at the foot of the volcano, the visitors center features color posters of the eruption, and a short film shows the power of nature and how the region rose from the ashes. The movie hall seats 60 people, and the film is available in multiple languages, including English, German, French, Spanish, and Italian. The center is open 10am-4pm daily May, 9am-6pm daily June-August, 10am-4pm daily September, and 11am-4pm daily October-November and February-April.

Getting There and Around

Eyjafjallajökull is on the Ring Road, Route 1, and is 140 kilometers east of Reykjavík. Buses do not stop near the volcano, so if you want to get up close and personal, you need access to a car.

SKÓGAR

Skógar is a tiny village that fewer than 40 people call home. The town hit a major setback in the aftermath of the Eyjafjallajökull eruption of 2010, as it was covered in ash and life ground to a halt. Since then, the town has recovered, and tourism to the region is back in full swing. The Skógafoss cascade is the main

The massive ash cloud caused by Eyjafjallajökull's eruption is seen in this photo dated May 12, 2010.

draw, but there is also a folk museum worth checking out.

Sights
SKÓGAFOSS

Skógafoss is an epic waterfall, one of the biggest in the country. It looms 25 meters high and has a drop-off of 60 meters. According to Viking lore, a local settler buried a treasure chest in a cave behind the waterfall. The story continues that locals discovered the chest years later, but it quickly disappeared before they could grasp it. Because of the amount of spray the waterfall produces, as well as the changing weather from sun to rain, it's common to see rainbows over the falls. Be sure to have your camera ready. The waterfall is near the southern Ring Road in town.

SKÓGASAFN (SKÓGAR FOLK MUSEUM)

Skógasafn (Skógar Folk Museum) (Austur-Eyjafjöllum, tel. 354/487-8845, www. skogasafn.is, 10am-5pm daily May-Sept., 9am-6pm daily June-Aug., 11am-4pm daily Oct.-Apr., 1,750ISK) is a charming initiative that started in 1949 at the behest of resident Þórður Tómasson, who curated the museum from its inception until his retirement in 2013, at the age of 92. The museum, which houses relics of the past, including tools, fishing equipment, and a fishing boat, does a great job of showing what life has been like in Skógar over the last several decades. A little coffee shop serves a great cup of coffee and delicious pastries.

Hiking the Fimmvörðuháls Trail

The one-day trek through the Fimmvörðuháls pass from Skógar to Þórsmörk is one of the most popular hiking routes in the country. The trail takes hikers up from Skógar, along the Skóga River and its wondrous waterfalls, and up between the two enormous glaciers Eyjafjallajökull and Mýrdalsjökull. There, hikers can see recently formed lava and craters. Heading down from the craters to the stunning Þórsmörk glacier valley, there are some amazing views over the highlands and the surrounding glaciers.

The hike is demanding, with an elevation gain of over 1000 meters and a total distance of about 25 kilometers. It takes about 8-10 hours. It's recommended that you start the hike at Skógar and end at Þórsmörk. There are no shops along the route, so be sure to have enough food and water, as well as proper gear.

Skógafoss

Good hiking boots and waterproof clothing are required. Guided hikes are available through Icelandic Mountain Guides (tel. 354/587-9999, www.mountainguides.is) for 37,900ISK.

Accommodations and Food

Just a five-minute walk from Skógafoss waterfall, ★ Hotel Skogar (Skogum, tel. 354/487-4880, www.hotelskogar.is, rooms from 34,000ISK) offers 12 rooms with a minimalist Nordic design style that you would expect from a countryside hotel. The rooms are bright and airy with wood furniture and shockingly white bedding. It's clean and comfortable, with a beautiful in-house restaurant in a killer location. At the foot of Eyjafjallajökull, the hotel has stunning views. Breakfast is included, and guests have access to a sauna and outdoor hot tub. The Hotel Skogar Restaurant (entrées from 3,900ISK) offers a delicious selection of choice local meats and fish and fresh ingredients. You will find a lot of lamb and fish dishes, as well as a few vegetarian options. The restaurant is open for breakfast 8am-10am daily year-round, lunch noon-3pm daily June-August, and dinner 6pm-10pm daily year-round.

Getting There and Around

The tiny village of Skógar is 154 kilometers southeast of Reykjavík and is accessible by Route 1.

Some bus tours include Skógar in their itinerary. For instance, Bus Travel Iceland (tel. 354/511-2600, www.bustravel.is) offers a "Southern Iceland" nine-hour tour that includes Skógafoss along with the town Vík for 11,900ISK.

VÍK

Vík has that small-town feel—fewer than 400 people call it home. The main tourist draw is the Katla Geopark, a region that surrounds the mighty Katla volcano, which has wreaked havoc on the island over the centuries.

Sights
REYNISDRANGUR

Reynisdrangur is a cluster of striking basalt sea stacks that jut out from a sandy beach. The stacks sit under the mountain Reynisfjall just outside Vík. It's common to climb on the stacks and take photos, then roam the black-sand beach picking up stones and looking at the rock formations rising from the sea.

the Reynisdrangur sea stacks

KATLA GEOPARK

Vík is the gateway to the Katla Geopark. Iceland's first geopark was designated in 2011 to protect the natural environment, promote local sustainable development, introduce local culture, and emphasize nature tourism. The name comes from one of the island's volcanoes, Katla, which is situated under the glacier Mýrdalsjökull. The geopark is 9,542 square kilometers, which is 9.3 percent of the total area of Iceland. Within the geopark are glaciers, volcanoes, mountains, rivers, waterfalls, and miles of lava fields. Visitors can enjoy hiking, caving, angling, horse riding, glacier walking, and ice climbing. The geopark is open year-round.

One of the best tours offered in the region is a three-hour jeep tour from Katla Track (tel. 354/849-4404, www.katlatrack.is), which takes you takes you to see black beaches, the Katla glacier, and Reynisdrangur. The tour is available year-round and costs 24,900ISK per person for a local guide and the jeep. Be sure to dress in warm clothing, rain gear, and good shoes.

Accommodations

Hótel Edda Vik (Klettsvegur 1-5, tel. 354/444-4840, www.hoteledda.is, May-Sept., rooms from 16,300ISK) is a 41-room hotel featuring standard rooms that aren't much to look at but are clean and adequate. The hotel could use a renovation, and Wi-Fi and breakfast cost extra, but the location is great, and it is a decent place to lay your head.

Guesthouse Hátún 8 (Hátún 8, tel. 354/487-1211, www.guesthousevik.is, rooms from 13,000ISK) is operated by a delightful couple named Tanja and Johann, who offer two cozy bedrooms with comfortable beds.

There's a shared bathroom, and guests have access to free Wi-Fi, a common kitchen to prepare meals, and a dining room. The guesthouse is nothing fancy, but the warm owners and great location make this place a winner.

Food

★ Halldorskaffi (Víkurbraut 28, tel. 354/487-1202, www.halldorskaffi.is, 11am-10pm daily year-round, entrées from 2,000ISK) has it all for a tiny café. There are soups, sandwiches, pizza, hamburgers, and more upscale fish and lamb dishes. A children's menu offers chicken nuggets and hamburgers. The food is eclectic for a local café, and the owner is a big fan of garlic. The lamb sandwich with fresh, marinated lamb meat in pepper sauce with a salad and French fries hits the spot.

Suður-Vík Restaurant and Café (Suðurvikurvegur 1, tel. 354/487-1515, 11am-9pm daily Apr.-Oct., 6pm-9pm daily Nov.-Mar., entrées from 3,000ISK) burst onto the scene in Vík in 2014, offering some much-needed food diversity. The menu is eclectic and includes some tasty Thai dishes that are perfectly spiced. The restaurant is situated in an old house on the top of a hill with amazing views of the landscape, including the sea and mountains.

Getting There and Around

By car, Vík is 185 kilometers southeast of Reykjavík by Route 1. It's about a 2.5-hour ride.

The Strætó 51 bus (tel. 354/540-2700, www.straeto.is) departs daily from the Mjodd bus terminal in Reykjavík to Vík. It's about a three-hour ride and costs 5,600ISK.

Heimaey

The Westman Islands (Vestmannaeyjar) are chock-full of rocky ridges and bird-watching opportunities. Heimaey, the only inhabited island, is where all of the sights, restaurants, and museums are located. With fewer than 5,000 residents, Heimaey is an isolated community, surrounded by beauty. The other islands remain uninhabited and are typically seen from the sea during a boat tour.

SIGHTS
Eldfell

Eldfell, which means "fire mountain" in Icelandic, is a volcanic cone that reaches 200 meters high. It was formed after the 1973 volcanic eruption on Heimaey, which came without warning and displaced more than 3,000 Icelanders. Ash from the eruption fell for weeks, destroying homes, livestock and personal possessions. Most of Heimaey's residents left by boat, and thankfully there were no deaths.

Tourists can take a 30-minute ferry ride from Landeyjaharbor in the southern town Hvolsvöllur to Heimaey to get a close look at Eldfell. Eimskip (tel. 354/481-2800, www.eimskip.is) operates the ferry that departs five times a week May-September (1,000ISK).

Sæheimar (Natural History Museum & Aquarium)

Heimaey's museum of natural history and aquarium, Sæheimar (Heidarvegur 12, tel. 354/481-1997, www.saeheimar.is, 11am-5pm daily mid-May-mid-Sept., 1pm-4pm daily mid-Sept.-mid-May, adults 800ISK, children free) is in the center of town and a great spot to take kids. You will see tanks and tanks of live Icelandic fish, along with stuffed birds such as puffins and arctic terns. Kids tend to love puffins with their colorful orange beaks.

Surtsey Visitors Center

To get some background on Surtsey, Iceland's newest island, stop by the Surtsey visitors center (Heidarvegur 1, tel. 354/591-2140, www.surtsey.is, 9am-4pm daily June-Aug., 1pm-4pm Sat. winter, adults 900ISK, children free). Rising from the sea after a series of volcanic eruptions beginning in 1963, Surtsey is

the Westman Islands

a geology buff's dream. However, the island remains off-limits, so those interested can find out all about it from this museum. The visitors center has photographs, scientist accounts, and some video footage of the island. Surtsey is 21 kilometers south of Heimaey.

SPORTS AND RECREATION
Bird-Watching

The island's puffin population is the main attraction for tens of thousands of visitors. Puffins are cute, charismatic, and classically Icelandic. Their bright orange feet, round bodies, and striped bills are irresistible to children and adults alike. Take a walk along the sea cliffs and spend some time with the adorable birds. Prime puffin-watching season is June-August.

★ Boat Tour

Viking Tours (tel. 354/488-4884, www.vikingtours.is) offers a lovely boat tour departing from Heimaey harbor daily at 11am and 3:30pm (May-mid-Sept., 5,900ISK). On the tour you will see the rugged lava coastline, bird cliffs, and ocean caves. The 1.5-hour tour ends with entering a cave near the harbor, where you will hear the sounds of instrumental music to enjoy the acoustics in the cave. It's a wonderful way to spend a couple of hours.

Hiking

Heimaey has a little of everything. Because of its small size, it's impossible to get lost, but there are moments when you will feel completely isolated, and serene, on your hike. Many choose to roam the base of the Eldfell volcano, watch the personality-packed puffins in the summer, and stroll downtown. You won't find a plethora of arduous treks, but the island is an opportunity for casual strolls and prime picture-taking. There are about 12 kilometers of trails along the coast.

Swimming

The Heimaey Swimming Pool (6:15am-9pm Mon.-Fri., 9am-6pm Sat.-Sun. June-Aug., 6:15am-9pm Mon.-Fri. rest of year, 450ISK) has a large indoor swimming pool, three hot tubs, sauna, and a gym. There's a slide for children and it's family-friendly. It's open all year.

ACCOMMODATIONS

Árný (Illugagata 7, tel. 354/481-2082, www. arny.is, rooms from 16,000ISK) is a small guesthouse that favors wood decor and neutral tones. The beds and furniture are comfortable and homey, and guests have access to a shared kitchen and laundry facilities; bathrooms are also shared. A swimming pool is next to the guesthouse.

The Hótel Eyjar (Bárustígur 2, tel. 354/481-3636, www.hoteleyjar.is, rooms from 20,000ISK) boasts ample rooms with private bathrooms in the center of town. Located above a bookstore, the hotel features contemporary decor and standard beds. All rooms come with free breakfast and en-suite kitchenettes. Inquire about a special rate for groups.

Hotel Vestmannaeyjar (Vestmannabraut 28, tel. 354/481-2900, hotel@eyjar.is, rooms from 21,000ISK) offers clean, small rooms with shared kitchen and bathroom facilities. The hotel has a hot tub out back, arranges bicycle rentals, and has a tour desk that can book excursions.

FOOD

Café Kró (Smábátabryggja, tel. 354/488-4884, 10am-6pm daily, entrées from 1,100ISK) is a great place to grab a cup of coffee and a snack, and also to check out a documentary about the 1973 volcanic eruption (the café has regular showings). The café also serves light meals, including soup and sandwiches.

Café María (Skólavegur 1, tel. 354/481-3160, 11:30am-11:30pm Sun.-Thurs., 11am-1am Fri.-Sat., entrées from 1,800ISK) is the best known and most frequented restaurant on the island. Tourists have a lot to choose from, ranging from local cod and salmon to halibut and monkfish. For those who don't eat fish, puffin, lamb, and salads are on the menu. It's crowded in the summer months with both tourists and locals.

INFORMATION AND SERVICES

The tourist information center (Strandvegur, www.vestmannaeyjar.is, 9am-6pm Mon.-Fri., 10am-5pm Sat.-Sun. June-Aug.) is open during the summer months and is ground zero for pamphlets and booking tours.

GETTING THERE AND AROUND

Heimaey Airport (tel. 354/481-3300), which is roughly three kilometers from downtown Heimaey, hosts Eagle Air (tel. 354/562-4200, www.eagleair.is) with daily flights to and from Reykjavík. Flights are about 25 minutes and cost 20,000ISK each way.

By ferry, visitors can get to the island through the company Eimskip (tel. 354/481-2800, www.eimskip.is, 1,300ISK), which has frequent year-round service, daily May-September. Travelers can bring their cars on the ferry for an extra fee. The ferry departs from Landeyjahöfn in South Iceland, and the ferry ride is about 35 minutes. Landeyjahöfn is a town 137 kilometers southeast of Reykjavík, and it's accessible by Route 1.

Snæfellsnes Peninsula and the Westfjords

Black-sand beaches, hot springs, quiet fishing towns, and a glacier accessible by foot await you, just 40 minutes from Reykjavík. A trip to West Iceland is ideal if you have limited time but want to see some of the countryside.

Perhaps the most beautiful park in Iceland, Snæfellsjökull National Park is the ultimate tourist treat. The glacier's ice-capped glory invites visitors to put on a pair of crampons and see it for themselves.

On the Snæfellsnes Peninsula, you can see the small fishing towns that serve as the backbone of the country, sustaining the island over the centuries. Without fish, there wouldn't be an Icelandic economy to speak of.

If you are in Iceland for an extended period of time, don't miss the Westfjords, where you'll find steep cliffs with millions of nesting birds, well-maintained hiking paths, quirky museums, and some of the most striking beauty on the island.

PLANNING YOUR TIME

Tourism in the west is still growing, especially in the Westfjords. Independent travelers who rent a car for a day out of Reykjavík frequently make their way to Akranes, Borgarnes, and the Snæfellsnes Peninsula, which gives casual day-trippers a great taste of what the west has to offer, including mountains and charming fishing villages. A trip farther northwest will treat you to pure beauty, with everything from whale-watching excursions to quirky museums to mountain climbing.

A day is enough for a taste of the west coast. To get a true sense of the western coast and the Westfjords, plan for at least 5-6 days, with one day in Akranes/Borgarnes, two days in the Snæfellsnes Peninsula, and 2-3 days in the Westfjords. While buses stop at several towns, you need a car to see some choice spots in the Westfjords—Hólmavík and Hornstrandir in particular.

Previous: puffins in the Westfjords; West Iceland landscape. **Above:** flowers blooming in the Westfjords.

Look for ★ to find recommended sights, activities, dining, and lodging.

Highlights

★ **Landnámssetur (Settlement Center):** This museum in Borgarnes offers a crash-course in the sagas and the earliest days of Icelanders. Visitors can enjoy interactive exhibitions and an audio tour (page 117).

★ **Hiking in Húsafell:** Húsafell is a gem of a town in the west, with well-maintained hiking trails that offer spectacular views of mountains and glaciers (page 121).

★ **Snæfellsjökull National Park:** This park gives you plenty to explore, including the giant glacier that was the setting for Jules Verne's *Journey to the Center of the Earth* and Djúpalónssandur beach, covered by small black stones shaped by the tides and the winds (page 123).

★ **Bird-Watching at the Látrabjarg Cliffs:** The Látrabjarg cliffs are one of the best spots on the island to see puffins. The charming black-and-white birds travel en masse to the region every June and stay until August (page 138).

Snæfellsnes Peninsula and the Westfjords

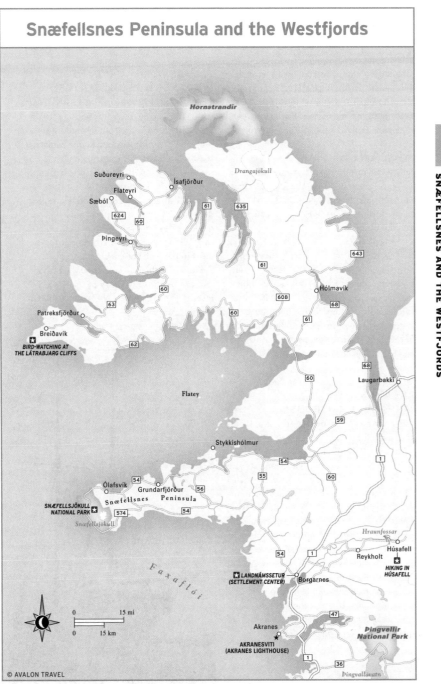

© AVALON TRAVEL

Akranes and Inland

Charming small towns await travelers who pass through the Hvalfjarðargöng (Hvalfjörður Tunnel) from Reykjavík. Before heading to the Snæfellsnes Peninsula, spend some time exploring the small fishing villages.

AKRANES

Just a 40-minute drive from Reykjavík, Akranes is a popular detour for those looking to explore the west coast. Start at Akranes, then continue on to Borganes, Snæfellsnes, and the Westfjords.

A town of 6,600 people, Akranes is a classic west coast fishing village that also has deep industrial roots. The town is home to the country's only cement factory, and an aluminum smelter lies just outside the town. It's peaceful, friendly, and home to a lighthouse that is regularly open to tourists. Scale the top of the lighthouse to get spectacular views of Snæfellsnes on clear days.

Sights
AKRANESVITI
(AKRANES LIGHTHOUSE)

The Akranes Lighthouse (Breid 2, 10am-4pm daily June-Aug., rest of year by request, free) is a delightful place to visit any time of year. Away from bright lights, tourists and townfolk flock to the site in winter to catch a glimpse of the northern lights dancing in the sky. In the summer, you can see locals having a picnic outside the lighthouse, and when it is open, guests are invited in and can climb to the top. On clear days you can see the Snæfellsnes Peninsula and a spectacular view of Mount Akrafjall. Built in 1947, the lighthouse has been used in recent years to host concerts and art exhibitions. In 2013, the Icelandic band Amiina filmed a video here for a single off of their album *The Lighthouse Project*.

SAFNASVÆÐIÐ Á AKRANESI
(AKRANES MUSEUM CENTRE)

The Akranes Museum Centre (Garðar, tel. 354/431-5566, www.museum.is, 10am-5pm daily June-Aug., 1pm-5pm daily Sept.-May, 500ISK) comprises three museums: the Icelandic Sports Museum, dedicated to the town's rich sports history (primarily soccer); Mineral Kingdom, which features an extensive mineral collection and is housed in the same hall with the sports museum; and the Akranes Folk Museum, which explores what Akranes was like in the days of settlement in the 10th century.

Outdoors, there are a few houses and boats that are key to the history of the town. For instance, the red house Neðri-Sýrupartur

ship at the Akranes Museum Centre

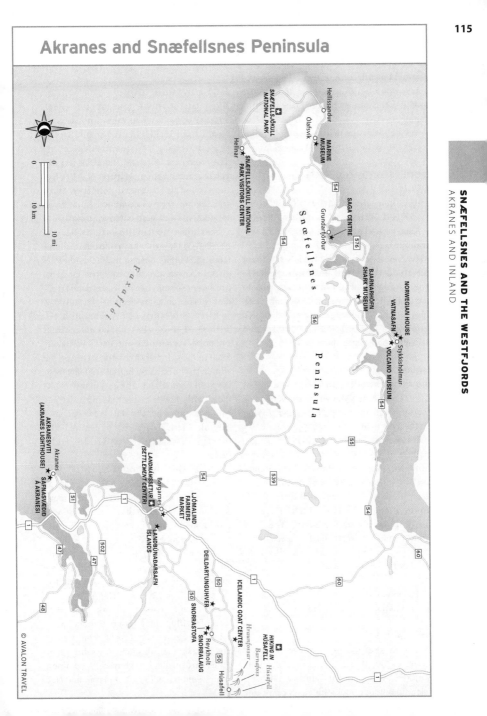

Akranes and Snæfellsnes Peninsula

Hellissandur
Ólafsvík
MARINE MUSEUM
SNÆFELLSJÖKULL NATIONAL PARK
Hellnar
SNÆFELLSJÖKULL NATIONAL PARK VISITORS CENTER

54

Grundarfjörður
SAGA CENTRE

576

Snæfellsnes

BJARNARHÖFN SHARK MUSEUM
NORWEGIAN HOUSE
VATNASAFN
Stykkishólmur
VOLCANO MUSEUM

56

54

Peninsula

55

Faxaflói

ARKANESVITI (AKRANES LIGHTHOUSE)
Akranes
SAFNASVÆÐID Á AKRANESI

51

1

47

502

47

48

LANDNÁMSSETUR (SETTLEMENT CENTER)
Borgarnes
LJÓMALIND FARMERS MARKET
LANDBÚNAÐARSAFN ÍSLANDS

54

539

54

60

1

DEILDARTUNGUHVER

50

SNORRASTOFA
50
Reykholt
SNORRALAUG
ICELANDIC GOAT CENTER
50

1

60

Hraunfossar
Barnafoss
HIKING IN HÚSAFELL
Húsafell
Hvítá

0   10 km
0   10 mi

© AVALON TRAVEL

was built in 1875, and it's considered the oldest wooden house in the town. Visitors can go inside the houses and explore. The grounds also hold a collection of fishing boats, and a new wood building was erected in 2013 to house the annual Nordic blacksmithing competition.

A café inside the main museum building serves coffee, soft drinks, and cakes.

Sports and Recreation
GOLF

The 18-hole course Garðavöllur (Garðar, tel. 354/431-2711, www.leynir.is), in Akranes, is known as a challenging course with several bunkers, scattered trees, and bodies of water. The scenery is beautiful, with Mount Akrafjall, sheep, and horses in the background. Clubs and golf carts are available to rent. Call ahead for a tee time. Hours are 8am-1pm Monday-Friday (greens fee 4,000ISK), 1pm-6pm Monday-Friday (6,000ISK), and 8am-6pm Saturday-Sunday (6,000ISK).

HIKING

Mount Akrafjall is the pride and joy of Akranes residents. Many locals have memories of foraging for seagull eggs and playing on the mountain as children.

It's known as a relatively easy climb, especially from the Akranes car park. A shorter climb will take you to Haihnukur (555 meters), which has a nice view of the outskirts of town. It's about two hours round-trip. If you're up for a longer climb, the highest peak is Geirmundartindur (643 meters). The views from the top are breathtaking, especially on clear days when you can see Snæfellsjökull. It's about five hours round-trip for a leisurely climb.

The mountain can be reached by Route 51 and is 11 kilometers east from the town.

SWIMMING

The Jadarsbakkar Pool (Innesvegur, tel. 354/433-1100, hkj@akranes.is, 6:15am-9pm Mon.-Fri., 9am-6pm Sat.-Sun., 400ISK) is a splendid outdoor pool with views of Mount Akrafjall. Take a dip in the geothermally heated outdoor pool or soak in one of the hot tubs.

Accommodations

Akra Guesthouse (Skagabraut 4, tel. 354/587-3901, www.akraguesthouse.com, rooms from 13,500ISK) is a small, family-run guesthouse with countryside charm. The rooms are large and make you feel like you're staying with grandparents. Akra features wood floors, muted wallpaper, and a friendly staff. There's a common dining room for guests as well as an outdoor eating area.

Akranes Hostel (Sudurgata 32, tel. 354/868-3332, www.akraneshostel.is, rooms from 13,500ISK) opened in 2009 and offers guests access to two fully equipped kitchens, a television lounge, free Wi-Fi, and laundry facilities. The rooms are clean, bright, and cozy.

Birta Guesthouse (Vogabraut 4, tel. 354/695-6255, www.birtabirta.is, rooms from 14,500ISK) is dormitory accommodation offered in the summer (May-Aug.). During the winter, the guesthouse houses students from the local high school. The guesthouse is no-frills, with double beds or sleeping bag accommodations, but the staff is friendly and helpful. Guests have access to private bathrooms with a shower, a small fridge, and a stove.

The Little Guesthouse by the Ocean (Bakkatun 20, tel. 354/695-6255, www.leopold.is, rooms from 10,500ISK) is a three-room guesthouse situated on the shore of the town. The rooms are small but bright and comfortable, with double beds and a sink en suite. Guests have access to shared bathroom facilities, a large, well-equipped kitchen, and an outdoor eating area to enjoy in good weather.

Teigur Guesthouse (Háteigur 1, tel. 354/431-2900, www.teigur-akranes.com, rooms from 10,800ISK) is a two-room guesthouse that has the comforts of home. Guests have access to a full kitchen, washing machine, garden, and large terrace. A common living room has a TV, DVD player, and free Wi-Fi.

Food

★ **Galito Restaurant** (Stilholt 16-18, tel. 354/430-6767, www.galito.is, noon-10pm daily, entrées from 1,800ISK) is the most upscale restaurant in Akranes, but its prices are reasonable. Diners can choose traditional options like shrimp soup and saltfish entrées or hamburgers, pizza, and an array of sandwiches. The decor is modern and the staff is friendly.

Gamla Kaupfelagid (Kirkjubraut 11, tel. 354/431-4343, www.gamlakaupfelagid.com, 11:30am-10pm daily, entrées from 1,500ISK) is a cozy restaurant situated downtown, close to the tourist office. An eclectic menu ranges from fresh salads to Indian-inspired naan bread sandwiches, and the restaurant is not short on imagination. Icelandic staples include lamb and fish dishes, but hamburgers and tandoori-oven cooked pizzas are on the menu as well.

Information and Services

The **information center** (Sudurgata 57, tel. 354/433-1065, www.west.is, 10am-4pm daily) is stocked with brochures on the western coast, offers access to the Internet, and has a staff happy to assist you in booking tours.

Getting There and Around

Akranes, which is about a 40-minute, 48-kilometer drive from Reykjavík, is accessible from Route 51.

Many people make a stop in Akranes before heading on to the 39-kilometer journey to Borgarnes, which takes about 30 minutes.

The **Strætó** 57 bus (www.straeto.is, 800ISK) runs from the bus station Mjodd in Reykjavík to Akranes in a little over an hour.

BORGARNES

About a 75-minute drive from Reykjavík, Borgarnes is a picturesque town that is home to about 2,000 people. Those traveling on the Ring Road will reach the town by one of the longest bridges on the island, which is an architectural feat for the country. Fans of the sagas will want to visit the town, as much of *Egil's Saga* takes place in the region. Film buffs may recognize Borgarnes from scenes in Ben Stiller's 2013 movie *The Secret Life of Walter Mitty.*

Sights

★ **LANDNÁMSSETUR (SETTLEMENT CENTER)**

The **Settlement Center** (Brákarbraut 13-15, tel. 354/437-1600, www.settlementcentre.is, 10am-9pm daily, 2,500ISK) is the place to get a crash-course in the sagas and the earliest days of Icelanders during the settlement—including what everything on the newly discovered island was like, ranging from food to fashion. Interactive displays and recreated dwellings are on exhibit. Audio guides available for the exhibition come in 10 languages. A gift shop sells everything from gourmet salts to woolen goods, and a restaurant serves up lamb, fish, and sandwiches.

LANDBÚNAÐARSAFN ÍSLANDS (AGRICULTURAL MUSEUM OF ICELAND)

The **Agricultural Museum of Iceland** (Hvanneyri, tel. 354/844-7740, www.landbunadarsafn.is, noon-5pm daily June-Aug., 500ISK) is dedicated to the farming history of Iceland during the 19th and 20th centuries. The museum holds an extensive collection of farm artifacts, including the first plows and other horse-driven equipment used in Iceland. The museum also has the first tractors imported to Iceland, as well as farming equipment of the present day.

EDDUVERÖLD (EDDA'S WORLD)

Edda's World (Skulagata 17, tel. 354/437-1455, www.Edduverold.is, 10am-11pm Sun.-Thurs., 10am-1am Fri.-Sat. May-Aug., free) is a café/museum that focuses on Norse mythology. Several large wall hangings depict striking images from Iceland's rich folklore. The centerpiece of the museum is a large model of the ancient world designed by local artist

Haukur Halldórsson. Tourists can enjoy a 20-minute audio guide, which is available in English, German, Norwegian, and Icelandic. Inside the museum is a café that offers lights meals, including soup and sandwiches.

LJÓMALIND FARMERS MARKET
Ljómalind Farmers Market (Brúartorg 4, tel. 354/437-1400, www.ljomalind.is, 11am-6pm daily) is a farmers market collective started by a group of 10 women in 2013. Situated on the main stretch of road in Borgarnes, the market sells fresh cream, eggs, jam, local meat, fresh produce, woolen goods, and souvenir trinkets. In the summer, you can find sunflowers and local tomatoes on offer.

Sports and Recreation
GOLF
Golfklúbbur Borgarness (Borgarnes Golf Club) (Hamar, tel. 354/437-1663, May-Sept., greens fees 9,000ISK) is an 18-hole course situated on the property of Icelandair Hótel Hamar. The course, which is great for beginners, also has a driving range area and an 18-hole putting course. It's also easy to walk. Call ahead for a tee time.

SWIMMING
The **Borgarnes Swimming Pool** (Þorsteinsgata 1, tel. 354/433-7140, 6:30am-10pm Mon.-Fri., 9am-6pm Sat.-Sun., 500ISK) is open year-round and has an outdoor swimming pool, slide, a hot tub, and a gym.

Accommodations
Borganes Hostel (Borgarbraut 9-13, tel. 354/695-3366, www.borgarneshostel.is, rooms from 16,000ISK) offers 20 rooms ranging from single rooms to triples. The hostel is centrally located with a quick walk to the harbor and Settlement Center. Guests have access to two fully equipped kitchens, laundry facilities, a computer room, free Wi-Fi, and a common living room.

Hótel Borganes (Egilsgata 16, tel. 354/437-1119, www.hotelborgarnes.is, rooms from 10,000ISK) is a 75-room no-frills hotel

perfect for short stays. It offers small, comfortable rooms with private bathrooms, and an in-house restaurant serves up a delicious breakfast buffet included in the price of the room.

Icelandair Hótel Hamar (Hamar, 310 Borgarnes, tel. 354/433-6600, www.icelandairhotels.com/en/hotels/hamar, rooms from 27,000ISK) was built on an 18-hole golf course and is in an especially scenic part of Borgarnes. Situated among waterfalls and lava fields, the 44-room hotel offers comfortable rooms with double beds and private bathrooms. There is an abundance of local art around the hotel, and it has a modern, yet country, atmosphere. The in-house restaurant is open 11am-10pm daily, serving everything from an Asian-inspired cod dish to lamb filets.

Food
Búðarklettur (Brákarbraut 13-15, tel. 354/437-1600, open 10am-9pm daily, entrées from 1,800ISK) is the restaurant housed above the Settlement Center. The menu is chock-full of Icelandic staples like fish soup, mashed fish, and Icelandic meat soup. Burgers and sandwiches are on the menu as well, and there are vegetarian options and a kids' menu. For a quick snack, the freshly baked cakes are delicious.

Geirabakari Kaffihus (Digranesgata 6, tel. 354/437-1920, geirabak@internet.is, 7am-5pm daily, entrées from 1,600ISK) offers light meals, including soups and sandwiches and an array of classic Icelandic cakes and pastries. The coffeehouse was used to film scenes from Ben Stiller's 2013 movie *The Secret Life of Walter Mitty*. Photos taken during filming are displayed throughout the coffeehouse.

Information and Services
Located in the Hyrnutorg shopping center, the **West Iceland Information Center** (Borgarbraut 58-60, tel. 354/437-2214, www.westiceland.is, 9am-10pm daily) has brochures, tour information, a gift shop, and free Internet access.

Getting There and Around

Borgarnes is about a 1.25-hour (75-kilometer) drive north from Reykjavík on Route 1.

The Strætó 57 bus (www.straeto.is, 1,600ISK) runs from the bus station Mjodd in Reykjavík to Borgarnes. The trip takes about 1.5 hours each way.

REYKHOLT

Reykholt is a placid, sleepy town about an hour from Borgarnes. However, that laid-back, quiet atmosphere is part of the town's charm. A couple of sights are connected to Snorri Sturluson, one of the most famous and important figures in Icelandic literature. Snorri penned *Edda, Egil's Saga,* and *Heimskringla* before his death in 1241. Tourists might also want to take a look at Deildartunguhver, the largest hot spring in Europe.

Sights

ÍSLENSKA GEITIN
(ICELANDIC GOAT CENTER)

The Icelandic Goat Center (Haafell, tel. 354/845-2331, www.geitur.is, 1pm-6pm daily June-Aug., 1,000ISK) was established to protect and maintain the goat stock in Iceland. Believe it or not, the Icelandic goat is an endangered species. Tourists are welcome to visit the grounds and meet the goats as well as other animals on the farm, including sheep, horses, and chickens. Workers at the center show an enormous amount of care for the animals. It's an especially great place to visit if you're traveling with children. The local food store sells many goat products, including cheeses, soaps, and handicrafts.

DEILDARTUNGUHVER

Geology buffs will want to take a look at Deildartunguhver, which is considered Europe's most powerful hot spring. It provides 200 liters per second of 100°C (212°F) hot water. Most of the water used for central heating in the West Iceland towns of Akranes and Borgarnes is taken from Deildartunguhver. The hot water pipeline to Akranes is 64 kilometers long, which is the longest in Iceland. The water is about 78-80°C when it reaches Akranes. Be sure to keep your distance, as there is a chance of getting splashed if you get too close. Visitors will see water bubbling up and splashing against moss and rock. Deildartunguhver is off of Route 50; the GPS coordinates are N 64.6631, W 21.4112.

Deildartunguhver, a geothermal hot spring

SNORRASTOFA

Snorrastofa (tel. 354/433-8000, www.snorrastofa.is, 10am-6pm daily May-Sept., 10am-5pm Mon.-Fri. Oct.-Apr., 1,200ISK) is the cultural hub of Reykholt. It was established in 1995 as an independent research center to investigate and collect information on the medieval era in Iceland, with particular focus on the legendary saga writer and politician Snorri Sturluson, who lived in Reykholt until his death in 1241. The building also holds a tourist information center, an exhibition on Snorri Sturluson's sagas, and a public research library, and it hosts courses and lectures. A gift shop sells books, CDs, and handicrafts. The GPS coordinates are N 64.6648, W 21.2937.

SNORRALAUG (SNORRI'S POOL)

Snorralaug, or "Snorri's Pool," is a geothermally heated pool preserved from Iceland's medieval period and is one of Reykholt's oldest structures. The hot tub was built with hand-hewn lava from the 10th century, cut and shaped to exact measurements. The hot water in the pool comes from the Skrifla hot spring through a canal. The site is open to the public, but visitors cannot enter the pool to bathe. The GPS coordinates are N 64.6640, W 21.2912.

Sports and Recreation
CAVE TOURS

Reykholt is home to **Víðgelmir,** the largest cave in Iceland. The cave is only accessible through a private guide: **Fljotstunga Cave Tours** (Fljotstunga, tel. 354/435-1198, www.fljotstunga.is, 10am, noon, 3pm, and 5pm daily May-Aug., 3,000ISK) can take you to explore the beautiful ice formations, including scores of stalactites and stalagmites.

Accommodations and Food

Fosshotel Reykholt (Hálsasveitavegur, tel. 354/435-1260, www.fosshotel.is, rooms from 20,000ISK) is the only hotel in the region. The 53-room hotel has dated furniture and carpeting but the dreary decor is made up for with free Wi-Fi, private bathrooms, free

parking and outdoor hot tubs. The included breakfast is adequate, but nothing to write home about.

Hverinn Restaurant (Kleppjárnsreykir, tel. 354/571-4433, www.hverinn.is, 10:30am-9pm Sun.-Thurs., 10:30am-1am Fri.-Sat. May-Sept., entrées from 1,800ISK) is a quaint farm-style restaurant serving up comfort food. The key is using organic ingredients from their farm and local meats in each dish, ranging from soups to salads to lamb and fish dishes. There are also sandwiches, hamburgers, and pizza on the menu.

Information and Services

Housed in the Snorrastofa complex, the **Reykholt Information Office** (tel. 354/433-8000, www.snorrastofa.is, 10am-6pm daily May-Sept., 10am-5pm Mon.-Fri. Oct.-Apr.) offers tourist brochures and art exhibitions, and at times there are lectures and concerts. The GPS coordinates are N 64.6648, W 21.2937.

Getting There and Around

Reykholt is 41 kilometers northeast of Borgarnes on Route 518.

The **Strætó** 81 bus (www.straeto.is, 800ISK) goes to Reykholt from Borgarnes.

HÚSAFELL

Húsafell is a tiny village surrounded by glaciers, ample hiking opportunities, and miles of lava fields. Most tourists make a stop to camp, visit two beautiful waterfalls, and check out some lava caves in nearby Reykholt or explore the newly opened Langjökull ice tunnel. Organized trips with a tour operator to Langjökull glacier are also available from Húsafell throughout the year.

Sights
HRAUNFOSSAR
(LAVA WATERFALLS)

The Lava Waterfalls are a series of waterfalls streaming over 900 meters out of a lava field. The lava flowed from an eruption from a volcano lying under the Langjökull glacier. The falls are beautiful to visit in any season, and rainbows are frequently seen near the falls on rainy/sunny days. Hraunfossar is 6.4 kilometers west of Húsafell on Route 518. The GPS coordinates are N 64.7028, W 20.9777.

BARNAFOSS (CHILDREN'S FALLS)

Barnafoss is a stunning waterfall named for children who disappeared from a nearby farm and drowned in the river. Lore has it that the mother of the disappeared children put a curse on the falls that people should not cross the river. Barnafoss is 6.2 kilometers west of Húsafell on Route 518. The GPS coordinates are N 64.7015, W 20.9727.

LANGJÖKULL ICE CAVE

For those looking for a little ice in Iceland, **Into the Glacier** (Viðarhöfði 1, tel. 354/578-2550, www.intotheglacier.is, tours from 17,900ISK) offers day tours to the world's largest man-made ice cave, Langjökull. A supertruck picks up visitors close to Hotel Husafell for a journey that will leave many breathless as they traverse the glacier to the base camp, which takes 25 minutes. The cave itself is an engineering feat where visitors are treated to views of crevices and the smooth ice walls. LED lighting embedded in the walls lights the ice nicely, and benches are scattered throughout the tunnel.

★ Hiking

Hikers have a number of options in Húsafell, ranging from easy walks to more challenging climbs. However, before you set out, be sure to check the weather forecast, bring the proper gear and plenty of drinking water, and let people know your whereabouts. The prime hiking season is June-August.

MOUNT STRÚTUR

While the climb to the summit of the 938-meter Mount Strútur isn't very difficult, it is quite long, as the summit is 938 meters. The hike takes several hours depending on the weather and your endurance. It is recommended to start from the low hill north of Kalmanstunga and to follow a track that leads up the mountain. The payoff for reaching the top is a spectacular view of mountains and the Borgarfjörður fjord. Kalmanstunga is 17 kilometers north of Húsafell and can be reached by Route 518.

Hraunfossar waterfalls and the Hvítá River in Húsafell

ODDAR

From the summerhouse settlement in the center of Húsafell, there are wooded paths heading westward for an easy walk along Oddar, a group of brooks with diverse birdlife. From there it is just a short walk upriver to the meeting point of two rivers: the Norðlingafljót and Hvítá. Just below Hvítá is the waterfall Hundavaðsfoss, which is a great place to stop and marvel at the region's beauty. The route then leads southeast along the sands, to a path leading back to the summerhouse settlement. The walk takes about 1.5 hours and is very easygoing.

Other Sports and Recreation

GOLF

The Húsafell Golf Course (Stórarjóður, tel. 354/435-1552, www.husafell.is, 8am-6pm daily May-Sept., greens fee 4,000ISK) is a nine-hole course situated on a gorgeous patch of land overlooking mountains and lava fields. You must call ahead for a tee time. The GPS coordinates are N 64.6991, W 20.8709.

SWIMMING

The Húsafell Swimming Pool (Stórarjóður, tel. 354/435-1552, www.husafell.is, 10am-10pm daily June-Sept., 1pm-5pm Sat.-Sun. rest of year, 800ISK) has two pools, two hot tubs, and a big water slide for kids.

Accommodations and Food

★ Hotel Husafell (Borgarbyggd, tel. 354/435-1551, www.hotelhusafell.com, rooms from 33,500ISK) is a new modern hotel that opened its doors in 2015. The location is unbeatable, as it is nestled in a scenic spot with stunning views of the mountain landscape, close to lava caves and glaciers. The rooms feature comfortable beds, private bathrooms, and modern design accents, including wood furnishings and large windows. A breakfast buffet is included in the room price, and 24-hour room service is available. A pool and hot tubs are on-site and the in-house restaurant is not to be missed. The menu features everything from tender lamb filet to fresh fish. Entrées start at 3,000ISK.

The Husafell Campground (tel. 354/435-1556, 1,400ISK) is an open campground surrounded by trees, which cuts down on the wind a bit. Caravans and tents are welcome, and the facilities include restrooms, showers, hot and cold water, and laundry machines. The site is a short distance to the swimming pool, golf course, and hiking trails.

Getting There and Around

Húsafell is 25 kilometers east from Reykholt on Route 518. There are no direct buses to Húsafell.

Snæfellsnes Peninsula

Snæfellsnes is considered the jewel of the western coast. In part, it's because the region has a taste of everything. If you're looking for mountains, they're there. If you want to attempt a glacier walk, Snæfellsnesjökull is your place. If whale-watching is what you're after, this region has it. There's a reason why many locals refer to the region as "Iceland in miniature."

If you're planning to visit Snæfellsnes while on the Ring Road, plan to spend some time here—at least two full days. It demands more

attention than a quick detour. The landscape is breathtaking, with the long volcanic ridge spanning miles with rocky lava fields and towering mountains. It's considered many an Icelander's favorite place on the island. Traveling to the region is not difficult, as there are numerous tours going to Snæfellsnes as well as buses. For a leisurely pace, you should rent a car.

The western edge of the Snæfellsnes Peninsula is home to the Snæfellsjökull National Park and small towns like

Hellissandur, Ólafsvík, and Grundarfjörður. The Snæfellsjökull glacier, which lies on top of a volcano in the center of the national park, is the main event for many. Tourists can book tours to walk on the glacier to explore some actual ice in Iceland. The small towns that dot the peninsula are charming fishing villages with ample hiking routes and quirky museums.

★ SNÆFELLSJÖKULL NATIONAL PARK

The Snæfellsjökull glacier became world famous after author Jules Verne described it in *A Journey to the Center of the Earth* as the starting point of the terrific journey in the book. Inside the park, there is plenty to explore. Take some time, wear comfortable yet sturdy footwear, and bring your camera. Plan at least one full day in the park.

Sights

SNÆFELLSJÖKULL GLACIER

The Snæfellsjökull glacier lies on top of a volcano, situated in the center of the national park. The glacier's peak reaches 1,446 meters, and it can be seen from Reykjavík on a clear day. The volcano is considered active, though the last eruption occurred 1,900 years ago.

It's about 190 kilometers from Reykjavík to the Snæfellsjökull glacier; the drive takes about 2.5 hours. From Reykjavík, take Route 1 north through the town of Borgarnes and then turn left onto Route 54. Head west on Route 54 across the peninsula for about 98 kilometers, connecting to Route 574. Continue west on Route 574 for about 35 kilometers. You'll find the road leading up to the volcano on the right-hand side, and signs are posted all the way up to a parking lot. Be sure to check the forecast before heading out.

DJÚPALÓNSSANDUR BEACH

Djúpalónssandur beach is one of the highlights of the Snæfellsnes Peninsula. The vast beach is covered by small black stones that were shaped by the force of the tides and whipping of the wind. Tourists love to wander among the frozen lava landscapes and interesting rock formations. A short paved road through lava fields leads directly from Route 574 to Djúpalónssandur beach, on the southwestern edge of the peninsula. The GPS coordinates are N 64.7493, W 23.9122.

VATNSHELLIR LAVA CAVE

The Vatnshellir lava cave, a site made available to the public in 2011, is another

a bird's-eye view of the Snæfellsnes Peninsula

highlight. The lava cave, which measures about 200 meters in length, has two main sections. The upper section showcases unique lava formations that are curved on the sides of the lava tube. The lower part of the lava cave, which can be reached by a long and narrow well-maintained staircase, takes tourists deep (about 35 meters) underground to a place hidden from the outside world for thousands of years, as local scientists believe the lava cave was created in an eruption between 6,000-8,000 years ago. The cave is accessible only through a guided tour from **Cave Vatnshellir** (tel. 354/665-2818, www.vatnshellir.is, 45-minute tours 2,500ISK). Tourists are required to have hiking boots, gloves, and warm clothing. The tour guide provides helmets and flightlights. The Vatnshellir cave is located in the southern end of the park, near Route 574.

Hiking

Many Icelanders say the beauty of Snæfellsnes is unrivaled, calling the region their favorite place in the country. Why? Snæfellsnes has it all. There are mountains to climb, lava fields to explore, and glaciers to scale, all accessible by countless hiking trails with varying degrees of difficulty. Specific information on trails can be found at the park's visitors center.

Feel free to roam and take in the sights. Whether you head out alone, with a small group, or with a tour, always go out for a hike prepared: Check the weather forecast, bring the proper gear and drinking water, and let people know your whereabouts.

A great moderate day hike of around 20 kilometers leads from **Hellissandur** village to the Eysteinsdalur valley. Hikers should take the unmarked secondary road near the campground, which leads towards Snæfellsjökull. The road becomes a hiking trail after about one kilometer and leads you to the **Prestahraun** lava field. Follow the trail to see a red scoria crater and rifts in lava and basalt rocks. The trail continues and takes you to see waterfalls, the glacial river Ljósulækir, and breathtaking views of the glacier. Detailed hiking maps are available from the tourist information office in Hellnar.

Glacier Climbing

It may seem obvious to some, but it cannot be emphasized enough: Be prepared! Glacier climbing is not to be taken lightly, and it's important to have the correct gear. It is highly recommended to join a tour, with experts who have years of climbing experience. Of the many tour operators available, a recommended one is **Arctic Adventures** (tel. 354/562-7000, www.adventures.is, 40,000ISK). A tour guide will pick you up from your hotel in Reykjavík and take you on a five- to seven-hour hike on the volcano that Jules Verne made famous in his book *Journey to the Center of the Earth*. The total elevation gain is 760 meters, and the total hiking distance is 7-8 kilometers.

Guided Tours

If you're after a more structured, guided tour, tour companies offer excursions. Check out **Reykjavik Excursions** (tel. 354/580-5400, www.re.is) for a list. They offer a 12-hour "Wonders of Snæfellsnes" tour from Reykjavík that includes a visit to the glacier, sandy beaches, craters, and fishing villages. The tour costs 18,900ISK and is available year-round.

Accommodations

Guests who stay at **Hótel Búðir** (Búðir, tel. 354/435-6700, www.hotelbudir.is, rooms from 35,000) are treated to a comfortable stay with spectacular views of the Snæfellsjökull glacier. The 20-room boutique hotel features clean and cozy rooms with private bathrooms. The hotel's top-notch breakfast is included in the price. It frequently hosts weddings and conferences. The hotel is 27 kilometers southeast of Ólafsvík on Route 54.

Hótel Eldborg (Laugagerdisskola, tel. 354/435-6602, www.hoteleldborg.is, rooms from 16,000ISK) is a charming 26-room countryside hotel with very large rooms and one of the friendliest staffs you will find. They are happy to arrange for tours ranging from horse riding to glacier walking. Guests have access to shared bathroom facilities, and budget-conscious travelers will be happy to hear that sleeping-bag accommodation is available for 4,200ISK. An in-house restaurant serves breakfast, lunch, a dinner buffet, and light meals throughout the day.

★ **Hótel Hellnar** (Brekkubær, tel. 354/435-6820, www.hellnar.is, May-Oct., rooms from 20,000ISK) is a beautiful 34-room country hotel that takes pride in the small things. Guests can find fresh flowers throughout the hotel, a warm staff, and a splendid in-house restaurant. It was renovated in 2011, and the owners added rooms, including a deluxe suite. Each room has a private bathroom, comfortable bed, and television. The restaurant uses fresh, organic ingredients with lots of fish and meat options.

Guesthouse Langaholt (Ytri-Garðar Staðarsveit, tel. 354/435-6789, www.langaholt.is, rooms from 22,000ISK) is a 20-room family-run guesthouse with spacious rooms, classic decor, free Wi-Fi, and a shared terrace. Amenities include an on-site restaurant, nearby golf course, plenty of free parking, and on-site camping facilities for budget travelers.

Food

Hótel Búðir Restaurant (Búðir, tel. 354/435-6700, www.hotelbudir.is, 4pm-10pm daily, entrées from 2,000ISK) features Icelandic staples like fresh cod and lamb dishes, but the chef likes to mix up the menu depending on the season. In the summer expect local puffin meat on the menu. The food is fresh, elegant, and memorable.

Hótel Hellnar Restaurant (Brekkubær, tel. 354/435-6820, www.hellnar.is, 8am-9pm daily May-Oct.) is open for breakfast, lunch, and dinner during the summer. Entrées start at 1,800ISK, and the fresh fish options are tempting. If you're not a meat eater, a few tasty vegetarian options are on the menu.

Information and Services

The **Snæfellsjökull National Park visitors center** (Brekkubær, tel. 354/436-6888, www.

ust.is, www.westiceland.is, 10am-5pm daily mid-May-mid-Sept., hours vary rest of year), in the village of **Hellnar** on the southern side of the peninsula, gives an overview of the history, flora, fauna, and geology of the park. The center also provides information on various hiking paths and the wildlife that can be seen in the park. The GPS coordinates of the center are N 64.7507, W 23.6525.

Getting There and Around

Snæfellsjökull can be reached by Route 574, which spans the perimeter of the park along the coastline. Please bear in mind that the road is unpaved and is not feasible for cyclists. However, Route 54 is a paved road that is very accommodating to cyclists.

Tour companies such as **Reykjavik Excursions** (tel. 354/580-5400, www.re.is) include stops at Snæfellsjökull. The **Strætó** 57 and 58 buses (tel. 354/540-2700, www.straeto.is, 3,500ISK) to Snæfellsnes can be taken daily in the summer from the bus station Mjodd in Reykjavík. The ride takes about three hours.

HELLISSANDUR

Hellissandur is a blink-and-you'll-miss it kind of town, but it's home to an interesting fishing museum (open in the summer) that's worth a stop if that strikes your fancy.

Sights
SJÓMANNAGARÐUR (HELLISSANDUR MARITIME MUSEUM)

Hellissandur Maritime Museum (Útnesvegur, tel. 354/436-6961, 9:30am-6pm Tues.-Sun. June-Aug., 700ISK) was established by the Council of Seamen of the towns Hellissandur and Rif to preserve the history of fishers and fishing stations in the region. One-stroke engines, a fishermen's house (called Þorvaldarbúð), and the oldest preserved fishing boat, Bliki, are on display, showing the rich fishing history of the town. The well-curated museum is a must-see for those interested in fishing history.

INGJALDSHÓLSKIRKJA (INGJALDSHÓLS CHURCH)

The other big draw in the town is Ingjaldshólskirkja (tel. 354/436-6970), which was, according to legend, the site where Italian explorer Christopher Columbus traveled in 1477 to meet with Icelanders. Columbus was interested in speaking with Icelanders whose ancestors had traveled to America. Today, there is a mural of Columbus meeting with Icelanders in the basement of the church. The church is a classic Icelandic structure that was built in 1903, and it has a white exterior and a red roof. However, the land has been a church site since the year 1317. The church is on Route 574, east of Hellissandur.

Accommodations and Food

Hótel Hellissandur (Klettsbúð 9, tel. 354/430-8600, www.hotelhellissandur.is, rooms from 25,000ISK) is a 20-room hotel with standard double rooms featuring private bathrooms and free Wi-Fi. Rooms are big but sparsely decorated, and the in-house restaurant serves adequate meals.

Kaffi Sif (Klettsbúð 3, tel. 354/577-3430, www.kaffisif.is, entrées from 1,200ISK) is an adorable café that serves up comfort food and a dynamite cup of coffee. If you're stopping in for a meal, the fish soup is superb.

Getting There and Around

Hellissandur is 9 kilometers northwest of Ólafsvík and 35 kilometers north of Hellnar. By car, take Route 574 to Hellissandur.

A couple of buses pass through the town. Check the bus schedule from BSÍ (www.bsi.is) to see departure times. Typically, buses depart from Reykjavík, Grundarfjörður, Ólafsvík, and Stykkishólmur.

ÓLAFSVÍK

Ólafsvík is a charming fishing village situated on the western end of the Snæfellsnes Peninsula. The small town has approximately 1,100 residents and is the main town of the Snæfellsbær municipality, which includes the villages of Hellissandur and Rif. Because of its proximity to the national park, Ólafsvík, which means "Olaf's bay," is often used as a base camp for travelers to stop for a bite to eat and to gas up their car.

Sports and Recreation

SWIMMING

The Ólafsvík Swimming Pool (Ennisbraut 11, tel. 354/433-9910, 8am-9pm daily, 500ISK) is popular among locals as well as tourists passing through. Amenities include an indoor 12.5-meter swimming pool, hot tubs, and an outdoor area for catching some sun (when it's out).

WHALE-WATCHING

While some say Húsavík is the best spot to go whale-watching in North Iceland, Ólafsvík might just be the best in West Iceland. Laki Tours (tel. 354/546-6808, www.lakitours. com, 2pm daily, 8,900ISK) operates three-hour tours from Ólafsvík from May 20 to September 5, and if luck is on your side, you'll catch a glimpse of sperm whales or killer whales. This is the only place in Iceland where you can see them. Seeing these majestic creatures with the Snæfellsnes Peninsula behind them is breathtaking—the setting with towering mountains, migrating birds, and looming glacier is gorgeous. If luck isn't on your side with killer or sperm whales, you also have a chance to spot minke, humpback, blue, and fin whales along with harbor porpoises and dolphins. Make sure you dress warmly and bring your camera!

Accommodations and Food

Hótel Ólafsvík (Ólafsbraut 20, tel. 354/436-1650, www.hringhotels.is, rooms from 20,000ISK) offers 48 rooms near the harbor, which is in the center of town. The rooms are large, bright, and comfortable. The decor is traditional and the staff is friendly. Most rooms have private bathroom accommodations, and breakfast is included in the price. The hotel's restaurant (dinner 6pm-10pm, entrées from 2,300ISK) is the only option for fine dining in the town, but its menu would stand up against competition. The menu features fresh, local ingredients, with an emphasis on fish, including cod, salmon, haddock, and langoustines. There are also meat dishes as well as a couple of vegetarian options.

Getting There and Around

Ólafsvík is 26 kilometers west of Grundarfjörður. By car from Grundarfjörður, Ólafsvík is reachable by Route 54 connecting to Route 574.

The **Strætó** 82 bus (tel. 354/540-2700, www.straeto.is) departs daily to Ólafsvík from Grundarfjörður (21 minutes, 400ISK) and Stykkishólmur (1 hour, 800ISK).

GRUNDARFJÖRÐUR

Centrally located on the northern coast of the Snæfellsnes Peninsula, Grundarfjörður is situated in a spectacular mountain range that includes Mount Kirkjufell, which has a steep and treacherous-looking peak. Those interested in spotting orca whales have a great shot in Grundarfjörður, as the majestic whales are found to feast on herring off the shores of the town. The town has a few interesting museums and a lot of hiking opportunities.

Sights
SÖGUMIÐSTÖÐIN (GRUNDARFJÖRÐUR HERITAGE CENTER)

The **Grundarfjörður Heritage Center** (Grundargata 35, tel. 354/438-1881, 9am-6pm daily June-Aug., 2pm-6pm Mon.-Thurs. Sept.-May, 800ISK) is a quaint museum focusing on saga stories, the town's fishing history, and life during the settlement era in the 9th century. There are fishing boats and equipment on display as well as recreated dwellings and artifacts. A café and a tourist information center are on-site.

Sports and Recreation
HIKING

Exploring the town by foot is far and away the most popular activity for tourists. At the center of it all is **Mount Kirkjufell**, which looms 463 meters high. From a distance the mountain looks quite daunting, and it is considered a difficult climb, with the trickiest points near the top. A climb, which takes about two hours, is advisable during the summer months, but it's still important to check weather conditions and bring proper gear with you. If you arrive in winter and the weather is good, a

Grundarfjörður in the winter

walk along the perimeter of the mountain is nice, but don't attempt a climb on your own.

SWIMMING

The **Grundarfjörður Swimming Pool** (Borgarbraut 19, tel. 354/430-8564, 7am-8pm Mon.-Fri., 10am-5pm Sat.-Sun. June-Aug., 500ISK) is a lovely local spot with a 16-meter outdoor pool, hot tubs, and a section for children.

Accommodations

Hótel Framnes (Nesvegur 8, tel. 354/438-6893, www.hotelframnes.is, rooms from 16,000ISK) offers 29 comfortable rooms with glorious views of the Snæfellsnes Peninsula. The room decor is effortless and authentically Scandinavian. All rooms come with a private bathroom, free Wi-Fi, and access to a sauna and hot tub. The in-house restaurant serves up tasty and elegant meals.

Grund Guesthouse (Grund, tel. 354/840-6100, www.resthouse.is, rooms from 17,000ISK) is a small, seven-room guesthouse just three kilometers east from downtown Grundarfjörður. Guests have access to shared bathroom facilities, a washing machine, free Wi-Fi, and an outdoor grill.

Grundarfjörður Hostel (Hlíðarvegur 15, tel. 354/562-6533, www.ubuntu65.com, beds from 15,000ISK) is in a cute countryside building that is painted bright red. In other words, you can't miss it. The staff is friendly and eager to give tips and help set up tours. Guests have access to a fully equipped kitchen, shared bathroom facilities, free Wi-Fi, and a common TV room.

Food

★ **Hótel Framnes** (Nesvegur 8, tel. 354/438-6930, www.hotelframnes.is, breakfast 7am-10am, dinner 5pm-9pm daily, entrées from 2,200ISK) is more than a hotel restaurant. The restaurant has a reputation among locals for delicious fish dishes. You will find fresh cod, salmon, and mackerel on the menu, but if you're not into fish, they offer lamb dishes as well as vegetarian options.

Kaffi 59 (Grundargata 59, tel. 354/438-6446, www.kaffi59.8.is, 10am-10pm Mon.-Thurs., 10am-1am Fri.-Sat., noon-10pm Sun., entrées from 1,800ISK) is the main choice for those visiting the town, other than the Framnes hotel restaurant. Icelandic staples on the menu include lamb and fish dishes, but there are also more casual options like hamburgers, sandwiches, and pizza. Kaffi 59 has a casual atmosphere with a friendly staff.

Information and Services

The **tourist information center** is housed in the **Grundarfjörður Heritage Center** (Grundargata 35, tel. 354/438-1881, www.grundarfjordur.is, 9am-6pm daily June-Aug., 2pm-6pm Mon.-Thurs. Sept.-May).

Getting There and Around

Grundarfjörður is 39 kilometers southeast from Stykkishólmur on Route 54.

The **Stræto 82** bus (tel. 354/540-2700, www.straeto.is, 800ISK) runs daily between Grundarfjörður and Stykkishólmur. The trip is about 40 minutes.

STYKKISHÓLMUR

Stykkishólmur is a placid, seaside town that hit it big when Ben Stiller decided to film crucial scenes in his 2013 film *The Secret Life of Walter Mitty* there. Since the movie's release, tourists have been flocking to the otherwise quiet town in droves. It's full of west coast charm, with brightly colored houses and quaint guesthouses along a looming mountain range.

Sights
NORSKA HÚSIÐ (NORWEGIAN HOUSE)

The **Norwegian House** (Hafnargata 5, tel. 354/438-1640, www.norskahusid.is, noon-5pm daily June-Aug., 800ISK) is known as the local museum of Snæfellsnes. Rotating exhibits focus on the fishing industry, the region's history, and art from regional artists. The building started out as the home of Árni Thorlacius, who was a local trader in the 19th century. The home, which was built in 1832, was extraordinary at the time because it was the first two-story home on the island.

BJARNARHÖFN HÁKARLASAFNIÐ (BJARNARHÖFN SHARK MUSEUM)

The Bjarnarhöfn Shark Museum (Bjarnarhöfn, tel. 354/438-1581, www.bjarnarhofn.is, 9am-6pm daily, 1,000ISK) is one of those interesting museums you won't see anywhere but Iceland. The museum is located on the farm of a family that has been shark fishing and processing shark meat for generations. The owners provide a guided tour of the museum, where you will see fishing boats and equipment used in shark fishing. The guide then takes guests to the drying house, where you can witness the process of preserving shark meat. You can even take a taste if you dare. If you'd like to take some with you, shark meat (*hákarl*) and dried fish (*harðfiskur*) may be purchased at the museum.

VATNASAFN (LIBRARY OF WATER)

The Library of Water (Bókhlöðustígur 17, tel. 354/430-2100, www.libraryofwater.is, 1pm-6pm daily June-Aug., 500ISK) is an ongoing exhibition created by American artist Roni Horn in a former library, reflecting her view of the geography, geology, climate, and culture of Iceland. The building overlooks the ocean and the picturesque town. Inside, there are 24 glass columns containing water collected from ice from some of the major glaciers around Iceland. The glass columns reflect the light onto a rubber floor filled with words in English and Icelandic that relate to the weather in Iceland. This is a unique spot and worth a visit if you're in town.

ELDFJALLASAFN (VOLCANO MUSEUM)

One of the town's newest sights, the Volcano Museum (Aðalgata 6, tel. 354/433-8154, www.eldfjallasafn.is, 11am-5pm daily May-Sept., 800ISK) was opened in 2013 to much fanfare. The museum showcases works of art, old and new, that depict volcanic eruptions, as well as artifacts and volcanic rocks. The museum is focused on volcanoes around the world, not just Iceland's volcanoes. If you would like an in-depth tour on the geology behind volcanoes, the museum offers geology excursions on Mondays and Tuesdays, which take you to interesting locales along the Snæfellsnes Peninsula. The eight-hour tour is about 20,000ISK.

Stykkishólmur

Sports and Recreation
BIRD-WATCHING
Seatours (Smidjustigur 3, tel. 354/433-2254, www.seatours.is, tours from 7,000ISK) runs a unique bird-watching tour by boat. The two-hour tour leaves from Stykkishólmur harbor, and tourists have a chance to see white-tailed eagles, shags, puffins (in the summer), eider ducks, and fulmars. While scouting for birds, guests are treated to stunning views of Snæfellsnes, including cool basalt rock formations.

SWIMMING
The **Stykkishólmur Swimming Pool** (Borgarbraut 4, tel. 354/438-1150, 7am-10pm Mon.-Fri., 9am-7pm Sat.-Sun., 500ISK) is an outdoor complex with a heated pool and hot tubs.

Accommodations
Hofðagata Guesthouse (Hofðagata 11, tel. 354/694-6569, www.hofdagata.is, rooms from 25,000ISK) is known as the oldest guesthouse in town, and the concrete structure might not be much to look at from the outside, but inside, it is warm and inviting. Rooms are decorated with great care, mixing warm hues with classic Scandinavian comfort. The four rooms include shared bathrooms, free Wi-Fi, and a hearty breakfast.

Holmur Inn (Skulagata 4, tel. 354/899-9144, www.holmur-inn.com, rooms from 14,500ISK) is a seven-room guesthouse on a quiet street in Stykkishólmur, just past the main road. Rooms are small but modern and comfortable. Guests have access to a common kitchen and shared bathroom facilities with showers. Breakfast is included.

The 11-room **Hótel Breiðafjörður** (Aðalgata 8, tel. 354/438-1417, www.hotel-breidafjordur.is, rooms from 21,500ISK) is a guesthouse that was converted from a local school and has been running for more than 30 years. Rooms are sparsely decorated with a lot of wood throughout the house and vinyl flooring. The staff is accommodating, but the guesthouse is quite basic and not memorable.

Hótel Stykkishólmur (Borgarbraut 8, tel. 354/430-2100, www.hringhotels.is, rooms from 20,000ISK) is chic, stylish, and inviting. All 80 rooms have a private bathroom, and rooms are tastefully decorated with large, comfortable beds. Guests have access to free Wi-Fi, free parking, an included breakfast buffet, and a hotel bar.

Food
Ocean View Restaurant (Borgarbraut 8, tel. 354/430-2100, www.hringhotels.is, breakfast 7am-10am daily, dinner 6pm-10pm daily, entrées from 2,000ISK) is delicious fine dining at its best. Located inside Hótel Stykkishólmur, the Ocean View Restaurant has a playful, eclectic menu featuring traditional, fresh Icelandic ingredients with an interesting Asian spin.

Narfeyrarstofa (Aðalgata 3, tel. 354/438-1119, www.narfeyrarstofa.is, noon-10pm daily, entrées from 2,200ISK) is an elegant restaurant serving Icelandic staples and savory comfort food. Guests can choose among Icelandic meat soup, cod filet, salmon, and lamb dishes, among many other tasty choices. Minke whale steaks and guillemot are also on the menu, as are hamburgers and fried fish. The meat soup is divine.

Information and Services
The **tourist information center** (Borgarbraut 4, tel. 354/433-8120, www.westiceland.is, 10am-5pm daily), located at the town's swimming pool complex, provides brochures on local sights as well as places to see in the surrounding area.

Getting There and Around
Stykkishólmur is approximately a two-hour drive from Reykjavík, traveling north along Route 1 and then west along Route 54, 165 kilometers via the Hvalfjörður tunnel.

The **Strætó** 58 bus (tel. 354/540-2700, www.straeto.is, 2,000ISK) runs between Borgarnes and Stykkishólmur five times daily. The trip is about 100 minutes long.

FLATEY

Flatey (Flat Island) is the largest of the western islands in Breiðafjörður, a bay that separates the Westfjords from the southern part of the country, reachable only by a ferry. The small island, which is north of the Snæfellsnes Peninsula and about one kilometer wide and two kilometers long, is an ideal visit for those seeking a spot in Iceland that is as old world as it gets—as in, not much has changed on this island in centuries. The colorful wood houses and single road evoke a simpler time, one that has not been overcrowded with industry.

Flatey is very much a seasonal destination, ideal for leisurely walks, birdwatching, and taking a break from some of the more popular attractions in the Westfjords. The island offers unspoiled nature at its best, with hordes of migrating birds coming to nest and few human souls occupying the island. Icelanders who own a second home on the island make regular trips in the summer, and only a handful of people remain during the winter months.

Flatey is a good place to spot puffins that migrate to the island in the summer (June-August), as well as other species, including arctic terns, seagulls, and oystercatchers.

However, take note that part of the island is restricted from mid-May to mid-July to protect nesting birds from outside interference.

Other sights include the **Flatey church,** which was erected in 1926. The exterior is classic minimalist Icelandic design, but the inside features paintings from Spanish painter Baltasar Samper, who captured scenes from the island in the 1960s. Baltasar is the father of renowned filmmaker Baltasar Kormakur, who directed movies like *101 Reykjavik* and *Contraband.* Across from the church is a small cemetery where people from several hundred years ago are buried.

The main hotel-restaurant on the island is only open for business during the summer, so plan accordingly if you want to venture out to the island in the winter.

Sports and Recreation
CAMPING

The Flatey **Krákuvör** campsite (tel. 354/438-1451, 1,200ISK) is small and as basic as it gets. It's an open area with no shelter, and the weather can be unforgiving. It's not recommended to camp unless you have top-notch equipment—including a waterproof tent that can withstand high winds.

isolated Flatey

Accommodations and Food

Hótel Flatey (tel. 354/555-7788, www.ho-telflatey.is, rooms from 25,500ISK) is housed in a traditional timber house, a type that is prevalent on the island. The rooms are small, yet tastefully decorated in a classic Scandinavian style—wood furniture, quaint white linens, and lots of minimalist charm. Each of the rooms is named after a different bird species that inhabits the island. The staff is accommodating and the house is centrally located in town. This place is a winner. It's open in the summer June 2-August 24. The in-house restaurant (9am-9pm daily in summer, entrées from 3,900ISK) is a favorite among tourists and locals, and the menu will make your mouth water. You'll find on the menu lumpfish caviar, mussels, lamb filets with blueberry salt, and a delicate pan-fried cod dish with lobster sauce.

Getting There and Around

There is one way to get to Flatey—by ferry. The *Baldur* ferry is operated by Seatours (www.seatours.is, round-trip 10,500ISK) and departs from the harbor in Stykkishólmur, where you can buy round-trip tickets. In the summer there are daily departures. The schedule in the winter varies. Be sure to check the website for up-to-date timetables.

The Westfjords

The Westfjords are simply beautiful. Endless coastlines, jaw-dropping bird cliffs, and gorgeous mountainous landscapes await those who make the trip. Rent a car to explore the region because bus service is limited.

ÍSAFJÖRÐUR

Ísafjörður is the unofficial capital of the Westfjords, but don't let that "title" fool you; it's just a tiny town of about 4,000 people. It's easy to feel isolated in Ísafjörður, but it's a feeling many tourists relish. The town itself is quaint, with a small downtown area with shops and restaurants, and the surroundings are picturesque with mountains in the background and a bustling harbor. A short drive outside town, you'll find towering mountains, interesting rock formations, and more sheep

view of Ísafjörður

The Westfjords

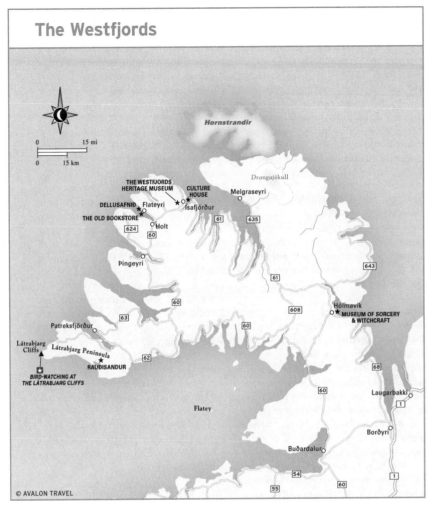

than people. Ísafjörður is a good base for exploring the Westfjords.

Sights

BYGGÐASAFN VESTFJARÐA (WESTFJORDS HERITAGE MUSEUM)

The Westfjords Heritage Museum (Neðstakaupstaður, tel. 354/896-3291, www.nedsti.is, 9am-6pm daily May 15-Sept. 15, 900ISK) pays homage to the old, traditional methods of fishing, with equipment and fishing boats used in the old days on exhibit. The museum is housed in an 18th-century building that sets the tone for the exhibits. There are also ship models on display, informative documentaries on view, and a special exhibition on the processing of sun-dried salted fish and its significance on the town.

GAMLA SJÚKRAHÚSIÐ (CULTURE HOUSE)

Ísafjörður's Culture House (Eyrartún, tel. 354/450-8220, www.safnis.is, 1pm-6pm

Mon.-Fri., 1pm-4pm Sat., free) was originally built in 1925 as the town's hospital, but it has morphed into Ísafjörður's library, with an art collection and photo archives that have a regional focus. The building itself is striking, with a white exterior and bright green roof. The interior is warm and cozy and a great place to hide out in for a couple hours when the weather is particularly bad. There are several computers available for use with Internet connection for a small fee, and many treasures wait to be discovered in the archives.

Sports and Recreation
SWIMMING
If the weather is particularly challenging, it's great to escape to the local indoor Ísafjörður Swimming Pool (Austurvegur 9, tel. 354/456-3200, 7am-9pm Mon.-Fri., 10am-5pm Sat.-Sun., 500ISK) for a few hours.

Accommodations
Hótel Ísafjörður (Silfurtogr 2, tel. 354/456-4111, www.hotelisafjordur.is, rooms from 30,000ISK) is the nicest hotel in town, but you will pay for that stay. The 36-room hotel is decorated in standard Scandinavian simplicity and has private bathrooms, free Wi-Fi, free parking, and a staff that is happy to arrange tours and make recommendations. The hotel is centrally located, and all the main attractions are within walking distance.

Hótel Edda Ísafjörður (Menntaskólinn, tel. 354/444-4960, www.hoteledda.is, mid-June-mid-Aug., rooms from 15,000ISK) is a 40-room hotel operated only during the summer months to accommodate the high season. The hotel offers 20 rooms with private bathrooms and 20 rooms with a wash basin and shared bathroom facilities. Rooms are bright, clean, and sparsely decorated. Most rooms have hardwood floors and Ikea-type furniture. A breakfast buffet is available for an extra fee, and there is free Wi-Fi in the hotel's public areas.

Gamla Gisthúsið (Mánagata 5, tel. 354/456-4146, www.gistihus.is, rooms from 20,000ISK) is a standard nine-room guesthouse that offers the comforts of home.

Rooms are small but clean and comfortable. The common lounge feels like you're visiting Icelandic relatives, with classic Scandinavian furniture and a reading corner with lots of books on the shelves. Guests have access to kitchen and laundry facilities.

Food
★ Tjoruhúsið (Nedstikaupstadur, tel. 354/456-4419, lunch noon-2pm and dinner 7pm-10pm daily, entrées from 2,500ISK) is a family-run restaurant that serves delicate, fresh fish in inventive ways. The rustic wood interior is cozy, the service top-notch, and the menu consists of the catch of the day. It could be haddock, cod, salmon, or other fish served with great care alongside fresh veggies. At night, there is an all-you-can-eat buffet for 5,000ISK per person, and it is well worth it.

Bræðraborg Café (Aðalstræti 22b, tel. 354/456-3322, www.boreaadventures.com, 9am-6pm daily, entrées from 1,500ISK) was a welcome addition to the town when it opened its doors in 2012. The cute café with bright blue tables, plush seating, and rustic hardwood floors is a great hangout spot that serves delicious snacks and light meals. Locals frequent the café for a coffee and freshly baked bread and jam in the mornings and the soup of the day for lunch. It's a cheerful place with a friendly staff and comfortable atmosphere.

Information and Services
The tourist information center (Aðalstræti 7, tel. 354/456-5121, www.westfjords.is, 8am-6pm Mon.-Fri., 10am-3pm Sat.-Sun.) offers tourists many services, including the option to rent camping equipment and bicycles. There are also brochures available on the region, and many tourists use the outpost as a place to join hiking groups.

Getting There and Around
Ísafjörður is accessible by Route 61. It's a little over five hours and 456 kilometers from Reykjavík.

There are buses to Ísafjörður by way of Reykjavík, Akureyri, Hólmavík, Patreksfjörður, Látrabjarg, and more during the year. The schedule changes often and can be viewed at www.isafjordur.is. The price from Reykjavík to Ísafjörður is 17,000ISK.

By plane, daily flights are available through Air Iceland (www.airiceland.is), which is operated at Reykjavík's domestic airport and Ísafjörður (tel. 354/570-3000). Depending on the weather, your 45-minute flight could be eventful due to wind conditions, but the view is amazing. A round-trip flight from Reykjavík is about 30,000ISK.

FLATEYRI

Flateyri was established as a trading post in 1792 and was a base of operations in the 19th century for whaling and shark-hunting. Most of the houses, some colorful, on Flateyri's seafront street, Hafnarstræti, were built between 1880 and 1915. Over the years, its fishing industry waned due to a major fish company closing, and the town has transformed itself to attract tourists in the summer months. Today, it's a popular place to visit for sea anglers and kayak enthusiasts. A couple of museums and its stunning landscape of mountains and endless ocean make the tiny town a place to see when traveling through the Westfjords.

Sights
GAMLA BÓKABÚÐIN (OLD BOOKSTORE)

Visitors to the Old Bookstore (Hafnarstræti 3-5, tel. 354/865-6695, www.westfjords.is, 11am-5pm Tues.-Sat., 2pm-5pm Sun. June-Aug., open by arrangement Mon. and rest of year, donations accepted) can have a look at an exhibition of the old living quarters of the merchant family who made their home in the building. It's a unique take on what life was like in the town a couple of centuries ago. The nondescript building also has an exhibition about dried fish, which was a big part of the town's history before Flateyri's fishing industry ground to a halt. Used books are sold by the kilo in the store, which also sells souvenirs and toys for kids.

DELLUSAFNIÐ (NONSENSE MUSEUM)

The Nonsense Museum (Hafnarstræti 11, tel. 354/894-8836, 12:30pm-5pm daily, 1,000ISK) is one of those quirky museums that tend to pop up in the countryside of Iceland. This museum is a labor of love for the owner, and its wackiness is worth a visit. There's no rhyme or reason to the collections, but they are certainly fun and/or unexpected. For instance, there are more than 100 police hats on display, from forces around the world. There are also collections of ship models (including a huge replica of the *Titanic*), teaspoons and sugar packets, matchboxes, salt and pepper sets, and lighters that belong to the owner. It's a fun place to peruse when weather is bad, or if you have planned an extended stay in the region.

Sports and Recreation
FISHING

Flateyri is a beautiful place to fish, with the chance to spot whales while angling for cod, haddock, and catfish. Iceland Pro Travel (Hafnarstræti 9, tel. 354/456-6667, www.icelandprofishing.com) is a local tourism company that runs sea angling day tours as well as longer package trips. Contact the company for detailed itineraries and prices.

KAYAKING

Flateyri's fjord is a popular place for kayakers to visit, and local company Grænhöfði (Hjallavegur 9, tel. 354/456-7762, jens@snerpa.is) offers half and full day trips around Önundarfjörður. Kayak enthusiasts are treated to calm waters amid stunning views of the fjord. The trips are run June-August, and prices start at 30,000ISK.

SWIMMING

The Flateyri Swimming Pool (Tjarnagata, tel. 354/456-7738, 10am-9pm Mon.-Fri., noon-4pm Sat.-Sun., 500ISK) is a central meeting place for locals, and tourists are more than welcome to take a dip and chat with the residents. The facility has a heated pool, hot tub, and sauna.

Accommodations and Food

Grænhöfði (Hjallavegur 9, tel. 354/456-7762, jens@snerpa.is, rooms from 20,000ISK) offers three apartments that can accommodate up to six people. The rooms are huge, and guests have access to a fully equipped kitchen, private bathrooms, and plenty of parking. The owners also offer kayaking tours, so be sure to inquire if that's of interest.

Vagninn (Hafnarstræti 19, tel. 354/456-7751, www.vagninn.is, 11am-11pm Sun.-Thurs., noon-2am Fri.-Sat., entrées from 1,000ISK) is your best bet to get a bite to eat when in Flateyri. Otherwise you will have to settle for fast food at the local gas station. But, just because Vagninn is the only game in town, doesn't mean that they don't go out of their way to please diners. The food is exceptional. The classic Icelandic fish and lamb dishes are delicious, and other options on the menu range from sandwiches to soup and hamburgers. The atmosphere is fun and easygoing, with live music on the weekends.

Getting There and Around

Flateyri is just 22 kilometers west of Ísafjörður and can be reached via Route 60.

There are three daily buses during weekdays between Ísafjörður and Flateyri (30 minutes, 1,000ISK).

ÞINGEYRI

Þingeyri is a tiny village of fewer than 300 residents that has scenic seaside views of the fjord Dýrafjörður. Tourism in the village isn't centered around museums or cultural exhibitions, but rather outdoor activities like hiking, swimming, and horse riding.

Sports and Recreation
CAMPING

The Þingeyri Campground (Þingeyra-roddi, tel. 354/450-8470, 1,400ISK) is close to the swimming pool, so there's a lot of foot traffic in the area. It's a small campsite with an adequate cooking area, toilets, and room for tents and RVs. The campsite is in an open field with no shelter, but it has stunning views of the fjord. It's open mid-May to mid-September.

HORSE RIDING

Riding horses along a scenic trail that includes moss banks, rocky ledges, and black sand is not to be missed. The tour company Westfjords Adventures (Aðalstræti 62, tel. 354/456-5006, www.westfjordsadventures.com) offers horse-riding tours that accommodate everyone from new riders to the more experienced. The four-hour "Valley Riding Tour" (17,900ISK per person) is available daily June-August. Tourists are urged to wear warm clothing and helmets; saddles and guides are made available.

SWIMMING

The Þingeyri Swimming Pool (Þingeyra-roddi, tel. 354/456-8375, 8am-9pm Mon.-Fri., 10am-5pm Sat.-Sun., 500ISK) is conveniently located right next to Þingeyri's campsite.

Accommodations and Food

Núpur Guesthouse (Dýrafjörður, tel. 354/456-8235, www.hotelnupur.is, rooms from 22,000ISK) offers 40 rooms ranging from singles to triples. The block-style buildings were once part of a school complex. The rooms are clean and neat, but nothing special. Guests have access to shared bathroom facilities, a kitchenette for use, and free parking. The in-house restaurant serves Icelandic staples with an emphasis on lamb and fish. The menu includes oven-baked leg of lamb, seafood soup, shrimp and monkfish with salad, and pineapple pan-fried cod with tartar sauce. The fish of the day costs 4,800ISK and the meat of the day 5,500ISK.

Við Fjörðinn (Aðalstræti 26, tel. 354/847-0285, www.vidfjordinn.is, rooms from 15,000ISK) offers eight rooms with standard beds and simple furnishings for a clean, no-frills stay. Guests have access to a kitchen to prepare meals and share bathroom facilities. There are also apartments available for larger groups. Breakfast is available for an added charge of 1,000ISK.

Simbahöllin (Fjarðargata 5, tel. 354/899-6659, www.simbahollin.is, noon-6pm daily June 1-June 15, 10am-10pm daily June 16-Aug. 15, noon-6pm daily Aug. 16-Aug. 31, snacks from 600ISK) is a charming countryside café located in a 1915 building that served as a grocery store. The old-fashioned atmosphere is adorable, the cakes and pastries fresh, and the staff makes you feel like family. The specialty is Belgian waffles with fresh rhubarb jam and cream. Try the waffles. Your taste buds will thank you.

Information and Services

The tourist information center (Hafnarstræti 5, tel. 354/891-6832, www.thingeyri.is, 10am-6pm Mon.-Fri., 11am-5pm Sat.-Sun. June-Aug., 3pm-6pm daily Sept.-May.) has brochures, suggestions for local tour operators, and Internet access.

Getting There and Around

By car, Þingeyri is 49 kilometers southwest of Ísafjörður and is accessible by Route 60.

While Þingeyri feels a bit off the beaten track, a bus operated by Westfjords Adventures (Aðalstræti 62, tel. 354/456-5006, www.westfjordsadventures.is) runs twice a day from Ísafjörður (1 hour, 3,800ISK) via Flateyri.

PATREKSFJÖRÐUR

Patreksfjörður is the kind of sleepy fishing town you have come to love and expect as you travel along the Westfjords. Many travelers use the town as a base while heading out on excursions and day trips—the new Fosshotel has something to do with that. Spend some time in Patreksfjörður if you're a sea angler or if you want to check out some choice scenic sights like the harbor area.

Sports and Recreation

FISHING

Sea angling in the Westfjords is an unforgettable experience, and Patreksfjörður has especially rich fishing grounds. West Tours (tel. 354/456-5111, www.westtours.is) offers a two-hour tour with a guide. Tourists are provided with gear and can fish for cod and haddock. The tour is offered May-November and costs 12,000ISK.

GUIDED TOURS

For hiking, biking, jeep and wildlife tours, Westfjords Adventures (Aðalstræti 62, tel. 354/456-5006, www.westfjordsadventures.com) is the main game in town. Based in Patreksfjörður, the company offers everything from all-day jeep tours on rocky terrain for action junkies (25,000ISK) to a leisurely three-hour hike around town (4,900ISK) with a guide pointing out the major sights, including the scenic harbor area and the fish market.

SWIMMING

The town has one of the nicest swimming pools in the region. Patreksfjörður Swimming Pool (Aðalstræti 55, tel. 354/456-1301, 9am-9pm Mon.-Fri., 10am-6pm Sat.-Sun., 500ISK) is an outdoor pool with hot tubs, a steam bath, and an indoor gym.

Accommodations and Food

★ Fosshotel Westfjords (Aðalstræti 100, tel. 354/456-2004, www.fosshotel.is, rooms from 24,000ISK), which opened in 2013, is one of the nicest Fosshotel chain hotels in the country. The lobby and rooms have an earthy, natural feel with warm hues and lots of wood accents. The beds are quite comfortable. Rooms are larger than average and have free Wi-Fi, private bathrooms, and flatscreen TVs. Meals are served in the cozy in-house restaurant (entrées from 2,400ISK), which specializes in fish. Entrées are light and fresh, and chefs have a classic sensibility when preparing the menu. Expect cod, salmon, lobster, and other fish on the menu, as well as meat and a couple of vegetarian options.

Stekkaból Guesthouse (Stekkar, tel. 354/864-9675, stekkabol@snerpa.is, rooms from 14,400ISK) is a cute countryside guesthouse run by a husband and wife who aim to make you feel at home. The rooms are on the small side, but tidy, and free Wi-Fi is included. The guesthouse is in a picturesque spot on the fjord, making it a perfect spot to spend the night before you continue on your journey. Breakfast is available for an added cost of 1,700ISK per person.

Information and Services

The **tourist information center** (Aðalstræti 62, tel. 354/456-5006, 10am-4pm) is in the Westfjords Adventures office in the center of town. The office allows you to book tours and has pamphlets about the region, hiking maps, and Internet access.

Getting There and Around

Patreksfjörður is 130 kilometers southwest of Þingeyri and is accessible by Route 60.

LÁTRABJARG PENINSULA

The Látrabjarg Peninsula is in the northwest fjord region near Patreksfjörður and has dramatic sea cliffs and an abundance of bird species, making it a paradise for bird lovers. June-August, the cliffs around the peninsula are home to numerous puffins, gulls, and kittiwakes.

Sights and Recreation

★ BIRD-WATCHING

Látrabjarg is one of the best bird-watching spots in the west, as millions of seabirds gather to nest each season. Puffins are a common sight in the summer months—you can see the adorable, bright-beaked birds May-August. You can also see fulmars, razorbills, and guillemots along the cliffs May-August.

The colossal rock formations of the **Látrabjarg cliffs** jut out of the earth at interesting angles, and the layered basalt forms intricate crevices that host bird nests. Trails allow you to access the cliffs by foot; stay on marked paths. Always be respectful of the area and be mindful where you step to avoid nests. The height of the cliffs is humbling, with some reaching up to 441 meters. The cliffs offer some of the most scenic views on the peninsula.

Even if you do trek the cliffs by foot, bird enthusiasts will want to have a pair of binoculars on hand to get a closer look. It's best to

Látrabjarg cliffs

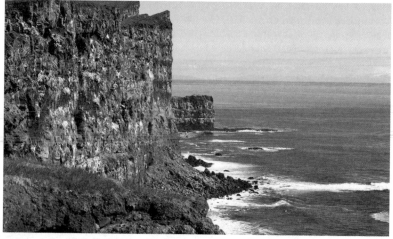

park your vehicle at the end of Route 612 and walk east toward the cliffs.

RAUÐISANDUR

Rauðisandur is a secluded beach with golden red sand and gorgeous views of the Látrabjarg area. Snæfellsjökull looms in the background. Take a walk along the shore, and be on the lookout for seals bobbing in the water. If you're lucky, you'll catch a glimpse. Route 614 takes you to the beach.

Accommodations and Food

Hotel Breiðavík (Breiðavík/Látrabjarg, tel. 354/456-1575, www.breidavik.is, rooms from 18,500ISK) is conveniently close to the Látrabjarg cliffs and offers darling accommodations for your stay. Double rooms look a little dated with bright carpet and old-fashioned linens, but the beds are comfortable, and some rooms with private bathrooms are available. All rooms have access to Wi-Fi, kitchen facilities, and a washing machine. The staff is warm and welcoming and the breakfast is hearty. For budget travelers, there are sleeping bag rooms as well as camping, but be sure to call ahead for availability. The in-house restaurant specializes in fish and lamb, but has other options. The salmon is fresh, seasoned

perfectly, and highly recommended. Entrées start at 2,200ISK.

Hótel Látrabjarg (Fagrihvammur, tel. 354/456-1500, www.latrabjarg.com, rooms from 21,000ISK) offers larger than average rooms with killer views from gigantic windows. Rooms are bright with standard beds (some are carpeted, which can feel old-fashioned), and all rooms have simple furnishings ranging from two-seat couches to armchairs. Breakfast is available for an added price of 1,800ISK per person.

Getting There and Around

You have one option to get to Látrabjarg, Route 612, which can be rough on your rental car as it's unpaved. Beware of steep drops and do not dream of exceeding the speed limit. Be safe. Látrabjarg is 59 kilometers southwest from Patreksfjörður on Route 612.

HÓLMAVÍK

Hólmavík, while a small town, is the largest in the Strandir area, which makes up the most eastern tip of the Westfjords. It's a popular stop for those looking to check out the unique Museum of Sorcery and Witchcraft and the cute Sheep Farming Museum, along with the beautiful coastline. Many travelers

on the way to Látrabjarg

choose the town as a base for spending the night while exploring nearby towns.

Sights

GALDRASAFNIÐ Á HÓLMAVÍK (MUSEUM OF SORCERY AND WITCHCRAFT)

The Museum of Sorcery and Witchcraft (Höfðargata 8-10, tel. 354/897-6525, www. galdrasyning.is, 9am-6pm daily, 900ISK) certainly has a name that grabs your attention, and the exhibits are truly unique. The main theme of the museum is based on Iceland's famous witch hunts in the 17th century. The two-story museum features wax figures, an audio tour, and information about spells and runes. It's the only museum on the island that gives a comprehensive overview of Iceland's witch hunts. The museum may be a little unnerving to children under the age of 12, as there are depictions of death and violence. If you still have an appetite, there's a gift shop and museum café that serves coffee and snacks.

SAUÐFJÁRSETUR Á STRÖNDUM (SHEEP FARMING MUSEUM)

The Sheep Farming Museum (Sævangur, tel. 354/451-3324, www.strandir.is, 10am-6pm daily June-Aug., free) is a region-specific museum that opened in 2002, and it's great if you're traveling with children. The museum focuses on Icelandic sheep and sheep-farming methods that have been employed in the Strandir region for centuries. A favorite among kids is feeding young sheep milk from a bottle while learning about the breed. There's also a souvenir shop and small café, where you can grab a coffee or cocoa and a snack.

Sports and Recreation

CAMPING

The town has a centrally located, well-maintained campsite, Hólmavík Campground (Jakobínutún, tel. 354/451-3111, 1,400ISK), that is close to the swimming pool. There are adequate cooking facilities and hot showers at this site. Tents and RVs are welcome to camp, and there are hookups available. The site is in an open field with no shelter, so be prepared for the elements if you're camping in a tent.

SWIMMING

The Hólmavík Swimming Pool (Jakobínutún, tel. 354/451-3560, 9am-9pm daily, 500ISK) is quiet and gets a bit of traffic in the summer because it's close to the campsite. There are a few hot tubs and a steam bath to enjoy as well.

Accommodations and Food

Finna Hotel (Borgabraut 4, tel. 354/451-3136, www.finnahotel.is, rooms from 15,700ISK) is a small guesthouse in a quaint yellow house on a quiet road in the center of town. Rooms are clean, smart, and furnished simply. The rooms on the second floor of the guesthouse underwent a recent renovation, and if you have a choice, request a room on the second floor. Amenities include free Wi-Fi, free parking, and shared bathrooms. Room rates with or without breakfast are available.

Hótel Laugarhóll (Bjarnarfjörður, tel. 354/451-3380, www.laugarholl.is, rooms from 23,000ISK) offers 16 rooms, and 11 have private bathrooms. The rooms are bright and tidy, with Wi-Fi access and free parking. The hotel is in a large white estate with a rocky landscape in the background. It's close to town (about 25 kilometers east of Hólmavík) but remote enough to maintain a countryside feel. The in-house restaurant offers a breakfast that's included in the room price, as well as a lunch and dinner menu. Entrées start at 2,000ISK and range from fish and lamb dishes to lighter items like soup, sandwiches, and vegetarian options.

Café Riis (Hafnarbraut 39, tel. 354/451-3567, 11:30am-10pm Sun.-Fri., 11:30am-3am Sat., entrées from 1,500ISK) is your only chance for a sit-down meal in town. The non-descript green building has a tourist-friendly menu ranging from traditional fish and lamb dishes to pizza, sandwiches, and snacks. On weekends, Café Riis serves as the main watering hole where locals congregate to grab some drinks and let loose.

Information and Services

The tourist information office (Höfðagata 8, tel. 354/451-3111, www.holmavik.is, 9am-4pm Mon.-Fri.) is in the center of town and offers Internet access, pamphlets about the region, and information on local tours and horse rentals.

Getting There and Around

By car, Hólmavík is a popular stop on the Westfjords for travelers coming from Ísafjörður, as Ring Roaders tend to need to gas up their cars. Route 61 connects Hólmavík, which is 223 kilometers southeast of Ísafjörður, to the Ring Road.

The Strætó 59 bus (tel. 354/540-2700, www.straeto.is, 4,400ISK) goes from Borgarnes to Hólmavík and takes about two hours.

HORNSTRANDIR

The Hornstrandir Peninsula is the northernmost part of the Westfjords, and it is idyllically isolated, a perfect spot to explore by foot, enjoying hiking paths and observing the rich birdlife. Nature rules in this spot of the Westfjords—you won't find museums or cultural attractions, but who needs them when you have millions of seabirds to see and arctic fox sightings are common. It isn't just foreign travelers making their way to these parts, but also Icelanders in search of pure solitude and striking beauty. On bird cliffs, the subjects of postcard-perfect photos, you can see puffins, kittiwakes, fulmars, and guillemots. A long sand beach is the perfect place to roam while basking in the shadows of sharp mountains and the jagged landscape.

Sights and Recreation

HIKING THE HORNSTRANDIR NATURE RESERVE

The Hornstrandir Nature Reserve, which was established in 1975, lies on the north edge of the peninsula. Be mindful that this stretch of land is fiercely protected; cars are banned within the reserve limits and fishing is strictly prohibited. Enjoy the land, but be respectful and obey the rules.

The hike between the small village Hesteyri and Aðalvík Bay at the tip of Hornstrandir is the most popular option, and it's about a half-day (5 hours) moderate hike, during which you can enjoy the cliffs, the rocky landscape, and unspoiled nature.

There are also longer hiking trails, but you must monitor weather conditions and be prepared. Good maps are necessary and can be found in the Online Shop at www.galdrasyning.is.

The terrain could be treacherous depending on the weather, so it's not ideal for casual hikers, but rather for more experienced trekkers. Because of its northern locale, the winds can be fierce and the rain plentiful. Make sure you are prepared with a good pair of boots, waterproof gear, and lots of layers because it can get really cold. Use common sense—there are streams that need to be crossed, sections can be slippery with ice, and crampons are necessary. Visitors must bring along their own tents if the plan is to camp overnight. Weatherproof equipment is necessary, as snow can be expected at any time of the year and storms can break with little warning. Thick fog often occurs in the region, and it's a good idea to have GPS with you.

If you are a novice hiker or would like the structure of an organized tour, West Tours (tel. 354/456-5111, www.westtours.is) offers packages and excursions throughout the year.

CAMPING

The campground Höfn in Hornvík (free) has basic camping facilities, including restrooms, a cooking area, and hot and cold water. Be sure to be respectful of the surroundings, dispose of your trash, and leave no trace. The campsite is in an open space with little shelter. The GPS coordinates are N 66.4232, W 22.4882.

Getting There and Around

Travel to Hornstrandir is very much seasonal, with the high season being from the middle of June to the end of August. Because of its northern locale, the weather can be especially cold, even in the summer, and very wet.

There are daily 45-minute flights from Reykjavík's domestic airport to Ísafjörður for 30,000ISK, and from Ísafjörður, you can catch a ferry operated by Sjóferðir (tel. 354/456-3879, www.sjoferdir.is) that stops at Aðalvík, Hornvík, Grunnavík, Hesteyri, and Vigur for 5,000ISK.

The easiest way to travel to the region is to book an excursion, as there are logistics involved and it's best to have a local tour company handle them. There can be delays because of weather, and travelers can avoid headaches by booking a tour. Local tour companies include Ísafjörður-based West Tours (tel. 354/456-5111, www.west-tours.is), Arctic Adventures (tel. 354/456-3322, www.adventures.is), and Borea Adventures (www.boreaadventures.com), also in Ísafjörður.

North Iceland

Look for ★ to find recommended
sights, activities, dining, and lodging.

Highlights

© AVALON TRAVEL

★ **Lystigarður Akureyrar (Akureyri Botanical Gardens):** The northernmost botanical garden in the world has an eclectic collection of native and international flora (page 165).

★ **Goðafoss:** Witness the thundering Waterfall of the Gods, a spectacular sight any time of year (page 176).

★ **Jarðböðin (Mývatn Nature Baths):** Just try to resist taking a dip in the soothing, heated waters of Mývatn. The water stands at 36°C (96.8°F) and the bottom of the lagoon contains healing minerals (page 177).

★ **Whale-Watching in Húsavík:** The unofficial whale-watching capital of Iceland offers the chance to view as many as 12 species of whale. Seeing these gentle giants up close is truly beautiful (page 184).

★ **Ásbyrgi:** This gigantic canyon features cool rock formations, looping walking paths, lush greenery, a lot of birds…and tons of photo opportunities (page 187).

★ **Dettifoss:** The largest waterfall on the island, and the most powerful in Europe, spans 100 meters wide and 45 meters high. It's common to see a rainbow or two depending on the weather (page 188).

There's a lot to explore in North Iceland, and Akureyri is the center of it all.

Iceland's second most populous city, Akureyri has a thriving art scene, gorgeous gardens, and restaurants that rival Reykjavík's. The harbor serves as a port for large cruise ships, and visitors are treated to views of the country's highest peaks and longest fjord.

Akureyri is a perfect place to base yourself when exploring the north. The open terrain from Akureyri to Siglufjörður, the northernmost town in Iceland, treats visitors to sights of traditional churches, wondrous waterfalls, and a dreamy seaside.

Farther west is Northwest Iceland. This region comprises sparsely populated farm country. In fact, depending on the time of year, you may see more seals, birds, horses, and whales than people in areas like Húnaflói and Skagafjörður.

Heading from Akureyri toward eastern Iceland, stops include Krafla's steamy lava fields, Lake Mývatn's lush lands, and the majestic Dettifoss waterfall, to name a few. In the summer, birders and geology buffs will want to stretch the drive out an extra couple of days.

From waterfalls and hiking trails to the best skiing on the island, the north has plenty to keep you busy.

PLANNING YOUR TIME

North Iceland is a huge chunk of land (for Iceland), but it's quite easy to split the sections, using a major town as a home base and doing day trips. For instance, Akureyri, Húsavík, and Mývatn are the largest and most frequented destinations for tourists, with museums, outdoor activities, and historical sites to visit.

If you're traveling the Ring Road, Northwest Iceland would be your first destination after visiting the Westfjords. The northwest offers some of the most exquisite scenery on the island in the small towns and counties including Hvammstangi, Blönduós, and Skagafjörður. Akureyri is a great base while visiting this area.

Akureyri rivals Reykjavík for the center of artistic life in Iceland. Plan to spend as much time as possible up here, with at least one day each in Mývatn and Húsavík and two days in Akureyri—three days if you want to include a trip to Grímsey.

Previous: central Skagafjörður; traditional Icelandic farm with mossy roofs in Glaumbær. **Above:** Dettifoss.

North Iceland

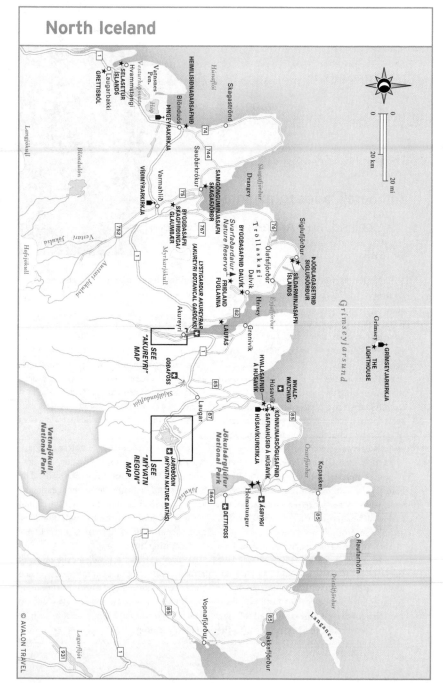

© AVALON TRAVEL

When driving in the north, it's important to take the weather into consideration. Some roads are impassable in the winter. It's possible to see much of North Iceland by sticking to the Ring Road, which is the best-maintained road in the region. However, always be sure to check the road conditions and weather forecast before heading out in a car.

Húnaflói Area

The northwest is steeped in saga history, as legendary hero Grettir the Strong was said to have lived in the area, but most people travel to the Húnaflói area for the charming fishing villages and wildlife-spotting opportunities in the form of whales, seals, and birds. Húnaflói is a large bay between the Strandir coast and the Skagaströnd region. It is about 50 kilometers wide and 100 kilometers long with the small towns Blönduós and Skagaströnd located on the bay's eastern side. The region is lush in the summer, with a majestic coastline, similar to the Westfjords.

VATNSNES PENINSULA

The Vatnsnes Peninsula is home to some of the best seal-watching opportunities in the north (in the summer, you have a good chance of spotting harbor and gray seals), and there's a museum with lovely exhibitions at the Icelandic Seal Center, which does research on local seal species. **Hvammstangi** is the largest town on the peninsula and the site of many tourist attractions. The Vatnsnes Peninsula juts out into Húnaflói, exposing jagged rocks and bobbing hills. Visitors can access Route 711 from the Ring Road to Hvammstangi and around the peninsula.

Sights
SELASETUR ÍSLANDS (ICELANDIC SEAL CENTER)
The **Icelandic Seal Center** (Brekkugata 2, Hvammstangi, tel. 354/451-2345, www.selasetur.is, noon-3pm Tues.-Sat. Apr., 9am-4pm daily May-Sept., open by request rest of year, 950ISK) is as cute as it sounds, if you like seals. There is a research component to the facility that is quite serious, but the museum section captures these lovable, adorable creatures

rock formation in the Húnaflói Bay

perfectly. Most of the exhibitions are geared toward children, and topics include the seals of the North Atlantic and the Arctic, the importance of seals in Icelandic culture and tradition, seal biology (with skeletons on display), and the evolution of seal hunting on the island. There are also documentaries on Icelandic seals in English. The main seals the center works with are harbor, harp, bearded, gray, hooded, and ringed seals. (There's also the odd walrus that comes ashore in Iceland from Greenland—the seal center is contacted in that event.) The staff has information on the best sites for seal-watching opportunities, and a small shop sells souvenirs and light meals. Check the website for current opening hours. For independent travelers, it is possible to go to the popular seal watching spots without a tour guide.

GRETTISBÓL (GRETTIR'S LAIR)

Grettisból (Laugarbakki, tel. 354/451-0050, www.grettistak.is) is an outdoor area and cultural center dedicated to the great saga hero Grettir "the Strong" Ásmundsson from Grettir's Saga. One of the most infamous outlaws of the sagas, Grettir was born on the farm Bjarg, which is only seven kilometers south of the site of this cultural center. There is a Viking garden at Grettisból, and from the road you will see a big Viking sword sculpture. In the summer months (June-Aug.), a Viking market in the house sells Viking-related wares, such as figurines, artwork, and woolen goods. The center is open all year long, and if you're a fan of the sagas, this should be on your itinerary.

An annual festival held at Grettisból in August is called Grettistak; locals have a strong-man competition in the spirit of Grettir.

BARDÚSA-VERSLUNARMINJASAFN (MERCHANT MUSEUM)

Merchant Museum (Brekkugata 4, Hvammstangi, tel. 354/451-2747, 10am-6pm Mon.-Fri., 11am-4pm Sat.-Sun. June-Aug.,

1,000ISK) is a small museum in Hvammstangi that is the remains of a shop that sold goods to locals in the early 20th century. Today, the museum keeps all the old goods that were key to society in the town, such as fishing equipment, kitchen utensils, and other home goods. The museum also sells Icelandic-made handicrafts.

Accommodations

Guesthouse Hanna Siggi (Garðavegur 26, tel. 354/451-2407, gistihs@simnet.is, rooms from 14,000ISK) offers six rooms, a common kitchen to prepare meals, and an outdoor hot tub. It's close to whale- and seal-watching opportunities. Rooms are small but clean, and guests share bathroom facilities. Free Wi-Fi is also available.

Hotel Hvammstangi (Nordur Runway 1, tel. 354/855-1303, rooms from 15,000ISK) is a 10-room guesthouse about six kilometers from the highway and in the middle of some great seal-watching spots. Rooms are small but neat and tastefully decorated. Each room has a private bathroom, there is a shared TV lounge with complimentary coffee and tea, and guests have access to free Wi-Fi. The town's public swimming pool, with hot tub and steam bath, is across the street from the hotel, and admission is free for guests.

Dæli Holiday Farm (Viðidalur, tel. 354/451-2566, www.daeli.is, rooms from 17,500ISK) has larger than average rooms, some wood-paneled, that are simple and smart. The 14 rooms have private bathrooms, TVs, and free Wi-Fi, and guests have access to a sauna, hot tub, minigolf, a playground for kids, and a café. A kitchen is available to prepare meals, and guests have access to a barbecue grill.

★ Gauksmýri (Þjóðvegur, tel. 354/451-2927, www.gauksmyri.is, rooms from 21,500ISK) is the best place to stay, hands down, if you love horses. The 24-room ranch offers cozy, comfortable rooms with adorably appropriate horse-print bedding. The beds are comfortable, the decor is rustic cool and the amenities are superb. Most rooms have private bathroom facilities, and all guests have access to free Wi-Fi and huge windows overlooking the gorgeous landscape. The owners are obviously horse enthusiasts and operate a horse-rental business as well. There are short guided horse tours and demonstrations showing the various gaits Iceland's horses are known for, and training and teaching facilities are on-site. Breakfast is included in the room price.

Ósar Hostel (Vatnsnesvegur, tel. 354/451-2678, www.hostel.is, beds from 3,300ISK) is just 20 minutes from the Ring Road, making this a popular choice in the area for budget travelers making the expensive trek around the island. Rooms are adequate but nothing to write home about. A few rooms have private bathrooms, but most share facilities. It's open May-September.

Food

Gauksmýri Restaurant (Þjóðvegur, tel. 354/451-2927, www.gauksmyri.is, 7am-9pm daily) is the in-house restaurant of the Gauksmýri guesthouse. In addition to breakfast, the restaurant does a nice lunch buffet that features soup, hummus, homemade bread, pesto, and a variety of salads. The main event, however, is the dinner buffet, which has lamb, horse, pork, chicken, and whale meat; trout, salmon, and cod; and a salad bar, along with homemade bread, baked potatoes, and vegetables. The emphasis is on local ingredients prepared in a traditional way.

Getting There and Around

By car, Hvammstangi is 190 kilometers north of Reykjavík on Route 1 and 200 kilometers west of Akureyri.

It's best to have a rental car to explore this region, but there is bus service from Akureyri. The Strætó 57 bus (tel. 354/540-2700, www.straeto.is) departs from Akureyri and travels roughly three hours to Hvammstangi for 3,600ISK.

BLÖNDUÓS

Blönduós is a tiny town that was built around a bridge that crosses the Blanda River

(Blönduós means "mouth of the river Blanda" in Icelandic). Home to just a few shops, private homes, and guesthouses, the town is a small spot that has a few attractions. If you are traveling on the Ring Road and have some time, think about visiting the Textile Museum and the local church, which is steeped in history.

Sights
HEIMILISIÐNAÐARSAFNIÐ (TEXTILE MUSEUM)
The Textile Museum (Árbraut 29, tel. 354/452-4067, www.textile.is, 10am-5pm daily June-Aug., 900ISK) is a quaint museum for fiber enthusiasts. On display are local crafts, Icelandic national costumes, looms of different sizes, and wonderful woolen products. The gift shop has a collection of cute wares, including wool for knitting projects and classically patterned Icelandic sweaters.

ÞINGEYRAKIRKJA (ÞINGEYRAR CHURCH)
Þingeyrakirkja (Austur-Húnavatnssýsla, tel. 354/895-4473, 10am-5pm daily June-Aug., open by request rest of year, free) offers one of the most beautiful panoramic views in all of North Iceland. Þingeyrakirkja was built out of stone in Romanesque style and was officially consecrated in 1877. The land surrounding the church was also the site of Iceland's first monastery, which was founded in 1133. An important place from the time of early settlement, Þingeyrakirkja is mentioned in the saga literature as a regional assembly site. Next to the church is a large circular structure, which is believed to be a judgment circle; it is listed as a heritage site. In the summer, tourists can enter the church and have a look.

Accommodations
Hótel Blönduós (Aðalgata 6, tel. 354/452-4205, www.hotelblonduos.is, rooms from 20,500ISK) is an upscale countryside hotel that features brightly painted walls, vintage furniture, and huge bathrooms. It's the poshest hotel in the region, but there isn't much competition. It seems pricey, but the service

is superior and the location great. Breakfast is included. **Gladheimar Guesthouse** (Brautarhvammi, tel. 354/820-1300, www.gladheimar. is, cottages from 18,000ISK) offers self-contained cottages that include private bathrooms, a patio, hot tub, barbecue grill, and proximity to the town's swimming pool. The cottages aren't luxurious, but it's a clean and convenient place to stay that won't break the bank.

Food
Potturinn Restaurant (Norðurlandsvegur 4, tel. 354/453-5060, www.pot.is, 11am-10pm daily, entrées from 2,300ISK) has a diverse menu including pasta, Indian-inspired dishes, pizzas, hamburgers, soups, vegetarian options, and a salad bar. There's something for everyone, and it's a great option for large groups. The monkfish with mango chutney sauce, sautéed vegetables, and rice is recommended.

Getting There and Around
Blönduós is 58 kilometers northeast of Hvammstangi on Route 1.

The **Strætó** 57 bus (tel. 354/540-2700, www.straeto.is) runs from Akureyri, takes 2.5 hours, and costs 2,400ISK. Be sure to check schedules, as they change frequently due to weather.

Skagafjörður

With sloping mountains, a beautiful coastline, and chunks of glacial ice dotting the fjord, Skagafjörður's landscape is heavenly. Skagafjörður is often described as horse country, and it's very true. Horse farms and horse tour operators abound in the region—and it's the only county in Iceland where horses outnumber humans.

Skagafjörður is just 40 kilometers long and 15 kilometers wide, with the towns of Sauðárkrókur and Varmahlíð the main areas for tourism. Here, farms reign supreme and all residents are involved in agriculture in one form or another. Tourism has picked up in recent years, and there are a few museums, some historical sites, and plenty of outdoor activities to keep visitors entertained.

VARMAHLÍÐ
Tourists don't typically travel to the town of Varmahlíð, but rather through it, as Varmahlíð is close to where Route 1 passes through the area. There's a historic church to check out, but those who stick around for a few hours are usually booked for a river-rafting or horse tour. The town has defined itself as a place for adventure activities over the past few years.

Sights
VÍÐIMÝRARKIRKJA (VÍÐIMÝRI CHURCH)
Just outside Varmahlíð lies **Víðimýrarkirkja** (tel. 354/453-5095, 9am-6pm daily June-Aug., 750ISK), one of the last few preserved turf churches in Iceland. The church, which features a frame made from driftwood, was built in 1834 and has turf walls but timber gables both back and front. Turf houses are representative of a very old building method. At the beginning of the 20th century, the church's fate was uncertain, but the National Museum of Iceland became responsible for its renovation and maintenance. The church still holds Sunday services at 11am, and tourists are welcome to attend. The GPS coordinates are N 65.5389, W 19.4710.

Sports and Recreation
HORSE RIDING
Skagafjörður is horse country. **Hestasport** (Vegamót, tel. 354/453-8383, www.riding.is) offers short and longer riding tours on scenic paths along the region. The staff clearly has a passion for horses, and guides are well informed, patient, and excited to take you to

some hidden gems in the area. Options range from one-hour to full-day tours, and the staff has all the equipment you need for your excursion—helmets, rain clothes, and all other necessary gear. Tours start at 6,000ISK per person.

RIVER RAFTING

Bakkaflöt Rafting (560 Varmahlíð, tel. 354/453-8245, www.bakkaflot.is) offers river-rafting tours on the Austari Jökulsá River and the Vestari Jökulsá River, which are fed from the Hofsjökull glacier. Five levels of rafting classes range from easy to very demanding, based on an individual's level of experience. Tours are three hours long and cost 11,900ISK.

Bakkaflöt is 37 kilometers from Sauðárkrókur, about 300 kilometers from Reykjavík, and about 100 kilometers from Akureyri. Once you arrive in Varmahlíð along Route 1, take Route 752 and follow that for 10 kilometers.

SWIMMING

The **Varmahlíð Swimming Pool** (560 Varmahlíð, tel. 354/455-6020, 10:30am-9pm Mon.-Fri., 10:30am-6pm Sat.-Sun. June-Aug., 9am-8pm Mon.-Thurs., 8am-2pm Fri., 10am-3pm Sat. Sept.-May, 600ISK) has two sections—one that is 12.5 by 25 meters for adults and a children's pool that's 12.5 by 8 meters. The children's pool is extremely popular among local families, and the slide is a favorite with kids. For adults, there are hot tubs and a sauna in the sports hall that's connected to the pool area.

Accommodations and Food

Located near Route 1, **Hótel Varmahlíð** (tel. 354/453-8170, www.hotelvarmahlid.is, rooms from 26,800ISK) is the only hotel in the area, and it's a lovely place to stay. The 19 rooms are cozy and modern with private bathrooms, TVs, free Wi-Fi, and gorgeous photographs of the area by locals adorning the walls. It is a comfortable spot with hospitable employees and an in-house restaurant serving yummy dishes. A breakfast buffet is included in the price of the room, and lunch and dinner menus focus on local ingredients found in the region, such as lightly salted cod heads, horse filets, and tasty rhubarb cobbler made from local farm products. The restaurant is open 7:30am-10pm daily.

Skagafjörður harbor

Information and Services

In the center of the village, the Skagafjörður tourist information office (tel. 354/455-6161, www.visitskagafjordur.is, 9am-6pm daily June-Aug., noon-6pm Mon.-Fri., 1pm-6pm Sat.-Sun. Sept.-May) has pamphlets about the region, Internet access, maps, and the ability to book tours.

Getting There and Around

Varmahlíð is 286 kilometers northeast of Reykjavík on Route 1 and 93 kilometers west of Akureyri on Route 1.

Varmahlíð is well connected with buses to and from Akureyri. The Strætó 57 bus (tel. 354/540-2700, www.straeto.is) has daily departures from Akureyri. Trips take a little over an hour and cost 2,000ISK.

SAUÐÁRKRÓKUR

Sauðárkrókur is Skagafjörður's largest town, but don't let that fool you—this is a tiny town of fewer than 3,000 people. The name means "sheep's corner" in Icelandic, but that's a bit misleading, as this remains more of a fishing town than sheep-farming town.

Sights

BYGGÐASAFN SKAGFIRÐINGA (SKAGAFJÖRÐUR FOLK MUSEUM)

The Skagafjörður Folk Museum (tel. 354/453-6173, www.glaumbaer.is, 9am-6pm daily mid-May-mid-Sept., 10am-4pm daily mid-Sept.-Oct., open by request rest of year, 1,500ISK) is an extensive exhibition that includes several buildings. The main event is the farmhouse, Glaumbær, which was built circa 1879. It was constructed from stones, turf, and timber, and the structures have been maintained incredibly well. Builders made do with what they had, as the estate provided little rock suitable for building purposes, but there was plenty of good turf, so the walls of the farmhouse contain relatively little rock. The farmhouse consists of 13 buildings, each of which had its own function, ranging from a kitchen to a sleeping room. According to the sagas, the first known inhabitants of

the Glaumbær farm lived there in the 11th century.

Also on the museum grounds at Glaumbær are two 19th-century timber houses, Áshús and Gilsstofa, that are typical of the timber houses built in the area at that time. Áshús contains exhibitions about the region and houses the museum's administrative offices.

Áskaffi is a café housed in a timber house that serves traditional light Icelandic cuisine, including soup and sandwiches. In Gilsstofa, there are offices, an information center, and a souvenir shop.

Also on the property is the Glaumbær church, which was built in 1926. Earlier churches at Glaumbær had been built of wood, and most of them were covered with turf for protection against the elements. However, the last wooden church was blown down in a storm. The church that currently stands is a more modern structure with a concrete base and wood over it.

The Heritage House showcases exhibitions that highlight four 20th-century tradesmen's workshops. Also on permanent display are objects from the private collections of novelist Guðrún from Lundur (1887-1975), composer Eyþór Stefánsson (1901-1999), and artist Jóhannes Geir Jónsson (1927-2003). Guðrún's books are still read widely today in Iceland, and Eyþór's songs are sung regularly around the country. Jóhannes Geir's paintings, on display, show saga scenes, depicting life in the 13th century.

From the Ring Road, head north on Route 75 to reach the Folk Museum. The GPS coordinates are N 65.6104, W 19.5036.

SAMGÖNGUMINJASAFN SKAGAFJARÐAR (SKAGAFJÖRÐUR TRANSPORTATION MUSEUM)

The Skagafjörður Transportation Museum (Storagerdi, tel. 354/455-6161, www.visitskagafjordur.is, 11am-6pm daily mid-June-Aug., 800ISK) is a great place to spend a little time inside if the weather is bad, admiring the large collection of classic cars under one roof. The makes and models

Glaumbær

of automobiles are vast, and there's also some farm machinery on display dating back from the middle of the last century. Car fans will be pleased.

Sports and Recreation
GOLF

The **Hlíðarendi Golf Course** (Rte. 75, tel. 354/453-5075, www.gss.is, greens fees 3,500ISK) is the longest nine-hole golf course in Iceland, located in picturesque country surroundings with mountains in the background and miles of gorgeous landscape. Be sure to call ahead for a tee time.

SWIMMING

The **Sauðárkrókur Swimming Pool** (Skagfirðingabraut, tel. 354/453-5226, 7am-9pm Mon.-Fri., 10am-5pm Sat.-Sun. June-Aug., 7am-8pm Mon.-Fri., 10am-4pm Sat.-Sun. Sept.-May, 600ISK) is a 25-meter outdoor pool with hot tubs, a sauna, and sun beds.

Accommodations

Hótel Mikligarður (Skagfirðingabraut 24, tel. 354/453-6330, www.arctichotels.is, rooms from 22,000ISK) offers 65 small rooms with private bathrooms, and not much else. There

aren't a lot of amenities, but the location is convenient and it makes for an adequate short stay. Free Wi-Fi is available, and breakfast included.

Mikligarður Guesthouse (Kirkjutorg 3, tel. 354/453-6880, www.arctichotels.is, rooms from 20,000ISK) does not get points for style—the decor is dated and the rooms are small and a tad depressing—but the rooms are clean and the staff is accommodating. Guests have access to shared bathroom facilities, free Wi-Fi, free parking, and a tasty breakfast included in the room price.

Hótel Tindastóll (Lindargata 3, tel. 354/453-5002, www.arctichotels.is, rooms from 25,000ISK) occupies two buildings next to one another. The first, a green house with a traditional look, has the distinction of being the oldest hotel in Iceland. It opened in 1884 and has undergone a number of renovations. The rooms are cozy, tastefully decorated, and have the feeling of home. In 2012, the second building opened, and rooms are spacious, bright, and modern with flat-screen TVs, free Wi-Fi, and private bathrooms. Breakfast is included.

Food

Hard Wok Café (Aðalgata 8, tel.

354/453-5355, 11:30am-9:30pm daily, entrées from 1,800ISK) is an interesting Asian/pizza fusion restaurant that seems out of place in a small town in Iceland, but it works. The food is surprising, with choices including fish-and-chips, stir-fry dishes, hamburgers, pizza, and Asian-inspired sandwiches. The restaurant opened its doors in 2011 and is a favorite among locals.

Ólafshús (Aðalgata 15, tel. 354/453-6454, 11am-10:30pm daily, entrées from 2,800ISK) offers the most elegant dining experience in town. The bright blue exterior looks cool and inviting, and the interior doesn't disappoint. The feel is rustic and homey. The menu mixes fresh and local ingredients with flavors you may not expect. For instance, the pan-fried catfish with scallops, leeks, and sweet peppers is surprisingly delicious, and the lamb filet with mushrooms and berry puree is splendid. Other options on the menu range from barbecue ribs to pizza and pasta dishes. There's something for everyone, and the prices won't break the bank.

Getting There and Around

By car, take Route 75 from the Ring Road. Sauðárkrókur is 25 kilometers north of Varmahlíð.

The Strætó 57 bus (tel. 354/540-2700, www.straeto.is) has daily departures from Akureyri. The trip takes a little over an hour and costs 2,000ISK.

If you're interested in flying, Eagle Air (www.eagleair.is) flies from the Reykjavík Domestic Airport a couple of times a week, which is about a 40-minute flight that costs 26,000ISK each way.

DRANGEY

Drangey is a small, rocky island, dotted with moss and grass, in the middle of Skagafjörður. It juts almost 200 meters out of the sea. The cliffs are steep. The island is home to pure natural beauty and thriving birdlife. In fact, Drangey is a favorite nesting spot for puffins and guillemots, along with razor-billed auks, ravens, gyrfalcons, and other seabirds.

Other than the secluded beauty and bird-life, Drangey is known for its inclusion in several sagas. Grettir Ásmundarson was said to have lived on the island for nearly three years with his brother Illugi. Grettir swam to Reykir (a farm) from Drangey to get equipment to make a fire, and his journey was pretty daring because the water temperature was so cold. However, in the year 1031, Grettir, his brother, and a slave were killed in his hut on the island.

During the summer months you can reach the island by boat from Reykir. Drangey Excursions (tel. 354/821-0090, www.drangey. net) operates daily boat trips (11am June-mid-Aug., 9,800ISK pp). The excursion takes about four hours, and it's a wonderful way to spend the day. Be sure to check the schedule, as it may change due to weather. It is not necessary to book in advance.

Tröllaskagi

Tröllaskagi (Troll Peninsula), which lies between the fjords Skagafjörður and Eyjafjorður, has a gorgeous mountainous landscape, with some mountains reaching over 1,400 meters above sea level. Several deep valleys throughout the peninsula were created by glaciers and rivers. Tröllaskagi offers opportunities for outdoor activities, including hiking and whale-watching.

DALVÍK

Dalvík is a small fishing town perhaps best known to tourists as the gateway to Grímsey and Hrísey islands, as the ferry departs from the Dalvík harbor. But it's also a great spot for hikers up for the challenge of navigating the hilly and mountainous landscape around the town. Every year in late June or early July, there is a "hiking week" in Dalvík, where groups get together and hike with a guide.

Sights
FRIÐLAND FUGLANNA (BIRDLAND EXHIBITION)

Just outside Dalvík is the Birdland Exhibition (Húsabakki, tel. 354/466-1551, www.birdland.is, noon-5pm daily June-Aug., open by request rest of year, 800ISK) is a charming museum that is a great place to take children. The family-friendly spot allows children to conduct experiments, learn about bird species, and check out an artistic bird egg display. It's a cute little museum, but not a must-see unless you're a real bird enthusiast. It's just a few kilometers south of downtown Dalvík.

SVARFAÐARDALUR NATURE RESERVE

The Svarfaðardalur Nature Reserve, in a valley just west of town, is about eight square kilometers of wetlands on the banks of the Svarfaðardalsá. The unspoiled environment is a perfect breeding ground for a number of bird species, including great northern divers and harlequin ducks. Be sure to watch where you walk to avoid nests. Wear rubber boots in wet weather.

BYGGÐASAFNIÐ DALVÍK (HERITAGE MUSEUM OF DALVÍK)

The Heritage Museum of Dalvík (Hvoli við Karlsrauðatorg, tel. 354/460-4928, www. dalvikurbyggd.is, 11am-6pm daily June-Aug., 2pm-5pm Sat. Sept.-May, 700ISK) has an extensive collection of photographs and objects, including tools and home furnishings, that relate to the life and work of residents in Dalvík over the years. A natural history collection contains taxidermy of Icelandic mammals and birds, along with eggs, rocks, shells, and grass/moss. Also on display are exhibits relating to renowned individuals that hail from the area, ranging from politicians to artists. The collection is vast and a bit quirky.

Sports and Recreation
CAMPING

The Dalvík Campground (Sundlaug Dalvíkur, tel. 354/460-4940, 1,200ISK) is close to the town's swimming pool. The facility is pretty basic with an adequate cooking area and warm showers. The campground, which accommodates tents and RVs (with hookups), is open June-August. The campground also has a nice playground for children nearby, a football pitch, and a basketball court, and the Dalvík Swimming Pool is only a few feet away.

Dalvík

GOLF

Just seven kilometers outside Dalvík is the Arnarholt Golf Course (Arnarholt Svarfaðardal, tel. 354/466-1204, year-round, greens fees 5,000ISK), which is a nine-hole course said to have been built above where 9th-century settlers have been buried. If that doesn't spook you, the course is well maintained, and carts, clubs, and equipment are available to rent. Be sure to call ahead for a tee time. An on-site restaurant is open 1pm-9pm daily.

HIKING

Dalvík is quite hilly, and locals love to hike. Every summer (late June/early July) locals and tourists gather for a "hiking week," which features nine different guided hikes over nine days on which hikers explore the mountains along Tröllaskagi. Hikes range 2-10 hours and vary in difficulty from leisurely walks along the Dalvík harbor to steep mountain climbing. Shorter hikes cost 1,500ISK and longer hikes are 3,000ISK. For more information, visit www.dalvikurbyggd.is/gonguvika.

SWIMMING

The Dalvík Swimming Pool (Svarfaðarbraut 34, tel. 354/466-3233, 7am-8pm Mon.-Fri., 9am-5pm Sat.-Sun., 550ISK) is close to the campsite, so expect a crowd in the summer months. The pool facility has an outdoor pool, hot tubs, a children's pool, water slide, sauna, and gym.

WHALE-WATCHING

Arctic Sea Tours (tel. 354/771-7600, www.arcticseatours.is) operates a three-hour whale-watching tour where you have a 98 percent chance to see whales or dolphins, according to the company. You might get to see white-beaked dolphins, minke whales, harbor porpoises, and, if you're lucky, a humpback whale and the enormous blue whale. At the end of the tour, you will have an opportunity to do some fishing, and the fresh catches (most likely cod) will be grilled back on land for all to enjoy. The tours leave from Dalvík harbor year-round and cost 9,000ISK per person.

Accommodations

Fosshotel Dalvík (Skiðabraut 18, tel. 354/466-3395, www.fosshotel.is, rooms from 16,000ISK) is your standard chain hotel in Iceland. The 30 clean and average-sized rooms have standard beds, private bathrooms, and free Wi-Fi. The rooms have a bit of a 1980s feel to them with red carpeting and gold accents. An on-site restaurant serves breakfast (included in the price of the room), and guests have access to free parking.

Ytri-Vík Lodge (Árskógsströnd, tel. 354/466-1982, www.sporttours.is, cottages from 20,000ISK) offers cottages that range from accommodations for two people up to a three-story house for a large group. The cottages are made from wood and have fully equipped kitchens, roomy sleeping spaces, and all the comforts of home. The cottages all have decks, which have glorious views of the sea with looming mountains in the background. It's a gorgeous scene to enjoy while sipping your morning coffee on the deck.

Food

Þula Café-Bistro (Goðabraut, tel. 354/897-9748, 11am-6pm Mon.-Fri., noon-5pm Sat.-Sun., entrées from 1,500ISK) is a lovely café housed in the Berg Menningarhus Cultural Center. The food is New Nordic cuisine at its best, with light and healthy meals ranging from salads to fish dishes. The food is inventive and incorporates the freshest, most local ingredients. They serve a lunch buffet as well as cakes, coffee, and pastries.

Gregor's Pub (Goðabraut 3, tel. 354/847-8846, noon-1:30am Mon.-Thurs.., 9pm-3am Fri.-Sat., 6pm-11pm Sun., entrées from 1,500ISK) offers a great casual dining experience ranging from soup to tender lamb filets. The menu also includes hamburgers, sandwiches, and pizza. At night the place transforms into a local bar where the locals gather to grab a pint and catch up.

Information and Services

The tourist information center is based inside the Berg Menningarhus Cultural Center (Goðabraut, tel. 354/846-4908, info@dalvikurbyggd.is, 9am-6pm Mon.-Fri., 1pm-5pm Sat.) and offers Internet access, pamphlets about the region, maps, and information about local sights.

Getting There and Around

By car, Dalvík is 34 kilometers southeast of Siglufjörður on Route 82; 18 kilometers south of Ólafsfjörður on Route 82; and 42 kilometers south of Akureyri, also on Route 82.

The Strætó 78 bus (tel. 354/540-2700, www.straeto.is) travels to and from Ólafsfjörður (400ISK), about 15 minutes away; Akureyri (1,200ISK), about 35 minutes away; and Siglufjörður (1,200ISK), also about 35 minutes away.

Most notably, the ferry Sæfari (www.saefari.is) provides daily trips from Dalvík to the islands of Grímsey (about 3.5 hours away) and Hrísey (a short 30 minutes away). Check the website for the latest timetable, as it tends to change.

HRÍSEY

Hrísey was established as a herring station and today is a major tourist draw for visitors exploring the north. Known as the "pearl of Eyjafjörður," the island, which is 35 kilometers north of Akureyri, has a lot of appeal for bird-watching enthusiasts. Hrísey is 7.5 kilometers long and 2.4 kilometers wide, and about 200 people call it home. Its population soars during the summer months when ferries full of tourists come to shore.

The attractions are minimal, but tractor rides on a hay wagon are quite popular, and there's a small exhibition on shark hunting. The tractor rides are about 40 minutes long and take visitors around the island. The rides can be arranged by calling 354/695-0077 and cost 1,000ISK. Jörundur Hus (The House of Shark-Jörundur) (Norðurvegur 3, 354/695-0077, www.hrisey.net, 1pm-5pm daily

June-Aug.) is a small museum that houses objects related to shark hunting. The house was owned and built by Jörundur Jónsson, called Shark-Jörundur, in 1885, using timber from Norwegian ships that had run ashore on Hrísey. In 1917 the house was moved down the hill to its current site, but a statue of Jörundur is based where the house was originally built.

The main reason tourists come to Hrísey is for the nature, and it's wise to budget one full day for the island.

Sports and Recreation
BIRD-WATCHING

About 40 bird species nest in Hrísey, and its populations thrive because hunting and egg collection are strictly prohibited and there are no predators on the island (such as mice, minks, or foxes). Hrísey is known for having the densest population of ptarmigans in Iceland during the nesting season.

CAMPING

The Hrísey Campground (tel. 354/461-2255, June-Aug., 1,200ISK) is small with adequate facilities. It's conveniently located next to the swimming pool. The campsite, which is in an open field, has showers, hot and cold water, and restrooms. The location in the center of town and close to the sea is lovely, but it can get quite chilly. Be sure to have appropriate gear for cold temperatures.

Accommodations and Food

Options on the island are limited—very limited. Many visitors opt to spend the day at Hrísey and sleep in Akureyri or Dalvík. If you would like to spend the night on Hrísey, Brekka Guesthouse (Brekkugata 5, tel. 354/466-1751, www.brekkahrisey.is, 20,000ISK) is the only game in town. The small guesthouse, situated in a white and yellow building, offers no-frills accommodations in double rooms. Some rooms have pallet headboards and wood furnishings, and all feature white linens and shared bathroom facilities. The in-house restaurant, Brekka

Restaurant (Brekkugata 5, tel. 354/466-1751, 2,000ISK), offers everything from hamburgers and sandwiches to fish and lamb entrées. The restaurant is open daily mid-May to mid-September, and by request the remainder of the year.

Information and Services
The tourist information office (Norðurvegur 3, tel. 354/695-0077, hrisey@hrisey.net) is open daily June-August, and you can book tours, buy tickets for the ferry, and get maps and information about the island.

Getting There and Around
There are two ways to get to the island. The first is the ferry from Dalvík, Sæfari (tel. 354/461-3600, www.landflutningar.is), which sails year-round. A round-trip fare costs 2,460ISK. The second is the ferry Sævar (tel. 354/695-5544, www.hrisey.net), which sails between the island and the nearby village of Árskógssandur, just a few kilometers east of Dalvík. Sævar sails year-round, and a round-trip fare costs 3,000ISK. Both ferry trips are less than 30 minutes and are subject to weather conditions. Be sure to call ahead for current departure times, as they tend to change often due to the weather.

ÓLAFSFJÖRÐUR
Between Dalvík and Siglufjörður is Ólafsfjörður, a small sleepy fishing village of fewer than 900 residents nestled under towering mountains and next to an active harbor. Ólafsfjörður, however, comes alive during the summer months because tourists tend to pass through the town or stop to gas up before continuing onto Siglufjörður or Dalvík.

Accommodations and Food
Hótel Brimnes (Bylgjubyggð 2, tel. 354/466-2400, www.brimnes.is, cabins from 26,000ISK, doubles in guesthouse start at 18,000ISK) is the only hotel in Ólafsfjörður, and it's truly a lovely place to stay. The facility includes 11 rooms in a guesthouse and

eight self-contained Finnish-style cabins. The cabins are wood-paneled and comfortable with private bathrooms, a cooking area, and cozy sleeping quarters. Also, each cabin has a hot tub on the patio area that's great to enjoy in any season. Fresh linens and towels are included free of charge in the cabins; however, breakfast and laundry services come with an extra fee. The hotel rooms are much more modern, with bright white walls, neutral bedding, and pops of color in pillows and design accents. The surroundings are secluded, with mountains as your closest neighbors. The cabins and hotel have beautiful mountainous views. As for dining, Brimnes's restaurant (lunch noon-2pm, dinner 5pm-10pm daily, entrées from 2,500ISK) offers classic Icelandic staples, including fresh fish, lamb, beef, and chicken options. The food is not very inventive, but it's hearty and tasty. Breakfast is included in the rate of hotel rooms, but not cabins.

Getting There and Around
Getting to Ólafsfjörður is pretty straightforward, as Route 82 connects with the town from the west and exits on the east as the central road that leads to Dalvík. From the north, Route 76 heads toward Siglufjörður, which is very close due to the tunnel. Be sure to check the weather forecast before heading out, as the winds and snow can be punishing in the winter. Ólafsfjörður is 17 kilometers southeast of Siglufjörður and 18 kilometers south of Dalvík.

The Strætó 78 bus (tel. 354/540-2700, www.straeto.is) goes from Akureyri to Ólafsfjörður, takes about an hour, and costs 2,000ISK. The same bus goes between Ólafsfjörður and Siglufjörður in about 20 minutes and costs 400ISK.

SIGLUFJÖRÐUR
Just a one-hour drive from Akureyri, secluded Siglufjörður is the northernmost town in all of Iceland. It's easy to fall in love with this beautiful harbor town.

Siglufjörður's marina is home to much of the activity in the small town, with bustling restaurants and a few town-specific museums focusing on the herring industry and local music scene. For much of the year, the town of less than 2,000 is quiet, as it endures a sometimes-punishing winter with wind that feels like it's cutting right through you. That said, skiers are attracted to the region, and there are a couple of trails to enjoy. In the summer, however, the town comes alive with exhibitions, concerts, and packed coffeehouses and restaurants.

Sights

SÍLDARMINJASAFN ÍSLANDS (HERRING ERA MUSEUM)

The Herring Era Museum (Snorragata 10, tel. 354/467-1604, www.sild.is, 10am-6pm daily June-Aug., 1pm-5pm daily May and Sept., by appointment rest of the year, 1,400ISK) is one of the most well done museums in Iceland. Yes, it's educational and it's about fish, but it's anything but boring. The main exhibition is based in a large red building named Róaldsbrakki, which is a former Norwegian salting station that was built in 1907. Inside await interactive exhibits of photographs and film clips showing how fish was processed and salted, which was the source of the town's livelihood for generations. There's a boat inside, along with a lot of fishing gear and equipment. It's clear that great care went into creating this museum. If you're in town, this is definitely worth a visit.

Buying a ticket for this museum also grants you entry into the Folk Music Center; the Icelandic Poetry Center (Túngötu 5, tel. 354/865-6543, noon-4pm daily), which houses numerous books of poetry and hosts events in Icelandic; and the Old Slipway (Snorragata 10, tel. 354/467-1604, 10am-6pm daily), a boat yard that includes an exhibition on the 200-year history of boat building in the town. There are displays of wood-working hand tools and of machinery—some nearly 100 years old.

ÞJÓÐLAGASETRIÐ SIGLUFJÖRÐUR (FOLK MUSIC CENTER)

The Folk Music Center (Norðurgata 1, tel. 354/467-2300, www.folkmusik.is, noon-6pm daily June-Aug., by request rest of year, 800ISK) is a charming two-floor museum set in what once was the private home of folklorist Reverend Bjarni Þorsteinsson (1861-1938). The museum showcases Bjarni's collection of classic Icelandic folk songs, along with interesting instruments, photographs, and film clips. You have the opportunity to listen to music that includes genres like hymns, the traditional chanting style called *rímur*, and nursery rhymes.

Sports and Recreation

CAMPING

The Siglufjörður Campground (Gránugötu 24, tel. 354/460-5600, mid-May-mid-Sept., 1,200ISK) is near the center of town, near the harbor with beautiful mountain views. It has a cooking area and hot showers. The campsite is located in an open field with little shelter and welcomes tent campers as well as RVs. The main museums and restaurants are all within walking distance.

SKIING

Iceland is not known for its skiing opportunities, but there are a few ski areas in the north, with the Siglufjörður Skiing Center (Tjarnargata 14, tel. 354/467-2120, 10am-4pm Mon. and Thurs.-Sun., 3pm-7pm Tues.-Wed. in winter, lift ticket 1,500ISK) being the best. Three lifts carry skiers up to the slopes, with the highest lift measuring 530 meters in length with a vertical rise of about 180 meters. The top of the lift is over 650 meters. It's obvious to say the scenery is breathtaking, but it needs to be said. All the equipment you need is available to rent, and there are instructors on-site. Snowboarding and cross-country skiing are also possible. It's typically open November-April, but that can change due to weather. Be sure to call ahead.

SWIMMING

The Siglufjörður Swimming Pool (Hvanneyrarbraut 52, tel. 354/467-1352, 7am-8pm Mon.-Fri., 10am-5pm Sat.-Sun, 600ISK) is a delightful place to spend a couple of hours when the weather is frightful. You will find a lot of locals and their children enjoying the pool. The facility includes a 10-by-25-meter indoor pool and a large hot tub outside.

Accommodations

★ Siglunes Guesthouse (Laekjargata 10, tel. 354/467-1222, www.hotelsiglunes.is, rooms from 16,000ISK) is hands down the hippest place to stay in the north, and it attracts a lot of young travelers. The interior is darling, with vintage wood furniture and cool rugs, art, and wallpaper. Ten rooms have private bathrooms. It's a mixture of vintage and retro furniture that works well. There's an old-fashioned piano and fireplace in the lobby area, which is a great place to relax after a day of exploring the sights. Rooms are larger than average, with comfy beds and an antique flavor to the decor. The in-house restaurant and bar is quite popular, and breakfast is included in the room price. While the guesthouse is hip, you won't find it noisy with a lot of partying.

Hvanneyri Guesthouse (Aðalgata 10, tel. 354/467-1850, www.hvanneyri.com, rooms from 20,000ISK) is a 23-room guesthouse with options ranging from singles to family rooms. It feels a bit like grandma's house, with velour bedding and old-fashioned design accents, but rooms are cozy and clean, and the staff is accommodating. Some rooms have private bathrooms. This is the mature alternative to the Siglunes Guesthouse.

Food

★ Restaurant Hannes Boy (Gránugata 23, tel. 354/461-7730, 5pm-10pm daily, entrées from 3,900ISK) cannot be missed. Literally. It's a bright yellow structure on the harbor that doesn't give much of a hint to what's inside. The interior is chic with roomy wood tables, antique furnishings, and a menu that rivals restaurants in much larger cities. The small courses, using fresh ingredients including mackerel, herring, and cod, are a great way to start the meal, and the main courses are hard to choose from as they sound so delicious. The pan-fried salted cod with mashed potatoes and fresh tomatoes is exquisite.

Kaffi Rauðka (Gránugata 19, tel. 354/467-1550, www.raudka.is, 11am-10pm daily, snacks from 600ISK) is hands down the best place to hang out in the summer. The outdoor seating area is filled with tourists and locals sipping coffee drinks or cocktails or enjoying light meals. Inside, the two levels are decorated in a rustic theme with lots of wood and loads of comfort. The bright red building is hard to miss, and it's owned and operated by the same folks who own Hannes Boy next door.

Harbor House Café (Gránugata 5b, tel. 354/659-1394, www.harborhouse.is, 10am-1am Mon.-Thurs., 10am-3am Fri.-Sat., 10am-1am Sun., entrées from 1,400ISK) is a small harborside café that sells light meals and coffee for lunch and delectable seafood dishes for dinner. The seafood soup with mussels, shrimp, and lobster is memorable. The café is small, but cozy, and the staff is very friendly. You will see a local or two with their laptop and a cup of coffee or tourists curling up with a book to get in out of the rain.

Torgið (Aðalgata 32, tel. 354/467-2323, 11am-7pm daily, entrées from 1,600ISK) is the best family-friendly option as well as the best place to grab a quick bite to eat before heading out to explore the surroundings. Tourist-friendly fare on the menu includes hamburgers, sandwiches, and pizza, as well as some seafood options.

Getting There and Around

Getting to Siglufjörður is a trying exercise at times. By car, a tunnel links Siglufjörður, Olafsfjörður, and Dalvík. Driving through the one-lane two-way tunnel can be heart-stopping, with cars turning into pockets on the side to let the driver going the opposite way pass by. Route 82 connects to Route 76 to Siglufjörður from Akureyri if the weather is cooperating. Akureyri is 76 kilometers southeast of Siglufjörður.

Ólafsfjörður is 17 kilometers southeast of Siglufjörður on Route 76.

The Strætó 78 bus (tel. 354/540-2700, www.straeto.is) goes between Ólafsfjörður and Siglufjörður, takes about 20 minutes, and costs 400ISK.

Grímsey

About 40 kilometers off the coast of Iceland, Grímsey is a windswept and secluded island, about five square kilometers in area, that is as striking in beauty as it is difficult to reach.

Just 100 people reside in Grímsey, and those who remain come from hardy stock, battling arctic temperatures and isolation. Fishers brave the elements, including frost and storms and waves that could reach 15 meters high. It's not an easy life.

Tourists come to explore the tiny island, bird-watch, and experience 24 hours of daylight in the height of the summer. Night does not reach Grímsey until late July, when the sun sets around midnight, only to rise a short time later. The island can be explored in one day.

SIGHTS
Grímseyjarkirkja (Grímsey Church)

Grímseyjarkirkja was built in 1867 from driftwood that washed ashore, then renovated and enlarged in 1932. The exterior is white with a reddish brown roof. The highlight of the church for many tourists is the altar painting, a copy of a Leonardo Da Vinci painting, that was done by a local artist in 1878.

The history of the church is interesting, as one of Iceland's early Catholic bishops, Jón Ögmundsson, consecrated a church on Grímsey in the 11th century, dedicated to St. Olaf, the patron saint of Norway. At the time, it was said that there should always be two priests at the church who should lead a

the cliffs of Grímsey

Crossing the Arctic Circle

Want to witness the **midnight sun**? That's when the sun remains above the horizon for a full 24 hours during the summer solstice on June 21. There's only one place you can experience this phenomenon in Iceland: where the Arctic Circle crosses the country's northernmost point, on Grímsey. (If you'd prefer nearly 24 hours of darkness, there's always **polar night**, on December 21.)

A small **symbolic bridge** to cross the Arctic Circle can be found at 66°33'N, north of the Grímsey's airport terminal, next to Guesthouse Básar. Beside the bridge is a pole showing the distance to many well-known cities in the world, including London and New York.

Tourists who make the pilgrimage can buy evidence of the trip in the form of a **diploma** in the local gift store **Gallerí Sól** (Sólberg 611, tel. 354/467-3190, gullsol@visir.is), which is open Monday, Wednesday, and Friday during the summer months (June-Aug.). You can also reserve your diploma at Gallerí Sól by phone or email. Diplomas cost 1,000ISK. Those who come to Grímsey on a tour receive a diploma free of charge.

daily mass (two a day on special occasions). However, today, a vicar from the mainland visits Grímsey to serve in the church approximately four times a year.

The Cliffs

The cliffs on the east side of the island are the highest, towering from 60 to 100 meters. In the old days, the basalt cliffs served as a major source of food as locals collected eggs along the rifts. It was a tenuous task; a rope would be lowered 60 meters down from the edge of the cliff while the individual collected eggs. There was a great risk that the rope would break or a large rock could break off, hitting and killing the climber. Today, the egg collection practice is safer and more modern, but the cliffs are a reminder of the past and the importance they served to feed the island. They're also interesting formations and serve as a great backdrop when photographing birds.

The Lighthouse

Bright yellow and close to the cliff's edge, Grímsey's lighthouse is one of the most significant buildings on the island. It was built in 1937 and is situated on the southeast corner of the island. It was originally operated manually with a gas lamp that had to be turned on and off by hand. Today, the lighthouse is automatic and still plays an important role in directing boat traffic along the

coast. Although the lighthouse is closed to the public, it's a popular destination to take a photo, capturing birdlife and the cliffs in the background.

EVENTS
Grímsey Day

Grímsey Day is an annual festival that takes place at the beginning of June each year over three days. It focuses on old traditions from Grímsey, like collecting eggs from the cliffs, as well as enjoying seasonal local food, local music, and art. Visit www.grimsey.is for information on the schedule of events.

SPORTS AND RECREATION
Bird-Watching

Grímsey is one of the best spots in North Iceland for bird-watchers interested in seabirds. The high season for birding is from April, when birds migrate to the island to nest, to August, when birds depart the island for warmer weather. Bird-watchers will have a chance to see arctic terns, black-legged kittiwakes, northern fulmars, razorbills, common guillemots, black guillemots, and murres. You can also see white wagtails, northern wheatears, and snow buntings.

The main attractions, however, are the adorable Atlantic puffins, as Grímsey is home to one of the largest colonies in Iceland. The birds, with their bright beaks and big personalities, are a delight to watch nesting and gliding along the cliffs. Please be aware of eggs and be careful not to disturb nesting areas.

Swimming

The Grímsey Island Thermal Pool (tel. 354/461-3155, 550ISK) is situated near the airport and is a quiet spot to take a dip. You likely won't find crowds here, and the hours change often. For current hours you should inquire at the tourist information office or ask an employee of your guesthouse.

ACCOMMODATIONS

Guesthouse Básar (tel. 354/467-3103, www. gistiheimilibasar.is, rooms from 16,000ISK), next to the airport, is an eight-room guesthouse just steps from the Arctic Circle. Literally. Rooms are simple and neat, and amenities include a common TV lounge and a fully-equipped kitchen. Breakfast is available for an added fee of 1,500ISK, and lunch and dinner can be requested as well. The guesthouse is open year-round.

Guesthouse Gullsól (Sólbergi, 354/467-3190, www.grimsey.is, rooms from 10,000ISK) offers four single rooms and two doubles in a charming wood house, one of the oldest structures on the island. Rooms are small, but clean and neat, and it's the closest guesthouse to the main area. Guests share bathroom facilities and have access to a fully equipped kitchen to prepare meals. It's open year-round.

FOOD

Restaurant Krian (Hafnargata 3, tel. 354/467-3112, www.grimsey.is, noon-midnight daily summer, entrées from 2,200ISK) is only open during the summer, but it will open to accommodate large groups on request. The menu focuses on local fare, chock-full of fresh fish and meat from seabirds, like pan-fried puffin. Standard options include sandwiches and hamburgers.

INFORMATION AND SERVICES

In 2009, the towns of Grímsey, Hrísey, and Akureyri voted to become a municipality overseen by Akureyri. After the financial crash of 2008, it made sense to form this relationship. As such, tourist information and ferry information can be found at the tourist information center at Hof concert hall by the harbor in Akureyri (tel. 354/460-1199, www.visitakureyri.is).

an Atlantic puffin colony on the cliffs of Grímsey

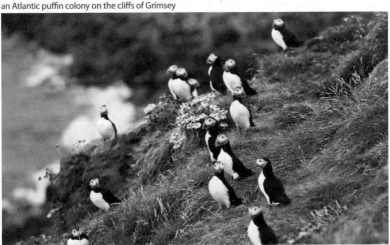

Safety

Weather can be your greatest enemy on the island, with unexpected wind gusts and horizontal rain. All children under the age of 14 must wear a lifejacket when in the harbor area, whether they are playing, walking, or about to board a ferry. It is island law. The ferry staff provides lifejackets at the harbor.

GETTING THERE AND AROUND
Sea

By sea, Sæfari (tel. 354/458-8970, www.land-flutningar.is) runs a ferry back and forth between Dalvík and Grímsey three days a week year-round. It takes about three hours each way, and the ferry can take 108 people. Book in advance in the summer months; tickets can be purchased at the tourist information office at Hof concert hall in Akureyri (tel. 354/450-1050, info@visitakureyri.is). A round-trip fare is about 9,960ISK. The departure times from Dalvík are Monday, Wednesday, and Friday at 9am; the ferry returns from Grímsey at 4pm. Check the website for up-to-date departure information. Schedules can vary due to weather.

Air

By air, the flight from Akureyri to Grímsey is one of the most beautiful 30-minute flights you will ever take. The jaw-dropping views of the landscape make the trip feel a tad too short. The landing is not for the faint of heart, as the small plane has to land on a small strip of grass on an island that looks like a rock in the middle of the ocean. During the summer (June-August), Air Iceland (www.airiceland.is) provides daily flights to Grímsey from Akureyri for 21,000ISK round-trip. For current departure timetables and precise ticket prices, check Air Iceland's website. There are four flights a week from September to May.

Akureyri

Akureyri is commonly referred to as Iceland's "second city," a moniker many of the town's 18,000 residents find amusing given its size. Akureyri has its own personality, and it looks and feels quite different from Reykjavík. Some might say Akureyri feels more low-key, more relaxed than the capital city. There are gorgeous gardens to explore around town, charming museums, paddleboats littering the fjord in the summer months, and a booming art

a view of Akureyri

their rental car to places like Húsavík and Mývatn.

Akureyri has gotten more traffic in recent years because it's becoming a popular stop for cruise ships, and word of mouth is spreading about what a charming and beautiful town this is. It's also surprisingly easy to get to. If you have the time, spend at least a couple of days here.

SIGHTS

★ Lystigarður Akureyrar (Akureyri Botanical Gardens)

The **Akureyri Botanical Gardens** (Eyrarlandsholt, tel. 354/462-7487, www.lystigardur.akureyri.is, 8am-10pm Mon.-Fri., 9am-10pm Sat.-Sun. June-Sept., free) are gorgeous, well-kept gardens, and it's hard to find a better place in the city to take a stroll. Known as one of the northernmost botanical gardens in the world, the public park was opened in 1912, and flowers and plants made their debut in the park in 1957. There are thousands of types of native and international flora in garden beds and the nursery. The gardens are considered a treasure by locals, and they're thrilled to share the beauty and tranquility with tourists. While roaming the gardens during the summer, you will see arctic poppy flowers, northern marsh violets, bilberry bushes, frog orchids, and hundreds of other species. The garden caretakers are always introducing new species to keep the collection fresh and eclectic. The gardens also have walking paths, bridges, and a fountain.

Akureyrarkirkja (Akureyri Church)

The **Akureyrarkirkja** (Eyrarlandsvegur, tel. 354/462-7700, www.akureyrarkirkja.is, 10am-4pm Mon.-Sat., 4pm-7pm Sun. June 15-Aug. 15, free) is in the center of the city, above the city on a hill. The steep steps up to the church from the middle of the city make for a great photo opportunity, with the church towering above. The church was designed by state architect Guðjón Samúelsson, who delivered a

Akureyri

scene. Akureyri has a tighter community than Reykjavík, and there is a lot support for local artists. Akureyri also boasts delicious restaurants and first-rate hotels, and its concert hall, Hof, is a must-see for architecture enthusiasts. Akureyri is a perfect place to base yourself while exploring Eyjafjörður, Iceland's longest fjord (60 kilometers).

Many tourists choose Akureyri as their home base when exploring the north, opting to spend nights in the town while booking day tours or putting some miles on

the Akureyri Botanical Gardens

design that is unique and Icelandic with stark white walls, wood pews, and a lot of windows. While the outside is beautiful, the interior is exquisite, complete with a 3,200-pipe organ and a large central window that once belonged to the Coventry Cathedral in England. The church, which was completed in 1940, is open to the public in the summer. The Sunday service is at 11am year-round, and tourists are more than welcome to join. Please note that the church is closed to tourists when there are funerals or other ceremonies.

Nonnahús (Nonni's House)
Nonnahús (Aðalstræti 54, tel. 354/462-3555, www.nonni.is, 10am-5pm daily June 1-Sept. 1, 900ISK) is a museum that was actually the childhood home of Jesuit priest and children's author Jón Sveinsson (1857-1944). The house was built in 1850, and it looks like a nondescript black wooden house from the outside. Inside, however, you get a sense of the life and work of one of Akureyri's most treasured sons. On the ground floor, there is a collection of Jón's books, from about 40 different countries where his books were published. Upstairs, which is a little cramped, you can get a look at his bedroom and some personal artifacts. The house gets its name from Jón's

nickname, Nonni, and it's one of the oldest structures in the town. A little gift shop sells his books in various languages.

Art Museums
Akureyri boasts a thriving art scene that rivals Reykjavík's. Painters, sculptors, and craftspeople occupy numerous private studios. The museums reflect the rich cultural landscape of the town, displaying works from some of the most varied and important artists from the region.

SJÓNLISTAMIÐSTÖÐIN (CENTER FOR VISUAL ARTS)
The Center for Visual Arts (Kaupvangsstræti 12, tel. 354/461-2610, www.listasafn.akureyri.is) comprises three art museums in three separate buildings. The first, the Listasafnið á Akureyri (Akureyri Art Museum) (10am-5pm daily June-Aug., noon-5pm daily May-Sept., free) hosts exhibitions in a variety of media, including landscape and portrait paintings, sculpture, photography, and other visual arts. The exhibitions focus on contemporary art. New exhibitions are revealed every eight weeks or so. The second building is the gallery Ketilhús (Kettle House), which serves as a space for local

Akureyrarkirkja

paintings, sculptures, drawings, models, books, dolls, tools, and toys. Every year there are about 15 new exhibitions on display delighting locals and surprising tourists with art you won't see anywhere else on the island. The museum is 12 kilometers from Akureyri on Route 1.

Friðbjarnarhús (Friðbjörn's House)

Friðbjarnarhús (Aðalstræti 46, tel. 354/863-4531, 1pm-5pm daily June-Sept., 2pm-4pm Sat. Oct.-May, 600ISK, free for children under 15) houses an exhibition of 20th-century toys owned by Akureyri resident Guðbjörg Ringsted. The museum, in an old house built in 1856, is great for kids and kids at heart, with dolls, toy cars, models, and hundreds of other toys on display.

Flugsafn Íslands (Aviation Museum)

The Aviation Museum (Akureyri Airport, tel. 354/461-4400, www.flugsafn.is, 1pm-5pm daily June-Aug., 1pm-5pm Sat. Sept.-May, 1,000ISK) is a small museum located at a hangar at the airport, dedicated to the planes and pilots who have flown the windy skies over Iceland. On display are a flying ambulance and Iceland's first gliders, as well as some relics from World War II, when U.S. and British troops occupied Iceland. There are lots of photographs and some recreated accounts from pilots.

Minjasafnið á Akureyri (Akureyri Museum)

The Akureyri Museum (Aðalstræti 58, tel. 354/462-4162, www.minjasafnid.is, 10am-5pm daily June-mid-Sept., 2pm-4pm Sat. mid-Sept.-May, 1,000ISK) has historical exhibitions including displays that feature nautical maps, 19th-century photography, and artifacts from everyday life in the settlement era. The exhibits also detail the region's geological background as well as saga story references. The museum grounds have a beautiful garden.

concerts and meetings, as well as art- and design-related events. Exhibitions in Kettle House are by invitation only and can include everything from painting exhibitions to performance art. The third building, Deiglan (Melting Pot), across the street from the Akureyri Art Museum, is devoted to young artists, giving them a platform to express and show their work.

SAFNASAFNIÐ (MUSEUM OF ICELANDIC FOLK AND OUTSIDER ART)

For something a little different, the Museum of Icelandic Folk and Outsider Art (Svalbarðsstrond, tel. 354/461-4066, www.folkart.is, 10am-5pm daily May-Aug., 1,000ISK) is one of those quirky museums that doesn't get the attention it deserves. The museum is the only institution on the island that collects and displays folk and outsider art. It houses 5,000 works from local artists, as well as a library and research facility. You will find

Iðnaðarsafnið á Akureyri (Akureyri Museum of Industry)

The **Akureyri Museum of Industry** (Krókeyri, tel. 354/462-3600, www.idnadarsafnid.is, 10am-5pm daily June-mid-Sept., 2pm-4pm Sat. mid-Sept.-May, 500ISK) displays relics from Iceland's industries, such as agriculture, fishing, and construction, throughout the years. Exhibitions include products, machinery, and photos of people hard at work in the region. It's a quaint museum with a passionate curator, but you can skip this if time is an issue.

Mótorhjólasafnið (Motorcycle Museum of Iceland)

The **Motorcycle Museum of Iceland** (Krókeyri 2, tel. 354/866-3500, www.motorhjolasafn.is, 10am-5pm daily June-Aug., 1,000ISK) is a small museum founded in the memory of local biker Heidar Johannsson, who died in 2006 after a motorcycle accident. The museum has about 50 bikes on display, including photographs, objects, and gear related to Iceland's 100-year history with motorbikes.

Jólagarðurinn (Christmas Garden)

If you're a fan of Christmas, do not miss the **Christmas Garden** (tel. 354/463-1433, 10am-9pm daily June-Aug., 2pm-9pm daily Sept.-Dec., 2pm-9pm daily Jan.-May, free), just a 10-minute drive from downtown Akureyri. The bright red house, which resembles a gingerbread house, has an astounding number of Christmas decorations, ranging from traditional to Icelandic-themed wares featuring the Yule Lads (Christmas elves). You can pick up a locally made trinket and buy some Christmas-themed candy or just enjoy the jolly atmosphere. A garden outside offers benches, local art, and a tiny place to buy waffles and coffee. It's a cute space.

The Christmas Garden is about 10 kilometers south of downtown Akureyri on Route 821.

ENTERTAINMENT AND EVENTS
Nightlife

Brugghúsbarinn (Kaupvangsstræti 23, tel. 354/896-6782, www.brugghusbarinn.is, 6pm-1am Sun.-Thurs., 6pm-4am Fri.-Sat.) is a small, hip bar in the city center that focuses on beer produced at the local brewery Kaldi. They serve light and dark beers, including seasonal beers around Christmas, Easter, and Þorrablót (the annual midwinter festival). Cocktails and coffee drinks are also on offer.

Götubarinn (Hafnarstræti 96, tel. 354/462-4747, 5pm-1am Sun.-Thurs., 5pm-4am Fri.-Sat.) is a wildly popular bar that has a great selection of beers and wines. It's situated in the city center in a nondescript green building, but the inside is warm, friendly, and crowded.

Græni Hatturinn (Hafnarstræti 96, tel. 354/461-4646), which means "The Green Hat," is a centrally located bar that features live music and DJs. The crowd tends to be on the younger side, and it can get very loud and very crowded on weekends. The opening hours vary depending on special events, but it's usually open 8pm-3am Friday-Saturday. Check local listings for concerts and events during the week.

Performing Arts

Hof (Strandgata 12, tel. 354/450-1000, www.menningarhus.is) is the striking building by the harbor that is home to Akureyri's big concert performances, including rock concerts, symphonies, and everything in between. Hof, which opened in 2010, also houses the restaurant 1862 Nordic Bistro and the main tourist information office. Even if you're not going to attend a concert, or pick up brochures at the tourist office, architecture buffs will want to visit this building for its unique round concrete design. The interior is amazing, with modern curved wood accents intertwined with metal. It's open 8am-10pm daily, or later when there is a performance.

Hof concert hall

Events

Dedicated to winter extreme sports, AK-Extreme (www.akx.is) is an annual snowboard and music festival held in Akureyri over four days in mid-April.

SPORTS AND RECREATION

Bowling

You won't find many bowling alleys in Iceland, and that's what makes Keilan Akureyri (Hafnarstræti 26, tel. 354/461-1126, www.keilan.is, 11am-11:30pm Mon.-Sat., 11am-10pm Sun.) so special. It has eight lanes, a restaurant serving snacks and light meals, and several arcade games. It has an old-fashioned feel and is a local hangout spot for teenagers. A game costs 900ISK.

Camping

There are two main campsites in town. The first, Thórunnarstræti Camping (Hafnarstræti 49, tel. 354/462-3379, 1,200ISK), is in an ideal location right next to the town's swimming pool and a stone's throw from shops, restaurants, and museums. The facilities are good, with hot showers and a decent

cooking area. The second campsite, Hamrar Camping (Kjarnaskógur, tel. 354/461-2264, 1,200ISK), is a little outside the city center, but it's a larger campsite and slightly less crowded. The facilities are similar, with hot showers and an adequate cooking area. Both campsites are open May-September, and both welcome tent and RV campers (hookups are available).

Fishing

Iceland Fishing Guide (tel. 354/660-1642, www.icelandfishingguide.com, tours 36,000ISK) provides guided fishing tours to lakes and rivers around Akureyri. You'll have a chance at reeling in salmon, trout, and arctic char, among other fish. The tours are suitable for beginners as well as experienced anglers, and you can choose from day tours or longer trips. The licenses needed for the tour are arranged in advance.

Golf

Akureyri Golf Course (Jadar, tel. 354/462-2974, greens fees 5,700ISK) is a wildly popular 18-hole golf course that has the distinction of being the most northerly course in the world. The par-71 course loops around broad ridges and is quite scenic with towering mountains in the background. Club and gear rentals are available on-site. Be sure to call ahead for a tee time. The course also plays host to the Arctic Open, held during the summer solstice.

Hiking

While Akureyri is known as more of an urban playground, similar to Reykjavík, there are some hiking opportunities on the outskirts of town, namely around Eyjafjarðardalur, which is a wide valley surrounding the Eyjafjarðará River. To get information on trails and pick up maps, visit the tourist information center at Hof. Most hikes are moderate.

Ice Skating

Skautahollin (Naustavegur 1, tel. 354/461-2440, 1pm-4pm and 7pm-9pm Fri., 1pm-5pm Sat., 1pm-4pm Sun. Sept.-May, 800ISK) is a delightful skating hall chock-full of local families. If the weather is bad outside, visit the hall, rent a pair of skates, and join the fun! The rink is closed June-August.

Skiing

The Hlíðarfjall ski area (tel. 354/462-2280, www.hlidarfjall.is) is just a few minutes outside town and offers more than a dozen well-kept trails. While Iceland isn't known for its skiing, if you're dying to ski on a glacier, this is your chance. Bear in mind that the trails are 1,000 meters at the highest, so don't be disappointed. A day pass costs just 4,000ISK, and a shuttle bus picks you up at the tourist information office for 1,500ISK round-trip, if you don't have a rental car. Other activities include snowboarding and cross-country skiing. You can rent all the equipment you need at the ski area. The season is November-April. Check the website for hours as they tend to change due to weather.

Swimming

If you're going to visit one swimming pool in North Iceland, the Akureyri Swimming Pool (Þingvallastræti, tel. 354/461-4455, 7am-9pm Mon.-Fri., 8am-6:30pm Sat.-Sun.,

600ISK) should be it. The fantastic facilities include two outdoor pools, children's pools and play areas, water slides, a sauna, and a steam room. Rain or shine, this is a great spot to relax and spend some time.

Tours

Saga Travel (Kaupvangsstræti 4, tel. 354/558-8888, www.sagatravel.is) is an Akureyri-based company that offers day tours from Akureyri and Mývatn, including horse-riding tours and hiking excursions. Day tours start from 34,000ISK.

Another Akureyri-based tour company is Nonni Travel (Brekkugata 5, tel. 354/461-1841, www.nonnitravel.is), which offers day tours in North Iceland, including visiting sites like Goðafoss, Dettifoss, Grímsey, and Lake Mývatn. Tours start at 14,800ISK.

ACCOMMODATIONS
Hotels

Hótel Akureyri (Hafnarstræti 67, tel. 354/462-5600, www.hotelakureyri.is, rooms from 17,000ISK) is a posh boutique hotel close to city center. The exterior looks quaint and old-fashioned, but the inside reveals modern and tastefully decorated rooms with standard beds, private bathrooms, free Wi-Fi, and free parking. For an extra fee, you can request a room with a beautiful ocean view. A standard breakfast buffet is included in the room price.

Hótel Edda Akureyri (Þórunnarstræti, tel. 354/444-4900, www.hoteledda.is, mid-June-mid-Aug., rooms from 16,000ISK) offers 204 rooms during the summer. The rest of the year, the hotel serves as accommodations for university students. For hotel guests, the digs are comfortable, with private bathrooms for 118 of the rooms (the rest have shared facilities), free Wi-Fi, and clean, minimalist decor. The rooms with private bathrooms are large with comfortable beds. The remaining no-frills rooms are small but clean and comfortable. A breakfast buffet is available for 1,750ISK per person.

Hótel Kea (Hafnarstræti 87-89, tel. 354/460-2000, www.keahotels.is, rooms from

34,000ISK) is posh, with modern amenities and first-class service. The 104-room hotel, which is a stone's throw from the Akureyri Church, features an elegant interior. Spacious rooms offer hardwood floors, big, comfortable beds, free Wi-Fi, satellite television, and private bathrooms. Some of the luxury stems from 24-hour room service and same-day dry-cleaning services. The hotel restaurant serves a hearty breakfast that's included in the room price.

Hótel Norðurland (Geislagata 7, tel. 354/462-2600, www.keahotels.is, rooms from 28,000ISK) is a 41-room hotel owned by the same folks as the nearby Hótel Kea. It's a more simple and affordable option, but the location is good, the staff is friendly, and the rooms are clean and adequate. All rooms have private bathrooms, free Wi-Fi, and satellite television. Breakfast is included in the room price.

★ **Icelandair Hótel Akureyri** (Þingvallastræti 23, tel. 354/518-1000, www.icelandairhotels.com, rooms from 24,700ISK) is one of Icelandair Hótels' latest additions, as it opened its doors in July 2011. The 99-room hotel is beautiful, with art and design accents touching every corner of the property. The lobby is rustic and Nordic chic with sheep and reindeer skins adorning gorgeous wood furniture. Rooms range from standard twins to family rooms and suites. The clientele ranges from business travelers in town for a night to families staying a week. The hotel restaurant doesn't disappoint; fresh and local ingredients go beyond traditional lamb and fish dishes. Breakfast is included in the room price.

Apartment Hotels

Hótel Íbúðir (Geislagata 10, tel. 354/892-9838, www.hotelibudir.is, apartments from 23,800ISK) offers 7 self-catering apartments ranging from studios to three bedrooms. Apartments are chic and modern with all the comforts of home. Guests have access to fully-equipped kitchens, comfortable beds and newly-remodeled bathrooms. There are balconies to enjoy the view of the city with mountains in the background.

Ráðhúsið Apartment Hotel (Brekkugata 1b, tel. 354/571-7201, www.radhusid.is, apartments from 26,000ISK) offers four apartments ranging from one-bedroom apartments to a three-bedroom luxury apartment. Apartments are stylish, and have everything you need for a self-catered, beautiful stay. Apartments include solid beds, free Wi-Fi, a balcony with beautiful views and a barbecue grill, and a fully equipped kitchen. Ráðhúsið also offers five double rooms with private bathrooms that start at 16,000ISK.

Guesthouses and Hostels

Akureyri Backpackers (Hafnarstræti 98, tel. 354/578-3700, www.akureyribackpackers.com, private rooms from 18,000ISK) caters to the twentysomething traveler looking for a fun atmosphere and a clean place to stay. Rooms range from privates to dormitory-style accommodations. However, tourists tend to stay here for the facilities and the opportunity to meet fellow travelers. The hostel's bar tends to get packed, its restaurant frequented by young guests. Tourist information services are top-notch; there's a desk for booking tours, buying bus and flight tickets, and renting cars. A common cooking area allows you to prepare your own meals, and laundry facilities are available. Recommended for young travelers.

Guesthouse Akurinn (Brekkugata 27a, tel. 354/461-2500, www.akurinn.is, rooms from 14,000ISK) is a cozy guesthouse within walking distance of city center. Rooms are small but clean, and a common living room is a great spot to relax after a long day exploring the town. Breakfast is included in the room price, and guests also get a 15 percent discount at the nearby restaurant Greifinn. Guests have access to free Wi-Fi and free parking.

Guesthouse Brekkusel (Byggðavegur 97, tel. 354/461-2660, www.brekkusel.is, rooms from 13,900ISK) is a charming, family-run guesthouse that offers bright, minimalist rooms for solo travelers, couples, or families. There are nine rooms, some with private bathrooms. Guests have access to a fully equipped kitchen, free Wi-Fi, and a beautiful common garden where it's nice to drink your morning coffee or read a good book. Breakfast is included.

H104 Guesthouse (Hafnarstræti 104, tel. 354/469-4104, www.h104.is, rooms from 17,900ISK) provides small, tidy rooms in the best part of town. Located on the main street in Akureyri, the guesthouse stands out with "Apotek," which means pharmacy in Icelandic, in big block letters on the exterior of the white building. Inside, there are 19 rooms, five of them with private bathrooms. The guesthouse doesn't get many points for the decor, but it's clean and adequate for a short stay.

FOOD
Fish
Rub 23 (Kaupvangsstræti 6, tel. 354/462-2223, www.rub23.is, 11:30am-10pm Mon.-Fri., 5:30pm-10pm Sat.-Sun., entrées from 4,190ISK) is your best bet if you're looking for fresh and eclectic fish dishes. The restaurant, which also serves scrumptious sushi, specializes in cod, arctic char, blue ling, and salmon with a choice of "rubs," including citrus rosemary, Indian, sweet mango chili, Texas barbecue, and Asian fusion, among others. Meat dishes include lamb, chicken, beef, and minke whale with your choice of rub. Dinner for two, with drinks, can be pricey, but if you want a taste, the lunch menu (available on weekdays) is glorious as well.

Casual
Íslenska Hamborgarafabrikkan (Icelandic Hamburger Factory) (Hafnarstræti 87-89, tel. 354/460-2000, www.fabrikkan. is,11am-10pm daily, entrées from 1,600ISK) is the best spot to grab a hamburger in Akureyri. The family-friendly joint offers 120-gram hamburgers on a square bun, ranging from traditional beef burgers to more exotic whale-meat burgers. There's something for every meat eater here. The "surf and turf burger" is glorious, with a beef patty, tiger prawns, Japanese seaweed, cheese, red onions, lettuce, tomatoes, and a garlic-cheese sauce. Other combinations include a barbecue burger, a lamb burger, and a Mexican-inspired salsa burger.

Bautinn (Hafnarstræti 92, tel. 354/462-1818, www.bautinn.is, 11:30am-10:30pm daily, entrées from 1,600ISK) is a typical casual eatery with plenty of tourist-friendly fare. You will find hamburgers, pasta, pizza, sandwiches, and soup on the menu, as well as more traditional Icelandic cuisine such as lamb, horse, whale, and beef steaks and an array of fish dishes. This is a popular place for locals as well as large tourist groups. The service is friendly and accommodating.

Nætursalan (Strandgata 6, tel. 354/462-4020, 8am-11:30pm Mon.-Thurs., 10am-5am Fri.-Sat., and 11am-10pm Sun., entrées from 1,000ISK) attracts locals and tourists with its no-frills fast food. Stop by here for some decent fried chicken, sandwiches, and hamburgers. Because of its late hours, the place attracts Akureyri's bar/club crowd on weekends, and it's usually packed with teenagers during the day in the summer months.

Greifinn Restaurant (Gléragata 20, tel. 354/460-1600, www.greifinn.is, 11:30am-11:30pm daily, entrées from 1,400ISK) feels like the Icelandic version of TGI Friday's. There are mozzarella sticks, hamburgers, nachos, soups, sandwiches, burritos, and even pizza. It's casual and quick with no surprises.

Strikið (Skipagata 14, tel. 354/462-7100, www.strikid.is, 11:30am-10:30pm daily, entrées from 3,000ISK) does a nice job with lamb and fish dishes, some more traditional, others with a Middle Eastern and Italian flair. The restaurant occupies one of the highest buildings in Akureyri, giving a fantastic view of the town. There's a lovely three-course menu available that really hits the spot—ginger and lemongrass shellfish soup, fresh fish of the day, and warm chocolate cake with ice cream for dessert.

Mediterranean
Bryggjan (Strandgata 49, tel. 354/440-6600, www.bryggjan.is, 11:30am-10pm daily, entrées from 1,800ISK) is known for its perfect

pizzas in just about any combination of ingredients you could imagine. You can go the traditional route with a ham and pepperoni pizza, or more exotic with a shrimp, tuna, onion, and tomato pie. If you're not up for pizza, there are soups, sandwiches, and starters, such as mozzarella sticks and nachos.

La Vita é Bella Ristorante (Hafnarstræti 92, tel. 354/461-5858, www.bautinn.is, 6pm-11pm daily entrées from 2,500ISK) is a delightful Italian restaurant that serves all the traditional favorites: lasagna, spaghetti Bolognese, and even pizza and calzones. It's a cute, family-style restaurant with a friendly staff and casual atmosphere.

Icelandic

The restaurant ★ **1862 Nordic Bistro** (Strandgata 12, tel. 354/466-1862, www.1862. is, 11:30am-9pm Mon.-Sat., 11am-9pm Sun. summer, 11:30am-6pm Mon.-Sat., 11am-6pm Sun. winter, dinner buffet 5,990ISK) is housed in Hof, the main concert hall in Akureyri that is right next to the harbor. The restaurant is known for its dinner buffet, which features Icelandic delicacies, including smoked guillemot with horseradish cream, prime filet of lamb, salmon, catfish, traditional Iceland fish gratin, and marinated herring. If you want to sample fresh Icelandic ingredients served in traditional as well as innovative ways, check this place out. The *skyr* cheesecake with blueberries is a perfect way to end the buffet.

Kaffi Ilmur (Hafnarstræti, tel. 354/571-6444, www.kaffiilmur.is, daily 8am-11pm, entrées from 1,200ISK) is a delightful little café off the main street in town. You will find soups, sandwiches, salads, snacks, and fresh pastries, along with a great cup of coffee. Situated in a nondescript house, it's a great, quiet spot to have a light meal in the heart of downtown Akureyri.

Asian

Indian Curry Hut (Hafnarstræti 100b, tel. 354/461-4242, daily 4pm-11pm, entrées from 1,500ISK) is a surprisingly wonderful Indian takeaway restaurant housed in a small shack-like structure on the main street. Don't be fooled, though; this is a great spot to get a tasty, affordable meal. The food is fantastic, with cooks specializing in perfectly spiced chicken and lamb dishes.

Krua Siam (Strandgata 13, tel. 354/466-3800, www.kruasiam.is, 11:30am-9:30pm Mon.-Fri., 5pm-9:30pm Sat.-Sun., entrées from 1,600ISK) has all the main dishes that you'd expect to see at a Thai restaurant, without many surprises. The mainstays are there, such as spring rolls, pad thai, fish in red curry sauce, and beef and curry with coconut milk. The lamb and fish are fresh, local, and divine.

Pengs (Gléragata 36, tel. 354/466-3800, 11:30am-11pm Sun.-Thurs., 11:30am-midnight Fri.-Sat., entrées from 1,400ISK) is an unconventional Chinese restaurant serving up southern Chinese food. Mainstays include fried rice and noodles, but some surprising dishes mix local ingredients with traditional Chinese flavors. For instance, the salmon and ginger sauce entrée is delightful. Iceland certainly isn't known for its Chinese food, but Pengs offers a decent meal for a good price.

Cafés

Bláa Kannan Café (Hafnarstræti 96, tel. 354/461-4600, 8:30am-11:30pm daily summer, Mon.-Fri. 9am-11:30pm, 10am-11:30pm Sat.-Sun. winter, 1,800ISK) is a charming café housed in a bright blue building on the main street, one of the oldest structures in the city. The interior is quaint and cozy, and the friendly staff serves freshly baked bread, pastries, soups, and sandwiches. The café tends to get crowded during lunchtime, when fresh soup is served with bread and butter. During the summer, chairs and small tables are outside, where locals and tourists can be seen sipping drinks and soaking up the sun. Its central location and simple, good food make this place a winner.

Kaffi Akureyri (Strandgata 7, tel. 354/461-3999, 3pm-1am Sun.-Thurs., 3pm-4am Fri.-Sat., 1,500ISK) is a café by day, serving delicious coffee drinks and snacks, and a raucous club by night, blasting the latest music and catering to the teens and twentysome-things in town.

Te og Kaffi (Hafnarstræti 91-93, tel. 354/540-2180, www.teogkaffi.is, 1,000ISK) is housed in the front of the Eymundsson bookstore on the main street. There's a decent selection of teas, coffee drinks, and fresh pastries on offer from this popular chain shop. You'll see locals perusing magazines while sipping on lattes.

Ice Cream

Ice cream is serious business in Iceland, and the holy grail is **Brynja** (Aðalstræti 3, tel. 354/462-4478, 350ISK). Icelanders are known to enjoy ice cream in any type of weather, and Brynja has been supplying locals with delicious creamy concoctions since 1942. In the summer, it's common to see a line outside the shop, which is not something you can see in many places. In short, the ice cream is fantastic. Try a scoop or two.

INFORMATION AND SERVICES
Tourist Information

The **tourist information office** (Strandgata 12, tel. 354/460-1199, www.visitakureyri.is, 10am-5pm daily) is based in Akureyri's main concert hall, Hof, by the harbor. There, you can find pamphlets on tours and seasonal events, along with a gift shop that sells unique Icelandic wares. Just a few steps from the information center is a restaurant, 1862 Nordic Bistro, that sells snacks and light meals and has a buffet.

Medical Services

Akureyri Hospital (Eyrarlandsvegur, tel. 354/463-0100, www.fsa.is) is North Iceland's largest hospital. The hospital provides general and specialized health care services and emergency care.

Akureyrarapótek (Akureyri Pharmacy) (Kaupangur, tel. 354/460-9999, www.akap.is, 9am-6pm Mon.-Fri., 10am-4pm Sat., noon-4pm Sun.) is close to the swimming pool and camping area.

If you have a medical emergency, dial 112 for help.

GETTING THERE
Air

By air, Air Iceland operates daily flights from Reykjavík City Airport, which take about 45 minutes. The flight offers spectacular views of the landscape when the weather is clear. **Akureyri Airport** sits at the base of Eyjafjörður, just three kilometers from city center, and is a quite small commuter airport. It's a 30-minute walk or a 5-minute drive. Taxis can be hired at Hof, by the harbor, or arranged by your hotel or guesthouse. Check flight schedules and book tickets at **Air Iceland** (tel. 354/460-7000, www.airiceland.is, starts at 16,000ISK each way).

Car

By car, Akureyri is 391 kilometers from Reykjavík on Route 1. In good weather, it will take you about five hours.

Bus

By bus, travelers have a few options. In the summer, **Sterna** bus service (tel. 354/551-1166, www.sterna.is) leaves from Harpa concert hall in Reykjavík Monday-Friday, bringing you to the Akureyri campground in about six hours for 8,000ISK. The schedule changes often, so make sure you check the website for departures. The **Strætó** 57 bus (www.straeto.is) leaves the Mjodd bus station in Reykjavík a couple times a week, reaching downtown Akureyri in about six hours for 8,800ISK. Check the website for details. **SBA-Norðurleið** bus service (tel. 354/550-0770, www.sba.is) runs daily to Akureyri on its Kjölur (Highlands) route. The ride from Reykjavík is about 10.5 hours to Akureyri (17,000ISK). The bus runs during the summer only.

Sea

Arriving to Akureyri by sea is becoming more common, as cruise ships are increasingly adding Akureyri to their port stops. Most cruise ships dock at Strandgata, and downtown Akureyri is just a few steps away.

GETTING AROUND
Bus
Akureyri is small and walkable, but if you want to hop on a local city bus, they are free of charge. The yellow buses run 6:25am-11pm on weekdays and noon-6pm on weekends and holidays. The schedule can be obtained from your hotel or guesthouse or from www.straeto.is.

Taxi
BSO (Strandgata, tel. 354/461-1010, www.bso.is) is the only cab company in Akureyri, and it provides service 24 hours a day. It's possible to get taxis that can take up to eight people and also special cars for people with disabilities.

Car
Parking in Akureyri is considered a sport by some. If you are a local with a personal parking space, you're in the clear. Tourists, however, must be mindful of where they park and how long they have left the car. To deal with the limited parking spaces, the town has instituted a system where you must retrieve a small cardboard clock that has movable hands from the tourist information center or local gas stations. Before you leave your car in a designated parking area, move the hands of the clock to show the current time and display it clearly on the dashboard. Most spaces allow for two-hour parking, but make sure. Also, parking attendants closely monitor the clocks, and if you are past the time, or the attendant cannot see the clock, you will be issued a fine, which is 10,000ISK.

OUTSIDE AKUREYRI
Laufás
Laufás (tel. 354/463-3196, www.laufas.is, 9am-5pm daily June-Aug., 1,200ISK) is an ancient farm estate that gives a peek inside what life was like in the region as far back as the settlement era, complete with turf-covered houses that you can enter. The farm is even mentioned in historical records soon after the settlement of Iceland (874-930). The current church was built in 1865 and contains a pulpit dating from 1698, and the rectory at Laufás

Laufás

was rebuilt in 1853. There have been numerous churches built, and then rebuilt, over the centuries. It's a lovely place to spend a couple of hours, soak in the scenery, and reflect on what farm living looked like in the 19th century. There's a café in the service center, along with a small souvenir shop.

The farm is just 30 kilometers north of Akureyri and can be reached by Route 83.

Grenivík

Less than 400 people call Grenivík home, but the small, close-knit village is a popular place to stop to take some photos of the stunning fjord and mountainous landscape or to climb **Mount Kaldbakur,** which stands at 1,167 meters. Hikers rave about the view from the top, where on clear days you can get a glimpse of Hrísey Island. For hiking routes, stop by the tourist information office at Hof by the harbor in Akureyri (tel. 354/460-1199, www.visitakureyri.is). Also, **Kaldbakur Tours** (tel. 354/837-3770, www.kaldbaksferdir.com) offers snow-cat and sledding tours from January to May starting at 6,500ISK.

Grenivík is 38 kilometers north of Akureyri via Route 83.

BETWEEN AKUREYRI AND MÝVATN

The stretch between Akureyri and Mývatn is a beautiful drive with the must-see thundering Goðafoss waterfall.

★ Goðafoss

In a country full of spectacular waterfalls, what sets Goðafoss apart is the sheer width of the tumbling falls. White water surges over the rim, thundering down, crashing into rocks and water. The water of the Skjálfandafljót River falls from a height of 12 meters over a width of 30 meters. It's quite a show. Plan to spend some time here, walking along the perimeter, snapping photos, and taking in the beauty.

Goðafoss, which means "waterfall of the gods," comes from Iceland's long history with Christianity. In AD 1000, lawyer Þorgeir Þorkelsson made Christianity the official religion of Iceland. After his conversion, Þorgeir threw his statues of the Norse gods into the waterfall. The name Goðafoss was born.

ACCOMMODATIONS AND FOOD
Guesthouse Fosshóll (tel. 354/464-3108, www.godafoss.is, rooms from 17,000ISK) is just 500 meters from Goðafoss. The charming yellow house offers 21 rooms, including singles, doubles, and triples. Rooms are simple, bright, and cozy, with standard beds. Some rooms have private bathrooms, and guests have access to free Wi-Fi and free parking. It's also near a gas station and a grocery store, which is a plus. The guesthouse is only open mid-May to mid-September; book early, as rooms tend to sell out.

Restaurant Fosshóll (tel. 354/464-3108, 8am-10pm daily mid-May-mid-Sept., entrées from 1,800ISK) is the restaurant on the ground floor of the guesthouse. Clientele consists of tourists looking for a good meal in an isolated spot. The cooks do a nice job with Icelandic staples like salmon, cod, and lamb filets.

GETTING THERE
Goðafoss is located just off Route 1, 50 kilometers east of Akureyri and 49 kilometers west of Reykjahlíð. It's 46 kilometers from Húsavík via Route 85 and then Route 845.

Laugar

Laugar is a tiny stretch of land that is the closest town to Goðafoss. Granted, there isn't a lot to do or see in Laugar, but its proximity to Húsavík and Mývatn makes it a place to gas up the car and perhaps stay a night at the town's hotel, Fosshotel Laugar.

ACCOMMODATIONS AND FOOD
Fosshotel Laugar (tel. 354/562-4000, www.fosshotel.is, rooms from 20,000ISK) is another outpost of the popular Fosshotel chain. Rooms are clean, bright, and predictable, with simple furnishings and standard beds. The 57-room hotel is a popular stop

when continuing onto to Húsavík or Mývatn or if you're looking to spend some time at Dettifoss or Goðafoss, as they are quite close. Guests have access to free Wi-Fi, free parking, and a convenient restaurant and bar. Breakfast is included. The hotel is only open to tourists during the summer, June-August. In the winter, it serves as a dormitory for students.

Your only chance at a sit-down meal is at Fosshotel Laugar's restaurant (10am-10pm Mon.-Fri., noon-10pm Sat., noon-8pm Sun., entrées from 1,600ISK), which is open only June-August. The food is adequate, but nothing special, with hamburgers, sandwiches, and pizza on the menu. There are a few fish and lamb dishes as well.

GETTING THERE

Laugar is located on Route 1, about 65 kilometers east of Akureyri and about 35 kilometers west of Reykjahlíð. It's about 40 kilometers from Húsavík following Route 85 and then Route 845.

Mývatn Region

Mývatn is one of the fastest growing tourist destinations in the northeast. Visitors are lured by gorgeous hiking trails, rich birdlife, activities along Lake Mývatn, and the soothing Mývatn Nature Baths. The region has been shaped over time by punishing volcanic eruptions. Visitors come to soak in the rugged landscape, with its vast lava fields, gigantic craters, soaring mountains, and, of course, the 36.5-square-kilometer lake that is home to scores of bird and fish species.

The Mývatn region is perfect for the independent traveler who prefers to roam on their own time. Jump into a rental car and discover everything from the charming town of Reykjahlíð, on the northeastern shore of Lake Mývatn, to roaring waterfalls, volcanic craters, and black lava rock pillars. Alternatively, tours in the region include bird-watching, whale-watching, and jeep tours.

SIGHTS
★ Jarðböðin (Mývatn Nature Baths)

Despite obvious comparisons to the Blue Lagoon, Mývatn Nature Baths (tel. 354/464-4411, www.jardbodin.is, 9am-11:30pm daily June-Aug., noon-9:30pm daily Sept.-May, 3,500ISK), three kilometers east of Reykjahlíð, have their own unique personality and atmosphere. There's more room to wade and fewer people in the locker rooms, and the steam baths are far from full.

The bathing experience is heavenly, soothing your skin and relaxing every inch of your body. The views of the landscape are striking, with the volcanic crater of Hverfjall and the edge of Lake Mývatn in the background.

The milky-blue water, which stands at 36°C (96.8°F), comes from the National Power Company's borehole in Bjarnaflag. The water temperature reaches a scorching 130°C (266°F) when it arrives to the basin next to the lagoon, but it cools significantly before filtering into the glorious man-made hot spring. Overall, the basin and lagoon hold about 2.5 million liters of water.

The bottom of the lagoon is covered by gravel and sand, and it contains a large amount of minerals. Because of its chemical composition, vegetation and bacteria are not a problem. There is some sulfur in the water, which is beneficial for skin problems such as eczema and psoriasis, as well as respiratory issues. However, it's not a good idea to wear silver or brass jewelry in the water, as the pieces can become damaged from the sulfur.

Kaffi Kvika (11am-9pm daily June-Aug., noon-8pm daily Sept.-May) serves light, healthy meals while visitors overlook the lagoon.

Mývatn Region

© AVALON TRAVEL

Dimmuborgir

Dimmuborgir, which means "dark cities" or "dark castles," comprises interesting rock formations jutting out of the ground, resembling a fort from an ancient city. The black lava pillars were born from a collapsed lava tube from a large volcanic eruption more than 2,000 years ago. Scientists have said that lava pooled over a small lake in the region, and as it crossed wet land the water started to boil, with vapor emitting from the lava, forming pillars.

Some pillars reached several meters in height. There's a popular photo opportunity in the structure known as Kirkjan (The Church), which is a lava tube that is curved resembling a steeple. While it's tempting to scale many of the structures, climbing is strictly prohibited.

To get there, head south from Húsavík, turning off onto Route 87; keep straight once you reach the first junction at Lake Mývatn and then follow it around the eastern edge. It is about a 45-minute drive from Húsavík.

Hverfjall

Hverfjall (or Hverfell, depending on which Icelander you ask) is the largest tephra crater in the Mývatn region. Tephra craters are created from volcanic debris. The crater is striking because it's almost a perfect circle, and considering its size (140 meters deep and 1 kilometer across), it's quite impressive. Scientists have said that the crater was formed after repeated eruptions over 2,500 years ago. There are two walking paths around the rim, one on the north side and one on the south, and it takes about 15 minutes to climb. It gives you a good view of the landscape.

Take Route 1 to get to Hverfjall. It's 15 kilometers east of Mývatn off of Route 848, about a 20-minute drive. The GPS coordinates are N 65.6061, W 16.8751.

Krafla

The Krafla lava fields are home to Víti (Hell), one of the best-known craters in Iceland. Víti is huge, about 300 meters in diameter, exposing interesting formations that resulted from lava flows and water over the ages. The area is another reminder of how active this island has been, and continues to be, with spectacular eruptions resulting in the reshaping of land. Tourists come to the region to get a glimpse of the crater, hike around the area, and take in the very much alive hot springs and mud pools. The crater was formed during a massive volcanic eruption in 1724. The eruption continued for five years, and Víti's bubbling cauldron of mud boiled for more than a century after that.

Krafla is 24 kilometers northeast of Mývatn off of Route 1, about a 25-minute drive. Víti is situated near Krafla, and a road leads up to it from Route 1. The car park area is right next to the rim, and you should spend at least an hour to walk around the rim.

Námaskarð

Námaskarð is a big draw for tourists because of its sheer otherworldly atmosphere. The yellow and brown colors of the clay along with the gray mud pools look like a movie scene from another planet. A path loops around the region; be sure to stay on it for safety reasons, as the mud pools can get up to 100°C (212°F). The area is secluded and the smell of sulfur can be a bit much for some, but it's worth a visit.

Námaskarð is 15 kilometers northeast of Lake Mývatn on Route 1.

Fuglasafn Sigurgeirs (Sigurgeir's Bird Museum)

Sigurgeir's Bird Museum (Ytri-Neslond, tel. 354/464-4477, www.fuglasafn.is, noon-5pm daily mid-late May, 9am-6pm daily June-late Aug., noon-5pm daily late Aug.-Oct., 2pm-4pm daily Nov.-mid-May, 1,000ISK) is Iceland's largest privately owned taxidermy bird collection. It is at the farm Ytri-Neslond near Lake Mývatn. The museum features about 180 species of birds and more than 300 birds in total, ranging from goldeneye ducks to puffins. The birds are in glass displays, and they are labeled with information about the species. An on-site café serves coffee and snacks. Binoculars are available to use for bird-watching outside the museum. The museum, which opened its doors in 2008, was created in honor of Mývatn resident Sigurgeir Stefansson, who had a passion for birds and died tragically in an accident in 1999 at the age of 37.

Take Route 1 to reach the bird museum, which is on the north side of the lake. The GPS coordinates of the museum are N 65.6288, W 16.9951.

SPORTS AND RECREATION
Bird-Watching

Iceland has been established as a bird-watchers' paradise, but Mývatn gets props for getting a view of a few species not found in much of the island, namely the duck species—gadwell, shoveler, and common scoter. In the bay of Neslandavík, you can seen large flocks of greater scaup, Eurasian wigeon, and tufted duck species, as well as common pochard and ring-necked ducks. The Laxa River

The Disappearing *Marimo* in Mývatn

A rare form of algae is disappearing from Lake Mývatn. The algae, called *marimo* (which means "water plant ball" in Japanese), is a round spongy moss that collects on the bottom of lakes. It exists only in this part of Iceland and parts of Japan, Scotland, and Estonia.

The *marimo* in Mývatn was discovered in 1978, and you can see the moss gently roll back and forth in the waves. Iceland's *marimo* can be found in water that is about two meters deep, and they grow at most to 12 centimeters in diameter. The lake balls are a curiosity, as they can grow only in very specific conditions with the right amount of sediment, certain light conditions, and lake current. Perhaps most curious, for non-scientists, is the Icelandic translation: Lake balls are called *kúluskítur*, which means "ball of shit" in Icelandic. The numbers of *marimo* have been declining, and scientists are unsure why.

is a popular spot for locals to bring a pair of binoculars and a pair of boots to walk along the perimeter in search of harlequin ducks. Other waterbirds that are common to the area include the red-breasted merganser, whooper swan, and great northern diver. Short-eared owls are seen rarely, so hopefully you will be lucky. Keep your eyes peeled.

The best season for bird-watching is from the beginning of May to the middle of August, as that's the high nesting season, but some species, such as geese, remain in the autumn. Remember that the lake is a protected area, and some regions are off-limits to cars. Stop by the tourist information office in Reykjahlíð (Hraunvegur 8, tel. 354/464-4390, www.visitmyvatn.is) for maps and tips on where to catch certain species, and always remember to be careful of nests.

Camping

There are a couple of camping opportunities around Mývatn, but it's important to note that they become quite full during the summer months.

The Bjarg campsite (tel. 354/464-4240, May-Sept., 1,200ISK) is situated perfectly, right next to the lakeshore of Lake Mývatn near Reykjahlíð. It's close to shops, the tourist information office, and excellent hiking trails. The facilities are top-notch, with laundry facilities, a cooking area to prepare meals, hot showers, and a place to rent bicycles. It's in

an open field with no shelter. Tents and RVs are welcome.

Hlíð (tel. 354/464-4103, www.myvatnaccommodations.is, 1,200ISK) is a campsite that includes cottages for rent. The camping section is on the northern shore of Lake Mývatn, and it's a short five-minute walk to the grocery store and tourist information office. It's in a open field with no shelter, in a pretty space close to the lake. It has an adequate cooking area, warm showers, and an area for tents and caravans. There are laundry facilities on-site. Cottages cost 15,000ISK per night and are available June-early September.

Hiking and Biking

Hike and Bike (tel. 354/899-4845, www.hikeandbike.is) is a Mývatn-based tourism company that offers a range of tours, including three- to four-hour day tours and overnight tours that allow you explore the region by mountain bike, by foot, or both. The company provides all the gear you need, and there are tours available for all levels of experience. A popular tour is the "Bike and Bath," which is about three hours and costs 9,900ISK per person. A guide takes you by mountain bike to sites including an old steam bath, the fissure of Grjotagja, ancient bathing caves, and ultimately the Mývatn Nature Baths for an hour of soaking in the milky-blue, geothermally heated water.

Jeep Tours

Sel Hótel Mývatn (tel. 354/464-4164, www. myvatn.is) offers action-packed super-jeep tours year-round. They range from riding on mountain tracks in the summer to navigating on top of fresh winter snow. Tours take you to the rock formations of Dimmuborgir, the crater at Hverfjall, and some hidden places that the local tour guide knows well. It's a great option to get out and explore nature with an experienced guide who has all the safety equipment needed due to possible difficult weather conditions. Tours are about three hours and cost 25,000ISK per person.

Swimming

If you aren't up for a dip in the Mývatn Nature Baths, but want to swim, the **Mývatn Swimming Pool** (Mývatnssveit, tel. 354/464-4225, 8am-8pm Mon.-Fri., 10am-7pm Sat.-Sun., 600ISK) is just outside Reykjahlíð. The GPS coordinates are N 65.6431, W 16.8932.

ACCOMMODATIONS
Hotels

Hótel Gígur (Skútustaðir, tel. 354/464-4455, www.keahotels.is, rooms from 27,000ISK) is in a dynamite location near the southern shore of Lake Mývatn. The 37 rooms, mostly doubles, have private bathrooms, free Wi-Fi, free parking, and an in-house restaurant. The hotel feels a bit dated, especially the restaurant, but it's clean, centrally located, and a convenient place to spend a couple of nights. The staff is friendly, and breakfast is included in the room price. It's open from the middle of May to the end of September.

Hótel Reykjahlíð (Kísilvegur, Reykjahlíð, tel. 354/464-4142, www.myvatnhotel.is, rooms from 32,000ISK) offers nine rooms on two floors. The four rooms on the top floor are larger and slightly nicer than the five on the ground floor, but overall, this is a great place to stay in town. Rooms are neat and clean, furnished in a tasteful manner, and overlooking the lake. Breakfast is included, and guests are invited to have coffee or tea any time of day in the restaurant, free of charge.

Hótel Reynihlíð (Kísilvegur, Reykjahlíð, tel. 354/464-4170, www.myvatnhotel.is, rooms from 32,000ISK) is a smart and modern hotel with spacious rooms, killer views, and an accommodating staff. Rooms have big, comfy beds and huge windows overlooking gorgeous scenery. The hotel restaurant serves up a delicious breakfast that is included in the room price. And the dinner menu has all the lamb and fish dishes you'd expect.

Sel Hótel Mývatn (Skútustaðir, Mývatn, tel. 354/464-4164, www.myvatn.is, rooms from 34,000ISK) is halfway between a modern and quaint hotel. The exterior is a gray block structure that looks fairly new, while rooms boast vintage furniture, dainty linens, and all the comforts of home. The in-house restaurant does a fantastic Icelandic dinner buffet.

Guesthouses

Dimmuborgir Guesthouse (Geiteyjarströnd 1, Mývatn, tel. 354/464-4210, www.dimmuborgir.is, rooms from 13,000ISK) offers eight double rooms with private bathrooms, as well as nine cottages. Rooms are bright and clean with simple furnishings and free Wi-Fi. A living room has a television. Cottages are roomy and wood-paneled, and half have a private bathroom. The owners are warm and friendly and have a long tradition of smoking trout in a nearby smokehouse that they love to show tourists. Breakfast is included.

Eldá Guesthouse (Helluhraun 15, Mývatn, tel. 354/464-4200, www.elda.is, rooms from 20,000ISK) offers rooms in several small houses with a breakfast buffet included in the room price. It's possible to rent an entire house that has a fully equipped kitchen, private bathrooms, and all the comforts of home.

Vogafjós Guesthouse (Vogafjós Vegur, Mývatn, tel. 354/464-4303, www.vogafjos.net, rooms from 18,000ISK) has been owned and operated by the same family for more than a century. With spectacular views of mountains and lava fields, the guesthouse offers 10 rooms in log cabins. All have private bathrooms, and breakfast is included.

FOOD

Restaurant Myllan (Kísilvegur, Reykjahlíð, tel. 354/464-4170, 6:30pm-9pm daily, www. reynihlid.is, entrées from 3,000ISK), located in Hótel Reynihlíð, is the fanciest restaurant in Mývatn. The food is fresh and hearty, with dishes like lamb shoulder with bell peppers, red onion, and potatoes, and fried char with almonds, grapes, and hollandaise sauce.

Sel Mývatn Restaurant (Skútustaðir, Mývatn, tel. 354/464-4164, www.myvatn.is, 8am-11:30pm daily summer, 10am-9pm daily winter, entrées from 2,000ISK), at Sel Hótel Mývatn, is your best bet for a traditional Icelandic dinner buffet featuring key island delicacies, such as smoked trout and marinated salmon, and more exotic dishes, such as shark, blood pudding, smoked lamb, liver pudding, and sheep's head jelly. But if you're not after something so exotic, don't fret, because there are plenty of fish and lamb dishes on the menu.

Kaffi Borgir (tel. 354/698-6810, www. kaffiborgir.is, entrées from 1,500ISK) is conveniently situated near the Mývatn Nature Baths, which means this place can get crowded in the summer months. It's a cafeteria-style café that serves hot meals like lamb or fish, coffee, and pastries. Good for a quick bite to eat. It's open from April until Christmas and is closed the remainder of the year.

Vogafjós Café (Vogar, tel. 354/464-4303, www.vogafjos.net, 7am-11:30pm daily summer, 9am-7pm daily winter, entrées from 1,200ISK) is a cute and quirky café based in a dairy barn. While enjoying your meal of sandwiches, salads, or hot food, you can watch dairy cows get milked from the other side of a glass partition (milkings are at 7am and 6pm). The fresh mozzarella is surprisingly good.

INFORMATION AND SERVICES

Mývatn's **tourist information center** (Hraunvegur 8, Reykjahlíð, tel. 354/464-4390, www.visitmyvatn.is, 9am-4pm daily May, 7:30am-6pm daily June-Aug., 9am-4pm daily Sept., 9am-noon Mon.-Fri. Oct.-Apr.) offers Internet access, pamphlets about the region, and the chance to book tours in the area.

GETTING THERE AND AROUND

It's best to have a car to explore the region or to book a tour from Akureyri.

By car, Lake Mývatn is 92 kilometers east of Akureyri on Route 1. The town of Reykjahlíð connects to Route 848, which follows Lake Mývatn's northern edge. The lake's perimeter is about 40 kilometers.

Strætó (www.straeto.is) has departures on the 56 bus from Akureyri and Egilsstaðir in the east. It's about one hour from Akureyri and two hours from Egilsstaðir. Be sure to check the website for current timetables. Buses stop in Reykjahlíð and cost 2,400ISK.

Húsavík

Húsavík has transformed itself from a placid small town with little appeal to the outside world to a must-see destination for tourists interested in some of the best whale-watching opportunities on the island. Húsavík is home to under 3,000 full-time residents, but in the summer the numbers spike dramatically, as Icelanders from other towns, tourists coming in on bus tours, and independent travelers converge on Húsavík's harbor. The main draw for tourists is of course whale-watching tours, but the charm of the small town, with tasty restaurants and classic Icelandic hospitality, makes this a destination to consider even if you're not up for a boat tour.

SIGHTS
Hvalasafnið á Húsavík (Húsavík Whale Museum)

The Húsavík Whale Museum (Hafnarstétt 1, tel. 354/414-2800, www.whalemuseum.is, 8:30am-6:30pm daily June-Aug., 9am-4pm daily Apr.-May and Sept., 10am-3:30pm Mon.-Fri. Oct.-Mar., 1,400ISK) is a comprehensive museum on Iceland's most famous marine mammals. The exhibits have been developed and maintained with great care, and the curator clearly has a passion for whales. The museum, which is housed in a huge building that used to be a slaughterhouse, provides information on the whale species that inhabit the waters off Iceland's coasts as well as whale ecology and conservation. There are 10 different whale skeletons to check out, as well as a sperm whale jaw bone that is the size of a car. It's incredible to stand next to it. Short films available in English teach about whales, and a library has a large selection of marine-related books. If you're going to go to one museum in Húsavík, this should be it.

Könnunarsögusafnið (Exploration Museum)

The Exploration Museum (Héðisbraut 3, tel. 354/848-7600, www.explorationmuseum. com, 9am-6pm daily, 1,000ISK) is a great spot to see something a little different in Iceland. The museum focuses on various types of exploration, from Vikings coming to Iceland to Americans landing on the moon. Maps and photographs are on display, and documentaries about Apollo astronauts training in Húsavík before a mission are available in English. It may not sound like it makes sense, but the exhibits work, doing a nice job of tying Viking exploration, Arctic explorers, and astronauts together.

Safnahúsið á Húsavík (Culture House at Húsavík)

The Culture House at Húsavík (Stóragarði 17, tel. 354/464-1860, www.husmus.is, 10am-6pm daily June-Aug., 10am-4pm Mon.-Fri. Sept.-May, 600ISK) features two fantastic exhibitions that give a window into life in Húsavík over the ages. The first exhibit has a maritime theme and includes a number of boats, many of which were built in Húsavík. Other displays include fishing equipment, tools used for seal and shark hunting, and photos and documentaries in English. The second exhibit focuses on daily life and natural history in the region. Here you can view homemade objects and crafts and learn about subsistence farming. Regional archives and a library are on-site.

Húsavíkurkirkja (Húsavík Church)

Located close to the harbor, the Húsavíkurkirkja (9am-11am and 3pm-5pm daily June-Aug., free) is one of the most significant landmarks in the town. Built in 1907, it stands 26 meters high and has a white exterior with reddish brown trim and a dark green steeple/roof. The interior features strong wood beams, beautiful windows, and red cushioned pews. Icelandic state architect Rögnvaldur

Ólafsson designed the church, and all of the wood used to construct it was imported from Norway. The painting behind the altar is revered by town locals. Icelandic artist Sveinn Thórarinsson was commissioned to portray the resurrection of Lazarus for the church. His work incorporated Iceland's landscape, including mountains and mist from Dettifoss.

SPORTS AND RECREATION
Camping

The **Húsavík Campground** (Héðinsbraut, tel. 354/845-0705, mid-May-mid-Sept., 1,200ISK) regularly gets kudos for being a well-maintained, large, and efficient facility that is wildly popular in June and July. The kitchen area is great and the showers are steaming hot. The campground, which is close to the center of town, is situated in an open field with no shelter. Tents and RVs and welcome.

Swimming

The **Húsavík Swimming Pool** (Héðinsbraut, tel. 354/464-1144, 9am-7pm Mon.-Fri., 10am-5pm Sat.-Sun., 600ISK) is close to the campsite, which means it can get pretty crowded. Besides the pool, a couple of hot tubs also draw a crowd.

★ Whale-Watching

Come to Húsavík for the whale-watching tours. If you leave without getting on a boat to view these gentle giants up close, you're missing out. The main whale-watching season runs from the middle of May to the end of October, but the high season is June and July. That time is your best chance to see as many as 12 species of whale, with the most common being minke and humpback whales. If you're lucky, you'll spot fin whales, orcas, and blue whales. You can always count on sighting dolphins, as they love to hang out close to the bay. Many of the guides are passionate about whales and love relaying stories to tourists about up-close-and-personal encounters.

Three main companies offer whale-watching

Húsavíkurkirkja

tours. The tours are about three hours and depart daily.

- **Gentle Giants** (tel. 354/464-1500, www.gentlegiants.is, 10,300ISK), April to mid-November
- **North Sailing** (tel. 354/464-7272, www.northsailing.is, 10,500ISK), mid-March to November
- **Salka** (tel. 354/464-3999, www.salkawhalewatching.is, 9,950ISK), mid-May to mid-September

Bring your camera, plus a pair of binoculars if you're inclined, and dress warmly, even in the summer. The wind at sea can be punishing.

ACCOMMODATIONS
Hotels

Fosshotel Húsavík (Ketilsbraut 22, tel. 354/464-1220, www.fosshotel.is, rooms from 23,600ISK) is a 70-room hotel, with 44 standard rooms and 26 superior rooms with king-sized beds, satellite TV, and private bathrooms. The hotel is decorated in nautical accents, and superior rooms have a fun and fresh whale theme to the decor. The hotel's bar is appropriately called Moby Dick, and the restaurant, Terian, serves fresh fish and other traditional Icelandic cuisine. Guests have access to free Wi-Fi and free parking, and breakfast is included.

Húsavík Cape Hotel (Höfði 24, tel. 354/463-3399, www.husavikhotels.com, rooms from 17,000ISK) is housed in a historic 1950 building that was owned by the Húsavík Fishing Company. The house was renovated in 2012, transforming it into a smart and rustic hotel, complete with standard beds, hardwood floors, and simple furnishings. Guests have access to free Wi-Fi, and breakfast is included.

Guesthouses

Árból Guesthouse (Ásgarðsvegur 2, tel. 354/464-2220, www.arbol.is, rooms from 18,100ISK) is a quaint guesthouse close to the center of town. Some of the rooms have the look of a hunting lodge with wood-paneled rooms, while others look like you're staying at your grandmother's house. The rooms are clean and comfortable and a bit larger than average. All rooms share bathroom facilities, and breakfast is included.

Húsavík Guesthouse (Laugarbrekka 16, tel. 354/463-3399, www.husavikguesthouse.is, rooms from 17,000ISK) is a family-run guesthouse that offers seven rooms ranging from singles to family rooms. The atmosphere looks and feels very much like you're staying in a comfortable, well-loved home. There's art on the walls, jam-packed bookshelves with everything from novels to travel guides, and comfortable guest rooms. Guests share bathroom facilities, and breakfast is included.

Guesthouse Sigtun (Tungata 13, tel. 354/846-9364, www.guesthousesigtun.is, rooms from 17,500ISK) has eight rooms ranging from singles to family rooms, just minutes from the harbor. Rooms are cozy and the amenities are great, with free Wi-Fi, access to a fully equipped kitchen, a computer for use, a washing machine to use free of charge, and a grill.

FOOD

Gamlí Baukur (Hafnarstett 9, tel. 354/464-2442, www.gamlibaukur.is, 11:30am-11pm Sun.-Wed., 11:30am-1am Thurs., and 11:30am-3am Fri.-Sat., entrées from 3,200ISK) is a unique restaurant built from driftwood found along the coastline of Húsavík. The rustic vibe continues inside, with large tables and

whale-watching in Húsavík

photos of the town's fishing history adorning the walls. The food is hearty, and the fish and lamb dishes hit the spot. The meat soup is also divine. The casual ambiance of the restaurant carries over to the evening, when it transforms into a concert venue for local and visiting Icelandic acts. The combination of good music and good beer is hard to beat.

Salka Restaurant (Garðarsbraut 4, tel. 354/464-2551, 11:30am-10pm daily, entrées from 2,300ISK) is a harborside restaurant that is owned by a whale-watching company. The food is good, but predictable, but the pizzas are quite nice. There are also soups, sandwiches, hamburgers, and fish and lamb dishes on the menu. The restaurant is proudly whale-friendly, so whale meat is not an option.

★ **Naustið** (Naustagarður 2, tel. 354/464-1520, noon-11pm daily, entrées from 2,800ISK) is a new kid on the block, having opened its doors in 2011, but it quickly became a town favorite. Known for its seafood, the restaurant uses fresh ingredients and local fish including cod, salmon, and blue ling. An outdoor eating area is delightful in good weather, and local musicians often play concerts. The interior is rustic, with wood-paneled walls and seafaring-related artwork.

Fish and Chips (Hafnarstett 19, tel. 354/464-2099, flokiehf@simnet.is, 11:30am-8pm daily June-Aug., entrées from 1,400ISK) serves quick and fresh fried cod and french fries from a harborside hut. The best fast food option in Húsavík by far.

INFORMATION AND SERVICES

The **tourist information office** (Hafnarstett 1, tel. 354/464-4300, www.visithusavik.is, 10am-4pm daily June-Sept.) is close to the harbor and offers Internet access, pamphlets about the region, and the opportunity to book tours.

GETTING THERE AND AROUND

By air, **Eagle Air** (tel. 354/562-4200, www.eagleair.is) offers 10 flights a week from Reykjavík. It's about a 45-minute flight and costs 22,000ISK each way. Húsavík Airport is 10 kilometers south of the center of Húsavík.

By car, Húsavík is 90 kilometers northeast of Akureyri via Route 85, and it's 56 kilometers north of Mývatn on Route 87.

Strætó (tel. 354/540-2700, www.straeto.is) offers year-round bus service from Akureyri to Húsavík on the 79 bus, which takes about two hours (2,400ISK). Check the website for recent timetable schedules. From mid-June to mid-August, **SBA** (tel. 354/550-0700, www.sba.is) runs daily bus service from Akureyri to Húsavík, with other stops at Dettifoss and Mývatn (3,330ISK). Check the most recent timetables on the website.

Jökulsárgljúfur National Park

The **Jökulsárgljúfur National Park** was established in 1973 and joined with **Vatnajökull National Park** in 2008, making it the largest national park in Europe. The park has some of Iceland's most visited sites in the north within the park limits, including Dettifoss and Ásbyrgi. Several well-maintained hiking trails travel along the perimeter of waterfalls, rivers, and canyons. Many tourists opt to stop at Dettifoss to photograph the powerful waterfall, but the park has other treasures. If you have the time, plan to spend some of it here. The landscape is breathtaking, with mountains, rivers and canyons, but if you don't have an extended period of time in Iceland, try to spend at least one day in this area.

Note that hikers must register with the park office at Ásbyrgi before they set out on their journey. Safety first.

SIGHTS
★ Ásbyrgi

Ásbyrgi (Shelter of the Gods) is an enormous canyon full of interesting rock formations, lush grass, well-maintained walking paths, thriving birdlife, and several bodies of water, including rivers and waterfalls. The horseshoe-shaped canyon, which is part of Vatnajökull National Park, measures roughly 3.5 kilometers in length and 1.1 kilometers across.

Scientists have said that Ásbyrgi was most likely formed by glacial flooding of the Jökulsá á Fjöllum River after the last Ice Age, and again some 3,000 years ago. However, Icelandic folklore has a different explanation for the unique shape of the canyon.

The canyon has been nicknamed Sleipnir's Footprint, as folklorists have said that the canyon was formed when Odin's eight-legged horse, Sleipnir, touched one of its feet to the ground, which created the depressions. Folklore also stipulates that the canyon is the central meeting point of the *huldufólk* (hidden people) who live among the cliffs.

Tourists make the trek to Ásbyrgi to take in the steep rock formations and to enjoy a hike. In some spots hikers have to be careful in navigating the rocks. Be sure to wear proper footwear and take caution over any slippery-looking patches. One easy hike, which is about one kilometer and takes 30-60 minutes, starts at the car park at Ásbyrgi and leads to a platform at a small pond named Botnstjörn. Along the way are lots of trees, shrubbery, and rock formations. A lovely view over the pond takes in ducks and other birds as well as the view over the western side of the canyon.

To reach the visitors center in Ásbyrgi from Húsavík, take Route 85. Ásbyrgi is 65 kilometers south of Húsavík.

Hólmatungur

Hólmatungur is an area on the western side of the canyon of the glacial Jökulsá River that has breathtaking basalt column formations, along with choppy streams and the wondrous waterfall Rettarfoss. It's a beautiful spot in the national park that offers scenic views and a wonderful spot to walk around and take photos.

To reach Hólmatungur from Ásbyrgi and Route 85, head south on Route 862, which is on the west side of river Jökulsá. Route 862 is a gravel road between Route 85 and Dettifoss. Hólmantungur lies along this unpaved stretch. (Heading south of Dettifoss to Route 1, the road is paved.) The gravel road

the rock formations of Ásbyrgi

is passable for normal vehicles, but it's closed during wintertime, due to snow or wet conditions, and does not open until late May or early June.

★ Dettifoss

Dettifoss, which means "tumble falls," is the largest waterfall on the island, and the most powerful in Europe, with an average flow of 200 cubic meters of water per second. During an especially rainy day, it can get up to 500 cubic meters per second. It's not because of its height, but width. Spanning 100 meters wide and 45 meters high, Dettifoss is gigantic. Tens of thousands of tourists catch a glimpse from several viewing platforms. The grayish color of the water comes from sand and rocks that get picked up along the way only to tumble a punishing depth.

Because of the waterfall's size and sheer beauty, plan to spend at least a couple of hours here to take it all in. This is an open, slippery spot with lots of steps and minimal guardrails. Be careful. If you are visiting on a windy day, expect to get hit with spray—but that's part of the fun, to really experience the falls.

For tour companies, Dettifoss is considered to be part of the "Diamond Circle," which is a popular route around the Mývatn region and Húsavík, based in Akureyri. For a day tour, check out Reykjavik Excursions (tel. 354/580-5400, www.re.is).

Dettifoss is 28 kilometers south of Ásbyrgi. From Ásbyrgi and Route 85, head south on Route 862 on the west side of river Jökulsá. Route 862 is a gravel road between Route 85 and Dettifoss. (Heading south of Dettifoss to Route 1, the road is paved.) The gravel road is passable for normal vehicles, but it's closed during wintertime, due to snow or wet conditions, and does not open until late May or early June.

ACCOMMODATIONS

You won't find any hotels or guesthouses within the park limits, so if you want to spend the time, your only option is camping at the Ásbyrgi campground (tel. 354/470-7100, 1,500ISK). The site, which is situated in an open field, is open from mid-May through September and allows for 350 tents as well as caravans (with hookups). There are adequate

Dettifoss

cooking facilities, hot showers, and a small shop that sells some food and hiking gear. Bring all the food, water, and supplies you need with you.

INFORMATION AND SERVICES

The national park's tourist information center (tel. 354/465-2195, www.ust.is) is based at Ásbyrgi, which is open year-round.

GETTING THERE AND AROUND

It's best to have a car to explore the park. Keep in mind that while Jökulsárgljúfur is open year-round, the roads beyond Ásbyrgi, including Route 862, are closed during wintertime, due to snow or wet conditions, and do not open until late May or early June.

If you don't have a car, a tour could be a great option. For instance, Akureyri-based SBA (tel. 354/550-0700, www.sba.is) offers a Dettifoss Grand Tour (13,000ISK) from mid-June to mid-September. The tour departs from the Reykjahlíð information center and takes you from Mývatn to Dettifoss, Ásbyrgi, Húsavík, and back to Mývatn.

The Northeastern Corner

The northeastern corner is one of the least populated, most desolate regions of Iceland. There is no mad tourist rush here. Þórshöfn is a small fishing village in the area, located on the northern coast of the Langanes Peninsula on the Þistilfjörður bay. Fewer than 400 people live on the peninsula.

LANGANES

Langanes (Long Peak) is a 40-kilometer-long, narrow peninsula, situated between two bays (Þistilfjörður and Bakkaflói), that is shaped like a goose with a very large head on the end. Some may be quick to dismiss the area, but the sloping coastal landscape is ideal for bird-watching and photographing steep sea cliffs. If you are driving through, it's worth a stop to take some photos of gannets, terns, gulls, and guillemots.

Be aware that the main road on Langanes is challenging to drive on, as it's extremely rocky in some spots. This is something to consider if you rented a compact car; four-wheel drives fare much better in this region. For those who do make the journey, at the end of the peninsula there is a charming lighthouse that was erected in 1950. If you are passing through in the winter, the lighthouse is a perfect place to catch a glimpse of northern lights (if the forecast is favorable).

Accommodations

Ytra-Lón Hostel (tel. 354/468-1242, www. hostel.is, double room 11,000ISK, studio 16,000ISK, apartment 20,000ISK) underwent an extensive renovation in 2010 and now offers nine self-catering apartments for 2-4 people with private bathrooms and a fully equipped kitchenette. The overall facility has beds for 50 people with some dormitory-style rooms. The hostel is remote, with the nearest grocery store and restaurants about 14 kilometers away, so bring food and supplies with you, or shop early because stores in this region tend to have wacky hours. Ytra-Lón is on Route 869, which is 14 kilometers northeast of Þórshöfn.

GETTING THERE AND AROUND

Langanes is 252 kilometers northeast of Akureyri via Route 85 and 69 kilometers north of Vopnafjörður (in East Iceland) on Route 85.

East Iceland and the Eastfjords

East Iceland is where you find the actual "ice" of Iceland, including Vatnajökull glacier, a giant white spot on the map that is truly breathtaking in person. You can drive or hike right up to the glacier's edge in Skaftafell National Park.

In the summer, the only practical time to tour this region, it can be crowded with fellow travelers, but there are plenty of detours to take to avoid the hordes. Lacking buildings and people, the east is the most remote part of the island, and travel is difficult in winter.

One of the least visited destinations in Iceland is one you should keep on your radar: the Eastfjords. If you're looking for remote, unspoiled beauty, it's here. The Ring Road weaves through the fjords, where you will see gorgeous mountains, charming fishing villages, and thriving wildlife. It's not easy to get around the region (you need a car), but it's worth the costs and trouble.

The east is also home to one of the most active volcanic areas on the island, and Vatnajökull National Park deserves its own day (at least) in its own right. Navigating the glacier (with a guide and proper equipment) is one of those unforgettable, bucket-list excursions.

East Iceland is often overlooked but has some of the most pristine, untouched nature in the country. If you can spare a couple of days, spend some time hiking and photographing the Eastfjords. Even during the high season, there's a good chance you won't bump into many other tourists. The east can be your own private treasure.

PLANNING YOUR TIME

East Iceland is not conducive to tight schedules, as weather can be unpredictable and winds punishing. It's best to visit in summer. Winter in particular can make travel to the area challenging. The wind and snow can make travel difficult at best, dangerous at worst. Monitor weather conditions closely and check to see if roads have been closed.

The Ring Road (Route 1) takes you through the east, and most people choose either Egilsstaðir and/or Seyðisfjörður as a base. Both towns are complete with guesthouses, bus stations, and airports. Some guesthouses and restaurants operate only June-August. To spend a lot of time in the Eastfjords, Seyðisfjörður is the best option.

Previous: a sheep pausing on a rocky hillside; traditional turf houses at a farm near Skaftafell National Park. **Above:** a glacier lagoon in Vatnajökull National Park.

Look for ★ to find recommended
sights, activities, dining, and lodging.

Highlights

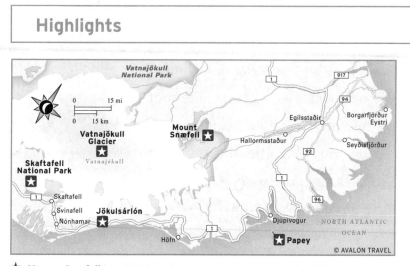

★ **Mount Snæfell:** The highest mountain (excluding glaciers) in Iceland towers a whopping 1,833 meters, but it's only a moderate hike to the top, where the view spans from the highlands to Vatnajökull and all the way out to sea (page 200).

★ **Papey:** Small Papey is affectionately called "Bird Island" because 30,000 pairs of puffins occupy the island during the summer. Eider ducks and black-legged kittiwake birds also nest here (page 211).

★ **Vatnajökull Glacier:** Covering about 8 percent of the country, the Water Glacier is the biggest glacier in Europe and a fantastic region to visit. Under the ice cap are still-active volcanoes (page 218).

★ **Jökulsárlón:** This Glacier Lagoon is not very wide, but it is up to 250 meters deep, which makes it the deepest lake in Iceland. Huge blocks of ice constantly break off the glacier, and large icebergs float along the lagoon (page 218).

★ **Skaftafell National Park:** Skaftafell is one of East Iceland's most beautiful places, with striking white glaciers against a backdrop of green fields and black sands (page 219).

East Iceland and the Eastfjords

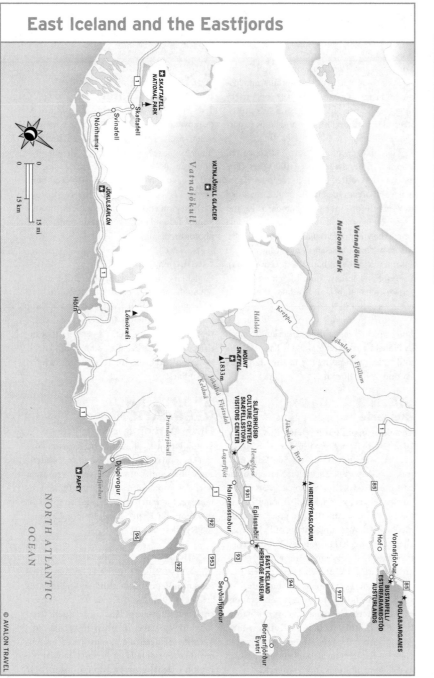

SKAFTAFELL NATIONAL PARK

Skaftafell

Svínafell

Nónhamar

JÖKULSÁRLÓN

Höfn

Lónsöræfi

Vatnajökull

VATNAJÖKULL GLACIER

Vatnajökull National Park

Hálón

Kreppa

Jökulsá á Fjöllum

MOUNT SNÆFELL
▲1833m

Kelduá

Jökulsá á Brú

Jökulsá í Fljótsdal

SLÁTURHÚSIÐ CULTURE CENTER/ SNÆFELLSSTOFA VISITORS CENTER

Hengifoss

Lagarfljót

STÖÐVARFJÖRÐUR

Breiðdalur

Breiðdalsvík

Djúpivogur

PAPEY

Berufjörður

NORTH ATLANTIC OCEAN

Hallormsstaður

Egilsstaðir

EAST ICELAND HERITAGE MUSEUM

Seyðisfjörður

Á HREINDÝRASLÓÐUM

Hof

Vopnafjörður

BUSTARFELL/ ESTURFARAMIÐSTÖÐ AUSTURLANDS

FUGLABJARGANES

Borgarfjörður Eystri

15 mi

15 km

0
0

© AVALON TRAVEL

Vopnafjörður (Weapon Fjord) is full of picturesque mountains, pure waterfalls, and historical farms. It's one of the best spots to try to get a glimpse of killer whales. It's pretty, steeped in medieval history, and home to gorgeous wildlife.

The history of the town, also called Vopnafjörður, dates back 1,100 years. The bay was first settled by Viking seafarers from Norway. Foreign merchants frequently sailed to Vopnafjörður in the early modern age, and a settlement gradually formed on a peninsula where the village of Vopnafjörður now stands. It became one of Iceland's major harbors for commerce in the 18th and 19th centuries. In the last half century, the fishing industry has grown considerably, and is today the largest business sector in the area.

As for the town's impact on literature, *Independent People,* the epic Icelandic novel by Nobel Prize winner Halldór Laxness, was said to be inspired by life in the highlands around Vopnafjörður.

SIGHTS
Bustarfell

The old farm of Bustarfell (off Rte. 85 about 20 km south from Vopnafjörður, tel. 354/471-2211, www.bustarfell.is, 10am-5pm daily mid-June-mid-Sept., entrance 700ISK) is one of the best-preserved of the traditional Icelandic turf houses, which Icelanders called home for centuries. The museum offers a great opportunity to see how people's ways of living have changed through the centuries. The rooms are furnished in the style of centuries past, giving an authentic look into what homes were like. The foundations of the current house are from 1770, but the house has undergone alterations over the years. The museum covers life from the 18th century to the mid-20th century. A café within the museum is a good spot to enjoy coffee, light meals, and yummy pastries as well as exhibitions from local artists.

Vesturfaramiðstöð Austurlands (East Iceland Emigration Center)

The East Iceland Emigration Center (Kaupvangur 2, tel. 354/473-1200, www.vesturfarinn.is, 1pm-6pm Mon.-Wed. and Sat. June-Aug., free) is dedicated to the emigration years 1875-1914, the years after the great Askja eruption of 1875 that displaced hundreds. The center is focused on the history of the region and renewing contact with emigrants' descendants. There are documents and photos on display.

Fuglabjarganes

Fuglabjarganes is a prominent cliff that juts out on the northern coast of the town. You can get a good look at it from a marked hiking path from the Strandhafnarvegur road, which is along the Fugla River. The scenery is beautiful, with white beaches, stone wall fences, towering cliffs, and impressive rock caverns and pillars.

SPORTS AND RECREATION
Bird-Watching

Vopnafjörður is a bird-watcher's dream. You can see a mix of seabirds, waterfowl, waders, passerines, and raptors. The Tangi Peninsula north of Vopnafjörður is a beautiful and remote spot to watch seabirds, and a big habitat of various duck species can be found around the Nypslon estuary.

Fishing

The Hofsa River is just a 15-minute drive east from Vopnafjörður, and the angling area stretches 19 miles in a wide valley. Anglers can try their hand at landing a salmon from July 1 to September 20, when the season ends. Permits are needed and must be secured in advance. For details on permits, look at the region's website (www.vopnafjordur.com/

activities/angling). The Sela River is a 10-minute drive north from Vopnafjörður and has long been one of the most popular of Icelandic salmon rivers. Fishing is fly only, and the river has a flexible catch-and-release system. Guides are available. The Vesturdalsa River is a 15-minute drive south from Vopnafjörður. It originates from the runoff of Lake Arnarvatn in the highlands above Vopnafjörður, flows 34 kilometers to the lowlands, and empties into Nypslon estuary. The fishing area reaches 27 kilometers up to a waterfall not accessible to salmon. A catch-and-release policy is in effect.

Hiking

Vopnafjörður offers several hiking routes that vary from easy to challenging. Beginners will find a wide range of mapped routes and marked trails that offer scenic views of the whole of Vopnafjörður—the bay, the Tangi Peninsula, inland areas, and mountains. Hike to the end of the Tangi Peninsula to find interesting rock formations and beaches. Another easy route is around Drangsnes Peninsula and to the towering waterfalls at Gljufursa River, which is popular among locals.

More experienced hikers looking for a challenging trail should hike to the top of Krossavik Mountain, which stands at 1,080 meters. The mountain stands opposite the village on the other side of the bay. Other challenges at a similar level include Svinabakkar Mountain (south of Krossavik Mountain) and many longer but less steep hikes in Vopnafjörður's valleys and highlands.

For maps and detailed trails, visit the tourist information center (Hafnarbyggd 6, tel. 354/473-1341, www.vopnafjordur.is), and always be sure to check the weather forecast and report your itinerary.

Swimming

The local swimming pool is called Selárlaug (3.5 km from Rte. 85, tel. 354/473-1499, 10am-7pm daily, 520ISK), where you will find locals taking a dip and socializing with friends and family.

ACCOMMODATIONS

Hotel Tangi (Hafnarbyggd 17, tel. 354/473-1840, hoteltangi@simnet.is, rooms from 18,000ISK) is a standard countryside hotel with 17 rooms, a restaurant, and a bar. The exterior isn't much to look at as it's a blue block building, but the inside is comfortable, with standard beds and IKEA-like furniture. There are single and double rooms, some with shared bathroom facilities.

Sireksstadir Farm Cottages (Sireksstadir, tel. 354/473-1458, www.sireksstadir.is, rooms from 11,000ISK) offers two cottages for families or groups intended for 4-6 people, as well as seven double guest rooms. The cottages are cozy and have a large deck and a barbecue grill. Guests are invited to observe farm activities, and the rooms are available year-round. The staff is friendly, welcoming, and inclusive.

Syðri-Vík (tel. 354/473-1199, www.farmholidays.is, early Mar.-late Oct., rooms from 12,500ISK) is a six-room guesthouse based on a working farm. Guests have access to a fully equipped kitchen, common dining and living rooms, and shared bathroom and laundry facilities. The owners are very friendly, and it's a lot of fun to stay in such an active farm. The owners also rent out two summer cottages for families or large groups of people. Syðri-Vík is eight kilometers from the village Vopnafjörður, located near Route 85.

FOOD

Cafe Hjaleigan (tel. 354/471-2211, www.bustarfell.is, noon-6pm daily mid-June-mid-Sept., entrées from 1,000ISK) is the café at Bustarfell museum (off Rte. 85 about 20 km south from Vopnafjörður). It serves coffee, soft drinks, and light meals such as sandwiches, as well as pastries.

Ollasjoppa (Kolbeinsgata 35, tel. 354/473-1803, 9am-11pm Mon.-Sat., 10am-11pm Sun., entrées from 1,200ISK) is a tiny café that offers quick fare including pizza, hamburgers, sandwiches, and pitas, along with hot dishes with lamb, fish, and chicken.

INFORMATION AND SERVICES

The main tourist information office is housed in a huge yellow building (Hafnarbyggd 6, tel. 354/473-1341, www.vopnafjordur.is, 10am-5pm Mon.-Fri., noon-4pm Sat.-Sun.) in the center of town. It has brochures and maps about the region, as well as a small food store to stock up on essentials if you're staying at a self-catering guesthouse or farm.

GETTING THERE AND AROUND

By air, there are flights from the northern town Akureyri to Vopnafjörður

Airport (354/570-3075), which is situated at the bottom of the fjord. Daily flights are about 45 minutes. By car, Route 85 connects Vopnafjörður with Bakkafjörður, a small fishing village 34 kilometers south of Vopnafjörður. Route 1, in the south, connects to Egilsstaðir (75 minutes). For the most scenic route, Route 917 is an unpaved road over the mountains.

Travel to Vopnafjörður by bus is possible in the summer months. June through early September, SBA (tel. 354/550-0700, www.sba. is) operates daily trips from the northern town Akureyri. The three-hour trip costs 5,760ISK each way.

Fljótsdalshérað

Fljótsdalshérað is a municipality that encompasses about 3,500 inhabitants, most of whom reside in the towns Egilsstaðir and Fellabær, which form the largest urban center in East Iceland. The region supports a strong rural community that stretches from Biskupsháls in the west and Héraðsflói, a bay in the north, to the mountain ranges surrounding the central eastern fjords in the east and to Vatnajökull and Öxi in the south. The area encompasses 8,884 square kilometers and has a varied landscape that includes Hallormsstaður, which is Iceland's largest forest, as well as lakes, mountains, and waterfalls.

EGILSSTAÐIR

Egilsstaðir is considered the unofficial capital of East Iceland, but don't let that fool you; it's a "capital" with fewer than 3,000 residents. The quaint town earned its name based on a reference to the nearby farm Egil's stead, which appears in saga stories. The community began developing and growing after Iceland gained complete independence from Denmark in 1944. The town today remains sparsely populated, but the harbor welcomes thousands of visitors who come to Iceland via ferry from mainland Europe.

Sights

MINJASAFN AUSTURLANDS (EAST ICELAND HERITAGE MUSEUM)

The East Iceland Heritage Museum (Laufskógar 1, tel. 354/471-1412, www.minjasafn.is, 1pm-5pm daily June-Aug., 800ISK) showcases how life was lived in the region over the last 200 years. The main exhibition features objects including clothing, food, and tools, as well as items used for hunting, crafts, food production, and hobbies. Tourists are also welcome to enter a room of a 19th-century farmhouse that was moved from the countryside into the museum. The room depicts a small bedroom/living room, with sparse furnishings. It's an interesting view into what life was like in this remote part of Iceland—a hardscrabble, difficult existence.

SKRIÐUKLAUSTUR CENTER OF CULTURE & HISTORY

The Skriðuklaustur Center of Culture & History (Skriðuklaustur, tel. 354/471-2990, www.skriduklaustur.is, 10am-6pm daily June-Aug., 1,000ISK) is an impressive historical site that includes the ruins of a 16th-century monastery as well as the home of the celebrated

Northeastern Iceland

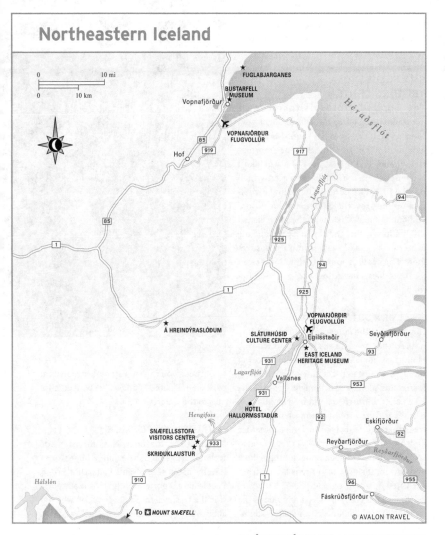

© AVALON TRAVEL

writer Gunnar Gunnarsson, a novelist who wrote *Af Borgslægtens Historie (Guest the One-Eyed)*, the first Icelandic book made into a movie. Gunnar's home was built in 1939 and was donated to the state by the writer in 1948. You can view photographs and objects that belonged to Gunnar Gunnarsson, and the building also serves as a cultural center where various events and exhibitions are held throughout the year.

SLÁTURHÚSIÐ (SLAUGHTERHOUSE CULTURE CENTER)

The **Sláturhúsið Culture Center** (Kaupvangur 7, tel. 354/471-1479, www.slaturhusid.is) injected some much needed culture into Egilsstaðir. Founded in 2005, the "slaughterhouse" cultural center is home to theater and dance productions as well as workshops, performances, lectures, and exhibitions. An artist residency available to locals and visitors provides an artist studio for tuition. The concrete building is cold and nondescript, but one might expect that from an old slaughterhouse.

SNÆFELLSSTOFA VISITORS CENTER

The Snæfellsstofa visitors center (Skriðuklaustur, tel. 354/470-0840, 10am-4pm Mon.-Fri., 10am-6pm Sat.-Sun. May-Sept., by appointment in winter) is the information center for the east area of Vatnajökull National Park. The visitors center, which opened in 2010, houses a fascinating exhibition on the area, the glacier, and local flora and fauna. Snæfell is one of the most visited destinations within the national park, and the center gives you a preview into the vast region. The center's souvenir shop focuses on local products, including woolen goods and food products.

HALLORMSSTAÐUR

In surveying the landscape, you've certainly noticed that trees are a rare sight in Iceland. Hallormsstaður has the distinction of being the largest forest in the country, but it is small. It stretches along a 35-kilometer-long glacial lake called Lagarfljót and by a small cove; it's beautiful to roam among native birch trees that have survived inclement weather and found a way to thrive. There are also scores of imported species, including willow and rowan. It's possible to rent horses from Riding Iceland (tel. 354/859-3560, www. riding-iceland.com) for a leisurely ride in the forest. Hallormsstaður is 23 kilometers southwest of Egilsstaðir on Routes 1 and 931, about a 20-minute drive.

HENGIFOSS

After roaming Iceland's largest forest, take a walk to the opposite side of the lake and look at the 120-meter towering waterfall Hengifoss. The landscape reveals a layer of basalt above ancient tree trunks. Have your camera ready. Hengifoss is 34 kilometers from Egilsstaðir on Route 931. The walk to Hengifoss from Hallormsstaður is 12 kilometers. For a closer

Hengifoss

look by car, you can stop at the designated car park off of Route 931 and walk about 40 minutes to the waterfall.

LAGARFLJÓTSORMUR

Scotland has the Loch Ness monster and Iceland has Lagarfljótsormur, a huge wormlike monster said to call Lagarfljót home. People have reported spotting the monster inside the freshwater, glacier-fed lake, which is about 30 kilometers long, as well as outside the body of water. It is said to have many humps and slither in a slow fashion. The tale is part of Icelandic folklore, and locals have a sense of humor about "sightings." If you do happen to see the monster, make sure you report it to the local heritage museum in Egilsstaðir.

Sports and Recreation
CAMPING

The Egilsstaðir Campsite (Kaupvangur 10, tel. 354/471-2320, mid-May-mid-Sept., 1,200ISK per adult, free for children under 14) can be quite busy in the summer. The campsite is close to town, and amenities include hot showers and adequate cooking facilities. There are areas for tents and RVs, with hookups. The campsite is situated in an open field with trees along the perimeter. You must pay at the tourist information center (Kaupvangur 10, tel. 354/471-2320, www.east.is, 8am-10pm daily summer, 9am-6pm Mon.-Fri., noon-4pm Sat.-Sun. winter).

GOLF

The **Ekkjufell Golf Course** (Fellabær, tel. 354/894-0604, 2,500ISK) is the sole course operated in the town. It's open year-round and is frequented by locals, so be sure to call ahead for a tee time.

HORSE RIDING

Those interested in a horse-riding tour have a great option with the travel service at **Sandfellsskógur** (17 km south of Egilsstaðir on Rte. 1, tel. 354/471-2420), which also offers horse rentals. Beautiful trails roam the forest and tour hills and valleys. You can rent a horse for 1-4 hours, and there's even a midnight summer tour available. Horse tours are available June through mid-September and cost 5,000ISK for a one-hour rental.

SWIMMING

The **Egilsstaðir Swimming Pool** (Tjarnarbraut 26, tel. 354/470-0777, 7am-9:30pm Mon.-Fri., 10am-7pm Sat.-Sun., 550ISK) is one of the nicest in the region, with a 50-meter heated pool, water slides for kids, hot tubs, and a fitness center.

Accommodations

Guesthouse Egilsstaðir (Fagradalsbraut, tel. 354/471-1114, www.farmholidays.is, rooms from 22,000ISK) is a charming countryside guesthouse based in a stately white building with a striking red roof. The 18-room guesthouse may be situated on a working farm, but it has some amenities that rival guesthouses in more urban locations, such as free Wi-Fi, a comfy bar and lounge, and

a common conference room with Internet access. The restaurant serves up classic comfort food, and the staff is warm and accommodating. The guesthouse is close to a swimming pool, a horse rental facility, and a golf course.

Hótel Eyvindará (Eyvindará 2, tel. 354/471-1200, www.eyvindara.is, Feb.-Oct., rooms from 25,000ISK) is a ranch-style guesthouse that offers 28 rooms and seven cottages. Rooms are decorated tastefully with cozy country accents and large windows that overlook a gorgeous view. Most of the rooms have private bathrooms, but a handful have shared facilities. The hotel's restaurant serves breakfast daily, and dinner is available late May through early September. The dinner menu emphasizes fish and lamb dishes but has a few vegetarian options.

★ **Icelandair Hótel Herað** (Miðvangur 5-7, tel. 354/471-1500, www.icelandairhotels.is, rooms from 22,900ISK) is the town's most upscale hotel option. The 60-room hotel, which is pretty huge for the location, is chic, modern, and has that classic Nordic style you'd expect to see in Reykjavík. But, this is an Icelandair Hótel, so the sleek interior and rooms are to be expected. The decor is heavy on wood, with gorgeous hardwood floors throughout the building, classic Scandinavian wood furnishings, and even modern wood art. The restaurant offers an eclectic menu featuring local ingredients.

Hótel Edda Egilsstaðir (Tjarnarbraut 25, tel. 354/444-4880, www.hoteledda.is, June-mid-Aug., rooms from 21,700ISK) is an adequate 52-room hotel just outside of town. What the hotel's rooms lack in luxury, is made up for with the location, if you want to be close to nature. The hotel is close to a 25-meter outdoor swimming pool, a nine-hole golf course, and a scenic stretch in the fjord where you can spot seals and take woodland walks. Rooms have standard beds and basic furniture, but all rooms have private bathrooms and there is free Wi-Fi in common areas in the hotel. The hotel restaurant serves a breakfast buffet 7am-10am that includes waffles, fresh fruit, and oatmeal, and a dinner buffet is available 6:30pm-9pm.

Húsey (Hróastunga, tel. 354/471-3010, husey@simnet.is, beds from 20,000ISK) is a 20-bed youth hostel that was converted from an old farmhouse. It's in an isolated part of the village, and there are great opportunities for spotting seals and hiking remote paths. The hostel has a common kitchen available to prepare your own meals. Sheets are available for a fee, and there is a barbecue available.

Food

★ **Icelandair Hótel Hérað** (Miðvangur 5-7, tel. 354/471-1500, www.icelandairhotels. is, 8am-10:30pm daily, entrées from 2,700ISK) is the most upscale dining you will find in the town, and the chefs do not disappoint. The hotel restaurant cooks up dishes with fresh ingredients that you'd expect, like fish and lamb, but there are some surprises, including reindeer meat, which is local to the area. You will find reindeer steaks, burgers, and pâté on the menu. If you're not game for reindeer, the arctic char with baby potatoes is recommended.

Café Nielsen (Tjarnarbraut 1, tel. 354/471-2626, www.cafenielsen.is, 11:30am-11:30pm Mon.-Fri., 1pm-11:30pm Sat.-Sun., entrées from 3,150ISK) is a small café serving flavorful dishes ranging from reindeer steaks to fresh mussels in a tomato-garlic sauce. The food is surprising and very tasty, with an interesting mix of ingredients. The pan-fried salted cod with garlic, chorizo, and olives is recommended.

Information and Services

Egilsstaðir's **tourist information center** (Kaupvangur 10, tel. 354/471-2320, www. east.is, 8am-10pm daily June-Aug., 9am-6pm Mon.-Fri., noon-4pm Sat.-Sun. Sept.-May) is the largest and most comprehensive in the region, and one of the largest in the country. You will find hiking maps, basic travel supplies, a café and souvenir shop, Internet

access, and a booking center for an array of tours. The site is also home to the bus station and the local campsite.

Getting There and Around

By car, Route 1 connects Egilsstaðir with the North Iceland town Akureyri, which is 3.5 hours and 266 kilometers away.

The **Strætó** 56 bus (tel. 354/540-2700, www.straeto.is) operates from Egilsstaðir to Akureyri all year. It takes about four hours from Akureyri and costs 7,200ISK each way.

Egilsstaðir Airport (354/424-4040) is in the heart of town, and there are daily flights by **Air Iceland** (www.airiceland.is) from Reykjavík's domestic airport. Flights take about one hour and cost 17,000ISK each way.

★ MOUNT SNÆFELL

Mount Snæfell (Snow Mountain) is the highest mountain, excluding glaciers, in Iceland. Despite towering 1,833 meters, it's fairly easy to scale. The dormant volcano offers spectacular views over the highlands, down Fljótsdalur valley, and of Vatnajökull glacier. You can see rivers, canyons, and valleys—and you may even catch a glimpse of a reindeer herd. Climbing doesn't get better than Mount Snæfell.

To get to the base, take Route 910 to Route F909. Getting to the base requires a rugged four-wheel drive, as the roads are at best challenging and at worst treacherous. Don't try to make it in a compact rental car or you'll wind up stranded. Don't be foolish.

A well-kept trail begins at the base station and continues to the top. Hiking groups start at the mountain hut **Snæfellsskáli** (tel. 354/575-8400); the GPS coordinates are N 64.8042, W 15.6418. The mountain hut offers basic amenities including beds, bathrooms, and cooking facilities. The cost is 5,800ISK per night. The whole area is open only in the summer.

The moderate hike is about eight kilometers and takes about 8-9 hours. The top of the mountain is snowcapped all year long. Bring good boots and waterproof gear, alert people of your travel plans, and monitor the weather closely. If conditions are not good, do not attempt a climb.

There is also a challenging trek from Mount Snæfell to **Lónsöræfi** that is about 55 kilometers and takes 3-7 days. Hikers can experience steep hills, glaciers, and waterfalls amid the rocky landscape.

The Eastfjords

The Eastfjords are some of the most remote and unspoiled parts of Iceland. In all, there are 14 fjords, each with its own charm and tiny population. There are waterfalls among small fishing villages, and unique museums lure tourists off the Ring Road. If you're on an extended trip to Iceland, you should make time to explore this wonderful land where wildlife greatly outnumbers humans.

BORGARFJÖRÐUR EYSTRI

This fjord is a prime destination for hiking, as there are numerous well-maintained trails, gorgeous mountains, and deserted bays. The big draw is the spectacular scenery that you don't have to share with hordes of tourists, which is common in other parts of the country.

Sights
KJARVALSSTOFA (KJARVAL MUSEUM)

Kjarvalsstofa (Fjarðarborg, tel. 354/472-9950, www.dyrfjoll.is, noon-6pm daily June-Aug., 500ISK) is a small museum dedicated to the work of celebrated artist Jóhannes Kjarval, who lived 1885-1972 and is known for his haunting landscape paintings as well as paintings that depict saga stories and Iceland's folklore.

Sports and Recreation
BIRD-WATCHING

Birdlife thrives in the area. About 10,000 pairs of puffins nest every summer in Borgarfjörður Eystri from mid-April to mid-August. Other common bird species nesting there are fulmars, kittiwakes, and eider ducks. A great

horses grazing in the Eastfjords

The Eastfjords

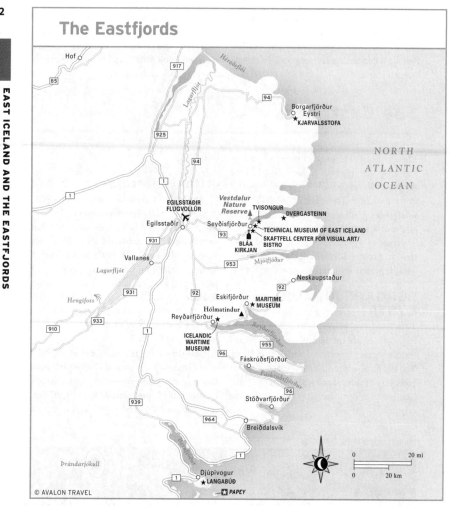

Hof
917
85
Héraðsflói
Lagarfljót
94
Borgarfjörður
Eystri
KJARVALSSTOFA
925
NORTH
ATLANTIC
OCEAN
94
1
1
EGILSSTAÐIR
FLUGVOLLÜR
Vestdalur
Nature
Reserve
TVISONGUR
DVERGASTEINN
Egilsstaðir
Seyðisfjörður
TECHNICAL MUSEUM OF EAST ICELAND
93
SKAFTFELL CENTER FOR VISUAL ART/
931
BLÁA
KIRKJAN
BISTRO
Vallanes
953
Mjóifjörður
Lagarfljót
Neskaupstaður
931
92
Hengifoss
933
92
Eskifjörður
MARITIME
MUSEUM
Hólmatindur
910
1
Reyðarfjörður
Reyðarfjörður
ICELANDIC
WARTIME
MUSEUM
955
96
Fáskrúðsfjörður
Fáskrúðsfjörður
96
939
Stöðvarfjörður
964
Breiðdalsvík
1
Þrándarjökull
0   20 mi
Djúpivogur
0   20 km
LANGABÚÐ
PAPEY
© AVALON TRAVEL

observation platform at the marina connects to a small islet that puffins love, giving you a close view, about two meters away. The islet is a photographer's dream; the birds are plentiful and the scenery breathtaking.

HIKING

Borgarfjörður Eystri is home to numerous well-maintained hiking trails and has earned the nickname "Paradise of the Hiker." There are 27 day routes in the region where hikers can see black-sand beaches, towering mountains, ancient farm ruins, and colorful hills and valleys. The region is also known for its exceptional hiking facilities, including lodges and restrooms at certain points. There is a hiking map for sale at local tourism businesses as well as the information center in Egilsstaðir. The hikes vary in degree of difficulty and length, so be sure to consult the maps closely.

Accommodations and Food

Alfheimar Guesthouse (Brekkubær, tel.

354/861-3677, www.alfheimar.com, rooms from 13,700ISK) is a 28-room remote guesthouse situated by a nearby puffin colony. The hosts, a husband and wife, are friendly and inviting, making you feel like you're staying with friends. The rooms are spacious and have the comforts of home. The free Wi-Fi is surprisingly strong for the region, and the inhouse restaurant has some delicious options. Breakfast is included.

Blábjörg Guesthouse (Gamla Frystihusid, tel. 354/861-1792, www.blabjorg.com, rooms from 10,000ISK) offers 11 rooms in an unexpected building, a renovated fish factory. Don't let that turn you off, though. The rooms are bright and cozy, and six rooms have beautiful seaside views. Amenities include a common kitchen and dining room, shared bathroom facilities, and free Wi-Fi throughout the building. The first floor features a spa and wellness center that has hot tubs and saunas.

Álfacafé (Iðngarðar, tel. 354/472-9884, alfacafe@simnet.is, 10am-8pm daily mid-May-mid-Sept., entrées from 1,500ISK) is a charming small café that serves delicious fish soup, salted cod snacks, and fresh pastries and breads.

Getting There and Around

By car, Route 94 connects to Egilsstaðir, which is about an hour away. Borgarfjörður Eystri is 70 kilometers north of Egilsstaðir.

Daily buses offered by SBA (tel. 354/550-0700, www.sba.is) operate in the summer June through early September. The five-hour trip from the northern town Akureyri costs 8,370ISK each way.

SEYÐISFJÖRÐUR

Seyðisfjörður gets a lot of traffic for a tiny town of fewer than 1,000 residents. This is due to the harbor acting as the main ferry terminal that shuffles passengers to and from continental Europe. You may be arriving as a point of necessity, but the darling town has lots of reasons to stay a couple days and explore.

Sights

BLÁA KIRKJAN (BLUE CHURCH)

The Bláa Kirkjan (Hafnargata 44, tel. 354/470-2308,www.blaakirkjan.is) is a quaint blue wooden church built in 1922 that hosts a series of concerts during the summer months. Concerts range from classical music to choral to jazz. Concerts are on in July and August and cost 2,000ISK. Check the website for

the Bláa Kirkjan

the summer schedule. If you like traditional churches, be sure to check it out, but if you're not seeing a concert here, you can skip it.

TÆKNIMINJASAFN AUSTURLANDS (TECHNICAL MUSEUM OF EAST ICELAND)

The **Technical Museum of East Iceland** (Hafnargata 44, tel. 354/472-1596, www.tekmus.is, 11am-5pm Mon.-Fri. June-mid-Sept., 1,000ISK) is home to the first telegraph station in Iceland along with exhibitions that depict the technical innovations from 1880 to 1950. There are tools on display, a letterpress machine and type, as well as equipment used for the fishing industry. It's an unexpected museum due to the remote surroundings, and it's worth the trip. A couple of exhibitions are meant for children.

TVÍSÖNGUR (SOUND SCULPTURE)

Tvísöngur is a sound sculpture by German artist Lukas Kühne that is situated on a mountainside of Seyðisfjörður. The concrete structure consists of five interconnected domes of different sizes ranging 2-4 meters. Each dome has its own unique resonance that corresponds to a tone in the Icelandic musical tradition of five-tone harmony, and the dome works as a natural amplifier to that tone. Guests can experience an acoustic sensation that can be explored and experimented with. The site's remoteness and serenity offer a perfect setting for playing music or singing—alone, in harmony, or even for an audience. To visit Tvísöngur, guests need to walk a gravel road that starts across from Brimberg Fish Factory (Hafnargata 47). It takes 15-20 minutes and is a moderately difficult walk. Make sure you have good shoes.

MYNDLISTARMIÐSTÖÐ AUSTURLANDS (SKAFTFELL CENTER FOR VISUAL ART)

The **Skaftfell Center for Visual Art** (Austurvegur 42, tel. 354/472-1632, www.skaftfell.is, 10am-4pm Tues. and Thurs.-Fri., 10am-6pm Wed., free) works hard to bring contemporary art exhibitions to a predominantly rural area. And they succeed. The center hosts exhibitions by local artists and visiting artists from an art residency program as well as a permanent exhibition of contemporary art featuring Icelandic and international artists.

VESTDALSEYRI NATURE RESERVE

The Vestdalseyri Nature Reserve, which is about one kilometer north of the town, is a valley known for its many waterfalls and rich birdlife. It's a beautiful place to roam and take in the mountain scenery. There's an easy hike up the nature reserve that is one of the most popular trails in Seyðisfjörður. You can start at Vestdalseyri entrance and follow the trail. After a few glorious waterfalls, you will arrive at a small lake, Vestdalsvatn, which remains frozen most of the year. The hike is about four kilometers and takes about 2.5 hours.

DVERGASTEINN (DWARF BOULDER)

Dvergasteinn (Dwarf Boulder) (Vesturgata 12) was once the site where a church sat, with the boulder behind it. The town's church moved, but the boulder remained, and folklore enthusiasts say the stone is inhabited by dwarves, or "hidden people."

Sports and Recreation

CAMPING

You have the option to camp close to the town center at the **Seyðisfjörður Campsite** (Ranargata 5, tel. 354/472-1521, May-Sept., 1,250ISK per adult, free for children under 14), in a facility that has showers, hot and cold running water, and shared kitchen facilities. There's also a free Internet connection. The campsite accommodates tents and RVs, and hookups are available.

FISHING

Sea Angling Seyðisfjörður (at the marina, tel. 354/471-3060) is a company operated by local fisherman Haraldur Arnason, who will take you out to fish, observe bird settlements, and enjoy the open sea. You can have your catch prepared at Hótel Aldan's restaurant for a fee. The tour is available all year but is dependent on the weather conditions. Call for the schedule and rates, as they vary depending on the time of year.

HIKING

There are quite a few trails in Seyðisfjörður to choose from; they range from easy to more challenging. Hiking maps are available at the town's tourist information center.

For an easy lowland hike, start from the parking area by Austdalsa River and head to the nature reserve Skalanes, where there is a guesthouse and museum. This hike includes views of the gorgeous Skalanesbjarg bird cliffs, where you can see nesting eider ducks May-July. Please be mindful of nests and eggs and be careful where you step along the way. It's about a 90-minute hike and a distance of 4.5 kilometers.

A more challenging trail starts from Skalanes and goes up along the edge of the cliffs to the Skollaskard pass, which is steep. You continue on into a valley, Afrettadalur. The landscape is breathtaking, but be careful to monitor weather conditions. The hike is about four hours and the total distance is 8.5 kilometers.

The hike through Brimnes is another gem of a trek. Brimnes is on the north shore of Seyðisfjörður and was for centuries one of the major fishing villages in East Iceland. Start at the Selsstadir farm, 10 kilometers from the center of town, and you'll find ruins of old buildings and a small orange lighthouse. A walk out to Brimnes in good weather with good visibility is memorable and worth it. Be sure to have your camera ready. The moderately difficult hike is about two hours and a distance of 5.5 kilometers.

Experienced climbers with endurance should check out the historical trail that leads from the Austdalsa parking area, up past the abandoned farmstead Austdalur. It's extremely important to follow the trail posts down into the Brekkugja opening, as well as to be careful when crossing the snowbanks above it, before continuing down Brekkudalur valley to the Brekka settlement, a historic village. The seven-hour, 12-kilometer hike has some steep climbs; make sure you head out in good weather. Check the forecast.

SKIING

The Stafdalur Ski Area (tel. 354/898-2798, stafdalu@stafdalur.is, May-Dec.) is nine kilometers southwest from Seyðisfjörður and has a 1,000-meter ski lift, as well as a lift for children. Cross-country skiing and snowmobiling are possible from the ski area because there is excellent access for snowmobiles from the ski area to magnificent mountains, deserted fjords, and the famous Dyrfjoll mountains. Lift tickets are 4,000ISK.

SWIMMING

The town swimming pool, Sundhöll Seyðisfjarðar (Suðurgata 5, tel. 354/472-1414, 10am-7pm daily, 500ISK) is small, but it's frequented by locals and their children. If the weather is bad, a dip in one of the hot tubs is divine.

Accommodations

★ Hótel Aldan (Norðurgata 2, tel. 354/472-1277, www.hotelaldan.com, rooms from 27,900ISK) is an adorable guesthouse that features seven double rooms and two triples with vintage furniture, antique lamps, and modern amenities, including Wi-Fi, mini bars, private bathrooms with showers, TV and DVD players, and laundry service. The rooms are tasteful, charming, and authentically Icelandic. Breakfast is included in the room rate, and the hotel is open year-round.

Hótel Snæfell (Austurvegur 3, tel. 354/472-1277, www.hotelaldan.com, rooms from 23,900ISK) is operated by the same owners as Hótel Aldan. This guesthouse, however, is based in a large three-story wooden house and offers 12 rooms. The rooms are bright and spacious and feature comfortable beds, but they lack the charm of rooms at Hótel Aldan. Guests have access to free Wi-Fi, a private bathroom with a shower, a small television, and laundry service. Breakfast is included. **Skalanes Mountain Lodge** (Skalanes, tel. 354/861-7008, www.skalanes.com, May-Sept., rooms from 9,800ISK) is a 1927 farmhouse that underwent an extensive renovation in 2007 to include a comfortable library, sauna and hot tub, and a lounge with a classic wood-burning stove. Rooms are small but clean and orderly, and common areas are equipped with Wi-Fi. The deck, which overlooks the sea, has an outdoor fireplace and is a perfect place to curl up with a book when the weather is pleasant. Skalanes's restaurant serves baked cod, lamb fillets, and vegetarian options like veggie burgers.

Hafaldan Seyðisfjörður Hostel (Suðurgata 8, tel. 354/611-4410, www.hafaldan.is, rooms from 6,500ISK) offers rooms in two buildings. Halfaldan Harbor Hostel is on the north side of the fjord, just two minutes from the town center, offering twin, double, and four-bed rooms, all with shared bathroom and kitchen facilities. The second location, Hafaldan Hospital Hostel, occupies a historic former hospital building. It was renovated in 2013 and offers private double rooms as well as double, twin, and dormitory rooms with shared facilities. In both locations, the dining and living rooms are lively and great places to meet fellow travelers. Rooms aren't pretty, but they are clean and adequate. The guests tend to be young budget travelers.

Food

Cafe Lára El Grillo Bar (Norðugata 3, tel. 354/472-1703, 11:30am-1:30am Mon.-Thurs., 11:30am-3:30am Fri.-Sat., 12:30pm-1:30am Sun.) is a relaxed café in town where you can see locals meet up for a cup of coffee, watch a football game, and dine outside when the weather is nice. You can buy coffee, cakes, soups, sandwiches, and other light meals. At night, the place turns into the local bar, and locals gather to drink a few pints and listen to music.

The ★ **Skaftfell Bistro** (Austurvegur 42, tel. 354/472-1633, www.skaftfell.is, noon-9:30pm daily, entrées from 1,500ISK) is a unique, cool spot to grab a bite to eat. The bistro is decorated with artwork by the artist Dieter Roth, and there are shelves of art books to check out while you dine. Sandwiches, pizza, pastries, and soup are on offer.

Information and Services

The **tourist information center** (Hafnargata 44, tel. 354/470-2308, 9am-4pm Mon.-Fri.) is at the ferry terminal by the harbor. You can find brochures about the region, ferry timetables and rates, hiking maps, road maps, and stamps. There's also free Wi-Fi, and a small café serves coffee, soft drinks, and snacks.

Getting There and Around

Seyðisfjörður is 27 kilometers east of Egilsstaðir, the nearest hub. By car, Route 93 is your only option to get to Seyðisfjörður.

FAS (tel. 354/893-2669) operates a year-round daily bus connecting Egilsstaðir's airport to Seyðisfjörður. Each way costs 1,050ISK, and the trip takes about one hour. For information on schedules, visit www.visitseydisfjordur.com/project/local-bus-schedule.

By ferry, **Smyril Line** (tel. 298/345900, www.smyrilline.com) operates a ferry from Denmark to the Faroe Islands to Iceland, with weekly departures from Hirtshals, Denmark. The trip from Denmark to Iceland is approximately 47 hours and costs 90,000ISK each way. For more information, check the rates and schedule online.

REYÐARFJÖRÐUR

Reyðarfjörður's population hovers around 1,000, and locals are amused by the attention their tiny town has been getting of late. The longest and widest of the eastern fjords, Reyðarfjörður has the charm you'd expect from a small town with quaint accommodations and scenic mountain walks.

Sights

ICELANDIC WARTIME MUSEUM

The **Icelandic Wartime Museum** (Spitalakampur, tel. 354/470-9063, 1pm-5pm daily June-Aug., 1,000ISK) may seem like an odd museum to be based in one of the most peaceful countries in the world. Iceland has never had its own military, but British and American troops were based in Iceland for decades leading up to and following World War II. This museum is dedicated to the old days when Allied troops were stationed in the region during World War II. You can find photos, models, weapons, uniforms, and information on how troops passed their time in the small fishing village.

Sports and Recreation
HIKING AND WALKING

Reyðarfjörður is the perfect town for taking leisurely strolls. For instance, lovely slopes above the village include a trail beginning along the southern part of the Búðará River. Above the residential area, you will find delightful areas to explore, such as the Icelandic Wartime Museum.

Accommodations and Food

Hotel Austur (Búðareyri 6, tel. 354/474-1600, rooms from 11,600ISK) looks and feels like a hunting lodge with dim lighting, lots of wood furnishings, and a remote location. Rooms are average-sized and sparsely decorated, and Wi-Fi is available. It's close to a host of activities, including horse riding, golf, skiing, and fishing. The room price includes a breakfast buffet, and the **restaurant** (6pm-10pm daily, entrées from 1,900ISK) serves classic Icelandic food for dinner with lots of fish and lamb on the menu.

Hjá Marlín Guesthouse (Vallargerdi 9, tel. 354/474-1220, rooms from 14,700ISK) is a cozy guesthouse that features singles, doubles, and dorm accommodations. Rooms are small and no-frills, but some rooms have private bathrooms. Guests have access to a fully equipped kitchen, TV lounge, sauna, and laundry facilities. The **restaurant** (5pm-8pm daily, entrées from 2,000ISK) serves lots of lamb dishes as well as fresh fish, including lobster, scallops, cod, and salmon.

Tærgesen Guesthouse (Buðargata 4, tel.

354/470-4444, www.taergesen.is, rooms from 13,900ISK) is an old-fashioned guesthouse that features rooms with standard beds, free Wi-Fi, and wood furnishings. Some rooms have spectacular views of the landscape. The in-house restaurant offers classic Icelandic cuisine, such as smoked leg of lamb and salted cod, but also tourist-friendly fare like hamburgers and pizza.

Getting There

Reyðarfjörður is 58 kilometers south of Seyðisfjörður on Route 92, the only way to the town. Be sure to check the weather forecast before you head out, as the road could be challenging—even dangerous—during wet weather.

ESKIFJÖRÐUR

Eskifjörður is a small, single road town that was established as a base of operations for Norwegian fishermen back in the day. Today, it's a quiet town of about 1,000 residents with a couple of guesthouses that draw tourists in the summer months. A few scenic hiking paths offer splendid views of the landscape and birdlife.

Sights
SJÓMINJASAFN AUSTURLANDS (EAST ICELAND MARITIME MUSEUM)

The **East Iceland Maritime Museum** (Strandgata 39b, tel. 354/470-9063, 1pm-5pm daily June-Aug., 1,000ISK) pays tribute to the town's rich fishing history with exhibits of items relating to fishing and seafaring, as well as artifacts of local trade, industry, and medicine from times past. The collection is housed in a black wooden building that was built in 1816, called **Gamlabúð**.

Sports and Recreation
GOLF

The **Byggðarholt** golf course (Strandgata 71a, tel. 354/892-4622, year-round, 5,500ISK) is a nine-hole course with yardage markers, a putting green, chipping green, and practice bunker area.

HIKING

Mount Holmatindur, which stands 985 meters high, towers over the fjord opposite the town. Locals take great pride in the peak, and while the trek to the top can be challenging to some, those who make it to the top can sign a log book declaring their achievement. Situated near Route 92 just 3.5 kilometers east from the center of town, it's quite easy to get to the mountain. There's a fantastic view of the east from the top. Check the weather forecast before you head out, bring the proper gear, and alert your hotel of your plans.

SWIMMING

The **Eskifjörður Swimming Pool** (tel. 354/476-1218, 6am-9pm Mon.-Fri., 10am-6pm Sat.-Sun. June-Aug., 6am-8pm Mon.-Fri., 1pm-6pm Sat.-Sun. Apr.-May and Sept.-Oct., 650ISK) features an outdoor 25-meter pool, a children's pool with three water slides, two hot tubs, a sauna, and a fitness center.

Accommodations and Food

Hotel Apartments in Eskifjörður (Strandgata 26, tel. 354/892-8657, www.hotelibudir.net, apartments from 12,300ISK) has four self-catering apartments for rent. The apartments are 60 square meters with one bedroom (two beds, extra beds and mattresses available), a living room with a dining area, a fully equipped kitchen, a laundry room, and a bathroom. The apartments have all the comforts of home, including free Wi-Fi. The location is perfect, in the center of town and close to the harbor.

Mjoeyri Guesthouse (Strandgata 120, tel. 354/477-1247, www.mjoeyri.is) offers two types of accommodations: standard rooms at the guesthouse (from 17,000ISK) and five self-catering cottages (from 28,000ISK) that were built in 2007. Cottages are equipped with a kitchen, dining room, one bedroom, and a balcony with a beautiful view of the landscape. Rooms are no-frills with standard beds and basic furnishings. The owners are friendly and accommodating.

The **Seahouse Restaurant** (Strandgata 120, tel. 354/477-1247, lunch and dinner daily in summer, entrées from 3,500ISK) offers local delicacies like shark meat, dried fish, pickled herring, and reindeer steaks as well as fresh fish from the fjord.

Getting There

Eskifjörður is 73 kilometers south of

Mount Holmatindur

Seyðisfjörður on Route 92. Be sure to check the weather forecast before you head out; the road could be challenging—even dangerous—during wet weather.

NESKAUPSTAÐUR

Fifty years ago, Neskaupstaður was only accessible by sea, making it the most remote and untouched spot in the Eastfjords. However, a tunnel was built that connected the town with Eskifjörður through Route 92. There isn't a lot to do, but there is a trio of museums to visit if you want to make a quick stop before continuing on the Ring Road.

Sights

The **Safnahúsið (Museum House)** (Miðstræti 1, tel. 354/ 477-1446, www.fjardabyggd.is, 1pm-5pm daily June-Aug., 1,000ISK) is home to three museums. The **Museum of Natural History** will be a winner if you're traveling with children, as a special exhibition allows them to touch different animals. There are also displays of Icelandic mammals, birds, insects, and shellfish, as well as exhibitions on stones and flora found in East Iceland. The **Josafat Hinriksson Maritime Museum** showcases relics relating to iron work, fishing, boat building, and the way in which people lived in East Iceland in the old days. The town's art museum, the **Tryggvi Olafsson Art Collection,** is dedicated to the works of local artist Tryggvi, who was born in the town in 1940. He is one of East Iceland's most revered contemporary artists. Tryggvi's style is bright, colorful paintings that mix abstract art with wildlife and landscape themes.

Accommodations and Food

Hótel Edda Neskaupstaður (Nesgata 40, tel. 354/444-4860, www.hoteledda.is, mid-June-mid-Aug., rooms from 19,500ISK) offers 29 rooms with private bathrooms and free Wi-Fi. Rooms are average-sized with bright white walls and bedding and a huge window overlooking the mountain landscape. A breakfast buffet is available for 1,750 per person, and the hotel's dinner menu consists of straightforward fish and lamb choices.

Getting There

Neskaupstaður is 72 kilometers southeast of Egilsstaðir on Route 92. Check the weather forecast before you head out, as the road could be challenging, perhaps dangerous, during wet weather.

FÁSKRÚÐSFJÖRÐUR

Fáskrúðsfjörður is a small village of fewer than 500 people nestled on a long fjord of the same name. And, it's the most "French" part of Iceland. The village was originally a base for more than 5,000 French fishermen who came every year in large numbers to fish the Icelandic waters. Some settled here in the late 19th century. The village had a hospital, chapel, and cemetery that were built by the French fishermen, and the history remains, as the streets of Fáskrúðsfjörður are marked in both Icelandic and French. The buildings still exist. If you visit in the last weekend in July, you can join in with the **French Days** festival, which celebrates the town's French history with French-inspired food and flags. A museum aptly named **French Fishermen in Iceland** (Hafnargata 12, tel. 354/470-9000, www.fransmenn.is, 1pm-5pm daily June-Aug., 600ISK) does a great job describing the history of the town and the importance of the impact of the French, and it even has a delightful little café, which is frequented by tourists and locals alike.

Getting There

Fáskrúðsfjörður is 50 kilometers south of Egilsstaðir on Route 92. Be sure to check the weather forecast before you head out because the road could be challenging and dangerous during wet weather.

STÖDVARFJÖRÐUR

Stöðvarfjörður is another minuscule village in the Eastfjords that has strikingly beautiful nature to explore, including a rocky landscape, mountains, and a gorgeous shoreline.

Sights
STEINASAFN PETRU STÖÐVARFIRÐI (PETRA'S STONE & MINERAL COLLECTION)

Petra's Stone & Mineral Collection (Fjarðarbraut 21, tel. 354/475-8834, www. steinapetra.is, 1,000ISK) is a stunning private collection of more than 1,000 stones that are cut and polished, revealing crystals and other beautiful parts of the stones. The owner started amassing stones in 1976, and the collection includes lava, crystals, basalt, pearls, granite, opals, amethysts, and others.

SAXA (SEA GEYSER)

Saxa is an interesting natural phenomenon where the waves crash into a rocky crevice and shoot high into the air, creating water "eruptions." The name Saxa is derived from the kelp and seaweed that are *saxað* (chopped) inside the crevices and then hurled into the air with the waves. The "sea geyser" is a cool sight and unique to the area.

Getting There

Stöðvarfjörður is 73 kilometers southeast of Egilsstaðir on Route 92. Be sure to check the weather forecast before you head out; the road could be dangerous during wet weather.

BREIÐDALSVÍK

Breiðdalsvík is a blip of a town with fewer than 200 residents. There's not much going on here, but a couple of guesthouses serve those who need a break from the Ring Road.

Accommodations and Food

Hótel Bláfell (Solvellir 14, tel. 354/475-6770, www.hotelblafell.is, rooms from 23,200ISK) is a darling 34-room country hotel offering singles, doubles, and family rooms that range from simple modern decor to wood-paneled, rustic chic. All rooms have private bathrooms, free Wi-Fi, and standard beds. The hotel also has a sauna, lounge with fireplace, and library with interesting books and even board games. The restaurant does a nice take on classic fish and lamb dishes, but the menu doesn't have any surprises.

Hótel Staðarborg (tel. 354/475-6760, www.stadarborg.is, rooms from 22,500ISK) offers 30 rooms ranging from singles with shared bathrooms to family rooms. Rooms are small but adequate, with minimal furnishings. There's a hot tub out back, but that's where the amenities end. The restaurant is pricey, as it costs 3,000ISK for breakfast and almost 6,000ISK for a meat or fish dinner. The hotel is located on Route 1, about seven kilometers from Breiðdalsvík. It's a fine spot to spend a night while navigating the Ring Road, but you'll pay quite a bit.

Café Margrét (Heimaleiti, tel. 354/475-6625, cafemargret@simnet.is, rooms from 18,000ISK) is a small four-room guesthouse right off Route 1. The guesthouse has standard rooms with shared bathroom facilities. The restaurant serves up classic Icelandic cuisine (lamb and fish) as well as soups, salads, and sandwiches.

Getting There

Breiðdalsvík is 83 kilometers southeast of Egilsstaðir on Route 1. Check the weather forecast before you head out because wet weather could make the road challenging—even dangerous.

DJÚPIVOGUR

Djúpivogur, a town of fewer than 500 people, has a long history of fishing and trading since 1589. A picturesque landscape is the backdrop to countless hiking trails, where you feel free to roam and explore. Mount Búlandstindur looms over the town, standing at 1,069 meters, dominating the landscape. A few museums are aimed at tourists looking to spend time indoors.

Sights
LANGABÚÐ

Langabúð (Búð 1, tel. 354/478-8220, www.langabud.is, 11am-6pm daily mid-May-mid-Sept., 750ISK) is the oldest building in the town, dating back to 1790, and it houses a heritage museum as well as an exhibition dedicated to a local sculptor. The folk museum contains an eclectic collection of pieces integral to the town's history, including fishing equipment such as whale harpoons as well as antique parts that belonged to early wagons. The collection may seem like there isn't a strong theme, but that's part of the charm, a mishmash of town history. As for the art portion of the building, artist Ríkarður Jónsson (1888-1974) was known as the founder of a national folk art movement in Iceland. Classic themes of work and family are depicted in his portraiture and wood sculpture, and the museum houses many of his wood carvings and tools he used in his work.

FUGLAVEFUR DJUPAVOGS (BIRD AND MINERAL MUSEUM)

The Bird and Mineral Museum (Bakka 1, tel. 354/478-89288, www.djupivogur.is, 10am-6pm daily in summer, 500ISK) holds about 130 species of stuffed birds, along with nests and eggs. There are also photos and books about birdlife and Icelandic minerals. The focus may seem random, but the curators have taken great care to unify the bird and mineral collections under one roof.

★ PAPEY

Papey is a small island south of Djúpivogur. It's affectionately called "Bird Island" by many due to the 30,000 pairs of puffins that occupy the island during the summer. Eider ducks and black-legged kittiwakes typically nest on Papey as well.

Papey is about two square kilometers, teeming with birdlife and seals basking on the island's reefs. The island's history has played an important role in constructing the history of Iceland, because Irish monks are believed to have lived there before the Viking settlement. The monks left when the Vikings came because they didn't want to share the land with unsavory fellows. The island is named after the monks, who were called Papar, and other local names like Papatættur and Írsku Hólar (Irish Hills) also reflect their presence.

Papey is home to the smallest and oldest wooden church in the country, which was built in 1807. North of the church is a beautiful hill called Einbúi (The Loner), where the church of the fairies is supposed to be located, according to Icelandic lore.

Papeyjarferðir (tel. 354/478-8119, www.djupivogur.is/papey) runs guided tours to the island at 1pm daily June-August from Djúpivogur Marina. During the boat trip, guests have the opportunity to see seals hanging out in the surf and on the rocks. Have your camera ready! The trip is four

Papey is home to the smallest and oldest wooden church in Iceland.

hours long and includes a guided hike on the island. This is your chance to visit the island, as the tour is the only opportunity to get a peek. The tour is 9,000ISK for adults, 4,500ISK for children aged 5-11 and free for children under 5.

Sports and Recreation
CAMPING
The **Djúpivogur Campground** (tel. 354/478-8887, May-mid-Sept., 1,000ISK per person) is conveniently situated close to Hótel Framtíð, which is where you have to pay to camp. At the height of the summer season (July), the site is littered with vans and campers, but it can feel like a little community and it's fun to meet fellow travelers. The facilities are decent, with an indoor cooking area and steaming hot showers. The campground is on an open field, and there is room for tents and RVs, with hookups available.

HIKING AND BIRD-WATCHING
Hiking the serene and well-kept trails around the flat **Bulandsnes Peninsula** is a must for bird-watchers. There are two different routes, and both begin and end at the cairn Bondavarða east of Djúpivogur. The longer route is about 10 kilometers, a moderate four-hour hike, and the shorter one is easier and approximately 5 kilometers, which should take about two hours.

For the bird-watching enthusiasts, most of the birds nesting in Iceland can be seen on or around Bulandsnes during the migration period in the summer. The most interesting places for bird-watchers are the lakes Breidivogur and Fyluvogur. On these two lakes, you can see species of ducks such as tufted ducks and pintails. In this area there are also less common species, including red-throated divers and black-tailed godwits.

If you opt for the shorter route, you must turn on Ulfseyjarsund (a fork) and continue to the airstrip, then to the lakes Breidivogur and Fyluvogur and back to where you started.

If you choose the longer route, you have to turn near Ulfseyjarsund, go to the airstrip, and

from there hike to Ulfsey. At the southwest tip of Ulfsey, there is a sign, and from there you can choose which way to go: to view Ulfsey, Hvaley, or Sandey. Then you go back the same way from the sign in Ulfsey, to the airstrip and then to the lakes Breidivogur and Fyluvogur and back to Bondavarða. Ulfsey, Hvaley, and Sandey are islets that are now connected to the land but were once separated by sea.

SWIMMING
On a rainy day, the **Djúpivogur Swimming Pool** (Varða 6, tel. 354/478-8999, 7am-8:30pm Mon.-Fri., 10am-6pm Sat.-Sun, 500ISK) is a great option. In the winter, you will see locals and their children taking a dip in the heated pool or one of the hot tubs, but the summer gets a lot of traffic from tourists.

Accommodations and Food
★ **Hótel Framtíð** (Vogalandi 4, tel. 354/478-8887, www.hotelframtid.com, rooms from 26,000ISK) is the place to go if you want to stay in town. This is the only close option. The 42-room hotel has wood-paneled rooms that remind you of a hunting lodge, standard beds, and simple furnishings. The **Framtíð Restaurant** features a three-course menu (from 4,780ISK) starting with a fish soup or soup of the day. Entrées include baked fish with white butter sauce, chicken breast with salad and potatoes, and lamb filets with fresh vegetables and potatoes. Desserts are scrumptious, including whipped *skyr* with cream and mixed berries and apple cake with fresh cream.

Berunes Hostel (Berufjörður, tel. 354/478-8988, www.berunes.is, Apr.-Sept., rooms from 10,500ISK) is a charming converted farmhouse just outside Djúpivogur. The hostel offers rooms that accommodate 1-4 people as well as five self-contained cottages that can house 2-5 people. Rooms are small but comfortable, and some of them remind you of a guesthouse out of the 1970s. Berunes serves meals in a building next to the hostel. **Gestastofa Café** serves breakfast daily, and a three-course dinner is served in July and August.

Langabúð (Búð 1, tel. 354/478-8220, 10am-6pm Mon.-Thurs., 10am-11:30pm Fri.-Sat., 10am-6pm Sun. mid-May-Sept., meals from 1,400ISK) is a tiny café that serves pastries, coffee, and light meals that hit the spot. The cakes are hard to resist, and the ingredients for the soups and sandwiches are local and fresh.

Information and Services

The **tourist information center** (Bakka 3, tel. 354/478-8204, www.djupivogur.is, 9am-5pm Mon.-Fri., noon-4pm Sat.-Sun. mid-May-mid-Sept.) offers hiking maps, brochures about the region, and Internet access.

Getting There

Djúpivogur is 86 kilometers south of Egilsstaðir on Route 1.

SBA (tel. 354/550-0700, www.sba.is) operates daily bus trips from Egilsstaðir to Djúpivogur June through mid-September. The three-hour trip costs 5,040ISK each way.

The Vatnajökull Region

In the Vatnajökull region, Iceland earns its ubiquitous "fire and ice" nickname. You'll see the glacier descend into black sands and hot streams erupt from frozen banks of ice.

The region is easy to access, as there are frequent flights and buses between Reykjavík and Höfn. For flights, check out **Eagle Air** (www.eagleair.is), and for buses, try **Strætó** (www.straeto.is) and **Reykjavik Excursions** (www.re.is). Höfn is the best gateway to the region and the perfect town to base yourself in.

HÖFN

Höfn, which means harbor, is the gateway to Vatnajökull glacier, and guesthouses and cafés accommodate the growing number of tourists to the region. There are fewer than 2,000 residents of Höfn, which makes it quite a sleepy town, but it comes alive in the summer, when legions of tourists from around the world gear up to scale the glacier. The town has a few small museums, including a spectacular one dedicated to the looming Vatnajökull.

Höfn harbor

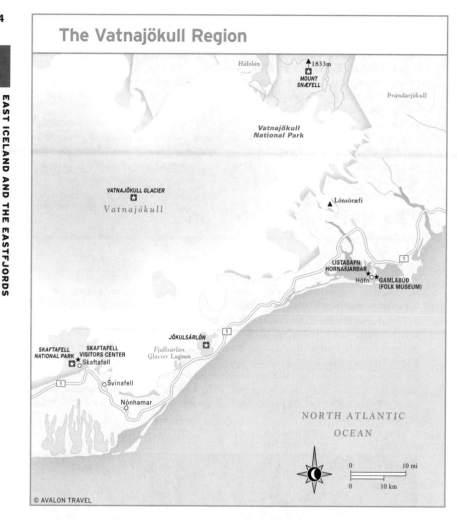

The Vatnajökull Region

Hálslón

▲1833m
✠
MOUNT
SNÆFELL

Þrándarjökull

**Vatnajökull
National Park**

VATNAJÖKULL GLACIER
✠
Vatnajökull

▲ Lónsöræfi

LISTASAFN
HORNAFJARÐAR
★
Höfn ○★ GAMLABÚÐ
(FOLK MUSEUM)

1

JÖKULSÁRLÓN
✠
Fjallsárlón
Glacier Lagoon

1

SKAFTAFELL   SKAFTAFELL
NATIONAL PARK   VISITORS CENTER
✠   ★ ○ Skaftafell

1   ○ Svínafell

Nónhamar ○

**NORTH ATLANTIC
OCEAN**

0   10 mi
0   10 km

© AVALON TRAVEL

Sights
JÖKLASÝNING (GLACIER EXHIBITION)

Höfn's **Glacier Exhibition** (Hafnarbraut 30, tel. 354/478-2665, 10am-6pm daily June-Aug., 1pm-6pm daily May and Sept., 1pm-4pm daily Oct.-Apr., 1,200ISK) is a great option to learn all about the glacier and check out photos and a film about the 1996 eruption, without getting up close and personal. And even if you do hike the glacier, the exhibition is still worth visiting to get a sense of the history and environment of the region.

GAMLABÚÐ (FOLK MUSEUM)

The **Folk Museum** (Hafnarbraut, tel. 354/478-1833, 10am-5pm daily year-round, free) has a small collection of artifacts that shows how life was like in one of the most isolated parts of the country from the 19th century on. You will find objects related to the old ways of farming, including antique tractors and cars. The museum is small, and free, but don't feel bad if you miss it.

LISTASAFN HORNAFJARÐAR (HORNAFJÖRÐUR ART MUSEUM)

The Hornafjörður Art Museum (Hafnarbraut 27, tel. 354/470-8000, 9am-4pm Mon.-Fri., 11am-4pm Sat.-Sun. May-Sept., 9am-4pm Mon.-Fri. and by request rest of year, free) displays the work of celebrated local artist Svavar Gudnason, who had a strong connection to his hometown Höfn and the Vatnajökull region. Svavar was born in Höfn in 1909 and spent

his youth there before moving to Reykjavík in 1928. He had been introduced to landscape painting at an early age, and his work depicts the natural surroundings in Southeast Iceland, portraying the sea, glaciers, lakes, and mountains. In the winter months, other artists are displayed alongside Svavar.

Sports and Recreation

BIRD-WATCHING

Bird-watchers must head to Ósland, a conservation area in the south of Höfn that was once an island but is now connected to the

Visiting Vatnajökull National Park

Vatnajökull National Park

Vatnajökull National Park (www.vatnajokulsthjodgardur.is) is huge, covering 13 percent of the island and 13,700 square kilometers, and is the largest national park in western Europe.

Skaftafell and Jökulsárgljúfur National Parks were combined with Vatnajökull glacier in 2008 to form the giant Vatnajökull National Park. Skaftafell and Jökulsárgljúfur are now considered the southern and northern divisions of Vatnajökull National Park.

Vatnajökull National Park has visitors centers in the south (Skaftafell visitors center), in the east (Snæfellsstofa visitors center at Egilsstaðir), and in the north (Jökulsárgljúfur National Park's visitors center at Ásbyrgi).

There are no roads in the national park except for the tracks leading up to private farms. Wardens operate in the park, assisted by park rangers during the summer months (June-August). Visitors are encouraged to seek information and advice from park staff. Hiking trips led by park rangers give visitors the opportunity to get to know the area and find out about its history, ecology, and geology, in the company of a well-informed guide. The hikes follow a variety of routes, and everyone should be able to find a suitable outing.

an arctic tern during nesting season

mainland (you can reach it by walking from the harbor in Höfn). Arctic terns are a common sight during their nesting season, which takes place early in the summer, and there are walking trails along the perimeter of a pond they frequent. Located on the hill Óslandshæð is a memorial to fishermen lost at sea and an information board about the surrounding natural area, including details on the flora and fauna.

CAMPING
The **Höfn Campground** (Hafnarbraut 52, tel. 354/478-1606, June-Aug., 1,100ISK per person) is one of the nicer ones in the region and gets quite a bit of traffic when it's open in summer. Campers have access to steaming hot showers and a nice cooking area, washing machines, and the Internet. The site accommodates tents and RVs, with hookups available.

GOLF
The **Silfurnesvöllur** golf course (Dalbraut, tel. 354/478-2197, 4,000ISK) is on the outskirts of Höfn. It is a well-kept nine-hole course open year-round that stretches along the shore with a breathtaking view over Vatnajökull glacier and mountain ridge.

SWIMMING
The local **Höfn Swimming Pool** (Víkurbraut 9, tel. 354/470-8477, 7am-9pm Mon.-Fri., 10am-7pm Sat.-Sun. mid-May-Sept., 7am-9pm Mon.-Fri., 10am-5pm Sat.-Sun. Oct.-mid-May, 600ISK) isn't as spectacular as some of the other pools in the region, but it's a nice spot to take a dip when taking a break from hiking and touring.

Accommodations
Hótel Edda Höfn (Ranarslod 3, tel. 354/444-4850, www.hoteledda.is, mid-May-late Sept., rooms from 22,500ISK) is a chain hotel offering 36 rooms that are spacious and bright, but devoid of character. But the amenities are good, and each room has a private bathroom. Guests have access to free Wi-Fi and parking, and a yummy breakfast buffet is available for 1,750ISK per person.

Hótel Höfn (Víkurbraut 20, tel. 354/478-1240, www.hotelhofn.is, rooms from 21,600ISK) is a 68-room hotel that is looks and feels like a chain hotel designed for business travelers. The rooms are sparsely furnished with standard beds, hardwood floors, flat-screen TVs, and free Wi-Fi. The in-house restaurant serves classic Icelandic cuisine ranging from fresh fish to lamb dishes. There are a couple of vegetarian options.

Höfn Inn Guesthouse (Ránarslóð 2, tel. 354/478-1503, www.hofninn.is/hvammur, rooms from 24,000ISK) is a cute guesthouse that is decorated with local art and furnishings. The 30 single, double, and family rooms have wash basins but share bathroom facilities.

Nýlibær Guesthouse (Hafnarbraut 8, tel. 354/478-1736, www.hostel.is, rooms from 24,000ISK) is in a pretty location, just a two-minute walk to the harbor. Rooms are small but brightly decorated, and guests have access to free Wi-Fi and free parking. Bathrooms are shared, and guests can use a common coffee area. Breakfast is included.

Food

★ **Hótel Höfn** (Víkurbraut 20, tel. 354/478-1240, www.hotelhofn.is, 6pm-10pm daily, 3,900ISK) has quite an eclectic menu for a hotel restaurant. There are quite a few lobster dishes on the menu, and you can't go wrong with any. The chili and garlic roasted lobster tails are divine. Other menu options include "tapas for two," featuring cod, lamb, beef, and shrimp options; pizza; vegetarian entrées; and pasta.

The **Víkin Restaurant** (Víkurbraut 2, tel. 354/478-2300, 9am-1am Sun.-Thurs., 9am-3am Fri.-Sat., 2,500ISK) is the local town watering hole as well as restaurant. Locals come for delicious lobster dishes and local fish entrées. The food is classic comfort food with no surprises.

Information and Services

The **tourist information center** (Heppuvegur 1, tel. 354/470-8330, www.visitvatnajokull.is, 8am-8pm daily June-Aug., 10am-6pm daily May and Sept., 9am-1pm daily Oct.-Apr.) has tourist brochures about the region and hiking maps as well as Internet access and booking information for day tours.

Getting There and Around

Höfn is on Route 1, 187 kilometers south of Egilsstaðir and 451 kilometers east of Reykjavík.

Höfn is challenging to get to if you aren't renting a car. **Strætó** (tel. 354/540-2700, www.straeto.is) operates one bus (bus 51) that leaves from the bus station Mjodd in Reykjavík every day, and it's about a seven-hour bus trip. The trip costs 11,600ISK each way.

By air, **Eagle Air** (tel. 354/562-4200, www.eagleair.is) operates daily flights from Reykjavík for 26,000ISK each way. The flight is about one hour long.

LÓNSÖRÆFI

Lónsöræfi is an isolated wildlife preserve in a raw part of the east, with birds outnumbering humans by the thousands. Bird enthusiasts looking for a glimpse of whimbrels will love Lónsöræfi. The brown and white waders with curved bills can be seen year-round.

The landscape is striking, but unforgiving, with strong winds and remnants of sub-glacial eruptions of the past. It's a beautiful patch of land, but be sure to monitor the weather closely before you head out for a hike, and keep in mind that there are not a lot of guesthouses or eateries nearby. You will feel like you're on your own, because in much of the area, you are. For accommodations, base yourself in Höfn.

Hiking from Mount Snæfell to Lónsöræfi

The trek from Mount Snæfell to Lónsöræfi is growing in popularity. The hike, which starts at the **Snæfellsskáli mountain hut** (GPS coordinates N 64.8042, W 15.6418; tel. 354/575-8400), is about 55 kilometers and takes 3-7 days, depending on your pace and what you want to see. It's challenging and for experienced hikers only.

The landscape is rocky and angular, with sweeping hills and vast valleys. Colors are muted, and the atmosphere is serene. Along the trek, hikers will see glaciers, waterfalls, and cliffs.

Make sure you have proper gear like

waterproof clothing for rain and wind, as well as enough water and food for the duration of the hike. There are mountain huts to stay in along the way; make sure you have maps and your itinerary set before heading out.

Getting There

The only road into the Lónsöræfi reserve is the F980, a rough road off of Route 1 that ends after 25 kilometers at Illikambur. As it's only drivable for super jeeps (which are huge and outfitted for rugged terrain) and experienced drivers, please do not attempt to take a compact car or SUV on the trip. There is a river crossing along the way, and you will get stuck.

★ VATNAJÖKULL GLACIER

Vatnajökull (Water Glacier) is a cool spot to visit—quite literally, as it's Iceland's remaining piece of the last ice age. Vatnajökull features miles of white, pure ice, intertwined with blue and smoky hues in interesting shapes formed by compressed ice. It's a wide-open space, sitting on top of active volcanoes. You will experience whipping winds, sky-high elevations, and cold temperatures.

Vatnajökull has the distinction of being the largest glacier in Europe and the third largest in the world (after glaciers in Greenland and Antarctica). The glacier spans 8,805 square kilometers, which covers about 8 percent of the country, and the average thickness is 400 meters.

Of the volcanoes, the most active is the system near Mount Grímsfjall (1,719 meters) at Grímsvötn (1,725 meters). Mount Barðarbunga (2,009 meters), which awakened in 2014, is another volcano fissure. There were thousands of earthquakes over the summer of 2014, stirring the sleeping giant awake. Mount Kverkfjöll (1,929 meters) and Mount Hvannadalshnjúkur (2,110 meters) also lie beneath the glacier.

Vatnajökull's vast, rugged terrain is a large draw for hikers and climbers around the world, but be sure you come prepared. Bring the necessary gear, monitor weather conditions, and alert people of your whereabouts.

Sports and Recreation

You can explore the glacier on a tour or with a private guide.

If you'd like to explore the glacier by snowmobile and jeep, Vatnajökull Travel (Bugðuleira 2, Höfn, tel. 354/894-1616, www.vatnajokull.is) offers tours all year. An 11-hour tour includes pickup at your hotel, jeep and snowmobile rides, and a boat ride on Jökulsárlón, which features large pieces of glacial ice that languish off-shore. It's a spectacular sight. It's a fantastic way to spend the day and explore the region. The tour costs 42,000ISK.

Atlantsflug (tel. 354/854-4105, www.flightseeing.is) offers flights from Skaftafell Airport, its private airport near Vatnajökull National Park, to various locations around Vatnajökull glacier, including locations like Grímsvötn (volcano), Katla (volcano), Eyjafjallajökull (volcano), Langisjór (lake), Laki (crater), and Lakagigar (crater). You'll get a spectacular aerial view of volcanoes, mountains, glaciers, lakes, and rivers. Flight tours start at 33,000ISK for 75 minutes.

★ JÖKULSÁRLÓN

Photos of Jökulsárlón (Glacier Lagoon) remind people that despite the lava fields and bright green landscapes in the summertime, there is quite a bit of ice in Iceland. You can view glacial landscapes up close with chunks of ice scattered about and walls of ice jutting up from the sea. It's a spectacular sight that begs to be photographed. Huge blocks of ice constantly break off the glacier, with icebergs varying in size floating on the icy water. The lagoon is not very wide, but it is up to 250 meters deep, which makes it the deepest lake in Iceland.

If you'd like a closer look at the icebergs, Glacier Lagoon (Jökulsárlón Ehf, tel. 354/478-2222, www.icelagoon.is, 9am-7pm daily June-Aug., 10am-5pm daily Apr.-May and Sept.-Oct., 4,000ISK) offers tours on

Glacial Floods

When Grímsvötn volcano erupted underneath Vatnajökull in 1996, the world watched in fascination as lava flowed from fissures and ash launched thousands of feet into the air. But another phenomenon captured the attention of millions—*jökulhlaup,* which is Icelandic for glacial floods. A glacial flood occurs when water dammed by a sub-glacial lake is released, triggered by volcanic eruptions. Glacial lakes can hold millions to hundreds of millions of cubic meters of water and can wreak havoc on surrounding areas when released.

Locals still talk about the 1996 eruption, and you have a chance to relive it through a film shown at the Skaftafell visitors center.

amphibious boats April-October. During the excursion, you sail among the huge icebergs, get to taste the 1,000-year-old ice, and, if you are lucky, might even see some seals bobbing in the lagoon. The tour takes about 40 minutes and includes an English-speaking guide who explains the geology of the lagoon. The tours depart depending on weather, so be sure to call ahead to check if the tour is going.

Jökulsárlón is a popular destination throughout the year, but it's quite crowded during the height of the summer season (July-August). It's close to Route 1, 80 kilometers west of Höfn and 377 kilometers east of Reykjavík.

★ SKAFTAFELL NATIONAL PARK

Skaftafell is one of East Iceland's most beautiful places, where visitors are treated to striking white glaciers against a backdrop of green fields and black sands.

A common draw for many tourists is the black-sand beaches, which are a result of glaciers grinding down the bedrock. It's particularly striking on clear days with the snowcapped mountains and blue skies in the background. Much of the black sand is carried to the sea by glacial rivers, the waves and winds shaping the sand into complex formations. In the most western part of the Vatnajökull region is 1,000-square-kilometer Skeiðarársandur, which is the largest black glacier sand area in the world. It can be accessed by Route 1.

Tourism companies offer everything from

ice walks to jeep tours. Icelandic Mountain Guides (tel. 354/587-9999, www.mountain-guides.is) offers a year-round guided tour walking on the Svínafellsjökull glacier tongue in Skaftafell National Park. The two-hour tours costs 8,900ISK.

Visitors Center

Whether you're just passing through, or planning a long hike, it makes sense to stop at the Skaftafell visitors center (Skaftafellsvegur, tel. 354/470-8300, www.vatnajokulsthjodgardur.is), which distributes maps and also has an exhibition on the geology and ecology found in the national park. The center is open 11am-4pm daily January and December, 10am-5pm daily February-April and October-November, 9am-7pm daily May and September, 8am-9pm daily June-August.

Waterfalls

Hundafoss (Hound Falls) was named after the many dogs that were swept over the edge during floods. Be prepared to take a lot of pictures here. The falls are gorgeous in all seasons. In the summer, the rocky terrain behind the falls are surrounded by beautiful greenery. The drop is steep and the roar is soothing. Þjófafoss (Thieves' Falls) is another smaller waterfall set against a backdrop of lava fields. Up ahead is the more spectacular Svartifoss (Black Falls) waterfall. Visitors are treated to sights of thundering white water falling over striking black basalt rock columns. At the visitors center in Skaftafell, you can get information on how to get to Svartifoss waterfall.

It's just 1.5 kilometers from the visitors center, and the trail is clearly marked. Svartifoss cannot be seen from the road, and the hike is about 90 minutes back and forth at a leisurely pace.

The hike is easy, and it may be a surprise that you're going upwards; the view from above will alert you. On your way back you can either return the same way or cross the river by Svartifoss and return back there. On that route you will get a closer look at Þjófafoss.

Accommodations and Camping

If you want to stay inside the park, the **Skaftafell Campground** (tel. 354/470-8300, May-Sept., 1,500ISK per night adults, 700ISK children 13-16, free for children under 12) is your only option. The campground is located next to the entrance gate to the park. Visitors should register prior to camping. Vehicle entry is allowed 7:30am-11pm. The facilities are great, but keep in mind that there is a distance between the facilities and where you set up camp. The campground offers hot showers and bathrooms (bring flip-flops; it can get pretty dirty during the height of camping season). Visitors can stock up on food and basic supplies at the visitors center, but it is advisable to bring what you need with you. The visitors center is also where you pay for your tent/camper entrance. The open field accommodates about 400 tents, and there is a section for RVs with the option to pay for electricity.

If camping isn't your thing, don't fret because there are nearby hotels and guesthouses outside the park.

Hótel Skaftafell (Skaftafelli 2 Freysnesi, tel. 354/478-1945, www.hotelskaftafell.is, rooms from 22,000ISK) is a 63-room hotel that looks a bit rustic, but it's comfortable and close to the national park. Rooms are standard with private bathrooms and classic countryside decor. A standard breakfast is included.

Hof 1 Hotel (Austurhus, tel. 354/478-2260, www.hof1.is, rooms from 26,900ISK) offers 37 rooms and a few self-catered cottages. The ranch-style countryside hotel has spacious, surprisingly modern rooms, a friendly staff,

Svartifoss

and a great breakfast buffet included in the room price. The hotel is about a 15-minute drive from Skaftafell.

Food

If you're not bringing your own food (which is a huge mistake), your only close option is the restaurant at Hótel Skaftafell (Skaftafelli 2 Freysnesi, tel. 354/478-1945, www.hotelskaftafell.is, 8am-9pm daily), which serves traditional lamb and fish dishes as well as a few vegetarian options. The restaurant has a huge banquet room that tends to fill up with busloads full of tourists.

Information and Services

The national park office (tel. 354/478-1627, 8am-9pm daily June-Aug., 10am-3pm daily May and Sept.), which is near the entrance to the park, also serves as the visitors center. Here, you will find information about the region, maps, and someone on hand to answer all your questions about the history and geology of the region.

Getting There

Skaftafell National Park is on the Ring Road, Route 1, about 330 kilometers east of Reykjavík and 130 kilometers west of Höfn.

Strætó (tel. 354/540-2700, www.straeto.is) operates a daily bus (bus 51) from the Mjodd bus station in Reykjavík. The trip takes about five hours and costs 8,800ISK each way.

ÖRÆFI

Öræfi is farm country. Comprising about 24 farms, the region is known for livestock farms and overcoming harsh weather, fallout from volcanic eruptions, and glacial floods. The region is known as "the land between the sands" for its striking black-sand beaches, and the region's residents come from hardy stock, as it has never been an easy place to live or make a living. With looming mountains and glaciers, locals are always reminded of the region's history, especially the 1362 eruption of Öræfajökull, which was one of the most destructive eruptions in Iceland's history thanks to devastating floods. The land was covered in ash, driving residents from their farms to rebuild and start anew. To give you an idea of the desolation of the area, the *öræfi* means "wasteland" in Icelandic.

Getting There

Öræfi is about 20 kilometers southeast of Skaftafell National Park on Route 1.

The Highlands

Iceland's uninhabited interior is home to an otherworldly landscape that must be seen to be believed.

It's full of dramatic and wild scenery, cut by endless wind and vast expanses of ice and desert, the most unique and unforgiving landscape on the island, complete with lava and volcanoes. The country's largest glaciers (Vatnajökull, Langjökull, and Hofsjökull) are the backdrop to the region.

The isolation seems romantic to some, especially travelers who seek to explore a region relatively free of fellow tourists. But the highlands are not for tourists seeking easy hiking trails with lush greenery and gorgeous fjords in the background. The region is largely devoid of plant life because it's pretty dry throughout the year—the highlands are essentially a desert. That said, if you are an avid hiker and looking to explore something different in Iceland, the highlands may be for you.

PLANNING YOUR TIME

Planning a trip to the highlands depends very much on what you want to do. If you want a peek at the interior, take a day tour to see glaciers, volcanoes, and the landscape. Most of the companies offering tours to the highlands are based in Reykjavík. Others like to plan five-day hikes throughout the interior. If you are keen on a lengthy hike, be sure to plan thoroughly, bring adequate supplies, and take proper safety precautions.

Travelers have fewer choices for accommodations (mainly huts) and food, and they must stay abreast of the weather forecast. Be prepared for anything in the highlands, and make sure to book your accommodation or campsite ahead of time.

SAFETY

Navigating the highlands should not be taken lightly. The roads are rough, the wind punishing, and the weather can be unpredictable—it can snow any day of the year. Pay close attention to road closures, and if a road calls for a super jeep to traverse, don't attempt the ride in a smaller car. You will likely damage your car. (A super jeep is a huge jeep with gigantic tires outfitted to handle rough terrain.) The best plan is to discuss your itinerary with the rental company and see if a super jeep is necessary for your plan. Do not guess; a mistake will be costly. Also, be mindful of filling up

---

Previous: a super jeep at Langjökull Glacier; the volcanic landscape of the highlands. **Above:** flowers growing in Askja's lava field.

Highlights

© AVALON TRAVEL

★ **Ódáðahraun:** The largest lava field in Iceland is actually considered an Arctic desert. See unusual lava and sand formations shaped by eruptions (page 227).

★ **Laugafell:** This popular geothermal hot spot is a desert oasis in an isolated stretch of the highlands (page 228).

★ **Hiking Mount Askja:** Hiking the rim of this volcano offers sensational views—and a can't-miss adventure (page 229).

★ **Langjökull Glacier:** Iceland's second-largest glacier, this mammoth ice cap beckons hikers and glacier walkers, but the crevasses and unpredictable weather should keep you on alert at all times (page 231).

your car with gas, because gas stations are few and far between in the highlands.

If you are planning a hike, be sure to wear appropriate windproof clothing, bring an adequate amount of water and food, and alert people of your trip itinerary. Bring maps and a compass, and know where all the emergency huts are located on your route. Be prepared for anything, and don't underestimate Iceland's weather. If you find yourself in an emergency, dial the emergency number 112.

GETTING AROUND

The highlands are a seasonal destination, and that season is short. Snow could fall at any time of year. If you are planning a trip in the summer, there still might be road closures due to a late snowfall or possible volcanic activity. Roads to the interior are typically open June-August, but check for closures before you head out. For up-to-date conditions, visit the Icelandic Road and Coastal Administration website at www.vegagerdin.is.

When it comes to car rentals, if you are planning to drive to the highlands don't skimp. It's best to drive a four-wheel-drive vehicle in the highlands, but if you want to go off the Kjölur route, a super jeep is necessary, because there are river crossings and harsh terrain. A lot of different insurance options are offered on car rentals, and be mindful that Reykjavík driving is very different from driving in the highlands. There can be sandstorms and wind damage, so pick the right insurance for the region you plan to travel to. Fill up with gas before you leave and take gas cans.

TOURS

If you don't want to worry about renting a car and navigating the highlands on your own, tour companies offer everything from day trips to several-day tours. These companies are recommended.

Reykjavik Excursions (tel. 354/580-5400, www.re.is) offers a 12-hour day tour through Landmannalaugar in the highlands, and also includes sights such as Mount Hekla and Þjórsárdalur in the south. Tours run from July to September and are 17,900ISK per person. Guests are picked up in Reykjavík.

Extreme Iceland (tel. 354/588-1300, www.extremeiceland.is) is a Reykjavík-based company that operates a two-day tour where you start off exploring the Golden Circle (Þingvellir National Park, Geysir, and Gullfoss) and continue to the geothermal area of Hveravellir in the Kjölur highlands. The tour (60,000ISK) includes hiking, sightseeing, and bathing in geothermal pools. Guests are picked up in Reykjavík. Extreme Iceland

Bárðarbunga Blows!

Iceland's most recent volcanic eruption began in August 2014 in the Bárðarbunga volcanic system. After a swarm of thousands of earthquakes over several weeks, the eruption began, emitting huge volumes of sulfur dioxide, impacting air quality in parts of Iceland, especially the east. The so-called fissure eruption occurred in the Holuhraun lava field, which is northeast of the Bárðarbunga caldera. Lava fountains shot several meters into the air from the crack in the earth.

The Holuhraun eruption did not occur underneath the ice cap, so there wasn't ash fallout. However, the airspace was closed three nautical miles around the eruption area up to 1,524 meters—meaning it did not affect commercial flights flying over Iceland.

The eruption ended in late February 2015 after six months of fiery lava shooting up from the earth. Locally, the event was referred to as a "tourist eruption," as tourists from around the world clamored to get a glimpse of the lava. But the only people allowed close to the site were journalists and scientists. Today, however, tours survey the area.

The Highlands

© AVALON TRAVEL

also offers a three-day trip (150,000ISK) that includes a super jeep ride to the Bárðarbunga eruption site. The price includes accommodations. Day 1 explores Landmannalaugur, day 2 the eruption site, and the last day takes guests to the Golden Circle.

Icelandic Mountain Guides (tel. 354/587-9999, www.mountainguides.is) runs a 12-day tour that hits all the hot spots in the highlands. Super jeeps will take you through the Kjölur and Sprengisandur routes, where you will see the Vatnajökull glacier, the Askja volcano, and the geothermal mountains of Kerlingarfjöll and Landmannalaugar. The package will run you 415,000ISK. Guests are picked up in Reykjavík.

Sprengisandur (Route F26)

Black lava, gigantic boulders, and towering mountains in the distance await you along Sprengisandur. Tourists travel to this region to check out what is essentially an Arctic desert. It's dry and barren with water trapped in the glaciers. Iceland's summer is warm enough for significant melting.

SIGHTS
Mount Trölladyngja

Mount Trölladyngja (Troll's Volcano) is the largest shield volcano in the country and connects the Grimsvotn and Bárðarbunga central volcanoes. Mount Trölladyngja (1,468 meters), which is still active, is 10 kilometers in diameter with a 100-meter-deep crater on top. Lava flowed from it in all directions, especially to the north and west. The Gaesavotn Route F910 passes through the north of it, and a four-wheel-drive vehicle is necessary. The GPS coordinates are N 64.8931, W 17.2547.

★ Ódáðahraun

Ódáðahraun (Crime Lava Field) not only is the largest lava field in Iceland, but also it's the largest desert in Europe, spanning over 6,000 square kilometers. Black, brown, and gray dominate the landscape. Visitors to the area will see kilometers of sand, vast expanses of lava, and interesting geological formations shaped by volcanic activity over the centuries. The lava shapes range from flat and smooth

Sprengisandur's designated parking area

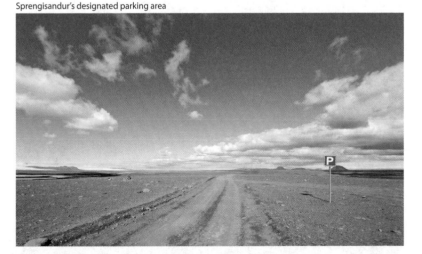

to rough and jagged. The region garnered its name "crime lava" based on lore that numerous criminals hid out in the area trying to elude the authorities. The wind blows strongly, and there always seems to be a chill in the air. It's an eerie place to visit—the isolation is overwhelming. Route F88 takes you to Ódáðahraun.

★ Laugafell

Laugafell (Bath Mountain) is situated near the northeast of the Hofsjökull glacier and about 20 kilometers southwest from the end of Eyjafjarðardalur, a valley. What makes this area so spectacular is that the mountain (879 meters) is adjacent to a geothermal hot spot. Three mountain huts are open during the summer with cooking facilities and a geothermal nature pool outdoors. Hot springs are on the northwestern region of the mountain. It's a special place in the vast barren stretch of the highlands. Patches of grass and plants with bubbling pools make it a desert oasis. Laugafell's GPS coordinates are N 65.0278, W 18.3319, and the region is accessible by Route F821.

Askja

Askja is a caldera in the Dyngjufjöll Mountains. Calderas are dramatic volcanic features that were formed by collapsing land after a volcanic eruption; they are essentially huge volcanic craters. The area is remote and awe-inspiring. Askja (1,510 meters) emerges from the Ódáðahraun lava field, and the terrain is quite rocky. Víti is a tremendous pale blue lake-filled crater that emerged after the great eruption of the Askja volcano in 1875. It's possible to take a dip in the water, which reaches a temperature of about 30°C (86°F).

Askja is one of the most popular destinations in the highlands. There are two mountain huts (the Dreki huts) on Route F88, about 100 kilometers from the Ring Road. From there, it's an eight-kilometer drive up into the Askja caldera. It is a walk of about 2.5 kilometers from the car park to Víti. Keep in mind that the roads are usually only open for about three months, from late June until September, depending on the weather. It could be longer or shorter.

Kverkfjöll

The Kverkfjöll volcano (1,764 meters) includes two calderas that are filled with ice. The area is striking for its colors. The deep black background gives way to gorgeous blues and icy white. The main event

the Víti crater

is ice caves that were created by hot springs slowly melting the ice into interesting shapes. However, please observe the caves from the outside; you never know when the ice mass could give way. Stay safe. The GPS coordinates for Kverkfjöll are N 64.7475, W 16.6315. To get to Kverkfjöll, take Route F910 southeast to Route F902.

SPORTS AND RECREATION
★ Hiking Mount Askja

Passionate hikers will want to walk the rim of Askja. The difficult eight-hour hike offers some slopes and ultra-rocky terrain along with spectacular views of lava fields, mountains, and the mighty Víti crater. While the trail is well maintained, the main challenge is weather. If the weather forecast calls for wind, it's best to skip the planned hike. Do not underestimate the power of Iceland's wind, especially in the highlands.

Askja is about a 30-minute moderate hike from the car park up to the caldera. If you are not planning to hike the rim, you can just explore near the car park. To reach the car park, take Route 1 to Route F88. The GPS coordinates are N 65.0300, W 16.7500.

ACCOMMODATIONS AND FOOD

Make sure to book your accommodation ahead of time.

★ **Hrauneyjar** (Route F26, tel. 354/487-7782, www.hrauneyjar.is, open year-round, 25,000ISK) offers 99 rooms ranging from doubles with shared bathroom facilities to double rooms with private bathrooms and free Wi-Fi. The GPS coordinates are N 64.1964, W 19.2655. Rooms are sparsely decorated with a bed, desk, and small table. It's not luxury, but it's adequate. Along with the guesthouse, Hrauneyjar has a restaurant, a gas station, and a tourist shop that offers food, maps, and a place to pay for fishing permits. It's a good idea to stop here to pick up essentials (like food, water, and gas) even if you don't plan to stay at the guesthouse.

There are mountain huts along the valley **Nýidalur** (tel. 354/860-3334, www.fi.is) that sleep 120 people; the GPS coordinates are N 64.7355, W 18.0725. The area can be reached by Route F26. The huts have cooking facilities, toilets, and hot showers. It costs 7,000ISK per night to stay inside the hut, and it costs 1,600ISK for tent camping outside in an open field. The shower costs 500ISK to use. The huts are open July-August.

an ice cave in Kverkfjöll

Navigating the Arctic Desert Safely

Safety needs to be your top priority. Every year tourists arrive in the highlands looking for a once-in-a-lifetime adventure but find themselves unprepared. Some tourists need to be rescued, and a few, unfortunately, don't make it out alive. Do not underestimate the weather in Iceland, even in the summer. Keep these things in mind—some may seem like common sense, but they're still important to note.

- Have an appropriate rental car. If the trail calls for four-wheel drive or a super jeep, take heed.

- Have enough gas for your trip. Gas stations are few and far between in the highlands.

- Dress the part. Make sure you have layers, warm clothing, and sturdy footwear.

- Bring adequate food and water. Don't count on buying food along the journey.

- Have maps, a compass, and a charged mobile phone on hand.

- If you find yourself in trouble, the emergency number in Iceland is 112.

The Laugafell huts (tel. 354/462-2720, www.ffa.is) are located about 15 kilometers northeast of Hofsjökull glacier and 20 kilometers southwest from the end of the Eyjafjarðardalur valley; the GPS coordinates are N 65.0269, W 18.3321. The huts can be reached by Route F752 or F881 from Route F26 or by F821. The accommodations are basic with gas available for cooking and restrooms near the swimming pool. It costs 7,000ISK to stay the night. The huts are open only during the summer.

The mountain huts closest to Askja are at Drekagil gorge. The Dreki huts (tel. 354/822-5190, www.ffa.is, www.nat.is) can be reached by Route F88 from the Ring Road east of Lake Mývatn or by Route F910 from Route F26; the GPS coordinates are N 65.0417, W 16.5948. There are two residential huts on the site that can accommodate 60 people. The huts make gas available for cooking and there are toilets and shower facilities. The Dreki huts are an ideal base for those interested in exploring the Askja caldera, which is an eight-kilometer drive. It costs 7,000ISK to stay the night. Showers cost an additional 500ISK. The huts are open only during the summer.

GETTING THERE AND AROUND

Route F26 is not for the faint of heart. It cannot be emphasized enough to have a proper vehicle to navigate this road—at least a four-wheel drive. The 200-kilometer route spans from Mount Hekla in the south to the glorious waterfall Goðafoss in the north. The route is not a year-round destination, and the road opens typically at the end of June. It could open later if the region had a particularly harsh winter with a lot of snowfall. To check road closures and opening date, visit the Icelandic Road and Coastal Administration website (www.vegagerdin.is).

Another important detail to keep in mind is that the only gas station along Route F26 is at Hrauneyjar. Be prepared and fill up before your journey.

To get there by bus, check out the schedule of Reykjavik Excursions (tel. 354/562-1011, www.re.is), which offers trips from early July to late August. The 10-hour trip costs 8,000ISK each way and the tour departs from Reykjavík. You can purchase a bus pass that allows you to hop off and on the bus.

Kjölur (Route F35)

For a less treacherous route to the highlands, Route F35 is your best bet. The majority of the route is flat and can be accessible up until October (depending on the weather, of course). This is a part of the interior where four-wheel drive is recommended but not necessary, as there are bridges and river crossings are not an issue. However, be safe, monitor weather conditions, and follow road conditions.

SIGHTS
★ Langjökull Glacier

At 952 square kilometers, Langjökull (Long Glacier) is the second largest ice cap in Iceland after Vatnajökull. Its volume is 195 cubic kilometers and the ice is quite thick, up to 580 meters deep. The highest point of the ice cap is about 1,450 meters above sea level. The rocky terrain and snowy patches are vast and haunting. Route F35 runs along the east side of Langjökull, between it and Hofsjökull. From Reykjavík, you head east on Route 1. Before you reach the town of Selfoss, you take a left turn on F35 and continue past Gullfoss for about 37 kilometers.

Hveravellir

Situated in the western highlands, the ★ Hveravellir Nature Reserve (Route F35, tel. 354/452-4200, www.hveravellir.is) is one of the last great wilderness spots in Europe. It's about 90 kilometers north of Gullfoss on Route F35. Hveravellir is a natural geothermal hot spot with smoking fumaroles and bubbling water holes, and it is a special experience to have a look around and see geothermal energy at work. There are private rooms (9,500ISK pp), dormitories (6,000ISK pp), a campsite (1,200ISK pp), and mountain huts (6,000ISK pp) available within the reserve. One bathable pool is situated close to the mountain huts. It's waist-deep and safe to take a dip.

Langjökull glacier

Hveravellir Nature Reserve

Kerlingarfjöll

The mountain range Kerlingarfjöll (Women's Mountains) shows all the characteristics of a matured caldera, including volcanic formations and geothermal spots. In short, this is a geology buff's dream. The towering mountains were created by eruptions from a large caldera lying under the mountains; while the caldera is still considered active, it has been silent for tens of thousands of years. Visitors will see steep slopes and pointy peaks dotted with ice, leading into a hotbed of geothermal activity. It's quiet and desolate with the earth steaming below. **Kerlingarfjöll** (tel. 354/664-7000, www.kerlingarfjoll.is) has a campsite for tents (1,500ISK) as well as 10 cabins (50,000ISK). To get to Kerlingarfjöll from Gullfoss, drive north on F35. For 15 kilometers the road is asphalt, and the remaining 38-kilometer secton is a gravel road. The GPS coordinates are N 64.6834, W 19.2999.

Hofsjökull Glacier

Hofsjökull (Temple Glacier) is the third largest glacier in Iceland after Vatnajökull and Langjökull. It is situated in the western highlands, north of the mountain range Kerlingarfjöll. The glacier covers an area of 925 square kilometers, reaching 1,765 meters at the top. It's vast and can be quite windy.

Also, visitors will have to be careful of huge crevasses in the ice. The GPS coordinates are N 64.8167, W 18.8167.

SPORTS AND RECREATION
Hiking

Hikers have many choices for roaming the interior. These popular options vary in scenery and degree of difficulty.

HVERADALIR

Hiking the geothermal area Hveradalir (Hot Springs Valley) is wildly popular and for good reason. The valley offers views of mountains, vast expanses of desert-like earth with steam erupting throughout the region (reminding visitors that the land is very much alive), and hot springs. Hveradalir is accessible off Route 1. The GPS coordinates are N 64.6453, W 19.2825.

A moderate hike begins at the car park by Neðri-Hveradalir (Lower Hveradalir) and takes you through the geothermal area Hveradalir, where ice and fire meet. The route is a three-kilometer loop and takes about three hours. Hikers will view the stark white glacial landscape and see the steam rise out of the ground near the numerous hot springs.

For a longer, more demanding hike (11.2

Hofsjökull glacier

kilometers), start at the car park called Keis, toward the bottom of Hveradalir, where you follow the Ásgarðsá River for 4.5 kilometers. The hike is an 11.2-kilometer loop. Being so close to the river, you will see plant vegetation, which is a rare sight in much of the highlands. During the hike, there will be points where you have to cross water, so dress accordingly. Hikers will pass hills and geothermal hot spots as the river twists and turns. Overall, it's a five-hour hike and moderately difficult.

KERLINGARFJÖLL

For a more difficult walk, start at the car park called Kastali and continue to Mount Lodmundur (1,432 meters), then to the highest peak of Kerlingarfjöll, Mount Snaekollur (1,460 meters). The trail is rocky and there are quite a few slopes, but the payoff is the gorgeous views of the barren landscape below and mountains in the distance. It's one of the best overviews of the highlands. This is a seven-kilometer hike, in a loop, which takes about six hours.

GETTING THERE AND AROUND

The 200-kilometer Kjölur route (Route F35) begins near the picturesque waterfall Gullfoss in the south and reaches to Blönduós in the northwest. This route is not a year-round destination: The road typically opens the middle of June, but it could be later if the winter was harsh. The road closes in September, but how early in September depends on the weather. It's best to have a four-wheel-drive vehicle for the journey. Be sure to gas up before you head to the highlands, as there are no gas stations in the region. Depending on the duration of your trip, it might be necessary to bring gas cans.

SBA (tel. 354/550-0700, www.sba.is) operates summer buses between Akureyri in the north and Reykjavík along the Kjölur route. The 10-hour, one-way trip, which is only available late June through early September, costs 14,000ISK. You can purchase a bus pass that allows you to make stops along the route. Be sure to have a copy of the most recent bus schedule. They tend to change.

Background

The Landscape

GEOGRAPHY

Iceland is the westernmost European country, situated in the North Atlantic between North America and Europe. Iceland is east of Greenland and south of the Arctic Circle, atop the northern Mid-Atlantic Ridge. It lies 859 kilometers from Scotland and 4,200 kilometers from New York City. The area of Iceland is 103,022 square kilometers, and a frequent comparison among Icelandic tour guides is that Iceland is roughly the size of the U.S. state Kentucky.

Climate

Iceland isn't as cold as you may think. The Gulf Stream swirls along the western and southern coasts and works to moderate Iceland's climate. But moderate doesn't mean calm, as the Gulf Stream is responsible for the frequent weather changes—as in lots of wind and rain. The biggest climate challenge is the unpredictability of it. The "summer" tourist season runs from the end of May to the beginning of September, and during that time, the climate ranges from rainy May days to the midnight sun in July to the possibility of snow in September. The winter climate brings colder temperatures, dark days, whipping winds, and the possibility of seeing northern lights flicker and dance on clear nights.

Weather

Weather in Iceland is not casual conversation, but serious business. Weather forecasts are frequent but largely hit or miss. The weather can change rapidly, from calm winds and sunny skies to rain, snow, sleet and back to calm wind and sunny skies, all in the same hour. It's unpredictable, frustrating, exhilarating, and confusing for many tourists, but Icelanders have learned to adapt and go with the flow. As a result, plans tend to be loose, whether it's for meeting friends for coffee or a job interview. If the weather acts up, locals understand.

Some of the most extreme weather you could experience on this island is wind—the type of wind in winter that could knock you off your feet. If the weather forecast is showing strong winds, especially in the countryside, alter your plans accordingly. Do not underestimate the wind, and heed any storm advisories. Be safe, smart, and prepared. The changing conditions are part of the experience of traveling to Iceland, and the key is being prepared with layers of clothing, proper footwear, and waterproof outerwear.

Geology

Iceland is a volcanic island constantly in flux, with magma breaking through fissures and periodic eruptions that redesign the rocky landscape. Iceland's land is made

winter in Iceland

Previous: horses grazing in southern Iceland; Skógafoss.

up of igneous rock, most of which is basalt, which forms from cooling magma. Most of Iceland's mountains were formed with basalt that has been carved by water and ice erosion. Earthquakes are a common occurrence, but tremors are rarely felt. At the time of this writing, a volcanic fissure eruption in Holuhraun has been ongoing for weeks, and there have been up to 1,000 tremors near the region per day.

VOLCANOES

Volcanic eruptions are a growing source of tourism for the country. Local travel companies offer helicopter, jeep and airplane tours when an eruption occurs. Most of Iceland's volcanic eruptions are fissure vents, like the 2014 Holuhraun eruption, where lava seeps out of the cracks in the earth's crust. Holuhraun produced fountains of lava shooting out of the earth, delighting photographers and keeping volcanologists busy trying to determine if the nearby Bárðarbunga volcano will erupt. At the time of this writing, it hasn't. The three most active volcanoes on the island are Katla, Hekla, and Eyjafjallajökull. Eyjafjallajökull erupted in 2010, grounding air travel in Europe for days thanks to a large ash cloud.

Residents have learned to adapt to eruptions, and most volcanoes are away from residential areas. In the case of the 2014 Holuhraun eruption, the surrounding area near Vatnajökull was evacuated of locals, and tourists and animals were moved from the area. The main threat was toxins in the air, and those close to the region were asked to stay indoors and turn up their heating if they were sensitive to air quality.

Air

When there isn't an eruption, Iceland's air is some of the cleanest and purest you will experience, as pollution is low and the Gulf Stream produces a strong, steady wind that blows toxins away. The main source of pollution on the island is from industry, mainly aluminum smelters.

Water

Like the air, Iceland's water is perfectly pure. There's clean, tasty drinking water on tap and geothermally heated water that powers swimming pools and hot water in homes. Snow can fall in any month of the year, but large snowfalls are uncommon in the Reykjavík area, at least during the last couple of decades. Ice covers about 11 percent of the country,

Eyjafjallajökull eruption in 2010

mostly in the form of Iceland's largest glaciers: Vatnajökull, Hofsjökull, Langjökull, and Mýrdalsjökull. Melting ice from the glaciers and melting snow form the rivers.

Iceland's water also serves as some of its tourist attractions. The manmade Blue Lagoon near Grindavík allows visitors to bathe in geothermally heated water, which soothes and heals the skin. Locals and tourists enjoy hot springs throughout the country, and spectacular waterfalls with roaring water tumble over basalt rock and earth. The largest and most visited waterfalls in Iceland are Gullfoss, Dettifoss, Goðafoss, and Skógafoss.

Northern Lights

The biggest winter attraction in Iceland is the aurora borealis (northern lights). People travel from around the world to catch a glimpse of the green, white, blue, and red lights dancing in the night sky. There's something very special about bundling up in your warmest winter gear, trekking outside main towns to avoid bright lights, and hunting for the aurora borealis. The phenomenon is caused by solar winds, which push electronic particles to collide with molecules of atmospheric gases, causing an emission of bright light. The best time to see northern lights is from October to March, and there are forecasts predicting visibility on the national weather website (www.vedur.is). When the forecast is strong, it's best to drive (or take a tour bus) to a dark area and look up. Northern lights tours are offered by Reykjavik Excursions (www.re.is).

PLANTS

Don't be fooled by photos of the vast, barren lava fields; there is in fact life thriving from Iceland's land. The most common plants in Iceland are the hundreds of species of moss found throughout the country, clinging to rocks, basalt columns, and the earth. It's common to find Icelandic moss, maritime sunburst lichen, dulse, rockweed, and several species of algae in Iceland.

Iceland has an abundance of rhubarb plants and bilberry shrubs (which Icelanders refer to as blueberries). Berry-picking season runs from late July to early August, but the season can be delayed if the winter was particularly bad.

As for flowers, the pale-pink glacier poppy is the country's national flower, and other common flowers are sea mayweed, alpine bartsia, meadow buttercup, and arctic poppy. Others include wood cranesbill, oysterplant, purple lupin, and blue grass.

the northern lights above a lighthouse on the Reykjanes Peninsula

ANIMALS

Iceland may not be known for its land mammals—other than sheep, cows, horses, reindeer, and arctic fox—but animals in the ocean and sky are varied and ample.

Fish

Fish are the lifeblood of Iceland, sustaining its inhabitants, as well as the country's biggest trade resource. In the waters surrounding Iceland, you will find cod, haddock, catfish, mussels, halibut, plaice, lumpfish, monkfish, skate, and Greenland shark. Native to Icelandic river waters are salmon, trout, and arctic char.

Seals

Several species of seals call Iceland home, with harbor seals and gray seals being the most common. There are seal-watching sites in the north of Iceland, and at Hvammstangi is a seal center that serves as a museum, information center, and seal-watching enterprise. Harbor seals are more common to spot because they spend more time on land, whereas gray seals like to spend more time out in the ocean. Harp, ringed, hooded, and bearded seals are also spotted in Iceland, but seeing one is a long shot.

Whales

Whale-watching is a spectacular way to spend an afternoon in Iceland, and there are several species to see, depending on where in Iceland you set out on your excursion. High season for whales around Iceland is May to October, and 14 species have been seen off the coasts of the island. The species in Iceland are: blue, fin, minke, pilot, humpback, sei, orca, sperm, bottlenose, beluga, and narwhal whales, as well as white-beaked dolphins, white-sided dolphins, and harbor porpoises.

Birds

Bird-watchers are delighted when they visit, as there are more than 300 species of birds in Iceland. The island serves as a stopover for birds migrating between North America and Europe, and common species are ravens, eider ducks, arctic terns, Iceland gulls, white gulls, black-headed gulls, skuas, white-tailed eagles, gannets, fulmars, kittiwakes, and oystercatchers.

The bird that has become synonymous with Iceland is the adorable puffin, with its black and white body, bright orange feet, and colorful red, blue, and orange beak. Puffins are remarkable swimmers and divers, able to stay underwater for up to a minute and

purple lupin blooming in the summer

a puffin in North Iceland

surface with as many as 10 small fish in their beaks. While exceptional in water, puffins are clumsy in flight and are known for their uneven landings on land. It's part of their charm. Millions of puffins call Iceland home, although their numbers have dwindled over the years. It's possible to see puffins during the summer in areas including the Westman Islands, Grímsey, and the Látrabjarg cliffs in the Westfjords.

History

SETTLEMENT

Iceland has the distinction of being the last country in Europe to be settled. The country is known for impeccable record-keeping, and for that reason, it's known that the first permanent resident in Iceland was Ingólfur Arnarson, who built a farm in Reykjavík in the year 874. The earliest settlers were emigrants from Norway who opposed the king, Harald, due to a blood feud, and they wanted to make a new life in a new land. In addition to the Norwegians, their slaves from Ireland and Scotland were brought along as well, which means Icelanders are a blend of Norse and Celtic stock.

As word got out about the new land, within a few decades most of the coastline was claimed, with farms and fishing stations popping up. A government wasn't formed until 930, when the Alþing (parliament) was created, but the new settlers in the meantime opted for each farmstead to have a self-appointed chief. Once the Alþing was established in Þingvellir, a legislative body was elected.

CONVERSION TO CHRISTIANITY

Christianity came to Iceland, some say, by force. By the 10th century, there was mounting political pressure from the king of Norway to convert to Christianity or face the consequences, which would be war. As the end of the first millennium grew near, many prominent Icelanders had accepted the new faith.

By the year 1000, the Alþing was divided into two religious groups: modern Christians and pagans. The two groups were steadfast in their beliefs, and a civil war seemed likely. The law speaker, Þorgeir Þorkelsson, was called upon for a decision. (The law speaker was appointed to office and was required to recite the law during parliamentary meetings.) Þorgeir decided that Iceland would be a Christian country, but that pagans could still celebrate their rituals in the privacy of their farms. Þorgeir was baptized in Þingvellir, and Christianity became the law of the land. Christian churches were built, a bishop was established in 1056, and the majority of Icelanders remain Christian today.

DANISH RULE

Iceland remained under Norwegian kingship rule until 1380, when the death of Olav IV put an end to the Norwegian male royal line. Norway (and by extension Iceland) became part of the Kalmar Union, along with Denmark and Sweden, with Denmark as the dominant nation. At this time, Iceland became effectively a colony of Denmark, with the king owning the land and the church's money. Iceland's government now answered to Denmark and did so for the next several hundred years.

Iceland was still very much centered on fishing and farming, and it was quite isolated from the dealings in mainland Europe. In 1602, the Danish government, which was pursuing mercantilist policies, ordered that Iceland was forbidden to trade with countries other than Denmark. The Danish trade monopoly would remain in effect until 1786.

INDEPENDENCE

Iceland began inching toward independence when it was granted a Minister of Icelandic Affairs in 1904, who would be based in Reykjavík. Hannes Hafstein was the first to serve in the minister position, and his place in Iceland's history is prominent. During this time, Iceland became more autonomous, building up Reykjavík's harbor, founding the University of Iceland, and eventually creating its own flag in 1915.

Over the next couple of decades, Iceland

stained-glass window in Hallgrímskirkja in Reykjavík

was taking more control of its affairs, and when World War II started, there was an economic opportunity for Iceland. Iceland was invited to join the Allied war effort by Great Britain, but Iceland's government refused, declaring its neutrality. Britain pushed for Iceland's cooperation, but ultimately British naval forces arrived in Iceland, began building a base near Keflavík, and occupied the country for its proximity to North America. In all, 25,000 British soldiers occupied Iceland, which created a significant number of jobs for Icelanders. The British left in 1941, but more than 40,000 American troops replaced them, continuing the economic win for Iceland. There were jobs, opportunity, an American radio station, and lots of money flowing into the tiny island nation.

Denmark took a step back from Iceland's affairs during World War II, and Icelanders eventually held a referendum on its independence. Almost 99 percent of the population voted in the referendum, 97 percent of which voted for independence. On June 17, 1944, Iceland became totally independent of Denmark. American troops maintained the Keflavík NATO base until 2006.

MODERN-DAY ICELAND

Iceland plodded along, building up its fishing resources, investing in infrastructure, and looking toward the future. During years of rule by the center-right Independence Party, banks were deregulated in the early 2000s and Iceland's financial sector began taking off at a rapid pace. Iceland was being lauded for its financial acumen, but it all imploded in 2008, when the country's three major banks failed, sending Iceland into one of the deepest financial crises in modern-day Europe. Today, Iceland is still rebuilding and is recovering.

One of the most divisive issues in Iceland has been whether to join the European Union (EU). Polls indicate that the majority of Icelanders are against joining, and the Independence/Progressive coalition that was elected in 2013 halted EU talks altogether. The debate continues to rage on as Icelanders demand a referendum on the matter, which was promised by the parties in power. It will be interesting to see how this plays out going forward.

Iceland today is reaping the benefits of increased tourism. People from around the world have become aware of and infatuated with Iceland for its raw nature, volcanic eruptions, and culture.

Government and Economy

GOVERNMENT

Iceland's government dates back to the year 930, when the Alþing (parliament) was formed, but its constitution was signed on June 17, 1944, when Iceland achieved independence from Denmark. The Alþing, which consists of 63 seats, meets four days a week near Austurvollur in the center of Reykjavík. Nine judges make up the High Court of Iceland and are appointed by the president. Iceland's president serves more of a ceremonial role, while the prime minister holds most of the executive powers. Other high-level cabinet positions are the Minister of Finance and Minister of Foreign Affairs.

Political Parties

Iceland's political party system is in double digits, with 13 main parties running for seats in the 2013 election. However, in the Alþing, six parties hold seats: Independence Party, Progressive Party, Social Democratic Alliance, Left-Green Movement, Bright Future, and the Pirate Party.

The Progressive Party (Framsóknarflokkurinn) is a center-right party that was formed to protect the interests of fishers and farmers. The current prime minister, Sigmundur Davið Gunnlaugsson, a former journalist, has served as leader of the Progressives since 2009. The Independence Party (Sjálfstadisflokkurinn), the second largest party in the country, was in power in the years leading up to the economic collapse of 2008. They were voted out of the majority in 2009 but regained seats, and power, in 2013. The Social Democratic Alliance, Bright Future, Left-Green Movement, and Pirate Party represent the more liberal political parties on the island. The sitting president, Ólafur Ragnar Grímsson, was a member of the now-defunct People's Alliance, and is known for having more liberal/moderate views. He was elected to a fifth term in 2012 and has stated that he will not be running for reelection.

Defense

Iceland does not have a military, but it hosted British and American troops in Keflavík during and after World War II. American troops remained in Iceland, on the NATO base, until 2006, at the height of the U.S. wars in Iraq and

Afghanistan. Iceland's Coast Guard oversees crisis management and protection along the coasts of Iceland and has been known to participate in daring rescues at sea. The Icelandic police force consists of fewer than 1,000 police officers, who maintain the peace. The crime rate is exceptionally low in Iceland, and police officers do not carry handguns.

ECONOMY

Iceland's economy is best known to tourists for taking a dive during the 2008 financial crisis. The island is still recovering from the collapse, and tourism is playing a large role in that recovery, along with alternative energy.

Banking Crisis

In early 2008, Iceland's currency began to take a dive compared to the euro, and that was the first international signal that there was deep trouble lurking in Iceland's financial sector. By the autumn, all three of Iceland's major banks had failed, lifting the veil on Iceland's house of cards. Following the collapse, unemployment soared, pension funds shrank, and inflation skyrocketed to more than 70 percent. Loans taken out in foreign currency became unmanageable to thousands of Icelanders, credit lines were cut off, and capital controls were put in place that restricted how much money Icelanders could move out of the country. It was dire. The IMF made an emergency loan of $2.1 billion in November 2008, and the country started to look to rebuild and recover.

Tourism

An increase in tourism made strides in Iceland recovering. In fact, the increase makes tourism the second-biggest revenue source after fish. In 2014, tourism agencies in Iceland predicted that one million tourists would land in Iceland, which is more than triple Iceland's population. Most of Iceland's tourists come from the United States, Great Britain, the Nordic countries, Germany, France, and Switzerland. Tourism is also increasing from Asian tourists. The issue going forward is how

protest signs outside Parliament

to keep tourism sustainable and to protect Iceland's land from too much traffic.

Fishing

It's no secret that fish are the lifeblood of Iceland. They nourish its residents and are Iceland's number one export. Iceland's biggest trading partners are within the European Union, which is interesting because the opposition to joining the EU, for many, is for Iceland to maintain complete control of its fishing stock. Cod is the most common fish export.

Energy

One of the perks of living on a volcanic island is having a hotbed of geothermal energy. About 98 percent of the island's energy comes from geothermal and hydroelectric sources, which accounts for low cost and low pollution. However, the pollution that does inhabit Iceland's airspace stems from an increasing number of aluminum smelters that have popped up in the last couple of decades. Foreign aluminum providers look to Iceland for its cheap energy and vast land. It's a trade-off that many Icelanders remain unhappy about, while the smelters do create jobs and revenue for the country. As of this writing, Iceland was in talks with the United Kingdom on how to export geothermal energy there.

Currency

Iceland maintains its own currency, as it is not a member of the European Union. The Icelandic króna has a small circulation and is pegged to the euro. Following the financial crisis, inflation soared more than 70 percent, and Iceland's currency took a dive. The uncertainty was a maddening time for many Icelanders. Inflation is still high, and exchange rates rise and fall. Capital controls were created in 2008 that limit how much money Icelanders can move out of the country, and they remain in place. If an Icelander is traveling abroad and wants foreign currency, they must present their plane ticket at their bank to receive foreign currency. Life has changed since 2008.

People and Culture

POPULATION

Nearly 330,000 people call Iceland home, and more than two-thirds live in the capital city, Reykjavík, and its outlying suburbs. Outside of Reykjavík, Hafnarfjörður, and Kopavogur, the most populated towns in Iceland include Keflavík and Selfoss in the south, Akureyri in the north, Akranes and Isafjörður in the west, and Höfn and Egilsstaðir in the east. More than 90 percent of the island population is composed of native Icelanders, but the foreign-born population continues to grow with migrant workers and refugees. Iceland is as multicultural today as it has ever been.

Native Icelanders have a genetic makeup that combines Gaelic and Norse heritage, and many Icelanders consider themselves Nordic instead of Scandinavian. Social lives center around family, as Icelanders tend to be a close-knit bunch. People tend to either know one another or have friends in common.

LANGUAGE

The official language of Iceland is Icelandic, which is considered a Germanic language. Icelanders like to think of their language as poetic and musical, and maintaining their language is an important part of Icelandic culture. Most Icelanders speak English and are happy to converse with tourists in English, but they are proud of their mother tongue and enjoy when foreign tourists give the language a go, even just a few words. The closest language to Icelandic is Faroese, which roughly 50,000 people speak, and the other close language spoken by a larger group is Norwegian. Many Icelanders can understand Norwegian, Swedish, and Danish due to some similarities. Learning Icelandic is a challenge for many foreigners because of the complex grammar and accent.

Alphabet

The Icelandic alphabet has 32 letters, including letters not known in the English language, such as Ð and Þ. The letter Ð represents the sound "th" as in "this," while Þ represents "th" as in "thin."

ICELANDIC NAMES

Iceland has a strident naming committee that must approve names parents wish to give their newborns, in the spirit of maintaining Icelandic culture. For that reason, you will find a lot of common first names, including Bjorn, Jón, Ólafur, Guðmundur, and Magnús for males, and Guðrun, Sara, and Anna for females. Very few Icelanders have surnames;

Best Festivals in Iceland

There's always something going on in Iceland—and whether it's the Viking Festival in June celebrating the country's roots, or the huge Iceland Airwaves music festival in the autumn, there's something for everyone.

FEBRUARY

Sónar Reykjavík (Reykjavík): This three-day music festival in mid-February features local and international rock, pop, and electronic bands.

Reykjavík Food & Fun Festival (Reykjavík): During this three-day festival at the end of February, world-renowned chefs occupy kitchens at trendy Reykjavík restaurants, using fresh local ingredients and lots of imagination.

MARCH

DesignMarch (Reykjavík): Typically held in early March over four days, DesignMarch showcases the newest and best Icelandic design in pop up shops, lectures, and fun events around the city.

APRIL

Reykjavík Blues Festival (Reykjavík): For a week in early April, blues music enthusiasts from around the world descend on Reykjavík for this annual festival that features international musicians and local artists.

AK-Extreme (Akureyri): Dedicated to winter extreme sports, AK-Extreme is an annual snowboard and music festival held in the northern city Akureyri over four days in mid-April.

MAY

Reykjavík Arts Festival (Reykjavík): For two weeks over late May/early June, Reykjavík is treated to exhibitions and outdoor installations of local and international artists.

JUNE

Viking Festival (Hafnarfjörður): Just outside Reykjavík, the annual Viking Festival in mid-June has fun reenactments of fights with traditional dress and weaponry, as well as food, music, and a market. The week-long festival is great for kids.

JULY

All Tomorrow's Parties (Keflavík): The major touring music festival found its way to Iceland

---

instead, Iceland follows a patronymic system in which children are given their father's first name followed by -son or -dottir. If a man named Einar has a son named Johannes and a daughter named Anna, their names will be Johannes Einarsson and Anna Einarsdottir.

RELIGION

Icelanders have an interesting relationship with religion. Most of the country identifies as Lutheran (more than 70 percent), but most Icelanders aren't known to attend church regularly or be very vocal about their religious beliefs. While the majority of the country identifies as religious, Iceland is considered a liberal nation. There is no separation of church and state in Iceland; the National Church of Iceland is subsidized by Icelanders through a church tax. However, non-Lutherans can choose to have their church tax donated to designated charities.

Of Iceland's religious minorities, Catholics

a few years ago. Local and international acts take the stage for three days in early July.

AUGUST

Reykjavík Jazz Festival (Reykjavík): It may seem unexpected, but Icelanders have an affinity for jazz music, and they put on a great annual festival over five days in mid-August that features local and international musicians.

Reykjavík Culture Night (Reykjavík): Held at the end of August, this day-long event is the biggest and most popular festival in Iceland, with more than 100,000 people participating. There's live music, food, and art to celebrate the end of the summer and Iceland's rich culture.

SEPTEMBER

Reykjavík International Film Festival (Reykjavík): Beginning at the end of September, this 11-day festival features short films, documentaries, and features from more than 40 countries.

the annual Viking Festival in Hafnarfjörður

OCTOBER

Iceland Airwaves (Reykjavík): The largest music festival of the year hits Iceland in late October/early November. More than 200 local and international artists perform at the five-day festival, which has attracted bands including Kraftwerk, Flaming Lips, and local band Of Monsters and Men.

are the largest minority at about 4 percent, and there are about 1,000 Muslims estimated to call Iceland home, as well as about 100 Jews. There is not a single synagogue in Iceland, as the Jewish population has not requested one, but a mosque was approved by Reykjavík in 2014, and construction is underway.

FOLKLORE

Icelanders have a spiritual connection to nature, which has been depicted through literature, paintings, and stories about the *huldufólk* or "hidden people." It's easy to understand why stories of *huldufólk* are prevalent once you experience the otherworldly nature of Iceland, including northern lights, crazy rock formations, howling wind, and desolate lava fields where it feels that anything can happen. Many of the hidden people stories originate in the lava fields, where unexplained phenomena, like broken farm equipment, could be explained away by saying

According to legend, if you make a pyramid out of stones it will change into a troll and bring luck.

"it must be the *huldufólk*." Indeed, Iceland's hidden people live among the rocks, and certain rocks are deemed "*huldufólk* churches." It's easy to dismiss the idea of hidden people, especially when the term is loosely translated as elves, but many Icelanders are not willing to deny the existence of hidden people. Does that mean that all Icelanders believe that elves physically walk among their human neighbors? Of course not. But it is part of their history and culture, and many Icelanders have a sense of humor about the foreign notion of *huldufólk*.

ARTS
Music

Music plays a large role in Icelandic society. There's still an emphasis on children learning to play instruments, and there are music schools around the country. It seems that everyone in Iceland is in at least one band. The earliest Icelandic music is called *rímur*, which is a sort of chanting style of singing that could include lyrics ranging from religious to descriptions of nature. Choirs are also very common in Iceland, and there are frequent performances in schools and churches that are usually well attended by the community.

As for modern music, Iceland boasts quite a few acts that have gained a following abroad. Of course, there's Björk, who put Iceland on the musical map back in the 1980s with her band, The Sugarcubes, and later her solo career. Icelanders tend to be quite proud of Björk, as an artist and an environmentalist. Sigur Rós became an indie favorite, and the band has been recording since 1994. Of Monsters and Men, Ólafur Arnalds, Amiina, Samaris, and GusGus are taking the world by storm. Reykjavík has cool venues to check out local bands and DJs and some great record shops to pick up the newest and latest Icelandic releases.

Literature

Iceland has a rich literary history. The sagas, considered the best-known specimens of Icelandic literature, are stories in prose describing events that took place in Iceland in the 10th and 11th centuries, during the so-called Saga Age. Focused on history, especially genealogical and family history, the sagas reflect the conflicts that arose within the societies of the second and third generations of Icelandic settlers. The authors of the sagas are unknown; *Egil's Saga* is believed to have been written by Snorri Sturluson, a 13th-century descendant of the saga's hero, but this remains uncertain. Widely read in school, the sagas are celebrated as an important part of Iceland's history.

Icelanders are voracious readers and prolific writers of prose and poetry. The nation's most celebrated author is Halldór Laxness, who won a Nobel Prize for Literature in 1951 for his cherished novel *Independent People*. His tales have been translated into several languages and center on themes near and dear to Icelanders—nature, love, travel, and adventure. Other authors who have been translated into English (and other languages) include Sjón, Arnaldur Indriðason, and Einar Már Guðmundsson, among scores of others.

Crafts (Knitting)

Icelanders have been knitting for centuries, and it remains a common hobby today. Icelandic sheep have been the source of wool that's been keeping Icelanders warm for generations, and a traditional, modern sweater design emerged in the 1950s or so in the form of the *lopapeysa*. A *lopapeysa* has a distinctive yoke design around the neck opening, and they come in a variety of colors, with the most common colors being brown, gray, black, and off-white. Icelanders knit with *lopi* yarn, which contains both hairs and fleece of Icelandic sheep. The yarn is not spun, making it more difficult to work with than spun yarn, but the texture and insulation are unmistakable.

Essentials

Transportation

GETTING THERE

Air

Keflavík International Airport (KEF, tel. 354/425-6000, www.kefairport.is), about 50 minutes west of Reykjavík, frequently gets kudos for being one of the best airports in Europe, and they're well deserved. Flying into Iceland is a pretty seamless experience. The country's main carrier, **Icelandair** (www.icelandair.com), serves more than 30 destinations in the United States, Canada, and Europe. Iceland's accessibility has been a main selling point as a travel destination because the country is just five hours from New York City and about three hours from London. Icelandair cleverly introduced an option years ago that allows North American travelers going on to Europe to stop over in Iceland for no extra cost. You can spend a couple days or longer to explore Iceland, and then continue on to your destination in Europe. The summer season is obviously the most expensive, with round-trip tickets that could exceed $1,000 from North America. Icelandair offers great deals during the winter months, when you can grab a round-trip ticket for around $500.

Sea

For those traveling from mainland Europe, a ferry can be a great option, especially if you want to bring a car, camper, or bicycle for the trip. **Smyril Line** (www.smyril-line.fo) is a Faroese company that runs the ferry *Norröna*, which goes to Iceland from Denmark, Norway, and the Faroe Islands. The ferry drops you off in Seyðisfjörður, in East Iceland, which is convenient for those traveling with cars and who want to spend time in the countryside. But, if you want to stay in the south, where Reykjavík and Golden Circle attractions are, a ferry may not be the best option. The timetable tends to change frequently, so check the website for the latest information.

GETTING AROUND

Air

Iceland is surprisingly easy to get around by plane—if the weather is cooperating, that is. **Reykjavík City Airport** (tel. 354/569-4100, www.isavia.is) connects travelers to Akureyri, Egilsstaðir, Isafjörður, Vopnafjörður, Grímsey, and Þórshöfn. **Air Iceland** (tel. 354/570-3000, www.airiceland.is) and **Eagle Air** (tel. 354/562-4200, www.eagleair.is) fly year round.

Car

Having access to a car gives you the ultimate freedom in seeing the island on your own schedule. However, if you plan to stay in Reykjavík for most of your trip or want to do short day trips in the southern or western parts of the country, it's not necessary to rent a car; you can book tours and travel by bus. But if you want a rental car and the freedom that comes with it, expect to pay dearly, especially in the summer months.

ROAD CONDITIONS

Road conditions in Iceland can change quite quickly, as the weather is unpredictable. As a rule, always check road conditions before you head out on a trip. The best way to get information about road conditions and the weather is to call 1777 (or tel. 354/522-1100). The line is open 8am-4pm in the summer and 6:30am-10pm in the winter.

The **Ring Road (Route 1)** is the most accessible and popular route around Iceland. It

---

Previous: a herd of sheep crossing the Ring Road in southern Iceland; traditional Icelandic sweaters for sale.

runs 1,332 kilometers and connects most of the most popular tourist attractions in the country. The Ring Road is paved for most of its length, but there are still stretches in East Iceland with an unpaved gravel surface. F roads are unpaved tracks that may only be driven in vehicles with four-wheel drive. Some F roads have river crossings, so trying to navigate with a compact car is dangerous.

GPS NAVIGATION

GPS coordinates are a popular way to navigate Iceland. You can input coordinates into navigational apps or GPS units for directions. However, it's important to keep in mind that sometimes roads are closed, so do some research on the route you plan to take, not just the shortest distance. You don't want to wind up stranded.

CAR RENTAL

Car rental prices remind you that you are very much on an island with very little price competition. In short, it's wildly expensive to rent a car and pay for insurance, and gas prices are sky high.

You can rent a car in advance or at the rental office at Keflavík International Airport, at BSÍ bus station, or within Reykjavík once you're settled. In the summer, with growing tourism, it is recommended to arrange your rental in advance as some dealers sell out early.

Choosing the right car for your trip depends on what you want to see and where you plan to go. If you plan on staying close to Reykjavík and traveling on well-paved roads, such as the Ring Road, a compact car is the best and cheapest option. However, if you plan on going out to the countryside or to the highlands, don't try to get away with renting the cheap option. If you try to bring a compact car into a region that requires four-wheel drive, expect damage to the car at best, and being stranded and needing to be rescued at worst. Be smart and be prepared.

For insurance, car rental companies provide "full insurance" for each rental, which is the basic third-party insurance option. For an extra fee, drivers have access to "extra insurance" that includes a collision damage waiver. However, be aware that you will *not* be covered for damage caused by rocks, snow, wind, ice, and all the other elements that could damage a vehicle. If you have any damage to a car, you will be charged...*a lot.* Be sure to choose the right insurance for the region you plan to travel to.

RULES OF THE ROAD

Always drive with headlights on (day and night). Do not drive off-road (expect heavy fines). Always wear your seat belt, and watch out for sheep and birds in the countryside.

Do not drink and drive. The law forbids any driving under the influence of alcohol, and police aggressively monitor drunk driving.

Do not speed. Always remember that roads are unpredictable and car accidents involving foreign drivers are quite common. You can be traveling on a quiet, scenic paved road that suddenly turns into an unpaved, rough section. You can lose control of the car quite easily. The maximum speed limit for the entire island is 90 kph (55 mph), but in towns and residential areas, it can be much less. Always respect the limit. If you do speed and are caught by a police officer, expect a huge fine and a stern talking to. Don't risk it.

Monitor the weather forecast. Driving in Iceland can range from peaceful to harrowing, depending on the weather. To check road conditions, visit the Icelandic Road and Coastal Administration website (www.vegagerdin.is). If there is an advisory, due to wind, rain, snow, or a volcanic eruption (it happens), stay off the road. Advisories are to be taken seriously.

Bus

The bus system in Iceland is surprisingly adequate, especially in Reykjavík.

BSÍ (Vatnsmýrarvegur 10, tel. 354/580-5400, www.bsi.is) is the main bus station in Reykjavík and serves as the first destination for many tourists in Reykjavík, as BSÍ is the first stop on the Fly Bus (tel. 354/580-5400, www.flybus.is) from Keflavík International Airport. One-way tickets on the Fly Bus cost 1,950ISK. (For an extra fee, the Fly Bus can connect to several different hotels and guesthouses in Reykjavík.) BSÍ also serves as a main departure site for many day-tour bus trips, such as the Blue Lagoon and Golden Circle, offered by companies such as Reykjavik Excursions (tel. 354/580-5400, www.re.is).

Strætó (tel. 354/540-2700, www.straeto. is) operates the city bus system in Reykjavík, with bright yellow buses running on numbered routes. The routes are quite comprehensive, linking downtown Reykjavík to outlying neighborhoods. Tourists can pay exact change for one-way trips (400ISK) or purchase a book of nine tickets for 3,500ISK. Hlemmur station is Strætó's central downtown bus station, where you can catch or connect to just about any bus line. Strætó's blue long-distance buses depart from Mjódd station, traveling to several regions around the country.

SBA-Norðurleið (tel. 354/550-0700, www. sba.is) is another bus company that offers day tours and bus service throughout the country.

There is a "bus passport" available through Reykjavik Excursions (tel. 354/580-5400, www.re.is) that allows unlimited travel on buses throughout the country for a specific period of time (7-15 days). The bus passport is available from June to September and starts at 58,000ISK. It's quite convenient for those traveling the Ring Road without a rental car, and many tourists love to meet fellow travelers along the way.

Cycling

Cycling in Iceland is a favorite pastime among locals and tourists. While seeing Iceland by bicycle can be exhilarating and budget-friendly, the downside is that the weather is unpredictable, even in the summer. There are summers that are relatively dry and sunny, but realistically, you need to be prepared for rain, and lots of it. Some cyclists are lured by gorgeous landscape photos and the thrill of long summer days, but are challenged by keeping themselves dry and motivated. Also, bike theft is rampant on the island, so you must be vigilant in keeping your bicycle and gear under lock and key. The plus side, however, is that you get to see the country powered by your own two feet, and you have the freedom to control how long you stay at sites without being tied to a tour bus. There are numerous well-kept bike paths throughout the country, and brochures with trail information are available at tourist information offices. The best advice is to plan, plan, and plan some more for challenging roads and unpredictable weather.

Hitchhiking

Hitchhiking is common practice, and legal, in Iceland, as it's a safe country with lots of drivers. If you are attempting to hitch along busier routes such as along the Reykjanes Peninsula, you will likely have more luck; however, in more remote destinations, it can be hit or miss. It's not advisable to be dependent on hitching in the winter months, because roads are less frequently traveled and the weather can be punishing. If you do score a ride, make sure you offer some cash for gas, as it's just good form.

Visas and Officialdom

VISAS AND PASSPORTS

Visitors to Iceland must have a valid passport that will not expire within three months of your scheduled departure. Tourists from the United States, Canada, Australia, and New Zealand do not need a visa if they are traveling to Iceland for fewer than 90 days. If you want to stay longer, you need to apply for a residence permit at the Icelandic immigration office (www.utl.is). For Europeans, Iceland is part of the Schengen Agreement, which allows free travel between Iceland and European Economic Area (EEA) and European Union (EU) countries; visas are not necessary.

EMBASSIES
Icelandic Embassies

Iceland has embassies in a number of countries, including:

- **Canada:** 360 Albert St., Suite 710, Ottawa, ON K1R 7X7, tel. 613/482-1944, www.iceland.is/ca

- **United Kingdom:** 2A Hans St, London SW1X 0JE, tel. 20/7259-3999, www.iceland.is/uk

- **United States:** 2900 K St. NW, Suite 509, Washington, DC 20007, tel. 202/265-6653, www.iceland.is/us

Foreign Embassies in Iceland

If you have an emergency while traveling in Iceland and require assistance (for example, if you lose your passport), contact your embassy for help. Embassies in Reykjavík include:

- **Canada:** Túngata 14, tel. 354/575-6500, rkjvk@international.gc.ca

- **United Kingdom:** Laufásvegur 31, tel. 354/550-5100, info@britishembassy.is

- **United States:** Laufásvegur 21, tel. 354/595-2200, reykjavikconsular@state.gov

CUSTOMS

Getting through Customs in Iceland is quite easy when compared to most other countries in Europe.

Travelers can import duty-free alcoholic beverages and tobacco products as follows: 1 liter of spirits, 1 liter of wine, and 1 carton or 250g of other tobacco products; or 1 liter of spirits, 6 liters of beer, and 1 carton or 250g of other tobacco products; or 1.5 liters of wine, 6 liters of beer, and 1 carton or 250g of other tobacco products; or 3 liters wine and 1 carton or 250g of other tobacco products. The minimum age for bringing alcoholic beverages into Iceland is 20 years; for tobacco, it's 18 years.

Iceland has a zero-tolerance policy on drugs, and all meat, raw-egg products, and unpasteurized dairy will be confiscated.

For additional information, visit the official Customs website (www.tollur.is).

Sports and Recreation

Iceland truly is a nature buff's playground. There is much to do, and locals are thrilled to have you explore their treasured land—safely and responsibly. If you are heading out on a hike or a climb, report your whereabouts. Also, be sure to closely monitor weather conditions, bring all the water and gear you need with you, and be careful. Iceland's rescue team is often called upon to save unprepared tourists in completely avoidable situations. Have fun, but be safe.

HIKING

Hiking is by far the most popular outdoor activity on the island. There are stretches of land in the north, south, Reykjanes Peninsula, west, east, and interior that are begging to be explored. Hikers have their

Best Day Hikes

Mount Akrafjall

Iceland is undeniably a hiker's paradise. The mountainous landscape begs to be climbed, lava fields invite you to explore, and the highlands offer the adventurous a place to conquer.

- **Mount Esja** is the picture-perfect backdrop to Reykjavík and a favorite among locals and tourists to hike. The hike is relatively easy, but be aware that it gets steeper as you get to the top. Along the way, you'll see a placid stream and gorgeous scenery. The view from the top is breathtaking, with views of Reykjavík across the bay.

- In the west, **Mount Akrafjall** offers moderate hiking, with two paths to choose from. The shorter climb (about two hours) is 555 meters and offers a lovely view of the outskirts of the town Akranes. If you're up for a longer climb (about five hours), a path leads 643 meters up, and on clear days you can see Snæfellsjökull glacier.

- For those who make it to the highlands, hiking the rim of **Mount Askja** is a must. The eight-hour trek is rather difficult, but the trail is well maintained and sees a bit of traffic among hikers. The hike offers special views of looming mountains, lava fields, and the spectacular Víti crater.

choice of terrain whether they're looking for vast lava fields, steep mountains, or enormous glaciers.

The key is to be well prepared, safe, and smart. Monitor weather conditions, have all the proper equipment with you, and alert authorities about your plans. While hiking is a beautiful way to explore the island, most emergency calls to the rescue service are due to ill-prepared tourists finding themselves in a predicament on a hiking expedition gone wrong. It cannot be overstated that you must respect Iceland's raw and sometimes treacherous nature.

Detailed maps are available at regional tourist information offices as well as online at the **Ferðafélag Íslands (Icelandic Touring Association)** (www.fi.is).

FISHING

Fishing is how many Icelanders make their living, so who has fishing rights can be political. Your best bet is to sign up for a tour with a local operator who handles the necessary permit as well as bait and gear. A good place to start is through the tour operator **Iceland Fishing Guide** (www.icelandfishingguide.

com), which offers fishing tours in Iceland's lakes, rivers, and streams. You have a chance at catching salmon, trout, and arctic char, depending on the tour location.

SWIMMING

Swimming is a big part of Icelandic culture. That may sound strange given the chilly temps compared to say, Spain or Florida, but an Icelander's local swimming pool is part of their social scene. If you visit a pool, you will notice groups of Icelanders, friends and family, sitting in hot tubs, sun rooms, or in the children's pool with their little ones. They love the water and they love to socialize. Pools are heated, and many have extensive facilities that include a gym, sauna, and several hot tubs. There are more than 120 swimming pools in Iceland, and they are well used, no matter the weather. Even outdoor pools can be full when there is a light snowfall.

The part about Iceland's swimming culture that frazzles some tourists is the communal showering that takes place before and after your swim. In the gender-divided locker rooms, you will see Icelanders showering stark naked—that's right, sans bathing

hiking in the highlands

suit—and you're expected to do the same. You must thoroughly clean yourself before you join the pool. At larger pools, there are often attendants who make sure that visitors shower. Locals are used to shy visitors and find it amusing, but at the end of the day, it just doesn't matter. After a couple of visits to the pool, you get used to it.

Accommodations and Food

ACCOMMODATIONS

Hotels

Iceland is not known for posh hotels offering every luxury that you desire. However, there is a good mix of "upscale" accommodations, mid-level boutiques, and budget hotels. The "fanciest" options on the island are in Reykjavík; namely 101 Hotel and Hótel Borg, which cater to guests who are willing to pay for top-notch service and amenities. Reykjavík also has midrange boutique or family-run options if you are looking for something a bit more formal than a guesthouse.

Outside of Reykjavík, hotels tend to be of the local chain-hotel ilk in the form of Fosshotels (www.fosshotel.is), Hótel Edda (www.hoteledda.is), and Icelandair Hótels (www.icelandairhotels.is). They are clean, comfortable, and reliable options.

When they compare hotel prices to those in other European countries, some tourists feel that they don't get their money's worth. In fairness, Iceland is a more popular destination than it was 20 years ago, but it's still not meant to be a budget destination. In short, accommodations do cost a lot. Be prepared for slightly shocking rates, especially in the summer months.

Guesthouses

The most prevalent form of accommodations on the island is the guesthouse set-up. Guesthouses range from comfortable bed-and-breakfasts that offer shared bathrooms and cooking facilities to more design-conscious options that are chic, modern, and fun. Some guesthouses in Reykjavík can still have "hotel-like" prices, as the competition for scoring a room in the high season has become almost a contact sport. Outside Reykjavík, however, guesthouses could be a good way to save a little money, depending on where you book. Always book a room in advance, as it's not recommended to leave where you will lay your head to chance.

Hostels

Hostels are another great option for the budget traveler, but as in guesthouses, beds tend to fill up, so make sure you book far in advance, especially in the summer. Some hostels in Reykjavík, like Kex Hostel and Loft Hostel, cater to young, music-conscious travelers, and beds are almost an afterthought. There is frequently live music in the lounge areas, and the bar is always packed with locals and tourists. Other hostel options cater to a more mature crowd looking to avoid the expensive hotel rates. Hlemmur Square would be a good option for those travelers. Outside of Reykjavík, hostels are prevalent and it's key to book ahead.

Sleeping Bag Accommodations

Some guesthouses and hostels around Iceland offer travelers sleeping bag accommodations, which can be great for the budget traveler. For a low price, guests are allowed to sleep in their sleeping bags and have access to shared bathroom facilities.

Mountain Huts

Not to be confused with emergency huts, mountain huts are similar to cabin-style accommodation, with many providing a cozy, hostel-like atmosphere with bunk beds. Huts have running water, and there is usually a shared dining hall. As tourism in Iceland has increased, it is necessary to book in advance to guarantee a place.

For more information, visit the website of Ferðafélag Íslands (Icelandic Touring Association) (www.fi.is), which runs several mountain huts around the country.

Camping

Camping can be a great option for some travelers, but be prepared. If you're going it alone with a tent, make sure you're ready for any type of weather—it can be unpredictable (even in summer), and you may be on the island during a good week, but maybe not.

There are campsites around the country that allow for tents as well as campers and caravans. Facilities vary; some campsites have top-notch cooking areas and steaming hot showers, while others have adequate cooking facilities and just toilets.

Most campsites are open mid-May to mid-September. It's not necessary to book a site well in advance. To see a list of campsites, visit www.nat.is/camping/camping_sites.htm.

The main camping information centers in Iceland are:

- Reykjavík: info@visitreykjavik.is

- Leifsstöð (Keflavík Airport): touristinfo@reykjanesbaer.is

- Reykjanesbær (Southwest Iceland): Icelandreykjanes@reykjanesbaer.is

- Borgarnes (West Iceland): tourinfo@vesturland.is

- Ísafjörður (Westfjords): info@vestfirdir.is

- Varmahlíð (Northwest Iceland): upplysingar@skagafjordur.is

- Akureyri (North Iceland): tourinfo@est.is

- Egilsstaðir (East Iceland): info@east.is

- Seyðisfjörður (East Iceland): ferdamenning@sfk.is

- Höfn (Southeast Iceland): tourinfo@hornafjordur.is

- Hveragerði (South Iceland): tourinfo@hveragerdi.is

FOOD
Typical Fare

The description of Icelandic food that you get depends on whom you ask, although it can't be disputed that fish and lamb take center stage. Typical fare can range from light to hearty. Local produce means what can survive outdoors (potatoes, rhubarb, moss) and what is grown in greenhouses (tomatoes, cucumbers,

campsite in Þingvellir National Park

broccoli, etc.). Most of Iceland's food is imported, and it isn't cheap.

Local fish includes cod (fresh/salted), salmon, lobster, mussels, halibut, trout, and haddock. A classic Icelandic dish is whitefish cooked in a white sauce with potatoes and onions. A popular snack is hardfish, which is like a whitefish jerky, where the fish is dried and seasoned.

As for meat, lamb is the most prevalent, but there is plenty of beef, pork, and chicken in the Icelandic diet. Some Icelanders also indulge in horse and whale meat as well.

Hot dogs are wildly popular among Icelanders. Called *pylsur,* Icelandic hot dogs are done up in a traditional bun with chopped onions, mustard, ketchup, crispy fried onions, and pickled mayonnaise. They're delicious.

Dairy is an important part of Icelanders' diets, including milk, cheese, butter, and the yogurt-like soft cheese called *skyr,* which you should try. It's very tasty and chock-full of protein. Icelanders are also known to eat ice cream all year long, despite the weather. There are quite a few popular ice cream shops around Reykjavík, and the ice cream sections in supermarkets offer an astounding number of locally produced choices.

Once a year, Icelanders celebrate the traditional foods of the nation, which sustained their ancestors through the ages. The winter festival, called Þorrablót, features *svið* (singed lamb head), blood pudding, lamb intestines and stomach, ram's testicles, fermented shark, seal flippers, hardfish, and rye bread. The food that gets the most attention from foreigners is rotten shark or *hákarl,* which is meat from Greenland shark. The flesh is put through an interesting process, where it is buried for at least two months and then is hung for another three or four months to cure. If you dare, *hákarl*

is available in small containers for sale. It is an experience you will not forget—if not the taste, then definitely the smell.

Finding a Restaurant

Reykjavík is home to some excellent fine dining establishments and casual eateries, but eating cheaply in Reykjavík, or on the island as a whole, is not easy. Hours tend to change depending on the season, but for the most part restaurants open their doors for lunch around 11:30am, and kitchens tend to close around 10pm.

Outside of Reykjavík and Akureyri, you will find a lot of fish and lamb restaurants that focus on local cuisine, but inside the two main cities, you have a lot to choose from. You will find sushi, tapas, Indian, hamburger joints, noodle bars, kebab houses, and Italian restaurants to name a few. International cuisine has been growing in popularity over the last 20 years, and new and interesting spots are always cropping up.

Drinking

The water in Iceland is pure and some of the tastiest in the world. Drinking from the tap is common and safe, and bottled water is frowned upon. Iceland is also a coffee-drinking nation. If you're a tea drinker, you will find some basic choices in coffee shops, but Icelanders are crazy about their coffee.

As for alcohol, Icelanders do have a reputation for indulging, but given the expensive prices, beer is the drink of choice when going out to a bar. And, believe it or not, beer is still relatively new to Iceland. A countrywide alcohol ban went into effect in 1915; the ban was relaxed in phases, with first wine and then strong liquors permitted, and beer eventually became legal to sell in 1989. Outside of bars, alcohol is available only at the government-run shops called Vínbúðin.

Travel Tips

WOMEN TRAVELERS

Iceland is regularly ranked as being one of the best countries in the world in which to be a woman and a mother. Icelanders are proud to have elected the first woman president in the world as well as the first openly gay prime minister (a woman). However, Iceland is not a utopia. Women are subject to incidents of theft, intimidation, and physical violence. Always keep your wits about you, and if you are a victim of crime, contact the police at the emergency number 112.

GAY AND LESBIAN TRAVELERS

Iceland is a leader in equality, and Reykjavík is one of the most gay-friendly cities in Europe. What many travelers find refreshing is that there is not just tolerance for gay, lesbian, bisexual, and transgendered individuals, but overwhelming love and acceptance of their fellow Icelanders. For instance, the gay pride festival, **Reykjavík Pride,** which takes place every August, attracts approximately 100,000 participants, for a country of just 320,000 people. Think about that. As for laws, the LGBT community is protected from discrimination, gay marriage was legalized in 2010, and hate crimes are few and far between. For such a small population, it's hard to say there's a "gay scene," but there is one gay bar in Reykjavík, Kiki Queer Bar. More information can be found at the **Pink Iceland** website (www.pinkiceland.is).

TRAVELING WITH CHILDREN

Children are the center of Icelandic society, and tourists traveling with children will feel right at home, whether in restaurants,

Reykjavík Pride festival

museums, or child-appropriate tours. The island is a safe place for children, and many foreign travelers raise an eyebrow at how carefree parents can appear—whether it's a child walking around a shop, or an unaccompanied pram outside a coffeehouse. It's not irresponsible parenting, just a reflection on how safe a society Iceland is. While Iceland is safe, it needs to be said to always take care to watch out for the elements, whether it's high winds, a slippery surface, or cracks in a walking path.

As for attractions and restaurants, there are frequently child rates for museums, tours, and children's options on menus. Discounts can be a great as 50 percent off for children under the age of 16.

TRAVELERS WITH DISABILITIES

Iceland has taken great strides in making as many tourist-related sites as wheelchair-friendly as possible. Visitors in wheelchairs will find that most museums, swimming pools, and restaurants provide access, as do transportation services. For instance, Keflavík International Airport and all domestic airlines can accommodate travelers in wheelchairs, and many buses come with automatic ramps to allow for easy boarding.

For more information on accessible travel, get in touch with the organization **Þekkingarmiðstöð Sjálfsbjargar** (tel. 354/550-0118, www.thekkingarmidstod. is). While the website is almost entirely in Icelandic only, information on traveling in Iceland has been translated into English (www.thekkingarmidstod.is/adgengi/accessible-tourism-in-iceland), and employees are happy to assist in English.

For information on services available to deaf travelers, contact the **Icelandic Association of the Deaf** (www.deaf.is), and for services for the sight-impaired, contact the **Icelandic Association of the Blind** (www.blind.is).

WHAT TO PACK

How you pack depends on where you plan to go and what you're going to do on the island. If you're going for a "city-break" long weekend to Reykjavík, you can afford to pack light; however, if you plan on an extended stay that includes camping, packing light is not an option. Here are some suggestions and tips for your time in Iceland.

Clothing

The key to dressing warm and being comfortable in Iceland is layers. Depending on the weather, it can be cotton T-shirt, fleece or sweater, parka or windbreaker, and perhaps a hat, scarf, and gloves. If it's summer and the sun is shining, it's common to see locals wearing a T-shirt in 15°C (60°F) weather. It's important to keep comfortable and add layers if the temperature warrants it. If you're out hiking, wearing waterproof gear along with proper hiking attire is key. Make sure fabrics are breathable and comfortable and under layers are cotton. Formal attire in Iceland is reserved for work or funerals, but if you want to bring a nice outfit along for a "fancy" dinner, by all means, pack something, but you won't find stringent dress codes anywhere on this island. Lastly, a bathing suit is necessary. Even if you think you won't take a dip in a pool or hot spring, the temptation might be too great. Pack at least one.

Outerwear

Because the temperature varies so much depending on time of day, season, and where you are in the country, it's a good idea to bring a hat, scarf, and gloves. As for jackets, the best advice is to bring something waterproof; whether it's a windbreaker for summer or a parka for winter, you are likely to encounter rain at some point on your trip. If you need to go shopping for warmer layers in Iceland, expect to pay. Clothes are not cheap in Iceland.

Footwear

Again, if you are staying in Reykjavík for the duration of your trip, and don't plan to climb mountains, you don't need to invest in an expensive pair of hiking boots. That said, if you do plan to be outdoors quite a bit, hiking boots are a great idea. You will need a pair of shoes that can withstand rain, rocks, ice, mud, puddles, sand, and sometimes snow. It's recommended to buy boots in your home country because shoes can be expensive in Iceland, and it's not the best idea to break in a brand-new pair of boots if you plan to do a lot of walking and/or climbing. Comfort is key. Socks are also important to consider. You want socks that are breathable yet thick enough to keep you comfortable in your shoes/boots.

Camping Gear

If camping is in your plan, don't scrimp on the quality of the tent you bring. And, make no mistake, you should bring the tent with you, as quality tents are, you guessed it, expensive in Iceland. You will need something waterproof that can endure punishing winds. A sleeping bag is necessary as well for campers. It's also great to have a sleeping bag on hand because some guesthouses and hostels still offer sleeping bag accommodations at a much lower price. Be sure to call ahead to see if they're available. Because of the likelihood of encountering rain, a sleeping bag made from a synthetic material is the best option, and it should be able to withstand -9°C (15°F) temperatures in the summer and -18°C (0°F) in the winter. If you decide to camp, be sure to monitor weather conditions and be safe.

HEALTH AND SAFETY
Medical Services

The Icelandic health-care system is top-notch, with hospitals in each large town and health clinics in smaller villages and hamlets. Most doctors, nurses, and emergency medical staff speak English, and non-EU citizens must pay for health services provided. If you are having a medical emergency, dial the number 112. Pharmacies (called *apótek*) hold everything from prescription medication to aspirin. Some tourists from North America find it frustrating that cold medicine and aspirin cannot be bought in supermarkets, just at the pharmacy. Pharmacies are typically open 10am-9pm Monday-Friday, 10am-4pm Saturday, and closed on Sunday and public holidays.

Weather

Weather is the number one safety concern in Iceland, trumping everything from violent crime to volcanic eruptions. The main danger is how fast weather can change. It could be a bright, sunny day when you head out on a trek in the highlands, but there could be a storm brewing that will bring high winds, rain, hail, and snow. And the storm could pass as quickly as it arrived. The joke among locals is that if you don't like the weather in Iceland, wait five minutes. The best defense against inclement weather is to closely monitor weather forecasts and obey advisories. You can check frequently updated forecasts at www.vedur.is. Icelanders deal with the weather by being flexible and never confirming plans far in advance. They learn to adapt after a lifetime of battling gale force winds.

Temperatures in Iceland can vary, but on average Reykjavík's winter season is warmer than New York City's. That said, always dress for the environment and the activity you are about to embark on. If you are staying within Reykjavík's city limits, dress comfortably with layers and waterproof gear. If you're out in the countryside in the evening, have a hat, scarf, gloves, and warm gear at the ready. It can get chilly and hypothermia can set in quickly.

Emergency Huts

Iceland's emergency huts are strictly for emergencies. Don't even think of staying in one unless you are, in fact, experiencing an emergency. The huts are painted bright orange and are based in isolated areas. Inside one of Iceland's bright orange emergency huts

the hut, you will find, water, food, bedding, and an emergency radio that will allow you to call for help. The huts can be located on maps as they are usually depicted as a red house. If you find yourself amid a storm, hunker down in an emergency hut and call for help. Dial the emergency number 112.

Crime

Crime is quite low in Iceland and is mostly limited to theft and vandalism; violent crime is rare. Be vigilant in protecting your possessions (especially bicycles) and trust your instincts. If you're out at night on Laugavegur in downtown Reykjavík on weekends, you might encounter loud and drunk locals or tourists. Don't engage with drunken people; continue about your business. If you are a victim of a crime, contact the police by dialing the emergency number, 112; all police officers are proficient in English.

Information and Services

TOURIST INFORMATION

Visit Iceland (www.visiticeland.com) is the main tourist information website for the country. The website has information on accommodations and activities for each region in Iceland.

MONEY

Iceland is not a cheap place to visit. Don't be fooled by the news stories that declared Iceland cut prices to accommodate tourists after its economic crisis of 2008. That period was brief, and Iceland remains an expensive destination. Prices on accommodations, food, gas, and everyday necessities remain high. Here is a list showing prices of common items.

- Milk (1 L): 131ISK
- Loaf of bread: 232ISK
- Dozen eggs: 514ISK
- Apples (1 kg): 388ISK
- Potatoes (1 kg): 223ISK
- Coke/Pepsi: 265ISK
- Meal for two: 10,500ISK
- Domestic beer: 900ISK
- Bottle of wine: 2,100ISK
- Pack of cigarettes: 1,200ISK
- Bus ticket (one way): 350ISK
- Gasoline (1 L): 250ISK

Currency

The official currency of Iceland is the króna (abbreviated kr or ISK). The króna fluctuates often; at the time of writing, the exchange rate was 125ISK to US$1.

There are banknotes in the amount of 500, 1,000, 5,000, and 10,000 and coins in the amount of 1, 5, 10, 50, and 100 kronur. Coins are handy for having exact change for the bus. Cash overall is not a popular payment method; locals are known to use debit and credit cards for just about every transaction.

Currency exchange is available at the airport and banks as well as tourist information offices. Your best bet to get the best exchange is to use your credit card. ATMs are available at all banks as well as supermarkets and other shops.

Banks

Banking hours are 9:15am-4pm Monday-Friday, and ATMs are available 24/7. There may be a limit on the amount of cash you can withdraw per your home bank's policy.

Tax-Free Shopping

As tourists encounter high prices for everything from accommodations to food, it only seems fair that you get a break when it comes to shopping.

A refund of local Value-Added Tax (VAT) is available to all visitors in Iceland. The refund will result in a reduction of up to 15 percent of the retail price, provided departure from Iceland is within three months after the date of purchase.

The fine print is that the refund does not apply to food or accommodations and the purchase must exceed 4,000ISK (VAT included) per store. Shops will provide you with a tax-free form (ask the store clerk for a "tax-free check"). Make sure you tuck the forms all away and redeem the rebate at the cash-refund office at Keflavík Airport before your flight. There, you will get an immediate cash refund.

You can also submit the receipts and paperwork by mail for a rebate on your credit card. This, of course, can take considerably longer.

Tipping

Tipping is very new to Iceland. Workers in bars, restaurants, and hotels, as well as taxi drivers, earn a living wage and are not dependent on tips. In recent years, tip jars have

Holidays in Iceland

Businesses in Iceland close on the following holidays:

- January 1: **New Year's Day**
- March or April: **Maundy Thursday**
- March or April: **Good Friday**
- March or April: **Easter Sunday**
- March or April: **Easter Monday**
- First Thursday after April 18: **First day of summer**
- May 1: **Labor Day**
- May or June: **Ascension Day**
- May or June: **Whitsun**
- May or June: **Whit Monday**
- June 17: **Icelandic National Day** (commemorates achieving independence from Denmark in 1944)
- First Monday in August: **Trading Day**
- December 24: **Christmas Eve**
- December 25: **Christmas Day**
- December 26: **Second day of Christmas**
- December 31: **New Year's Eve**

cropped up in coffeehouses and bars, but it's just tourists who tend to tip.

MAPS

To properly navigate Iceland, you need maps. That's a given. Lucky for you, they are available all over the island. You can pick up all-inclusive maps for the entire island as well as regional maps, road maps, and hiking maps at tourist information centers, bookstores, and gas stations. If you have the chance to purchase maps before your trip, do so, as they will likely be a lot cheaper in your home country. However, if you plan to stay in Reykjavík for the duration of your trip, it's not necessary to buy a map because quite a few free maps do a nice job detailing downtown Reykjavík.

COMMUNICATIONS AND MEDIA

Telephone

The country code for Iceland is 354. There are no area codes; if you are calling from within the country, just dial the seven-digit phone number and you will connect.

Icelanders love their mobile phones, and for that reason pay phones became obsolete several years ago. You can purchase international phone cards at local shops (called *sjoppas*) as well as the post office and gas stations. SIM cards are also available from providers **Vodafone** (www.vodafone.is) and **Siminn** (www.siminn.is) and can be purchased from phone retail shops, gas stations, and the airport.

Cell phone coverage in the countryside is surprisingly strong.

Internet Access

Iceland is wired, with Wi-Fi hot spots all over the country. Hotels typically have free Wi-Fi as do many coffeehouses.

Media

Given its small population, it's refreshing to see Iceland as such a die-hard newspaper town. Locals have several Icelandic-language print publications and websites to choose from, but publishers haven't forgotten about English-language readers. The *Reykjavík Grapevine* (www.grapevine.is) is the unofficial guide to music, museum exhibitions, restaurant reviews, and just about every cultural event in the city. The website is updated daily, and the free print edition comes out biweekly in the summer and monthly in the winter.

Iceland Review (www.icelandreview.com) is the main English-language glossy magazine on the island. You will find in-depth features on travel, culture, and business issues as well as gorgeous photography.

RUV (www.ruv.is) is Iceland's national public-service broadcasting organization, which consists of one television channel and two radio stations. RUV's television programs include news, dramas, documentaries, as well as programming from foreign countries, including the United States, Denmark, and Sweden.

TIME ZONE

Iceland uses Greenwich mean time (GMT). However, the country does not observe daylight saving time, so Iceland is either four or five hours ahead of New York time, depending on the time of year.

As for the amount of daylight, what you've heard is true. The summers are full of long days, and darkness reigns supreme in the winter. To give you an idea of what that means, here are daylight hours for Reykjavík at different times of year:

- January 1: sunrise 11:20am, sunset 3:45pm
- April 1: sunrise 6:45am, sunset 8:20pm
- July 1: sunrise 3:05am, sunset midnight
- October 1: sunrise 7:30am, sunset 7pm

WEIGHTS AND MEASURES

Iceland uses the metric system. With regard to electricity, the standard voltage is 230 V and the standard frequency is 50 Hz. The power sockets that are used are type F, for plugs with two round pins. If you forget to bring an adapter, they can be purchased in most bookstores and tourist shops.

Resources

Glossary

austur: east
bíó: movie theater
bær: farm
bíll: car
bjarg: rock, cliff
dalur: valley
ey: island
fjall: mountain
fjörður: fjord
fljót: river
flugvöllur: airport
foss: waterfall
gata: street
geysir: erupting hot spring
herbergi: room
hestur: horse
hraun: lava field
hradbanki: ATM
huldufólk: hidden people
höfn: harbor

Ísland: Iceland
jökull: glacier
kirkja: church
kort: map
laug: swimming pool
lopapeysa: Icelandic knitted sweater
lundi: puffin
norður: north
safn: museum
sími: telephone
stræti: street
strætó: bus
suður: south
sumar: summer
tjörn: pond
torg: town square
vatn: water
vestur: west
vetur: winter
veður: weather

Icelandic Phrasebook

Icelandic is not the easiest language to understand. It's a North Germanic language that is related to Norwegian, Danish, and Swedish, but it has the added difficulty of declensions that the other languages lack. Icelandic nouns are declined in four cases, which stumps many people. Fortunately, just about everyone in Iceland speaks English.

PRONUNCIATION

Pronunciation can be very tricky, but Icelanders are thrilled when tourists give their language a shot. Be warned, though: if you attempt to speak an Icelandic phrase, your accent will tell them you're a foreigner, and they most likely will answer you in English.

Vowels

Some vowels in Icelandic have accent marks that modify the sound of each vowel. Vowels can come in long or short forms. In Icelandic, all vowels can be long or short. Vowels are long when they are in single-syllable words or when they form the penultimate syllable in two-syllable words.

A a   like the "a" in "land"
Á á   like "ow" in "cow"
E e   like the "e" in "set"
É é   like "ye" in "yet"
I i   like "i" in "sit"
Í í   like "ee" in "feet"
O o   like the "o" in "not"
Ó ó   like the "o" in "flow"
U u   like the "u" in "put"
Ú ú   like the "oo" in "soon"
Y y   like the "i" in "sit"
Ý ý   like the "ee" in "feet"
Æ æ   like the "i" in "file"
Ö ö   like the "ur" in "lure"

Consonants

Ð ð   like "th" in "this"
J j   like "y" in "year"
R r   rolled, like Spanish "r"
Þ þ   like "th" in "thin"

BASIC AND COURTEOUS EXPRESSIONS

Hello *Halló*
Good morning *Goðan dag*
Good evening *Gott kvold*
How are you? *Hvað segir þu?*
Very well, thank you *Mjog gott, takk fyrir*
Good *Allt gott*
Not OK, bad *Ekki okei*
So-so *Bara fint*
OK *Allt í lagí*
And you? *En þu?*
Thank you *Takk fyrir*
Goodbye *Bless*
Nice to see you *Gaman að sjo þig*
See you later *Sjamust*
Please *Takk*
Yes *Ja*
No *Nei*

I don't know. *Ég skil ekki.*
Just a moment. *Augnablik.*
Excuse me. *Afsakið.*
What is your name? *Hvað heiti þu?*
Do you speak English? *Talarðu ensku?*
I don't speak Icelandic well. *Ég tala ekki íslensku svo vel.*
I don't understand. *Ég skil ekki.*
How do you say ... in Icelandic? *Hvernig segir maður ... á íslensku?*
My name is ... . *Ég heiti ... .*
What's your name? *Hvað heitir þú?*

TERMS OF ADDRESS

I *ég*
you *þu*
he/him *hann*
she/her *hun*
we *við*
they *þeir*
girl *stelpa*
boy *strakur*
man *maður*
woman *kona*
wife *eiginkona*
husband *eiginmaður*
friend *vinur*
son *sonur*
daughter *dottir*
brother *bróðir*
sister *systir*
father *pabbi*
mother *mamma*
grandfather *afi*
grandmother *amma*

ACCOMMODATIONS

hotel *hótel*
guesthouse *gistiheimilið, gistihúsið*
Is there a room? *Áttu laus herbergi?*
May I see the room first? *Má ég sjá herbergið fyrst?*
What is the rate? *Hvað kostar það?*
Is there something cheaper? *Ódýrara herbergi?*
single room *einsmanns herbergi*
double room *tveggjamanna herbergi*
bathroom *klósetti*

shower *sturtu*
towels *handklæði*
soap *sapa*
toilet paper *salernispappír*
sheets *rúmfötum*
key *lykill*
heater *hitari*
manager *framkvæmdastjóri*

FOOD

I'm hungry. *Ég er svangur.*
menu *matseðil*
May I have ...? *Get ég fengið ...?*
glass *glas*
fork *gaffall*
knife *hnifur*
spoon *skeið*
breakfast *morgunmatur*
lunch *hádegisverður*
dinner *kvöldmatur*
the check *reikninginn*
soda *gos*
coffee *kaffi*
tea *te*
water *vatn*
beer *bjór*
wine *vín*
white wine *hvítvín*
red wine *rauðvín*
milk *mjólk*
juice *safi*
cream *rjómi*
sugar *sykur*
eggs *eggjum*
cheese *osti*
yogurt *jógúrt*
almonds *möndlu*
cake *kaka*
bread *brauð*
butter *smjör*
salt *salt*
pepper *pipar*
garlic *hvítlaukur*
salad *salat*
vegetables *grænmeti*
carrot *gulrót*
corn *korn*
cucumber *agúrka*

lettuce *kál*
mushroom *sveppir*
onion *laukur*
potato *kartöflu*
spinach *spinat*
tomato *tómatar*
fruit *ávöxtum*
apple *epli*
orange *appelsína*
fish *fiski*
meat *kjöti*
lamb *lamb*
beef *nautakjöti*
chicken *kjúklingi*
pork *svínakjöt*
bacon *beikon*
ham *skinka*

SHOPPING

money *peningar*
What is the exchange rate? *Hvað er gengið á?*
Do you accept credit cards? *Tekur þú greiðslukort?*
How much does it cost? *Hvað kostar það?*
expensive *dýr*
cheap *ódýr*
more *meira*
less *minna*
a little *smá*
too much *of mikið*

HEALTH

Help me! *Hjálp!*
I am ill. *Ég er veikur.*
I need a doctor. *Ég þarf lækni.*
hospital *sjúkrahús*
pharmacy *apótek*
pain *verkir*
fever *hiti*
headache *höfuðverkur*
stomachache *magaverki*
burn *brunablettur*
cramp *krampa*
nausea *ógleði*
vomiting *uppköst*
antibiotic *sýklalyf*
pill *pilla*

aspirin *aspirín*
ointment *smyrsli*
cotton *bómull*
condoms *smokkur*
toothbrush *tannbursta*
toothpaste *tannkrem*
dentist *tannlæknir*

TRANSPORTATION

Where is the ...? *Hvar er ...?*
How do I get to ...? *Hvernig kemst ég til ...?*
the bus station *strætóstöðin*
the bus stop *strætóstopp*
Where is the bus going? *Hvert fer þessi strætó/rúta?*
taxi *taxi*
boat *bátur*
airport *flugvöllur*
A one-way ticket to ... *Einn miða, aðra leiðina til ...*
A round-trip ticket to ... *Einn miða, báðar leiðir til ...*
Stop here. *Hætta hér.*
I want to rent a car. *Get ég leigt bíl.*
entrance *inngangur*
exit *útgangur*
to the; toward the *til*
right *hægri*
left *vinstri*
straight ahead *beint áfram*
past the ... *framhjá ...*
before the ... *á undan ...*
opposite the ... *á móti ...*
Watch for the ... *Leita að ...*
intersection *gatnamót*
street *stræti*
north; south *norður; suður*
east; west *austur; vestur*

STREET SIGNS

Stop *Stans*
One Way *Einstefna*
Yield *Biðskylda*
No Parking *Engin Bílastæði*
Speed Limit *Hámarkshraði*

AT THE GAS STATION

gas station *bensínstöð*

gasoline (petrol) *bensín*
diesel *disel*
garage *verkstæði*
air *loft*
water *vatn*
oil change *olíu breyting*
tow truck *draga vörubíl*

VERBS

to buy *að kaupa*
to eat *að borða*
to climb *að klifra*
to do or make *að gera*
to go *að fara*
to love *að elska*
to want *að vilja*
to need *að þurfa*
to read *að lesa*
to write *að skrifa*
to stop *að hætta*
to arrive *til koma*
to stay *að vera*
to leave *að fara*
to look for *að leita*
to give *að gefa*
to carry *að bera*
to have *að hafa*

NUMBERS

zero *null*
one *einn*
two *tveir*
three *þrir*
four *fjorir*
five *fimm*
six *sex*
seven *sjo*
eight *atta*
nine *niu*
10 *tiu*
11 *ellefu*
12 *tólf*
13 *þrettán*
14 *fjórtán*
15 *fimmtán*
16 *sextán*
17 *sautján*
18 *átján*

19 *nítján*
20 *tuttugu*
21 *tuttugu og einn*
30 *prjatiu*
40 *fjorutiu*
50 *fimmtiu*
60 *sextiu*
70 *sjotiu*
80 *attatiu*
90 *niutiu*
100 *hundrað*
101 *hundrað og einn*
200 *tvö hundruð*
500 *fimm hundrað*
1,000 *púsund*
100,000 *hundrað púsund*
1,000,000 *milljón*

TIME

What time is it? *Hvað er klukkan?*
It's one o'clock. *Klukkan er eitt.*
morning *morgunn*
afternoon *eftir hádegi*
evening *kvöld*
night *nótt*
midnight *miðnætti*

DAYS AND MONTHS

Monday *mánudagur*
Tuesday *þriðjudagur*
Wednesday *miðvikudagur*
Thursday *fimmtudagur*
Friday *föstudagur*
Saturday *laugardagur*
Sunday *sunnudagur*
day *dagur*
today *i dag*
tomorrow *a morgun*
yesterday *í gær*
January *janúar*
February *febrúar*
March *mars*
April *april*
May *mai*
June *juni*
July *juli*
August *ágúst*
September *september*
October *október*
November *nóvember*
December *desember*
early *snemma*
late *seint*
later *seinna*
before *áður en*

Suggested Reading

Guðmundsson, Einar Már. *Angels of the Universe*. 1997. This is a startling tale of a young man struggling with mental illness, set in Iceland in the 1960s. The protagonist, Paul, retreats into his own fantasy world, while friends and family come along for the ride. The book is disturbing at times, funny at others, and almost impossible to put down. It was made into a film in 2000, which was wildly popular in Iceland.

Helgason, Hallgrímur. *101 Reykjavik*. 2007. The protagonist, Hlynur, is a lazy, unemployed twentysomething who lives with his mother, watches a lot of pornography, and hangs out in bars in downtown Reykjavík. His life takes a turn when a former girlfriend announces she is pregnant and Hlynur becomes obsessed with his mother's lesbian lover. It's a fun, unexpected tale that was made into a popular movie in Iceland.

Indriðason, Arnaldur. *Jar City*. 2006. Arnaldur is Iceland's leading mystery author. He pens about one book a year, which is great since his tales are so addicting. *Jar City* was the first of Arnaldur's books to feature detective Erlendur Sveinsson, who is a complicated man with a troubled relationship with his family and an obsession with solving

Reykjavík's violent crimes. Other characters include his partner, Sigurður Óli, and a female colleague, Elínborg.

Kellogg, Robert. *The Sagas of Icelanders*. 2001. This huge volume includes 10 sagas and 7 shorter tales that give a wonderful overview of Iceland's history and literature. If you're looking for a short introduction, this isn't it. It's comprehensive and glorious.

Laxness, Halldór. *Independent People*. 1946. Laxness remains Iceland's sole recipient of the Nobel Prize for Literature for his novel *Independent People*. The tale follows the life of a Bjartur, a sheep farmer, as he grapples with life, loss, and the sacrifices he made to achieve independence. If you're going to read one Icelandic novel, this should be it.

Internet Resources

Discover North Iceland
www.northiceland.is
This is the regional tourism guide for North Iceland, which includes information on towns including Akureyri, Mývatn, and Húsavík. You will find events listings, accommodations information, and a large list of tour operators.

Icelandic Tourist Board
www.visiticeland.com
Iceland's tourist board provides a website with pages and pages of information for travelers. The site offers information on festivals, shopping, national parks, and outdoor activities like hiking, birdwatching, whale-watching, and catching the northern lights in the wintertime. There's also information on accommodations, tour operators, and maps.

Iceland Review
www.icelandreview.com
Iceland's main English-language magazine provides features on everything from culture to travel to politics. The website underwent a revamp in 2014 and is worth checking out for in-depth articles as well as columns written by locals.

Reykjavík Grapevine
www.grapevine.is
Reykjavík's go-to English language newspaper,

which is published biweekly in the summer and monthly in the winter, also maintains a website. You can bone up on local news as well as check out a listings section that details concerts, art exhibitions, and bars.

Visit East Iceland
www.east.is
Covering everywhere from Egilsstaðir to the Eastfjords, this tourism guide lists camping options, weather advisories, outdoor activities, and tour operators.

Visit South Iceland
www.south.is
Covering the south as well as the Reykjanes Peninsula, this tourism site offers detailed information on driving routes, maps, accommodations options, and tour operators. This region encompasses the Golden Circle as well as the Blue Lagoon.

Visit West Iceland
www.west.is
This is a regional tourism guide for the western section of the country, including Akranes, Borgarnes, Snæfellsnes, and the Westfjords. The site lists upcoming festivals and events, tour operators, and travel information for the region.

Index

List of Maps

Photo Credits

Also Available

MAP SYMBOLS

▓▓▓▓▓	Expressway	○	City/Town	✈	Airport	⚲	Golf Course
▭▭▭	Primary Road	◉	State Capital	✗	Airfield	🅿	Parking Area
═══	Secondary Road	⊛	National Capital	▲	Mountain	▲	Archaeological Site
------	Unpaved Road	★	Point of Interest	+	Unique Natural Feature	⚱	Church
———	Feature Trail	•	Accommodation			🅶	Gas Station
- - - -	Other Trail	▼	Restaurant/Bar	⚐	Waterfall	⬮	Glacier
⋯⋯⋯	Ferry	■	Other Location	▲	Park		Mangrove
▤▤▤	Pedestrian Walkway			🎏	Trailhead		Reef
▥▥▥	Stairs	Λ	Campground	⛷	Skiing Area		Swamp

CONVERSION TABLES

°C = (°F - 32) / 1.8
°F = (°C x 1.8) + 32
1 inch = 2.54 centimeters (cm)
1 foot = 0.304 meters (m)
1 yard = 0.914 meters
1 mile = 1.6093 kilometers (km)
1 km = 0.6214 miles
1 fathom = 1.8288 m
1 chain = 20.1168 m
1 furlong = 201.168 m
1 acre = 0.4047 hectares
1 sq km = 100 hectares
1 sq mile = 2.59 square km
1 ounce = 28.35 grams
1 pound = 0.4536 kilograms
1 short ton = 0.90718 metric ton
1 short ton = 2,000 pounds
1 long ton = 1.016 metric tons
1 long ton = 2,240 pounds
1 metric ton = 1,000 kilograms
1 quart = 0.94635 liters
1 US gallon = 3.7854 liters
1 Imperial gallon = 4.5459 liters
1 nautical mile = 1.852 km

MOON ICELAND

Avalon Travel
a member of the Perseus Books Group
1700 Fourth Street
Berkeley, CA 94710, USA
www.moon.com

Editor and Series Manager: Kathryn Ettinger
Copy Editor: Deana Shields
Graphics Coordinator: Elizabeth Jang
Production Coordinator: Elizabeth Jang
Cover Design: Faceout Studios, Charles Brock
Interior Design: Domini Dragoone
Moon Logo: Tim McGrath
Map Editor: Kat Bennett
Cartographers: Lohnes + Wright, Brian Shotwell,
    Kat Bennett
Indexer: Deana Shields

ISBN-13: 978-1-63121-027-3
ISSN: 2470-0541

Printing History
1st Edition — March 2016
5 4 3 2 1

Text © 2016 by Jenna Gottlieb.
Maps © 2016 by Avalon Travel.
All rights reserved.

Some photos and illustrations are used by
permission and are the property of the original
copyright owners.

Front cover photo: ice cave on Svínafellsjökull
glacier © Peter Adams/Getty Images

Back cover photo: aerial view of Reykjavík © Alexey
Stiop/123rf.com

Printed in Canada by Friesens

All recommendations, including those for sights,
activities, hotels, restaurants, and shops, are
based on each author's individual judgment. We
do not accept payment for inclusion in our travel
guides, and our authors don't accept free goods
or services in exchange for positive coverage.

Although every effort was made to ensure that the
information was correct at the time of going to
press, the author and publisher do not assume
and hereby disclaim any liability to any party for
any loss or damage caused by errors, omissions,
or any potential travel disruption due to labor
or financial difficulty, whether such errors or
omissions result from negligence, accident, or
any other cause.

KEEPING CURRENT

If you have a favorite gem you'd like to see included in the next edition, or
see anything that needs updating, clarification, or correction, please drop
us a line. Send your comments via email to feedback@moon.com, or use the
address above.